Guide to
EFFECTIVE COACHING
Principles & Practice

Guide to EFFECTIVE COACHING Principles & Practice

SECOND EDITION

Billie J. Jones
Department of Movement Science and Physical Education, Florida State University

L. Janet Wells
Department of Movement Science and Physical Education, Florida State University

Rachael E. Peters
Former Coach and Director of Athletics, Annandale High School

Dewayne J. Johnson
Department of Movement Science and Physical Education, Florida State University

wcb
Wm. C. Brown Publishers
2460 Kerper Blvd.
Dubuque, Iowa 52001

Copyright © 1988, 1982 by Allyn and Bacon, Inc.

Copyright © 1988 by Wm. C. Brown Publishers. All rights reserved

Library of Congress Catalog Card Number: 87-14416

ISBN 0-697-06881-1

No part of this publication may be reproduced, stored in a retrieval system, or transmitted, in any form or by any means, electronic, mechanical, photocopying, recording, or otherwise, without the prior written permission of the publisher.

Printed in the United States of America by Wm. C. Brown Publishers
2460 Kerper Boulevard, Dubuque, IA 52001

10 9 8 7 6 5 4 3 2

Contents

Preface xiii

PART 1 The Coach   1

1 "Coach"

What Coaches Are Like 5
Qualities of a Good Coach 7
Obligation to Young People and Athletes 9
The Coach's Responsibilities 9

2 The Coach as a Person

Leader 13
    Role 13   Conflict 14
Follower 14
    Role 14   Conflict 15

Role Model 16
    Role 16   Conflict 17
Disciplinarian 18
    Role 18   Conflict 18
Psychologist 19
    Role 19   Conflict 20
Friend and Counselor 20
    Role 20   Conflict 22
Life Management Advisor 23
    Role 23   Conflict 24
Parent Substitute 24
    Role 24   Conflict 25
Family Member 26
    Role 26   Conflict 27
Single Person 28
    Role 28   Conflict 28
Summary 29

3 The Coach as a Professional   30

Administrator 31
    Role 31   Conflict 32
Personnel Manager 33
    Role 33   Conflict 33
Teacher 34
    Role 34   Conflict 35
Prudent Person 35
    Role 35   Conflict 36
Recruiter 37
    Role 37   Conflict 37
Trainer 38
    Role 38   Conflict 39
Public Relations Person and Fund Raiser 40
    Role 40   Conflict 41
Strategist and Tactician 41
    Role 41   Conflict 42
Summary 42

4 Professional Preparation   44

Pre-Service Preparation 45
    College Courses 46   Certification 46   Coaching Minor 47
    Clinics 48   Playing Experience 48   Volunteer Coaching
    Experience 48
In-Service Preparation 48
    School District Programs 48   High School Association

Clinics 50 *Agency Training* 50 *Professional Association Opportunities* 50 *Private In-Service Opportunity* 51 *Additional Formal Study* 51 *Commercial Products* 52 *Personal Continuing Study* 52
Summary 53

5 Should You Coach?   54

Balance Sheet 55
Should You Coach? 56
Summary 59

PART 2 The Coach and the Athlete   62

6 Biological Considerations   64

Children 65
   Maturation Rate 67 *Motor Development* 68
   Physiological Aspects 68 *Gender Differences* 72
Adolescents 73
   Growth Rate 74 *Body Build and Composition* 74
   Cardiovascular Endurance 76 *Muscular Development* 77
   Temperature Regulation 78 *Gynecological Considerations* 79
Race 81
   Biological Factors 81 *Experience Factors* 82
Summary 84

7 Meeting the Athlete   87

Preparation 88
   Notification 88 *Announcements* 89 *Time* 89
   Facility 89
The Meeting 89
   Equipment 91 *Agenda* 91 *Goals and Objectives* 92
   Personal Data 93 *Team Standards (Rules)* 93
   Eligibility 96 *Clearance Forms* 96 *Other Agenda Items* 97
Summary 98

8 Selecting the Athlete   99

Size of the Squad 100
Unstructured Selection 101
   No-Cut Policy 101 *Self-Cut Policy* 102 *Recruiting* 102

Structured Selection   103
    Objective Selection   103   Subjective Evaluation   105
    Personal Traits   106   Peer Evaluations   107
Informing the Players   108
Summary   108

9 Teaching the Athlete   110

Teaching/Coaching/Learning   111
    The Player   112   Teaching Skills   115   Practice   120
Summary   124

10 Motivating the Athlete   125

Motivational Planning   126
    Know Yourself, Be Yourself   127   Know Results of Current Research   127   Analyze the Situation   128   Be Aware of Personal Actions   131   Analyze the Results   131
Motivational Approaches   132
    Facilities and Equipment   132   Recognition   133   Practice   134   Player Involvement   135   Personal Touch   135   Feedback   136   Reinforcement   138   Preparing for the Game   138   Awards/Rewards   140   Rituals   140   Pride   141   Team Togetherness   141   Gimmicks   142   Slogans   142   A Change in Routine   143   Team Supporters   143   During Play   145   Half Time   145
Summary   146

11 Developing Appropriate Behavior   148

Discipline   149
    Basic Areas   150   Developing a Code   151   Rule Making   152
Planning Procedures   154
    Environments   155   Behaviors   155   Reinforcers   157   Control Variables   158   Inform the Team Members   160   Evaluate   160
Summary   160

12 Life Management Concerns   162

Drugs   163
    Coaches' Concerns   164   Coaches' Actions   166
Stress   169
    Coaches' Concerns   169   Coaches' Actions   171
Education   173
    Coaches' Concerns   173   Coaches' Actions   175
Summary   177

PART 3 The Coach as an Administrator   180

13 Fiscal Management   183

Financing   184
    Factors Affecting the Cost   184   Sources of Revenue   186
The Budget   195
    Types of Budgets   195   Budget Preparation   196
Summary   202

14 Purchasing Criteria   204

Justifications for Purchasing   205
    Safety and Performance   205   Rules Requirements   206
    Program Needs   208   Player Needs   209
Selection of Equipment and Uniforms   210
    Categories   210   Protective Equipment   212   General Considerations for Uniform Selection   214   Special Considerations for Uniform Selection   215
Summary   217

15 Purchasing Procedures   218

Equipment Management Cycle   220
    Inventory   221   New Equipment Information   221
    Requisition   223   Bulk Purchasing and Bidding   225
Purchasing Guidelines   227
    Standardization   227   Long-Range Planning   228   Where to Buy   229   Reconditioned Equipment   230
Summary   230

16 Equipment Management   231

Receiving, Controlling, Issuing   232
    Receiving   233   Controlling   234   Issuing   235
Planning for Care and Maintenance   236
    Annual Plan   237   Care of Uniforms   240   Care of Equipment   241
Summary   241

17 Schedule Planning   242

Planning the Schedule   243
    Time Frame   244   Academic Considerations   244   Equitable Competition   245   Factors Affecting Scheduling   246
Rules for Schedule Planning   248
    Game Balance   249   Classification Considerations   250
    Opponents with Good Fan Support   250   Multiple Scheduling of Contests   250

Special Situations 251
    Scheduling at a Coaches' Meeting 252   Completing a Partial Schedule 252   Scheduling for A Winning Season 253
Contracting Guidelines 253
    Between Competent Parties 254   Mutual Assent 254 Valid Considerations 255   Clarity 255   Legality 255 Other Information 256
Summary 256

18 Contest Management   258

Pre-Season 259
    Business Arrangements 260   Publicity and Public Relations 261   Security 262   Equipment and Facilities 263   Player Eligibility 263   Pre-Game and Half-Time Activities 263   Medical Supervision 264
Pre-Contest 265
    Home Team 265   Home and Visiting Teams 268   Visiting Team 268
Contest 269
    Coach/Player Schedule 270
Post-Contest 270
    Home Team 270   Coaches 273
Summary 273

19 Legal Aspects   274

Legal Liability 276
    Guidelines for Judgment 276   Guidelines for Coaches 277 Coach's Defense 279   Waivers and Consent Forms 279 Spectator Risk 279   Liability Insurance 281
Product Liability 281
    Guidelines for Defense 282   Guidelines for Coaches 282 Effect on Sports 282
Civil Rights 283
    Student Rights 283   Considerations 284   Due Process 284   Integration 285   Sex Equity 285
Summary 286

20 Transportation   288

Vehicles 289
    School Vehicles 289   Use of Private Cars 290   Commercial Transportation 292
Policies and Procedures 292
    Supervision 292   Schedules 293   Emergencies 295 Player Conduct 297   Other Concerns 298
Summary 299

PART 4 The Coach as a Personnel Manager 300

21 Planning with and for the Staff   302

Developing Philosophy and Objectives 303
    Philosophy 303   Objectives 304
Assessing Program and Staff Needs 304
    Budget 305
Determining Ways to Meet Objectives 306
    Pre-Season 306   Off-Season 306
Identifying Qualities Needed 307
    Professionals 307   Nonprofessionals 307
Selecting Assistant Coaches 308
    Personal and Professional Qualities 308   Sources of Staffing 310   Interpersonal Relations 312   Evaluation 314
Being an Assistant Coach 315
Being an Adjunct Coach 315
Summary 316

22 Support Personnel   317

Managers 318
    Desirable Characteristics 319   Recruitment and Selection 320   Duties 321   Direction and Organization 322   Rotation 322   Pride 324
Trainers 325
    Certified Athletic Trainers 325   NATA 325   Noncertified Athletic Trainers 327
Medical Personnel 329
    Securing a Team Physician 329   Policies 330
Maintenance Personnel 331
    Building Personnel 333   System Personnel 333   Cooperative System Personnel 333   Special Needs 334   When All Else Fails 334
Clerical Personnel 334
    Secretarial Staff 335   Purchasing Staff 335   Accounting and Pay Office Staff 335   Student Assistants 335
Summary 336

23 Support Groups   337

School Groups 338
    Faculty and Staff 338   The Band 344   Student Groups 345   Special Groups 346
Booster Clubs 347
    Functions 347   Organization 348   Advantages 348   Disadvantages 352

xii Contents

    Other Support Groups 353
        Parents' Clubs 353   Sports Club 353   Adopt-a-Team Concept 353
    Community Organizations 354
        Civic Clubs 354   Patriotic Clubs 354   Community Development Groups 355   Churches 355   Governments 355
    Summary 356

24 News Media   357

    Varieties 358
        Print Media 358   Nonprint Media 359
    Relationships 360
        Central Information Source 360   Ethical/Responsible Behavior 361
    Procedures 362
        Guidelines 363   Pre-Season 363   Season 364   Post-Season 366
    Summary 366

PART 5 The Inner Nature of Coaching   368

25 Why Coach?   370

    Advantages 371
        Satisfaction 371   Challenges 372   Intangible Rewards 373   Tangible Rewards 374
    Disadvantages 375
        Dissatisfaction 375   Lack of Challenge 376   Lack of Intangibles 376   Lack of Tangible Rewards 377
    Why Coaches Remain in Coaching 378
        Pride 378   Satisfaction 378   Challenge 378   The Money Is Adequate 378   They Would Miss It 380   They Are Winning 380
    Why Coaches Leave Coaching 380
        The Fun Is Gone 380   The Challenge Is Over 381   Family Obligations 381   They Lose 381
    Why You Should Coach 381
        Assist in Securing a Position 382   Satisfaction 383   Drive to Succeed 383   Association 383   Way of Life 383

    Index 385

Preface

There is a continuing interest in sports activity by all ages and both sexes, growing out of the boost given athletics by university and school programs, agency programs, and federal legislation in the 1970s. This tremendous growth—both in the number of activities and in the number of participants—has increased the demand for coaches and has, therefore, increased the need for their adequate preparation.

Many books have been written about how to coach a specific sport; these generally deal with a coach's approach to developing skills or teaching strategies. Other books have stressed the psychological aspect of coaching and have not touched on strategies, organization, or day-to-day problems. Still others have been written for the athletic administrator or trainer. Few, if any, have focused on the coach as a person who must deal with many tasks, responsibilities, and problems—both personal and professional—that actually require most of a coach's time.

This book, in its second edition as well as in its first, is designed to fill this void in the preparation of all kinds of coaches. Covering the roles of the coach as a person as well as a professional, it is based on practical experience gained through years of coaching, on reports and advice from active coaches and athletic administrators, and on sound theory about performance, management, and relationships. It does not contain guidelines on how to coach a specific sport, nor does it seek to promote the authors' styles of coaching.

New materials include a chapter titled "Life Management Concerns," which deals with drug abuse, stress, and increased academic requirements. Other chapters are updated to include emerging legal concerns, the value of computer use, the increase in employment of adjunct coaches, and other current issues and activities.

The information should be useful in both pre-service and in-service programs. Colleges and universities with curricula that include preparing students for careers in coaching will find it particularly useful in teaching about the role of the coach. It could supplement courses offered in programs that stress the coaching of a particular sport. This book should be of equal value for the practicing coach, athletic director, and community or industrial sports leader who is searching for new ideas and assistance. Finally, but certainly not least, the budding or novice coach working with players in the nonschool leagues, and parents or others interested in knowing more about the conduct of athletic programs should find the material valuable.

Because the coaching experience can be extremely satisfying or extremely frustrating, this book is offered to those from any background who believe that coaching can truly be the good life.

B.J.J.
L.J.W.
R.E.P.
D.J.J.

Guide to
EFFECTIVE COACHING
Principles & Practice

PART 1

The Coach

1

"Coach"

WHAT COACHES ARE LIKE
QUALITIES OF A GOOD COACH
OBLIGATION TO YOUNG PEOPLE
  AND ATHLETES
THE COACH'S RESPONSIBILITIES

"Coach" is a title indicating respect, affection, status, and responsibility that can stay with one long after actual coaching days are over. Once a coach, always "coach" to team members, colleagues, and the community.

Players believe that their coaches are authorities on everything. They quote their coaches' words as gospel, even after they are well into middle age—old enough to know that coaches are not really the fountain of all wisdom. Coaches' standards, procedures, and mannerisms will be transmitted as appropriate ways of behaving for teams that will come long after.

Those athletes who become coaches will remember how their coaches did it and will form their own style of working by modeling after, or reacting to, them. Some will want to be just like their coaches; others will swear never to do as he or she did; but all will be strongly influenced. Because of this, coaches bear a heavy responsibility and must be continuously aware of the possible effects of their words and actions.

Being a good coach requires more than possessing a cap, a whistle, and a clipboard. It is not enough to have played well, though this is very helpful. It is also not enough to have a commanding physical presence, though this may be helpful too. Being a good coach requires skill, knowledge, the ability to organize, and the talents of a great teacher.

A coach is always a teacher even though a teacher is not always a coach. All good teachers are concerned that their pupils, or athletes, perform well. Coaches have the additional opportunity of working with those who are willing to pay a price for excellence, those who are willing to do more than the minimum required. Teachers often have to deal with large numbers of students, but coaches can concern themselves with a smaller, self-selected group who will accept the need for practice, drill, and the search for better, faster, stronger ways to perform. This happy task, that of leading the chosen or self-chosen, is the major job difference between most teachers and most coaches.

It does not matter whether the responsibility is to coach the church league softball team for little girls, the soccer league pennant winner, the

Class AAAA state champion football team, or the coed country club swimming team—the basic relationships and responsibilities are the same. Little League coaches' basic concerns are very much like those of big league coaches, and helping the neighborhood runners can be very much like coaching the Olympic track team. The caliber of the talent and experience, the training of the coach, and the breadth of the audience are vastly different, but the basic functions and the basic joys and sorrows are the same.

It may be that the assignment is only to coach "Biddy Basketball," but young players can care as passionately about doing their best as any world-class athlete does, and so should their coaches. Players, at any level, deserve the best that can be given them; therefore, coaches are obligated to learn as much as they can so that the players derive maximum benefit from their leadership.

The opportunity to be a member of that long rank of coaches is open to everyone. To truly deserve to join that honorable association of experienced and dedicated men and women requires hard work and study. It requires strong personal commitment to helping boys, girls, men, and women in their search for athletic excellence at whatever level they choose to play. It also requires a large share of time, talent, energy, and probably money. Coaching is not an inexpensive profession in any way. Whatever the costs in time, talent, energy, and resources, there is always more needed.

If coaching is a vocation or an avocation that individuals think they want to pursue, this book can answer some of their questions about the tasks, the opportunities, and the good times and bad times that coaches have. Whether they are beginners or veterans, recreation league volunteers or paid professionals, they should be able to gain new or additional information about the profession. Part 1 of this book, entitled "The Coach," presents an overview of the coach's world to help individuals understand the basics of the job and decide if they want to enter the coaching field.

WHAT COACHES ARE LIKE

There seems to be a contemporary myth that says coaches are very conservative, traditional, and rigid in their dealings with athletes, colleagues, and the community. However, if coaches were as inflexible as the myth would have one believe, there would be little change in technique, strategy, or relationships. Common sense says that coaches are as willing to shift to a new strategy or technique as is any scientist, and that they do adjust to new styles in behavior. If they were inflexible in coaching procedures, they could not have flourished despite the "athletic revolution" of the late 1960s and early 1970s, the changes brought about by Title IX; academic reforms at local, state, and national levels; and the economic decline of the 1980s.

Although new or revamped programs have increased opportunities for boys and girls to participate in organized athletics, the National Fed-

6 *The Coach*

eration of State High School Associations (NFSHSA) reports a slight decrease in the number of participants. This may be the result of decreased school enrollments, or it may be that young people are opting "to do their own thing," which may not include highly organized athletic programs. In order to field full squads, coaches must keep abreast of new trends and conditions and be able to deal with continuous change.

Many persons believe that a school system's coaches form the last bastion of law and order in a world filled with disorder. For this, coaches receive both praise and blame. Archconservatives think that coaches are not tough enough, and liberals think that they are too tough. The probability is that coaches are very much like the general population from which they come and are pretty much middle of the road, as are most teachers. They may be more conservative than their players and more liberal than the town elders, but, generally, they are like anyone else.

The fact that coaches are in leadership roles may be because they are that kind of people to begin with—assertive, mature, and with leadership qualities that were inherent or that developed with the job. Because no coach can survive who is not intelligent, aggressive, tough minded, and self-controlled, most coaches have these characteristics.

Coaches are not alike; they come in many different packages and with varying abilities and talents. This book demonstrates that one does not have to fit into a particular mold but can possess or assume some of the best characteristics of all types.

QUALITIES OF A GOOD COACH

Many lists have been made as to what qualities a good coach or a good teacher should possess. After reading this chapter one may choose to make a personal list. The *Coaches' Manual,* an old but accurate and reliable publication, recommends the following as desirable qualities.

1. Reasonable flexibility and receptivity to attitudinal changes in society that affect youth.
2. An ability to understand and to cope with the problems and concerns of athletes.
3. A well-organized, logical, and rational approach to coaching which fosters mutual respect among the entire community.
4. An ability and willingness to communicate with team, parents, teachers, administrators, and the public.
5. Good judgment in the appropriate use of motivational techniques, particularly those having to do with encouragement, inspiration, and confidence.
6. A humanistic and ethical philosophy which emphasizes fairness, friendliness, and firmness.
7. An ability to innovate and to project within a sport setting and to envision any consequences to the total school environment.
8. Emotional stability and self-control in highly sensitive and involved situations associated with sports.

9. An ability to achieve educational objectives through the patient use of direct and indirect methods.
10. An excellent example in word, deed, and appearance.
11. An appreciation of the artistic viewpoint as related to athletics.
12. A belief in and practice of human dignity as a basic quality of man.[1]

The basic qualities of a good coach and teacher have been outlined and equated as being the same. These timeless qualities are:

1. Knowledge of the subject and intense interest and enthusiasm about it.
2. Willingness to share one's knowledge with anyone who is interested.
3. Communication skill.
4. A personality which demands, drives, stimulates, excites, or in some way pulls out of students levels of achievement beyond normal expectancy.[2]

Press Maravich, a noted coach, has said that coaches must have a thick skin, not gossip, not worry, develop a thorough knowledge of the game, be good and fair disciplinarians, be able to handle pressure, work at getting along with others, and have control and generosity of spirit.[3] Coaches do not last long if they do not enter the practice and game as a joint, enthusiastic, fun, hard-working venture. To criticize athletes, resist suggestions, or become defensive is the beginning of another failing coach.[4]

A compilation of competencies needed by high school coaches included the following as most important:

Care and prevention of injuries
Supervision
Consistent, firm, fair discipline
Presentation of fundamentals
Enthusiasm for the sport
Exemplary conduct during a game
Adherence to school policy
Knowledge of fundamentals
Communication with individuals, team, and the public
Organization of practice
Game preparation[5]

It should be apparent that the person seeking to enter the coaching profession must initially possess many good qualities and then strive to acquire the others. Coaches are developed, or develop themselves, through hard work and a determination to improve. Once the aspiring coach has selected a model—a coaching idea or ideal that he or she wants to become more like—then the path is set for achieving. After noting the characteristics already possessed, those desired, and those to be eliminated, then one can set about the task of becoming a top-flight coach.

OBLIGATION TO YOUNG PEOPLE AND ATHLETES

Coaches also have great obligations as molders of youth in the social and moral sense. They can no longer shrug off their own personal habits as not mattering to anyone but themselves, because now it does matter. Players will not hear what coaches say if it is different from what coaches do.

The health, training, and safety of players are also among coaches' responsibilities. Here, too, personal example as well as up-to-date information and close supervision are necessary. Those who coach cannot avoid the requirement of knowing the best methods of preparing players for participation and of putting their health and welfare first.

Although conscientious coaches will be concerned about athletes of all ages, they should be especially concerned about young athletes. A statement has been proposed in the *Youth Sports Guide for Coaches and Teachers* called a "Bill of Rights for Young Athletes." The good coach will follow these, which include:

1. Right of the opportunity to participate in sports regardless of ability level.
2. Right to participate at a level that is commensurate with each child's developmental level.
3. Right to have qualified adult leadership.
4. Right to participate in safe and healthy environments.
5. Right of each child to share in the leadership and decision making of their sport participation.
6. Right to play as a child and not as an adult.
7. Right to proper participation in the sport.
8. Right to an equal opportunity to strive for success.
9. Right to be treated with dignity by all involved.
10. Right to have fun through sport.[6]

THE COACH'S RESPONSIBILITIES

As a responsible person, a coach should exemplify the behaviors described in the National Code of Ethics for high school coaches whether coaching at the youth sport level, the school or college level, or the professional level. The Code of Ethics states:

As a professional educator I will

Exemplify the highest moral character, behavior, and leadership.
Respect the integrity and personality of the individual athlete.
Abide by the rules of the game in letter and in spirit.
Respect the integrity and judgment of sports officials.
Demonstrate a mastery of and continuing interest in coaching principles and techniques through professional involvement.
Encourage a respect for all athletics and their values.
Display modesty in victory and graciousness in defeat.

Promote ethical relationships among coaches.

Fulfill responsibilities to provide health services and an environment free of safety hazards.

Encourage the highest standards of conduct and scholastic achievement among all athletes.

Seek to inculcate good health habits including the establishment of sound training rules.

Strive to develop in each athlete the qualities of leadership, initiative, and good judgment.[7]

All of coaching's benefits, honors, and pleasures, as well as hard work, bad feelings, and sorrows, are not restricted to any one group. Individuals who enter the coaching profession will get the same kudos and knocks that their predecessors received. The title of "coach" can be earned by only those who truly want to wear it with pride.

The coaching game, a grand and time-honored profession, is deserving of the finest men and women the nation can provide because they will be dealing with the nation's most precious product—children and young people. It does not matter where coaches are, at what level they coach, or with whom they participate. If they work hard, become students of the game, and care about their players, they can become one of many who say with great pride, "I am a coach!"

ENDNOTES

1. National Association for Sport and Physical Education, *Coaches' Manual* (Washington, D.C.: AAHPER), pp. 9-10. (Undated revision of Florida D.O.E. Bulletin 741., 1959, n.d.)
2. J. D. Lawther, "Psychology of Teaching and Coaching," in *Proceedings of the Second National Institute for Girls' and Women's Sports* (Washington, D.C.: AAHPER, 1966), pp. 133-136.
3. P. Maravich. "What Every Coach Must Learn," *National Federation News* (November 1985): 28.
4. L. Leggett, "Why Coaches Fail," *Journal of Physical Education, Recreation and Dance* (April 1983): 62.
5. J. Gratto, "Competencies Used to Evaluate High School Coaches," *Journal of Physical Education, Recreation and Dance* (May 1983): 59.
6. J. R. Thomas, ed. *Youth Sports Guide for Coaches and Parents* (Washington, D.C.: AAHPER, 1977), p. 44.
7. NASPE, *Coaches' Manual*, p. 93.

2

The Coach as a Person

```
LEADER
FOLLOWER
ROLE MODEL
DISCIPLINARIAN
PSYCHOLOGIST
FRIEND AND COUNSELOR
LIFE MANAGEMENT ADVISOR
PARENT SUBSTITUTE
FAMILY MEMBER
SINGLE PERSON
SUMMARY
```

Each coach must wear many hats and play many parts in the complex activity called athletics. The potential coach must learn about the variety of roles and be prepared to change roles and scenes at a moment's notice. The drama of an athletic contest and season is very demanding of its participants. It is stressful at best, requiring continual success for both survival and acclaim, and discarding those who fail to meet its standards.

Shakespeare said that each man in his time plays many parts, and so it is with coaches. Sociologists define a role as a set of rights and obligations associated with a specific position within a social structure. No one has more specific positions or parts to play within a social structure than does a coach. This is due to the many tasks that a coach must complete, or see that they are completed, during the year. The types of tasks vary with the coach and the situation, but they are very much like those of the high school swimming team coach in Shawnee Mission, Kansas, listed in Figure 5-1, page 57.

The roles that coaches must play, and the kind of positions that they must fill, are presented in two chapters. This chapter deals with the coach as a person. It gives the duties, responsibilities, and conflicts of the coach as a leader, follower, role model, disciplinarian, psychologist, friend and counselor, life management advisor, parent substitute, family member, and single person. Chapter 3 discusses the role of a coach as a professional. Neither set of roles is more important or less important than the other; most will be filled by every coach, but not to the same level of competence.

Because some of the roles are overlapping—and therefore interfere with one another or with obligations outside coaching—role conflicts can arise. Role conflicts occur when the personal characteristics, goals, plans, and traditions of the coach are not in congruence with those of the institution, culture, or environment in which the coach functions. There are both inter-role conflicts and intra-role conflicts. Inter-role conflicts emerge when a person has two or more roles interfering with each other, such as teacher and coach. They are similar but it is difficult to do both well, and a conscientious person can be torn between two equally important duties.

The greatest inter-role conflict of all is overload, too many roles to play in too little time.[1] Intra-role conflicts occur when a person has difficulty in determining which way the role or position should be played. When there is uncertainty about the best way to select a team, to coach a game, or to play the role of coach, generally an intra-role conflict emerges. Both kinds of conflicts are uncomfortable and, until resolved, can interfere with the job to be done.

Experienced supervisors of student teachers and coaches know that beginners discover a real role conflict when they must change from student to teacher, from player to coach, and from follower to leader. These novices must learn to break away from old patterns, put social distance between themselves and their new students, and become mature, responsible faculty members.

Although less damaging than role conflict, role strain may occur in setting role expectations.[2] This difficulty is caused by the young person's not being sure what role he or she is expected to play, especially in moving from one position (student) to another (teacher/coach).

Roles, and the conflicts that may accompany each, are outlined in this chapter. The reader is invited to consider and debate the proposed possibilities in order to determine their validity for each person who considers coaching for a vocation or avocation.

LEADER

Role

The coach is placed in the role of a leader. To be "coach" is to be the "boss." This role of leadership goes beyond the authority of the position. As has been pointed out, "Few other members of the faculty display the degree of constructive leadership manifested by the coach. The testimony on this point is overwhelming and too many athletes have testified to the moral importance to deny it exists."[3]

Leadership is the quality of bringing people into the leader's way of thinking and behaving, and having them agree that this way is the path to follow. It is not a rule of fear but a rule of respect. While some coaches learn leadership from experience, many can profit from participation in leadership workshops.

When the group begins to work on a task, the true leader emerges—the one who knows the task, knows the group, and has a plan for accomplishing the task that is within the ability of the group. Knowing what needs to be done and being willing to work to get it done is the true essence of leadership. Many persons who know how to move a group to a solution hesitate to suggest the answer for fear of being made "chairperson of the committee" to do the job. Coaches should be ready to assume the leadership role and be prepared to carry the burden of work and responsibility it entails.

The skillful leader takes pleasure in seeing group members grow under the necessary restraints of group membership. There are circumstances when the leader must say no, and be firm, strong, and courageous. It is obvious in task-oriented groups, when decisions must be made quickly on the basis of experience, that pure democratic leadership cannot prevail.[4] It has been proposed that there are no democratic coaches; there are only degrees of autocratic coaches. This may very well be correct if one considers that player choices are usually available only within a framework constructed by a coach.

An analysis of leadership styles in coaching indicates that there are three general styles: the hard driver, the thoughtful persuader, and the friendly helper.[5] It should be noted, however, that inflexibility in leadership style can lead to conflict with athletes, other authorities, and the leadership role itself. After a person is made a coach and put into a leadership position, success depends on the capacity to perform, the experience brought to the job, the particular situation, coach-player and coach-administration relations, and the authority given the coach to do the job.

Conflict

The role of coach as leader carries with it the problem of being unable to please everyone all the time. Inevitably, some of the public—parents, players, reporters, principals, or boosters—will be annoyed or alienated. Decisions, nevertheless, ought to be made on the best evidence possible and on the best professional judgment of the coach. Coaches should do the best they can and then let the chips fall where they may. Those who believe that they are participating in a popularity contest and must keep everyone happy will soon be overcome by dissidents on all sides.

Another area of conflict is one between coach and young athlete. Most coaches believe that the majority of athletes find sports a meaningful experience, and they have difficulty in adjusting to the athlete who is resistant to direction or irreverent in his or her view of the coach's authority. Lacking self-discipline, the athlete may not be able to follow a routine, may have other interests, and may become a quitter; lacking patience, the athlete may want immediate independence and self-direction. Generally, coaches find it easier to work with the self-disciplined player or one who submits to directions than with one who is not interested in "paying the price." Athletes usually have to adjust to the coach, but in some instances the coach will have to adjust to the athletes. The higher up the competitive ladder one goes, the more this conflict appears. It is especially apparent in professional athletics; there many high-priced players are in open conflict with their coaches and managers.

FOLLOWER

Role

Not only should coaches be good leaders, they should also be good followers and good team members. Assistant coaches must cooperate with, and follow the directions of, the head coach. All are subject to the athletic director, sports supervisor, principal, president, and/or the board who employs or assigns them. If they expect players to respond to leadership directives, then they must also demonstrate how to follow.

Cooperation and teamwork to attain a common goal—major characteristics of sport and athletics—should be hallmarks of every coach. Re-

The Coach as a Person   15

Figure 2-1   Someone has to make the decision (Photo courtesy of The Florida State University, Tallahassee, Florida. Photographer: Ryals Lee)

sponsible, cooperative behavior as a part of a team is imperative for anyone who desires to be a coach.

Following is not a subordinate role. It is a necessary and integral function in any group, and the quality of the interaction between leader and group sets the stage for effective action.

Conflict   Following does not always come easily to the authoritarian coach. The personality who can be only chief and not Indian can quickly come into conflict with similar personalities in positions of authority. Those who firmly believe that no one else can understand as fully or perform as well may also irritate or alienate those for whom they are responsible or with whom they serve in a leadership or followship position.

Another potential area for conflict can occur when coaches are not experienced in carrying out orders, but only in giving them. Sometimes they can be so removed from the real details of the work to be done that they are incapable of carrying out the responsibility. The solution for this is that leaders should not ask followers to do anything that they are not prepared to do themselves.

ROLE MODEL

Role

Constantly in the public eye, coaches are expected to provide good examples for their players. They are always "on duty" as far as being role models for young people, even when they are not coaching and think they are "off duty." The requirement for exemplary behavior in all matters—social, business, and personal—cannot be ignored.

Young people model, or copy, the behavior of the significant people in their lives as they "try on" a variety of ways of behaving, searching for a style of their own. Coaches are prime examples of significant persons in the lives of athletes and thus become primary models for how to live.

Moral and ethical standards have to be lived if they are to be believable. Fair play and sportsmanship are caught as well as taught. The coach who is fair and courteous to players, opponents, and officials, and who requires this behavior from the team, can promote sportsmanship at every level. Although the evidence for specific transfer of sporting behavior from the field to the schoolroom or office is hard to find, it is an item of belief that good sports on the field are also good sports off the field.

Violence in sports is a serious concern. The coach who teaches or permits a player to injure another deliberately has lost all perspective as to what sport is all about. Concern for the safety and welfare of all players is the foremost duty of coaches, and the example of concern should be set by them to be observed by the players. A coach must not allow deliberate acts of violence either through commission of the act or through the omission of consideration for the safety of others.

Prohibition of the violation of the letter and the spirit of the rules is also a coach's responsibility. Rules and officials' judgments are designed to make the game operate smoothly and are to be obeyed. In a democratic society the defense against anarchy is law by the consent of the governed—so, too, in athletics. Coaches who have helped their team learn how to cheat or beat the rules are setting examples of unethical behavior for the team and for the community. Society cannot tolerate this, or perhaps even survive, if its strongest citizens believe that anything is acceptable if one does not get caught.

One of the great influences coaches have as models for acceptable behavior is in the way they behave before, during, and after a contest.[6] The coach and the coaching staff set the tone or atmosphere for the entire occasion. If the pep rally focuses on "our team" as the "good guys" and "their team" as the "bad guys," and the staff incites the student body to holy war, then they have failed to communicate that sport is a contest between equals under equal and honorable conditions. Those who deride the opposition during the game, lose their tempers, threaten the officials, scream and stamp the floor, and abuse players for mistakes set poor examples for the spectators also. This behavior is not acceptable, and "wanting to win" does not excuse it. The coach who thanks the opponents and congratulates them on a well-played game, shakes hands with the opposing coach, and, in general, acts like a lady or a gentleman instead of a spoiled child will help the players and spectators behave in the same manner.

All professionals expect their members to demonstrate high standards of conduct reflecting sound ethical judgments. The coaching profession is no exception to this principle, and, because of its nature, its members are subjected to unusually close scrutiny. This fact makes it imperative to project an image that reflects the highest credit on themselves, their teams, and their schools.

Good sportsmanship must be taught continuously if it is to be learned. Mere participation in sport does not guarantee the development of sporting behavior. Although every team should be coached to win, as that is the primary objective of competition, winning should always be accomplished through spirited fair play.

Realizing that they represent the coaching speciality in a teaching profession, a school, or an agency, coaches must insist that participants play their best, honor their opponents, and respect officials and their decisions. They must also exemplify emotional control, courteous behavior, and fairness at all times. This is why the first ethical standard for coaches reported earlier stated, "I will exemplify the highest moral character, behavior, and leadership."

Conflict

While there should be no conflict between the required exemplary behavior for a coach and the coach's usual behavior, it does happen, and novice coaches need to be prepared to deal with this. Always being on stage and observed by players, townspeople, and students can be a burden even when he or she is behaving properly according to the standards of the community, school, and ethical code. Having a personal life style that is not congruent with these standards can often create serious personal and professional problems.

Coaches can well complain that they should not have to be better, stronger, fairer, and wiser than the other adult citizens in the community, but, like it or not, being the good example is a coach's lot in life. The smaller the community, the greater the opportunity for on- and off-duty observation of the coach by the townspeople. The larger the community, the greater the opportunity to be lost in the crowd and to live far away from the school or agency population. A few coaches, deciding that serving as a good example during the school day and sport season is enough, may choose to live at some distance from the school and community in which they work. Assistants may be able to do this for a while, but head coaches need community support and cannot afford to be any distance from their power base.

The exemplary behavior of coaches at practices and contests may lead to conflict with the school administration or the townspeople. Many communities have long-standing feuds with neighboring communities with inter-city, inter-park, and inter-school rivalries. The generation of an artificial hatred is sometimes cherished and encouraged, and the conscientious coach who tries to modify this unsporting behavior may come in conflict with the community. Those who try to generate inter-community rivalry when the local population does not support this kind of activity can also conflict with local standards.

DISCIPLINARIAN

Role

Much has been written about the tough coach, and legends have been developed from the tactics of such noted "hard-nosed" ones as Vince Lombardi and Paul "Bear" Bryant. It is true that coaches typically exert authority far beyond that imposed by most other persons with whom athletes come in contact. They serve in a central position of authority, and response to authority is what discipline is all about.

The healthiest form of discipline for an athlete, or for anyone, is self-discipline. This is self-controlled behavior to meet an accepted goal or standard. It requires setting aside the immediate gratification of a want so that some larger or more valuable long-range plan can be fulfilled. Having self-disciplined athletes is usually a goal of every coach, so that each player can be relied on to run his or her life in ways consistent with accepted and agreed-on standards. The ability to discipline one's life is a primary mark of maturity and true adulthood. While young athletes are still maturing, their talent for self-direction should be developed.

Immaturity, the lack of self-discipline in most young athletes, or the lack of congruence in meaningful and significant goals between coach and athlete may require the imposition of a regime of discipline, or standards of behavior, by the coach. The business-oriented model of sport seems to be moving toward a "winning is the best thing" style and requires discipline imposed from above. The educational model of sport, in which playing is everything, should develop self-discipline.

Discipline can be defined as the attempt to set limitations and modify behavior. In athletics these limitations take many forms—the rules of the game, the authority of the officials, and the requests and demands of the coach for training, behavior, and performance.

Most young people want a framework within which they can operate freely. A structure with reasonable limitations can be provided so that the opportunity for stepping outside the framework is limited. There is nothing wrong in telling athletes what they may or may not do, as they need to learn to follow rules and to know the consequences of violating them. Procedures are discussed in Chapter 11.

Conflict

The coach may have serious conflicts with, and because of, discipline. One of these is found in the personality of the coach who can be so unyielding and authoritarian that the players are intimidated and humiliated. A second can be found in the coach who is so unsure of a direction that no firm guidelines are established; hence, the players have no framework in which to operate.

Another area of conflict is that between coach, as the maker of the rules, and the typical adolescent, who is trying to establish independence. In this situation both may lose because neither will bend or listen to reason. A fourth area of conflict sometimes arises when the demands of the coach run counter to those of the parents. Currently there is a tendency for parents to protect their children from the effects of their behavior, which is contradictory to the typical coach's idea of immediate payment for any violation.

PSYCHOLOGIST

Role

Many persons involved in athletic endeavors are convinced that sheer personal skills and strength are not enough for a winning performance and that the real game is in the player's mind, not in the body. If this is true, and it surely seems to be, then a coach has to be a sport psychologist and a social psychologist—as well as an educational psychologist or a teacher of skills—to elicit superior performances from players or to help them perform at their best. It is essential to understand human nature, the players, the opponents, and the interrelationships between them. The fact is that skill is not enough—motivation and "desire" must also be present.

Coaches should also understand how athletics can contribute to the personality and integration of each person and to the integration and cohesiveness of a team, as they are unavoidably involved in personality development. Personality development is strongly influenced by play, for it is in play that the individual is able to test skills and relationships under relatively safe, orderly conditions. The child and young adult can develop personal integration in physical, social, and psychological skills learned through exploration and practice in games. Individuals can learn much about life in a game—winning, losing, competing, and cooperating—which serves well in group situations as long as they live.[7]

As play is more institutionalized, it becomes sport that provides a stabilizing, organized force in a rapidly changing world. It provides an orderly framework within which an individual can grow. Sports remain a unique area where authority is accepted and acceptable; players are much more likely to listen to their coach than to anyone else. Faith in the coach can help young athletes meet crises and conquer them.

If sport is truly a central place for wholesome personality development, then the role of coach as psychologist is very important. Before the athletic program can be successful for coaches and players, in win-loss records, or in personal satisfaction and pleasure, the team must be developed into a cooperative, cohesive, contributing group. It has been stated that perhaps the greatest reward derived from membership on a team is the development of lasting friendships. These are the result of interactions taking place within a team as members help one another accomplish personal goals designed to enhance the total team picture. A coach as a psychologist will surely want to work to see that the players have respect for their peers' talents and contributions, share ideas with one another, have a keen sense of self-worth, have a commitment to shared goals, and know that they will all get just, equal, and fair consideration and treatment.

In the role of learning psychologist, the coach must be concerned with how motor skills are learned. Skill development is based on the readiness or the set of the individual to learn, on the potential the athlete possesses to learn (intellectual and physical endowments), the motivation or drive of the player, the opportunity to practice, and the environment in which the player works. This environment includes the physical as well as the social surroundings of teammates, coaches, and spectators.

All coaches should understand learning theory. Indeed, all teachers must take courses in educational psychology; and, if their background is limited or the material has been forgotten, they then have the obligation to learn, relearn, or upgrade such skills and knowledge. Information about teacher/learning is presented in Chapter 9.

Conflict

Personal and professional conflict can face those who attempt to apply a variety of learning and social theories but still have unsuccessful players and teams, dissension and strife, and low morale. No one can be comfortable or feel successful in such a situation.

Because a coach is primarily a teacher who is trained to elicit high-level responses from players, failure to succeed in this area causes personal frustrations. Professional conflict can also emerge when this lack of teaching/coaching skill, or at least the lack of results from athletes, is evident.

Coaches are also expected to be social psychologists who can mold a group of divergent personalities into a well-oiled machine—a team. Lack of success in this area can also cause personal and professional problems. When one player has problems and cannot function well in school, with teachers, with friends and teammates, or with a coach, there can be a personal conflict concerning the time devoted to the player and the results gained. When there is internal team conflict or team/coach conflict because of personalities, schedules, goals, and ineffective procedures, the coach will likely face great difficulties. If these personal conflicts are not resolved, practices and games can be nightmares, and a successful season is impossible.

FRIEND AND COUNSELOR

Role

Every athlete knows that a coach can be counted on to serve as friend and counselor. Coaches can get players out of trouble, lend them money, pat them on the back, laugh, cry, and cheer with them, and do not let anyone else talk about them. They are the ones that former athletes come back to see year after year, name their children after, and write to at Christmas. They can seem to be enemies when they require one more lap, but the truth is there for all to see—coaches are true friends.

Coaches are also in a particularly good position to counsel. They have a great deal of contact with people, under real-life conditions on the playing field, in the gym, and in other informal situations, while "official" counselors have only formal contact with students, or others under their care, and then only in the office by request.[8] Many teachers do not get to know students very well in a personal sense, but a coach who has built up rapport with students and athletes in real-life contexts is both exposed and accessible to those with troubles. The student and athlete come to know the coach, and the coach comes to know the young people.

To fill this strategic role of counselor, the coach must learn that each of the athletes is an individual with basic needs to find himself or herself and to learn "Who am I?" A related basic need is to be loved (fully respected and appreciated as individuals) by at least one person whom the player respects. The coach as a friend and counselor can meet this need.

Coaches must consider a series of behaviors if they are to develop as counselors and help athletes develop as persons. There must be a real and concerned interest in student/athletes and their problems. In hearing the athlete's concerns, the coach should express empathy and understanding and, when appropriate, give advice. If the athlete's problem is greater than the coach's skill to manage, he or she should know where to get professional help for the student and proceed to get it.

Figure 2–2 A coach's advice is valued (Photo courtesy of The Florida State University)

Problems—whether they involve players, faculty, administrators, or parents—can be settled more quickly and effectively in private. Calling the player aside and talking can frequently solve the issue. It is amazing how a player will level with a coach behind closed doors of an office where just the two of them can interact face-to-face.

A student/athlete pointed out one interesting communication and relationship problem between coach and athlete.[9] The athlete sees a one-to-one relationship with the coach; even when the coach speaks to the entire team, each member feels that the coach is talking on a personal basis and is aware of each athlete's thoughts and needs. On the other hand, the coach may be unaware of this feeling of a one-to-one relationship and thus ignores, or never even knows, the marvelous opportunity available for coach/athlete relationships.

High school coaches are influential persons in athletes' future educational and occupational plans. The advice that they give their players regarding their education beyond high school is positively related with the player's decision to attend college; however, players must be encouraged to make their own decisions about attending college and not to rely only on a coach's opinion. The coach who cares about the team and its competitive success will also care about the players and will listen, help, advise, and stand by the players as true friend and counselor.

Conflict

Any time the coach assists a player in resolving a difficulty, there is the possibility of conflict between the coach and player, and between others who may be involved. Some coaches take offense when good advice is not taken, and some players take offense when good advice is given; at times conflict is inevitable.

A classic area of conflict can occur when the coach, who considers himself or herself only a friend of an athlete as one among many athletes, is accused of playing favorites. This can be uncomfortable for both the coach and the player.

The other side of this conflict occurs when coaches really do have favorites that they obviously make concessions for. In some instances these relationships are friendships between mentor and protégé based primarily on common interests and skills. In other situations there are closer relationships with sexual connotations, either heterosexual or homosexual. Coaches cannot afford to date their students, as they would face strong disapproval from most school and community members.

There is another area of conflict between what may be good for the student academically and good for the student athletically. A fine athlete who could make a name for himself or herself, bringing glory to the coach as well, should be counseled carefully about the educational opportunities available. The question may be, "Should long-range goals of the player's life be interfered with by what may be short-range athletic goals?"

A fourth area of conflict lies in the realm of confidentiality. An ethical principle for a professional educator is to keep personal information about a student private and confidential, but coaches may be asked to testify in an action involving information learned through the counseling situation. Privileged communication is a formal, legal confidentiality extended to a few, such as priests, lawyers, and physicians, but it is not given to teachers and coaches. This may cause some conflict if a problem comes to court, but, fortunately, this type of testimony is usually not required.

Another conflict can arise when the student tells the coach confidential information that should be shared with parents or others in authority. The student should be told about the possibility of breaking a confidence in cases of drug abuse, child abuse, theft, and the like, as a coach must balance honoring confidentiality against the ultimate welfare of the athlete.

LIFE MANAGEMENT ADVISOR

Role   Not only do coaches have an obligation to fill all the roles of friend and counselor, they must also be concerned about drug abuse, effects of stress, and the value of an education. They are being charged by school boards and the public to take an active part in assisting young athletes to have full, productive, and healthy lives—to learn life management skills.

With the increased use of drugs by preadolescents and adolescents, coaches have a duty, imposed legally or socially, to help youth be drug-free and have the opportunity to do so. Apparently, the most widely abused drugs are alcohol, a licit drug, and marijuana, an illicit drug. However, the abuse of other chemicals such as stimulants, tranquilizers, steroids, and cocaine is prevalent, and being an athlete is no guarantee that an individual is drug-free. One has only to read or hear the sports news to know that many top-flight athletes have major problems.

A new duty placed on school faculty is that of recognizing and dealing with student stress. Particular emphasis is being placed on the reduction of teenage suicides through recognition of early signs of distress. Depression is a common emotional disturbance among competitive athletes; not being able to live up to expectations—theirs, their parents', the coaches', the hometown fans'—can be frightening. Frequently this situation is magnified because the individual is experiencing other major problems. Coaches are in a prime position to observe and alleviate stress in vulnerable young people.

Too many athletes able to perform well in a contest do not perform well in academic areas. Academics plus athletics can be a highly successful formula for educating youth, but many coaches, athletes, and parents utilize only the second half. The results are devastating as illiterate persons are "graduating" from high schools, and the careers of many athletes come to an abrupt halt as they find that they are not skilled enough to be professional athletes nor capable of continuing their education at a college or university. Also, they have no skills with which to make it in the work sector of the real world. Coaches may have a difficult time keeping their priorities straight because most are judged on their win-loss record. By placing the total education of the athlete at the top of their list, however, they are in a position to help students get their own priorities in order.

24 The Coach

Conflict

Some coaches do not follow sound life management practices themselves and thus face a conflict when trying to support these practices with their players. It appears that drinking alcoholic beverages, using tobacco and recreational drugs, and facing stress on the job are problems confronting coaches as well as students.

In addition, coaches are torn between duty to players and the pressure to win and keep their positions. Some drugs may enhance player performance temporarily, although be deadly in the long run, thus providing a winning edge. The conflict between personal and professional goals can be acute, but coaches must put players' health before their own gain. There is also the problem that coaches face when they discover players violating school rules about drug abuse. Should the violation be reported and the player lost for the season, or should no report be made and the team kept intact? This conflict can be resolved only by following school policy.

Stress among young people is a very serious problem, and the added stress of competition on athletes can accentuate it. Coaches who cannot serve as stress reducers and who do not know their players well enough to "pick up" on depression and personality change will be in conflict with their legal responsibility as well as with their professional obligation. No coach who really cares about athletes will knowingly continue to place them in highly stressful situations that cannot be handled well. Problems must be quickly recognized and either helped by a coach or referred to professionals who can help. Coaches have to realize that they are not "God" and that it is not necessary to know all the answers; however, it is important to know someone who may.

Regular academic progress for athletes is a major area of concern. Generally, coaches realize that academic work should take precedence over athletics, but frequently they just want to keep a player eligible. They may ask themselves such questions as: "Should I ask the faculty member to make an exception in this case?" "Should I encourage him to take this course because it is easy or the teacher gives no grade lower than a 'C'?" "Should I help her circumvent this policy to help her get into this particular university?" Logically, the answer is *no* to all of the above, but all too often logic is lost in a win-at-all-cost attitude.

Because many coaches are uninformed about drug use and abuse or are unaware of student stress and the possible results, most school districts now have optional, or required, teacher workshops. Regardless of their personal preference, coaches must take advantage of these opportunities so that they can better serve their athletes in managing their lives. For young people, as well as adults, life management knowledge and skills can be life savers. Refer to Chapter 12 for more in-depth information.

PARENT SUBSTITUTE

Role

In this current society the role of the family has changed. Instead of having strong family units that take the responsibility for their children's medical, moral, social, and ethical behavior, many families seem to be expecting the church, the school, and the community at large to assume these responsibilities.

This nation is also becoming one of single-parent families. While some of these are headed by fathers, the vast majority of single-parent homes are headed by mothers. When there is a broken home, the children are often not as closely supervised as the working parent would prefer, so schools and agencies must assist in this problem. Neglected or abused children also need assistance and support from outside the home if they receive none, or perceive that they receive none, from the family.

If children are to be stable they must have someone who cares about them who is important in their life. It is not enough just to have friends and be liked by teachers; one must have the love and concern of a significant other—someone who really matters. This person can be a parent, a relative, a teacher, a friend, or a coach. As coaches are high-status people in an athlete's life, they can serve as the admired authority figure, or significant other.

Coaches are generally admired, obeyed, and responded to as children typically respond to their loved parents. In fact, the male coach may be the only strong father figure with whom a young child may have personal and regular contact. Women coaches, whose players are more likely to have strong mother figures in their home, may still find their athletes turning to them as a parent figure for advice, security, care, and affection. A coach may be a more important influence than parents as he or she enters the world of a child when a normal striving for independence reduces parents' influence.[10] The young person may also look to the coach as a substitute for a parent who is missing either in a physical or psychological sense. Experienced coaches report that their parenting responsibilities include taking players into their homes, getting medical attention for nonathletic related problems, locating jobs for players, finding tutors to help them with their studies, and helping them make critical life decisions of all kinds.

This requires coaches of every age, not just grandparent age, suddenly to assume roles as parents and grandparents—becoming marriage counselors, baby sitters, and financial advisors. Individuals are marrying young and having children at an early age, but not necessarily in that order.

A serious problem facing coaches of some females is one of working with players (including those in junior high school) who have children and whose mothers (the babies' grandmothers) refuse to keep the children after school hours. Children at practice are an ever-present hazard and situation to be planned for, and special arrangements must be made for games. No coach of any other era has had to consider playpens and/or attendants for babies and toddlers.

So, for all these reasons, coaches must play the role of parent or grandparent. The team and the community view them as surrogate parents and expect them to function in that role, as part of the athlete's extended family.

Conflict

Several obvious reasons for conflicts arise from the parenting role. Primary among these may be rejection by a young coach of the necessity to be a parent to anyone and who, in fact, may still need parenting. Coaches who refuse this role or fail in it do not remain coaches long.

Another serious conflict can arise between the coach, acting as a parent, and the real parent(s) or guardian. Families may not lightly relinquish their authority over their children to a parent substitute. Jealousy can be a real problem if a player prefers the coach to the parent or, in the natural development of independence, rejects the parents' opinions and manners for those of the coach. There can also be a conflict between the values held by the parents and by the coach, and when dependence on the coach is detrimental rather than beneficial.

FAMILY MEMBER

Role

While a coach is busy filling all the roles mentioned previously, there is still one more role or obligation to consider—that of the family member. Coaches cannot spend all available time and energies on the job, or with other people's children, and not save time, energy, and devotion for their own spouses and children. This is true whether the coach has a Little League team or works with the pros.

Until the 1970s, as the majority of coaches were men the stresses and strains of marriage were focused on the coach and his wife. The advice of currently active coaches to ones entering the field is that it is important to seek a partner who fully understands all that coaching requires, including long hours, much time spent away from home, and the demands of the job. A new male coach should not assume that his bride will automatically become the perfect, understanding coach's wife. It is important that he make every effort to explain what the coaching profession is all about, that she must learn to ignore criticism, and that she must learn to live with the swing in mood that each coach goes through. She must learn that, to the coach, they are not just boys' games; they are his profession, and he cares very much about it. The stress of being on stage and evaluated at every contest, with his reputation on the line, is something each wife must understand.[11]

The married woman coach has all the problems that a male coach and family man has, plus some he does not have to face. Society still expects professional women to be professionals, and produce what the job demands, yet still be a wife and mother after work. The woman coach cannot play that dual role too well because of the time demands, so her husband and children must be willing to let her do her job, devoting her energies to coaching just as male coaches must. Women without children have fewer stresses than those with children, but the presence of children in the home does not present unsolvable problems, just different adjustments. Husbands of women coaches may have to be more adaptable than ordinary husbands and more willing to share in the homemaking responsibilities. Just as wives of coaches face special pressures, so do husbands of coaches.

The children of coaches have advantages that other children do not have, yet they face some disadvantages. The advantages are that coaches know about young people, have observed how others have reared their children, understand about school and competitive situations, and can usually provide a firm and stable home. Their children also get to participate in the world of sport and to know important adults in the sports community. Being the child of a coach can, however, have disadvantages because, while the parent is taking care of others' children, there may not be time for the children at home. The coach may unrealistically expect totally disciplined behavior and may also unrealistically expect that his or her children will all be highly skilled and totally interested in athletics.

All coaches' families must learn to accept the presence of athletes in their home for an evening, for a meal, for overnight, or for longer. Coaches get involved in their players' lives, and the athletes need and want to be with their coaches. Families must also learn to live with irregular schedules for appointments, meals, and for return from games because during the season nothing is fixed but the game time. They must learn to live in the public eye, hear derogatory remarks as well as praise about the parent, and know that their idle conversation may make headlines. They must accept the fact that they are expected to be full participants in community affairs—church, PTA, civic clubs, and fund-raising events, both charitable and athletic.

To be a family person and a coach is to be devoted both to coaching and to family, ensuring that each role gets its full measure of devotion. Being in the coach's family is an exciting and rewarding experience and always full of surprises—it is not always filled with waiting and cold suppers. The successful coach and family person shares this excitement and pleasure with a loyal and understanding spouse and children who care enough to live through the strife and stress that being a coach's family can bring. It may be necessary, though, to wait until the off-season to do things with the family and to share in family interests. There will surely be one.

Conflict

Although the joys of family life are many, the conflicts faced by the coach as a family person are very strong. A lack of understanding and appreciation of the peculiar demands and obligations of the coach's job on the part of the spouse and children is the greatest source of conflict, and all others stem from this.

When a coach devotes more than 12 hours a day (and up to 24 when on a trip) to teaching and coaching, working and coaching, or just coaching, there is little left for family time together. Families expect the coach to share time with them and can be upset when husband or wife, father or mother, is not home until late in the evening, day after day.

The coach's demand for athletic excellence from the children can create a real conflict if the children are neither skilled nor interested in sports or the parent's sport. An artistic or academically oriented or nonathletic child can become alienated from parents who consider nonathletic interests foreign to their way of life.

The greatest conflict may occur when the coach's spouse is concerned that the marriage is shaky. Because the coach is home so little, there may seem to be little basis for communication, understanding, or even for being married. This concern may bring the ultimate conflict and, if not resolved, can lead to the disruption of the home or divorce.

SINGLE PERSON

Role

Single coaches have a variety of life styles—some have solitary households; others are divorced or widowed with children; many have an apartment or housemates; a few live with parents or other close relatives. There is no stereotype of the single coach.

Those who have no children or household obligations are free to devote all their time and energy to the job. Many of these are younger men and women, often assistant coaches but frequently head coaches, who find their family in the team. As single persons they have the obligation to serve as social role models for the players, resist the opportunity to be one of the "boys" or one of the "girls," and always maintain a social distance.

Some single coaches also have children and/or older parents in their homes so they have the solidarity of a family but do not have the assistance of a spouse in meeting family obligations. Many of these single coaches are women, but both men and women can be overwhelmed by household responsibilities if there is no additional household support. It has been said that everybody needs a "wife"; obviously a single family head needs homemaking assistance if coaching duties are to be properly executed.

Conflict

The greatest conflict for the single coach is having a full-time, all-consuming job with no spouse to provide support, assistance, and companionship. Even if two coaches share a household, there is room for conflict because of differences in goals, schedules, and housekeeping abilities.

Single coaches, especially men, must be careful not to let too friendly behavior be exhibited to younger players and students. Even though drawn to attractive young women who admire them and seek them out, coaches must be careful to show only the exemplary behavior of a mature adult. Women coaches, too, must be above reproach, especially in their dealing with players and students. The loss of a job and a reputation are a high price to pay for a few instances of dallying with the girls or boys.

A conflict may arise if the community has higher standards of conduct for a single person than for those who are married. As discussed in the section "Role Model," coaches, teachers, and recreation leaders are expected to set a higher standard of behavior than ordinary citizens, and this too can cause conflict.

The overload of head of a single household and coach may create personal and professional difficulties. When there is just not enough time to do both jobs, one or both may suffer. All the problems outlined in the section "Family Member" exist but without a second pair of hands to share the tasks. Some must give up coaching; others cannot. Either way there is conflict.

SUMMARY

The personal qualities that must be possessed and the personal roles that must be played have to be considered by the aspiring coach. There is much to be gained by being a coach, but there are also some conflicts and perhaps even losses. Careful consideration of the obligations of a coach as a person may assist in making a wise choice about coaching as a vocation or an avocation.

ENDNOTES

1. D. E. Fuoss and R. J. Troppman, *Effective Coaching* (New York: John Wiley and Sons, 1981), pp. 24-26.
2. Ibid., p. 23.
3. J. A. Michener, *Sports in America* (New York: Random House, 1976), p. 254.
4. G. H. Sage, "Coach As Management," *Quest* XIX (January 1973): 24.
5. W. F. Straub, "How to be an Effective Leader," in *Sport Psychology: An Analysis of Athletic Behavior,* ed. W. F. Straub (Ithaca, N.Y.: Movement Publications, 1978), pp. 257-266.
6. H. B. W. Poindexter and C. Mushier, *Coaching Competitive Team Sports for Girls and Women* (Philadelphia: W.B. Saunders, 1973), p. 21.
7. A. Beisser, *The Madness in Sport,* 2nd ed. (Bowie, Md.: Charles Press, 1977), p. 130.
8. K. Clarke, *Drugs and the Coach* (Washington, D.C.: AAHPER, 1974), p. 49.
9. J. Cramer, "A Student Athlete's Viewpoint," in *Development of Human Values in Sports,* ed. R. Frost and E. Sims (Washington, D.C.: AAHPER, 1974), pp. 68-70.
10. F. L. Smoll, R. E. Smith, and B. Curtis, "Coaching Roles and Relationships," in *Youth Sports Guide for Coaches and Parents,* ed. J. R. Thomas (Washington, D.C.: AAHPER, 1977), pp. 7-23.
11. R. J. Sabock, *The Coach,* 2nd ed. (Philadelphia: W.B. Saunders, 1979), p. 104.

3

The Coach as a Professional

ADMINISTRATOR
PERSONNEL MANAGER
TEACHER
PRUDENT PERSON
RECRUITER
TRAINER
PUBLIC RELATIONS PERSON
  AND FUND RAISER
STRATEGIST AND TACTICIAN
SUMMARY

Not only must coaches possess many fine personal characteristics and play many roles as a person, they must also possess or acquire many skills and knowledges as a professional. In this chapter their roles as administrator, personnel manager, teacher, prudent person, recruiter, trainer, public relations person and fund raiser, and strategist and tactician are presented. As in the previous chapter, the potential conflicts are also discussed.

A professional is a person who spends years learning about relevant tasks and problems, who can operate independently on basic principles and be held responsible for decisions and outcomes, who assists in bringing promising new members into the profession, and who continues to study and seek new knowledge. Coaches, whether paid or volunteer, attempt to meet these criteria. Their roles described in this chapter demand the professional attention of professionals.

ADMINISTRATOR

Role

Because most coaches are appointed, not elected, they serve in the athletic world as managers serve in the business world, and they are just as responsible for team performance. A coach must therefore possess the abilities to plan and to organize people, events, space, time, travel plans, and money. The true administrator is a decision maker; the coach must also make many decisions and solve many problems.

One of the greatest problems facing the coach, the athletic director, the recreation superintendent, the principal, and the owner is money—how to get it, how to spend it, and how to get the most for it. The coach typically is concerned about expenditure and value, but securing the funds is often a concern too.

Budgeting and accounting (fiscal management), often considered dry, tedious jobs by some, are more important than ever in a period of low revenue. Projecting income and outgo, staying within this framework, and keeping records of every transaction are functions all coaches

Figure 3-1 There is always too much to do (Photographer: Mickey Adair)

must perform. The other functions of planning for and maintaining equipment, supplies, and facilities are likewise very important. Also important are the travel arrangements that every coach must make. All of these are part of the administrative role and are discussed fully in Part 3.

Conflict The coach who is not comfortable with other people's money, who is careless with receipts and equipment, or is not meticulous about details in planning is in trouble as an administrator. An even more serious conflict can arise when sloppy bookkeeping, or a touch of larceny in the heart, can lead to indictments for misappropriation of funds. Grand Jury investigations into the actions and transactions of superintendents, vendors, and coaches highlight the necessity for careful records and fiscal integrity.

Another area of conflict can emerge when coaches need and want sufficient funds to operate high-level programs but are not willing to raise or manage these funds. They believe that securing and managing adequate fiscal support is someone else's responsibility. These persons are deluded and misguided, as coaching does require management of funds and supplies.

PERSONNEL MANAGER

Role

Not only must coaches learn to work with money and equipment, they must also learn how to work with a wide variety of persons in a wide variety of jobs. The effective accomplishment of the role of personnel manager will assist in ensuring a harmonious staff and a successful season. Assistant coaches are the most obvious staff with whom a coach will work, but the responsibilities are much larger. The coach must also be able to secure and coordinate work and service from groundskeepers, other maintenance personnel, officials, lunchroom managers, bus drivers, trainers, and other medical personnel. In addition, a wide variety of auxiliary personnel such as program sellers, ushers, and concessionaires must be supervised.

A successful program is characterized by harmonious relations, mutual respect, and cooperative devotion to duty among the staff.[1] Professional respect should exist between the head coach and the assistants, among the assistants themselves, and among coaches of different sports. A head coach ought to support assistant coaches, give them proper credit for their work, encourage their growth and initiative, and promote their advancement within the profession. The entire coaching staff needs also to work cooperatively with the auxiliary staff, as all have a common goal.

A coach can prevent most jurisdictional disputes between assistant coaches and among other staff by clearly outlining duties and responsibilities for all personnel involved in the program. Salaries and levels of responsibility should be clearly understood, and differences of opinion need to be resolved in private.

Some successful head coaches like to think of the support personnel as partners and personal friends, certainly not rivals. They give all a job and let them work at it with the mutual feeling that they are helping each other. Loyalty is a two-way street. The head coach expects and must receive loyalty from every member of the staff, and, conversely, every member of the staff has a right to expect loyalty in return.

The coach has a serious responsibility for managing personnel so that the best program can emerge. Part 4 presents material on this important role.

Conflict

Unless coaches are very careful, they can inadvertently create a personnel chaos. A direct coach with an abrupt manner may have difficulty dealing with persons who work at their own pace or who march to a different drummer. The enmity of the janitor or the groundskeeper is to be avoided at all costs, and the violation of a union contract can wreak havoc on a program.

A most serious conflict can occur when the coach must arbitrate a dispute between assistants; then the wisdom of Solomon may be needed if a cohesive staff and a cohesive team are to result. Early clarification of assignments and responsibilities is most important.

There may be discrepancies between loyalties owed to a program or an individual. Each staff member must decide where the greater loyalty is due—to the program, to an individual, or to an ideal.

TEACHER

Role

The coach is also a teacher. Frequently he or she is a teacher in the traditional sense of being a faculty member on a school or college staff. Always the coach is a teacher in the true sense in that the entire function of coaching is to elicit superior responses and superior performances from often less than superior players. No coach can long survive who cannot carry out the job of the professional teacher, which is to diagnose the status or condition of the performer, to prescribe ways of increasing knowledge and improving skill performance, and to evaluate that performance in order to improve it.

Coaches have the opportunity to serve as teachers for volunteers who are already interested in performing better and who may already possess high levels of skill. The regular classroom teacher often has the harder role of educating all comers, the willing and unwilling, the quick and the slow, the skilled and the unskilled. Regardless of the clientele, however, the coach must learn and employ all the current information about how students learn motor skills; about practice, reinforcement, and feedback; and about the role of stress, fatigue, and motivation on performance. Chapters 9 and 10 contain material on these areas.

The teacher/coach has a double responsibility—to meet all the obligations and duties of a classroom teacher or professor and to meet the obligations and duties of a coach. Those who have teaching responsibilities should strive to provide the same level of excellence of instruction for their students as for their teams. They should continue to expand their knowledge and expertise in their academic subjects, and they should keep pace with changes in content, technology, and methodology in those areas as they keep pace with changing technique in the coaching field.

Because the athletic program is but one phase of the total program of education in a school, coaches must remember that they are first educators, then coaches. To successfully maintain their faculty status, they are obligated to perform the duties and responsibilities of the school staff. When faculty, students, and community understand that the coach is dedicated to excellence in the total school program, they are more interested in supporting the goals of the athletic phase.

The relationship of the teacher/coach to other faculty is very important, and a common sense of purpose should exist. Because of the nature of the coaching assignment, which removes coaches from some of the ongoing faculty business, it is important for all coaches to support the total academic program and all school policies. Increased graduation requirements, standardized tests, and increased collegiate admission requirements make it imperative that coaches and teacher/coaches see that players meet their scholarly obligations. All faculty and staff should support

Conflict

Massengale, a noted scholar in the field of role conflicts, stated that because of the uniqueness of the role of coach, conflicts cannot be avoided.[2] The teacher/coach is hired as a teacher but must survive as a coach. The reward system for coaches appears to favor nonacademic performance over academic performance in some situations, and this increases role conflict. This unique occupational role called coaching can result in acceptance or nonacceptance in the school hierarchy; the result may be faculty jealousy and misunderstanding.

There can be inter-role conflict when the teacher/coach has great personal dedication to both teaching and coaching and expends much energy in trying to be both an excellent teacher and coach. Many accomplish this goal, but some become victims of role-overload and are unable to meet all their expectations.

Some of the conflicts are as simple as that created when the regular faculty members must attend a faculty meeting and the coaches, because of their after-school responsibilities, do not attend. They should make every effort to avoid the appearance of receiving special consideration, even if they believe that the job requires additional effort and therefore differential treatment.

The teacher/coach must be diligent in attempting to reduce tension and conflict between the two roles that must be played between the coaching staff and the rest of the faculty and administration. This is necessary for the coach's sake and for the sake of the school, athletes, and program.

Coaches and other faculty must also join forces to improve players' academic standing. There can be, but should not be, conflicts over the requirement for improved educational accomplishments of the players. If a school's players are not admitted to college or university programs because they do not meet admission standards, the entire school is blamed; the disapproval of the community can cause further conflict. Coaches, in their role as teachers, must also be careful that in their zeal to help players they do not violate school policy by giving those students preferential treatment.

PRUDENT PERSON

Role

Because athletics are risk activities and an injury can happen to a player anytime, coaches have to consider the legal liability of their actions. They are responsible for acting as reasonable and prudent people would act under the same circumstances, and they cannot be sued for negligence if they adhere to the following principles:

1. The coach conforms to a standard of behavior which will not subject others to unreasonable risk or injury.

2. The coach observes due care for the rights and interests of participants.[3]

Negligence is thus based on carelessness and behavior that involves risks for others. In making a determined effort to avoid injury at all costs, coaches should consider the following:

1. Facilities. Are the fields, floors, and grounds safe and free from hazards? All hazards should be eliminated.
2. Equipment. Is everything in good repair? No faulty items should ever be used.
3. Protective Equipment. Are players required to wear protective items? These items should be available and in good repair.
4. Medical Assistance. Is trained first aid or medical assistance provided? The services of trained personnel should be utilized for all aspects of the program.
5. Proper Preparation. Are current, correct instructional sequences and training practices followed in preparing athletes for a contest? No player should be permitted to participate if his or her health and welfare are jeopardized.
6. Awareness. Are all players instructed about the hazards of their activity and warned of inherent dangers to be avoided? All players should know the risks present in their sport.

So, those who wish to take good care of their team and to avoid suits for negligence will be very careful in all practices and procedures. To prevent is better than to treat or to defend. Legal aspects are discussed fully in Chapter 19.

Conflict

The conflict between the coach as a prudent person and the coach as an imprudent person comes not because the coach wants anyone hurt but because, in the press of time, the work necessary to repair the bar, remove the glass, clean the floor, or follow current training and sequential instruction procedures does not get done. This time conflict must be resolved.

All institutions and personnel face a serious conflict in trying to determine how to spend limited funds in renovation and repair. Safety needs must come first, but it may be difficult to ascertain which safety need has priority. Who can say that the roof is less important than the surface of a field or floor?

The most serious conflict may occur between the coach and the player (or parents of the player) who sues for negligence when there is an injury. It may be a nuisance suit like the one brought against a physical education teacher because a boy skinned his hands when the class was playing monkey and walking on all fours (the teacher was found innocent of negligence), or a suit for millions of dollars for serious injury or death. In addition to caring for, and being prudent about, players, coaches can prove they are prudent about themselves by investigating the purchase of a professional liability insurance policy.

RECRUITER

Role

Recruiting, the securing of high-level performers, is a basic concern for many coaches. The youth sports coach rarely faces recruiting problems as the sponsoring agencies recruit the players and attempt to place them on teams in a fair and impartial manner, but most all other coaches must serve as recruiters or assist their athletes with recruiters. Surely those in high school and college have this responsibility. All coaches are now in the thick of the recruiting battle, and athletes are on the lookout for athletic scholarships. A well-known coach educator has stated that every high school coach in America has a moral obligation and duty to athletics to oversee the recruiting process in the school and to ensure strict adherence to the rules.[4]

Each agency or association that supervises competition has its own recruiting rules that must be observed. These are established to protect the athlete and to control the recruiters so that all have a fair opportunity to talk with the recruits. Violation of rules can result in penalties for the athlete, team, coach, institution, and/or school. High schools as well as colleges supervise the eligibility and recruitment of the players, and the papers are full of reports of institutions that are sanctioned for illegal recruiting and violations of standard academic practice. Coaches must protect their players from unethical and illegal procedures.

High school coaches can be faced with problems when college recruiters swarm after team "stars." They must protect the players from being exploited, missing classes because of interviews, believing their "press notices," and becoming alienated from team members.

The high school coach also has to fulfill an ethical obligation to athletes, parents, the school, and college recruiters that permits the athlete, not the coach, to decide on a college. An athlete must understand the seriousness of accepting a scholarship and the academic and athletic obligations this entails. Parents and the athlete must know the athlete's assets and limitations, chances for academic and athletic success, and the danger in being oversold by recruiters. The college recruiter is also due a fair and honest appraisal of the player's academic and athletic records.

College/university recruiters have the obligation of observing the letter and the spirit of the recruiting regulations of their associations and those of the school. The recruiter also has the obligation not to mislead the potential team member and not to take advantage of the player's or the parents' inexperience. It is both illegal and unethical to promise more than the regulations permit in terms of scholarship or other aids and gifts or in regard to academic admission or success. The high school coach must know all recruiting procedures and must ensure fair treatment for all athletes. Even in these days of business sport rather than educational sport, the basic goal of both coach and player should be a good education.

Conflict

No role is more filled with potential conflict than that of recruiter. The zeal with which some recruiters pursue their prey can lead the student, recruiter, and institution into serious trouble. It can also deprive the student of an education, a chance for athletic success, and a good life. The conflict is between ethical or nonethical behavior, between greed and true concern for the athlete, and between business sport for profit and educational sport for the development of the athlete.

Another personal conflict a coach may face is the loyalty felt toward Alma Mater when a star player is being recruited. For some coaches it is difficult to be fair to all college recruiters when their college comes around. They should make every effort to avoid encouraging the athlete to go in a particular direction, to avoid bending the rules for visits by a former coach, or to behave unethically in any manner.

A third conflict can arise when parents or players expect coaches to make final decisions about which scholarship to accept. If the athlete is athletically or academically unsuccessful at an institution chosen by the coach, then parents and the athlete will blame the coach. Coaches should always let parents and athletes make the choice, but they would be remiss if they did not make honest, objective recommendations.

A renewed emphasis on the requirement of normal academic progress both in high school and college can put pressure on a coach and a player. Conflicts can arise when a player does not understand the necessity for, and the value of, studying and passing, sees the chances for a college scholarship diminishing or disappearing, and then blames the coach for not "fixing it." Early insistence on studying and regular class attendance and participation may overcome this problem.

TRAINER

Role

If coaches are to help teams do their very best, then they must take into serious consideration the role of coach as trainer. The tasks are twofold: establishing a regimen that prepares a team physiologically for a performance, and preventing athletic injuries. If the athletic organization is large, the coach may have a trained and/or certified athletic trainer to assist in these two duties, though in many situations the trainer may limit services to the injury problem.

A medical specialty has emerged in this country and throughout the world—sports medicine. There are now physicians who are interested in the same tasks as the athletic trainer—preparing for a contest and caring for athletic injuries. If these specialists are available, the smart coach will call on them, not only for injuries but for advice and counsel as well.

Many books and articles tell how to prepare the athlete for a contest, generally, and for a particular sport, specifically. Each sport has training regimens that are closely related to the activity—so swimmers should swim, runners should run, pitchers should pitch, and kickers should kick. In addition, there are general areas of training that each coach should know in order to set up a basic training program. Chapter 6 is devoted to biological considerations.

It is necessary to have a trained first aider, trainer, or emergency medic—if not the coach, then someone else—at every practice and contest. Some state associations require that a school have the services of a

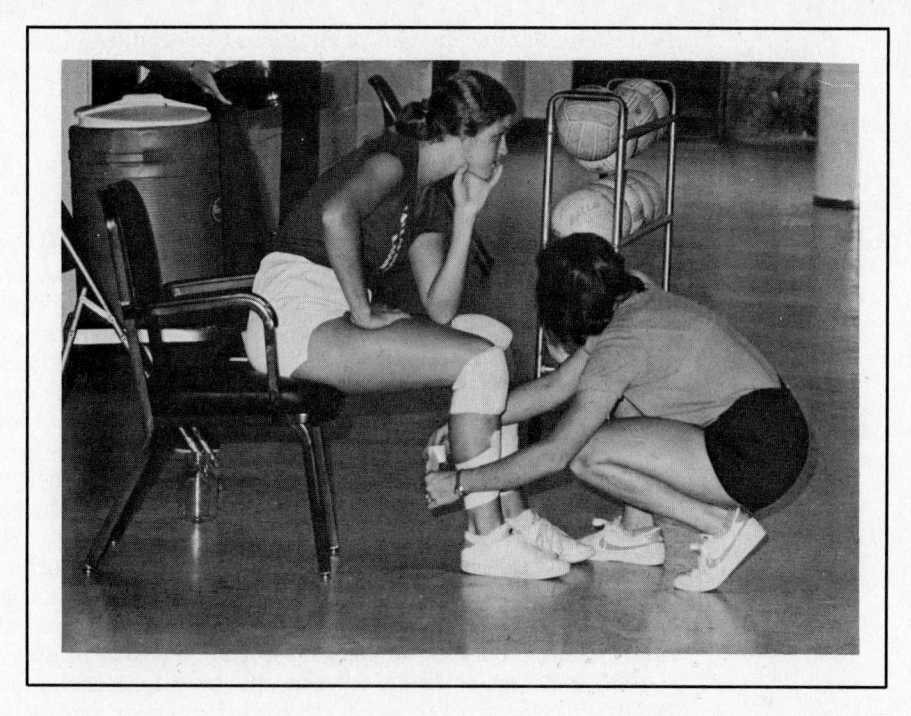

Figure 3-2   Someone has to get them ready for practice (Courtesy of Maclay School, Inc., Tallahassee, Florida. Photographer: Mickey Adair)

trainer available; other state associations are seriously considering adding this rule. If no such person is available, then the coach will have to rely on common sense and behave as a prudent person would.

Conflict   The conscientious coach may have personal conflicts between the ethical duty to take good care of the team and the practical requirement of playing an injured player to win. This demand for short-term results must never take precedence over the welfare of the player.

A similar conflict may arise when the use of stimulants is considered. Aside from the danger to the player, there is the other, ethical, consideration that sport is a contest between opponents under fair and equal conditions—not between a sky-high junkie and an unsuspecting opponent.

Conflicts may arise between coaches and players when training rules are imposed and violated. This classic confrontation can often be avoided if rules are sensible and understood, but such clashing can be a headache for any coach whose players refuse to be reasonable and mature.

Another area of conflict may come with parents whose family routine is disturbed by practice times, irregular meals, need for a new diet, or other changes in the accustomed procedure. Coaches should make every effort to include and consider parents when training rules are being established.

PUBLIC RELATIONS PERSON AND FUND RAISER

Role

Ever since the American public became addicted to sports and American newspapers steadily increased the news about sports, the coach has had a role to play in publicity and public relations. The coach and the team are news. Publicity is a part of, but different from, public relations. Publicity is the news and notoriety, and public relations is the larger field that uses publicity as a part of a good will and advertising campaign. Also, ever since the American public decided that sports programs at every level must pay their own way, the coach has been involved with fund raising, either alone or with a sponsor, an owner, a parents group, or a booster club. All these tasks fit together, and the coach has to wear all the hats.

Larger organizations may have Sports Information Directors (SID) to carry part of this burden, but coaches must always deal with the media themselves if they want an inch in the paper, a line on the radio, or a short scene on TV. It is suggested that a coach who wants publicity for a team will get to know all the sportswriters and sportscasters in the community so that they can share information and procedures. It must also be remembered that a team or a game must be newsworthy, and that even if the staffs of all the news media are coaches' friends, they cannot give time or coverage unless something interesting is happening.

It is imperative that coaches deal with the news media honestly and impartially if they want to be treated honestly and impartially. All media organizations should receive as much information as a coach has to offer and all the background that can be provided.

The coach has to be concerned with public relations, in addition to publicity, even though there may be a central public relations staff for the organization. Coaches, as public relations persons, cannot afford to be on bad terms with anyone, so most make themselves available and agreeable. This means speeches to civic clubs, participation in community affairs, mutual cooperation with the band and cheerleaders, and happy interaction with the faculty and staff.

The very best public relations program is an exciting team with skilled and interesting players and a good, sound athletic program. No amount of publicity, advertisement, or effort can substitute for skilled play and good games. Common courtesy and good treatment of spectators, participants, and visitors are a part of good manners as well as public relations.

When coaches are also charged with fund raising, they must cooperate with parents groups, booster clubs, and other support groups. A city league coach may need a sponsor only to provide uniforms and an entry fee, but the college coach is faced with the need to set up a program that costs more than gate receipts can ever pay for. Chapters 13 and 24 contain details on fund raising and relations with the media.

Conflict   Much of a coach's difficulty can come not from a team, a player, or a game, but from poor publicity. When a coach thinks that the team has been unfairly represented by the news media, the first inclination may be to make a rebuttal; but this can only create a conflict that the coach can rarely win. Parents may also feel that their child is not adequately publicized and may blame the coach instead of the media.

Another conflict can arise when the coach finds that a sportswriter is attempting to coach the team in the paper or on the air by second-guessing the coach's decision. This can undermine a coach's authority and influence and, if not resolved, can create a power problem. A winning season can, however, erase bad feelings and misunderstandings.

Shy, awkward, or unpolished coaches will have difficulty in public relations until they learn to speak well, turn aside criticism, recognize the power structure in the community, and make a joke. Deficiencies can be overcome through practice and experience.

The coach who is dependent on parents groups and booster clubs can be in conflict with them on matters of who plays and why, what teams are scheduled, and how the money is spent. This may also lead to problems about whether the coach is the employee of the boosters or whether the coach works for the school, college, or club.

STRATEGIST AND TACTICIAN

Role   It is as strategists and tacticians that coaches often make their reputation. Strategy is the long-range planning that goes into a winning season (or a losing one for that matter), and tactics are the short-range moves and skills that make the long-range strategy possible.

The coach who devises a new system of defense or offense, or who improves a new tactic or skill, is like the person who built a better mousetrap and the world beat a path to the door. Everyone wants to learn from him or her and to adapt and adopt the new system or method. Regardless of the level of coaching, the coach must be a student of how to outwit an opponent, using the team talents available, and how to win.

Entire libraries have been written by expert players and coaches in every sport, and it is outside the scope of this book to describe every strategy and tactic a coach may need. All aspiring coaches should build a personal collection of such books by the authorities in their field of interest. It is not unusual for a serious student of a sport to have several hundred volumes of materials on how to play and win in a sport.

When Amos Alonzo Stagg and Fielding Yost first used the forward pass, it put them in the record books as master strategists and tacticians. When Dick Fosbury's coach helped him perfect the famous backward "flop" high jump, a new jumping style was created. When Danny Litwhiler used the traffic radar gun at Michigan State to measure the velocity of a pitched baseball, he opened the door to a new way of determining the effectiveness of a pitcher. When Suzanne Tyler developed a new offensive system for field hockey, she altered a game that had not been drastically changed since Constance Applebee introduced it to the United States in the early part of this century. When Henry "Hank" Iba re-

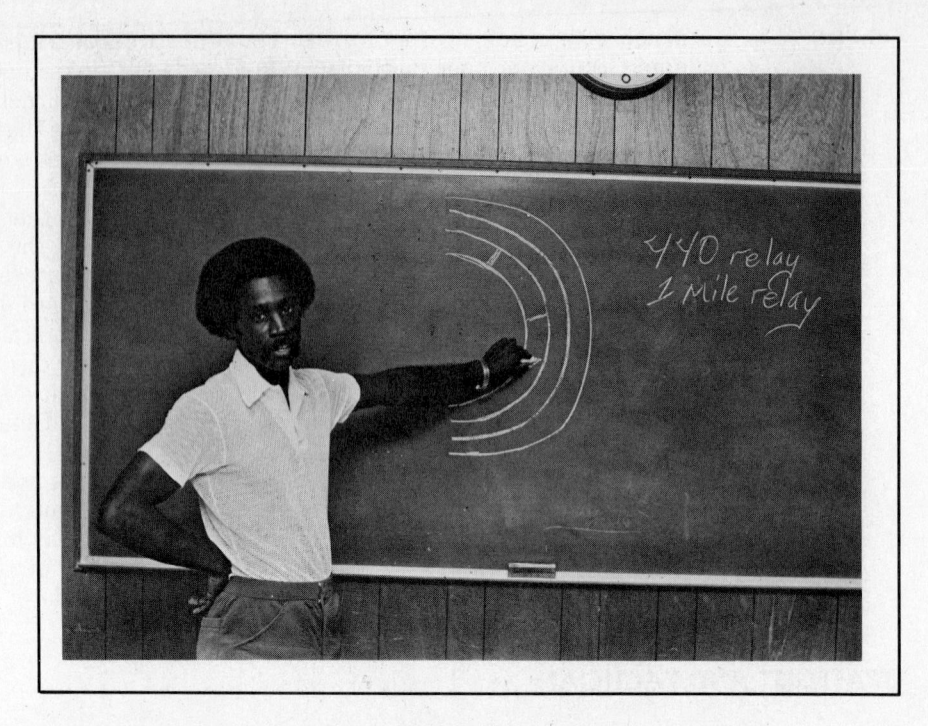

Figure 3-3 A good coach has a good plan (Photographer: Mickey Adair)

cruited Bob Kurland, a seven-foot basketball player, at Oklahoma A & M University, he revolutionized the game. And so it goes. Anyone can find a better way and it is the coach's ultimate task to continue to seek, experiment, and produce a new style, defense, gimmick, or method to gain the winning edge.

Conflict

Innovative coaches rarely have conflicts over new strategies and tactics if they are within the rules and are not harmful to the player. There can be conflicts and disagreements if the new procedure is on the borderline of a rules violation or if there is concern about the welfare of the athlete.

Alert coaches observe new formations, procedures, and tactics employed by winning mentors and quickly use them with their own teams. Modifying a new strategy soon becomes another new method as each coach adapts an idea to a specific group. A personal problem or conflict may arise for one that is not a true student of the game. That coach will be a plodder and, competing with innovative coaches, may fail to win and thus soon go.

SUMMARY

The coach who is a professional in intent if not in fact, whether paid or volunteer, must pay serious attention to all the duties and roles of coaches. A fledgling coach must learn to fill these roles; an experienced coach must improve performance in them. Generally, topflight coaches successfully fill these roles; they know their jobs and work hard at them.

All the roles described in Chapters 2 and 3 lead up to the ultimate role, that of a coach. The multifaceted person whose functions have been outlined here is not a super-person in the comic-strip sense, but a super-person in the real sense who plays a respected part in the lives of young people and communities throughout the country.

Anyone who truly wants to coach can be a coach. No one can be all things to all persons; but honest effort, study, and devotion to the task can carry most through to the goal—the development of athletes to their fullest potential and winning teams.

ENDNOTES

1. National Association for Sport and Physical Education, *Coaches' Manual* (Washington, D.C.: AAHPER, n.d.), p. 20.
2. J. D. Massengale, "Occupational Role Conflict and the Teacher Coach," *Phi Delta Kappan* (May 1977): 64–69.
3. NASPE, *Coaches' Manual*, pp. 71–72.
4. R. J. Sabock, "Recruiting," *Journal of Physical Education, Recreation and Dance* (August 1985): 26.

4

Professional Preparation

> PRE-SERVICE PREPARATION
> IN-SERVICE PREPARATION
> SUMMARY

A person desiring to be a coach may follow many routes to learn how to coach and how to fill the roles that must be played. The Little League coach may have learned on the job, read books on the sport, played as a younger person, and/or attended clinics. The school coach typically is a teacher, certified in some subject area, who has taken courses in how to coach and who usually has participated in athletics in high school and/or college. The college and university coach is generally one who took coaching courses, played at the college level, and had experience as a high school coach, as an assistant college coach, or perhaps as a professional athlete.

Preparation received prior to beginning a coaching career is called "pre-service" training because it occurs prior to entry into the profession. Preparation or training received after the job is begun is called "in-service" training because it occurs while the coach is already on the job or in service. Pre-service preparation may be of only a few years' duration, but in-service training is a lifetime affair. No coach can ever afford to stop learning.

PRE-SERVICE PREPARATION

An official recommendation was made by the American Alliance for Health, Physical Education and Recreation (AAHPER) about the professional preparation of coaches.[1] It stated that sports at every level should be conducted by professionally prepared personnel of integrity who are dedicated to the optimal mental, physical, and social development of those entrusted to their supervision. In addition to having a thorough knowledge of sports, a coach (in most school situations) must be a certified teacher with expertise in guiding students in the pursuit of excellence.

There are many areas of experience to be considered for pre-service training. The most common are college courses which can lead, in some cases, to certification as a coach. Other pre-service areas are clinics and schools operated by recreation departments, agencies, and sports associations. Athletic or team experience as a player, volunteer coaching experience, and advice or instruction from coaches in the field are additional sources for this preparation.

College Courses The Division of Men's Athletics of AAHPER outlined four basic areas for the professional preparation of coaches: biological sciences including anatomy, kinesiology, physiology, and physiology of exercise; safety including first aid, athletic training and conditioning, and care and prevention of injuries; foundations such as philosophy, principles, organization and administration, and psychology; and theory and techniques of coaching in selected sports.[2] In addition, it was emphasized that coaches must know about legal situations typical in athletics, about liability, and about the administrative aspects of budget, records, scheduling, and purchasing. Also called for were coaching internships similar to the field experience teachers must have.

A similar statement recommended competencies in five areas: medical-legal aspects of coaching, sociological and psychological aspects of coaching, theory and techniques of coaching, kinesiological foundations of coaching, and physiological foundations of coaching.[3] It also advocated that aspiring coaches gain practical knowledge through a variety of field experiences that included volunteer coaching, working as an assistant for a coach, attending clinics and seminars, and officiating. The statement also recommended that student coaches continue to increase their knowledge by reading professional journals.

Most physical education major programs include the courses suggested in both of these recommendations for the professional preparation of coaches, so persons preparing to teach physical education at the secondary level have already received the suggested pre-service preparation. The typical internship or field experience required for the certification of physical education teachers can also provide opportunities for practical experience in coaching.

Certification It has been stated that requiring certification for all interscholastic coaches would be a major step forward for the coaching profession.[4] There is even a proposal that criteria be established and that certification be required for all new public school coaches by 1995.[5] Eight states (Arkansas, Connecticut, Illinois, Iowa, Maryland, New Jersey, New York, and Wyoming) are already certifying full-time and part-time coaches. Four (Montana, North Dakota, Oregon, and South Dakota) require only that full-time coaches be certified, and four others (Idaho, Minnesota, New Mexico, and Utah) require certification of head coaches.[6] Other states have expressed interest in certifying coaches, but the great demand for coaches and the limited supply of those suitably prepared has caused some states to suspend this practice.

The concept of not requiring certification makes it easier for school boards to employ staff with limited training, which may not be conducive to good athletic programs. These nonqualified personnel are usually part-time and are not paid as teachers. Support for certification comes from the teaching and coaching professions. Opposition comes from school administrators who have difficulty in staffing their programs, but it is anticipated that increased litigation will accelerate the demand for certified and qualified coaches.

Canada has a five-level system of certification, with each level containing a theory, technical, and practical component.[7] The first three levels are administered by provinces, and the fourth and fifth are responsibilities of the federal government. Theory includes psychology of coaching, motor learning, sports medicine, bio-mechanics, exercise physiology, growth and development, and training methods. Technical courses deal with updated methods of teaching and learning new skills and strategies for a particular sport. The practical area requires application of knowledge in a coaching experience, which is evaluated.

Recreation departments and other youth agencies are moving rapidly to training, certifying, and/or using certified youth sport coaches to ensure having well-prepared leaders. Certification can be obtained from two organizations: the National Youth Sport Coaches Association (NYSCA), West Palm Beach, Florida, works cooperatively with the National Recreation and Park Association (NRPA), while the American Coaching Effectiveness Program (ACEP), Champaign, Illinois, trains YMCA staff among others.

The NYSCA program content, which is usually taught in clinics through membership organizations, typically chartered by recreation departments, includes psychology of coaching children, organization of practice, teaching proper techniques, and safety and first aid.[8] The ACEP curriculum includes courses on three levels. Level One contains coaching philosophy, sport psychology, sport pedagogy, sport physiology, and sport medicine plus sport specific content. These may be studied in a clinic or through a self-study program. Level Two has more advanced courses for experienced coaches, and Level Three is designed for coaches of elite athletes.[9]

The primary purpose for certification is to assure quality coaching. Also, a program that includes three aspects—instruction, assessment of players, and safety—can be effective in ameliorating law suits.[10]

Coaching Minor Assistant football coaches from Arkansas, Louisiana, Oklahoma, and Texas reported that they had been poorly prepared in physiology, anatomy, nutrition, athletic training, football tactics, principles and problems of coaching, coaching psychology, administration, and counseling. They supported certification of coaches and a coaching minor in college.[11]

Some institutions offer a coaching minor designed to serve as a substitute for an official state certification program. Such a curriculum can be found at Florida State University. Each "coaching minor," who is typically a student who is either planning to teach some subject other than physical education or do youth work in some form, must complete seven courses. They are: Principles and Problems of Coaching, Organization and Administration of Physical Education and Athletics, Care and Prevention of Athletic Injuries, Anatomy and Physiology, Sports Officiating, and courses in the theory and practice of two sports. Upon completion of the program a certificate is awarded.

As the demand for teams, for both males and females, has increased the need for additional coaches, the supply of teachers who can, or will, coach has not increased at the same rate. This makes pre-service training in coaching, for teachers of all subjects, imperative. It also points out the need for physical education teachers to be certified in more than one field to increase their employability and usefulness.

Clinics Most recreation departments, agencies, and sports groups provide coaching clinics for their participants. The sports director for each program regularly meets prior to a league season to talk with coaches and managers to ensure minimal understanding of routines, schedules, and coaching skills. This is not extensive preparation, but it does help fill in a knowledge gap before play begins.

Sports associations also prepare coaches or professionals for their jobs. Golf is an outstanding example of rigorous training for professionals. Novices must serve apprenticeships, attend schools, and pass difficult examinations before getting their "card."

Playing Experience Many believe that an integral part of a coach's preparation is participation in a sport or sports as an athlete. Although there are enough non-playing coaches to serve as exceptions to that rule, most successful coaches have had a solid background in sports activities as a performer. It is strongly recommended that aspiring coaches seek opportunities to play.

Volunteer Coaching Experience The field experience recommended for the preparation of coaches can be formal or informal. Most established coaches welcome volunteers and beginning coaches to assist in their programs. Assignments may consist of preparing equipment, scouting, running errands, or a host of other duties. These opportunities to learn at the side of experienced coaches should be sought. Practical experience is valuable because it broadens knowledge of the sport and players, and it expands the friendship and personal contact horizons of the novice.

Additional coaching experience can be gained as a Little League or an agency team coach. Any experience with athletics and with players of all ages is to be sought, as no one can ever learn too much too soon.

IN-SERVICE PREPARATION

Studying and learning need to be continuous. There are many opportunities for in-service training available to every coach, and all successful coaches follow a pattern of lifelong learning. Keeping up with each new system, strategy, and technique or learning to devise innovative tactics can provide the impetus for successful programs.

School District Programs Those persons already employed as teachers or youth workers who want to fill coaching positions need to participate in the kind of in-service program called "on-the-job-training." A study of in-service education for coaches outlined the procedures that several states and school systems

Professional Preparation **49**

Figure 4-1 High school playing experience is an integral part of a coach's preparation (Malvern High School, Malvern, Arkansas. Photographer: Susan Scantlin)

followed in preparing additional personnel to be coaches.[12] It reported the preparation of teachers, nonteachers, and full-time and part-time coaches. In almost every instance, training programs included those courses specified for pre-service coaches. They were: Principles and Problems of Coaching, Theory and Techniques of Coaching, Medical Aspects of Athletic Coaching, Kinesiological Foundations of Coaching, and Physiological Foundations of Coaching. These materials were offered in workshops, clinics, short courses, and night classes at times and places appropriate for the employee. Minnesota, which certifies head coaches only, permits school districts to contract with universities to help set up certification programs for coaching staffs. The courses include First Aid, Care and Prevention of Injuries, Sport Science Techniques, Psychology of Coaching, and a practicum.[13]

The need to prepare additional personnel is very great as there are not enough teachers available in most school systems to service all the teams needing coaches. Some districts hire part-time assistant coaches; others use volunteers; some must teach new skills to teachers—all are eager to have competent personnel who can safely and effectively supervise and enhance athletic endeavors. Because the need for coaches appears certain to increase, the demand for district in-service programs will increase.

It is not unusual for high school head coaches in some school systems to invite, or strongly urge, staffs of feeder schools and programs, junior high school coaches, and recreation league coaches to participate in pre-season planning and practice. This procedure, praised by some and condemned by others, is designed to ensure the same system of play over a long span of a player's athletic life. Young student coaches can also learn from these sessions.

Districts are also eager to upgrade the skills of their qualified coaches. Athletic supervisors or district athletic directors are expected to plan in-service programs to meet the informational and skill needs of their sports personnel.

High School Association Clinics

Most state high school athletic or activity associations provide clinics in all sports to upgrade the skills and knowledge of coaches in that state. Typically these clinics are held for fall sports, winter sports, and spring sports, with experts in all activities brought in to serve as clinicians, lecturers, and resource persons. It is customary to attend as many of these as possible, and most coaches eagerly look forward to the knowledge, the fellowship, and the chance to talk shop.

Agency Training

As indicated in the pre-service training section, many recreation departments and other youth-serving agencies provide training for new coaches, but it should be noted that they also have clinics for returning or continuing coaches and managers. Each sport season generally requires a training period for the volunteer coaches administered by the paid staff.

Coaches returning for a new sport season should take advantage of this training opportunity. Recreation league athletes deserve the best leadership; they value skillful play and a successful season as much as all other athletes do.

Professional Association Opportunities

Many opportunities for updating skills and knowledge are offered by sports associations or by coaches' associations. The U.S. Field Hockey Association regularly sponsors hockey camps, the Professional Golf Association has teaching clinics, the Gymnastics Association offers workshops for coaches; the opportunities are endless. Most groups, either single-sport or multi-sport, provide in-service training.

Professional Preparation 51

Coaches' associations, whether of single sports, such as the Football Coaches Association, or multi-sport, like state coaching associations, provide clinics and workshops to keep coaches up-to-date. The state, district, and national meetings of the American Alliance for Health, Physical Education, Recreation and Dance (AAHPERD) and the National Recreation and Park Association (NRPA) have special sessions for coaches as well as new information.

Whatever the opportunity, the serious coach takes advantage of it. Keeping up with the newest information is crucial to success.

Private In-Service Opportunity

In addition to the training offered by supervisory agencies and professional associations, there are many private opportunities for upgrading or updating information and skill. These private learning opportunities are connected with a business enterprise.

Coach's Clinic

Many successful college coaches have special clinics for which a fee is charged. Besides using their own staffs, they bring in other outstanding coaches and provide superior and popular in-service programs. Open to all coaches, these clinics are attended primarily by high school and college staffs.

Sports Camps

Some coaches, in conjunction with their summer sports camps for players, offer special instruction for coaches. These camps can be especially helpful when a young coach can enroll his or her team in the program and work alongside the entire camp staff. This saturation in a particular style of play can quickly provide new skills and techniques.

Professional Team Assistance

Coaches who live in areas that have professional teams may find that the players and coaches of those teams frequently offer clinics and workshops for local schools and recreation leagues. Soccer teams, eager to establish their sport in the United States, offer prime examples of this kind of cooperation and service, but any sport has its athletes who are willing to share their skills.

Visitation

Where funds and schedules permit, some head coaches and their staffs go in a group to visit a highly successful program in order to observe procedures and learn a particular system. This can provide a more personalized experience than the coach's clinic or camp.

The visitation may also be reversed. Head coaches or administrators can arrange for a visit from a highly regarded coach to the local site. This consultation can be expanded into a school or agency clinic for coaches and players, or it can be further expanded so that an entire system is served.

Additional Formal Study

Not all in-service training occurs in clinics and workshops or on the job. Coaches can also enter into a formal educational experience to upgrade their skills. This return to a campus does not necessarily have to lead to a degree; its purpose is to gain more useful information.

College Courses

Persons desiring to update their skills and knowledges often attend colleges or universities for special courses either as part of a degree program or for general information. Community or junior colleges may also offer courses through their adult program that have particular meaning to established coaches.

Advanced Degrees

Many colleges and universities are now offering graduate degrees, usually master's degrees, with specialties in areas useful for coaches or athletic directors. The educational specialist degree, a sixth-year program, is offered for those who want to move from coach to athletic director and want to have special training for it. The doctorate is available in the administration of physical education and athletics, but this degree is not usually sought by most coaches and athletic directors.

Commercial Products

Many commercial firms provide coaching films and equipment. Soft drink bottlers, breakfast cereal manufacturers, milk producers, and similar businesses are eager to assist coaches and players in the improvement of their programs. Equipment manufacturers, for gymnastics as an example, provide clinics and materials to make coaching better and easier.

Publishers are in business to sell materials that improve coaching and playing. Most are profit-making concerns, but some, like the Athletic Institute, provide excellent materials at minimal cost.

A trainers' supply company has done a notable job in presenting workshops and short courses for athletic trainers, and a floor-finishing supplier is always ready to assist coaches in learning how to maintain and refinish floors. Any coach who wants to can learn a great deal with the help of business and industry.

Many commercial firms have experts at conventions of coaches, teachers, and recreation associations. They frequently provide free materials and always display the latest in equipment, facilities, uniforms, and publications.

Personal Continuing Study

One of the important ways that coaches continue to improve is through reading coaching magazines and books and building a large personal library. The monthly publications can be general, such as the *Scholastic Coach*, *Women's Sport and Fitness*, and *Athletic Journal*, or such specific publications as *Runner's World*, *World Tennis*, and *Volleyball*. Personal libraries can be built on "book of the month" clubs for coaches or by general purchases from a bookstore.

Once booksellers learn a coach's name and address, they begin to send book announcements and advertisements for books and journals of various kinds. Then the coach has only to review these carefully to learn of new books or to read the book reviews in professional teacher magazines and journals to determine which to buy or read.

Serious students of a sport frequently have a personal library with hundreds of books in it. Beginning coaches can start their libraries as soon as they develop an interest in an activity; they will soon be possessors of extensive sports libraries.

SUMMARY

The professional preparation of a coach is a lifelong process. For the fortunate ones who know their goals and seek their opportunities early, preparation begins with pre-service training in some formal way and perhaps with personal athletic experience. For those who come to coaching some time later in their lives, the in-service route is easy to follow with many opportunities provided by school districts, agencies, associations, and private organizations. Regardless of when and how adequate preparation is obtained, its continuance is important. When coaches stand still, they lose ground; novice coaches should plan on upgrading their preparation forever.

ENDNOTES

1. *Professional Preparation in Dance, Physical Education, Recreation Education and School Health Education* (Washington, D.C.: AAHPER, 1974).
2. M. G. Maetozo, *Standards of Professional Preparation for Athletic Coaches* (Washington, D.C.: Division of Men's Athletics, AAHPER, 1971).
3. Ibid.
4. S. Adams, "Coaching Certification: The Time Is Now," *USSA News* 3 (1979): 1.
5. D. Lopiano, "The Certified Coach: A Central Figure," *Journal of Physical Education, Recreation and Dance* (March 1985): 34.
6. R. J. Sabock and P. Chandler-Garvin, "Coaching Certification: United States Requirements," *Journal of Physical Education, Recreation and Dance* (August 1986): 57.
7. G. D. Jepson, *In-service Education Programs for Coaches,* Eric Clearinghouse on Teacher Education (Washington, D.C.: AAHPER, 1978), pp. 37–40.
8. "Protect the Children, Protect Your Program," *Athletic Business* (March 1986): 12.
9. "American Coaching Effectiveness Program" *1985–86 Catalog* (Champaign, Ill.: Human Kinetics Publishers).
10. B. Van der Smissen, "Legal Liability," *Coaching: Women's Athletics* (January/February 1980): 16.
11. L. Fuller, "Professional Preparation of Interscholastic Football Coaches," *Journal of Physical Education and Recreation* (November/December 1979): 81.
12. Jepson, *In-service Education,* p. 1.
13. J. Johnson, M. Anderson, and R. Jonas, "The Minnesota Experience. Coaching Certification," *Journal of Physical Education, Recreation and Dance* (August 1986): 53.

5

Should You Coach?

BALANCE SHEET
SHOULD YOU COACH?
SUMMARY

The preceding chapters have presented an overview of what coaching is like and what the qualifications are. The novice may already know that coaching is for him or her or may still be wondering if coaching is the place to invest a lifetime.

A part-time or volunteer coach will not have to make a permanent career decision, just a temporary hobby choice. The novice or aspiring teacher/coach may very well make a permanent career choice. College seniors can look forward to professional lives of twice as long as they have already lived, and care should be taken that this career is productive and satisfactory for all concerned. Sensible and rational career decisions are imperative.

A survey of men and women students in six Kansas universities who wanted to be coaches revealed that the major reasons they wanted to coach were: (1) liking to work with young people, (2) having a keen interest in athletics, and (3) believing it to be a challenging profession. They agreed that coaching is more rewarding personally than financially and that a coach makes a positive contribution to the development of young people.[1]

It has been said that coaching is a complex, contradictory, and highly changeable profession. It consists of many diverse elements—effective and defective practices, victory and defeat, recruiting success and failure, community and school relationship, media obligations, and job loss and job gain.[2]

Although it is generally conceded that people change careers in midstream more now than in the first half of the century, early decisions are still important. All the pluses and minuses should be weighed before a commitment is made.

BALANCE SHEET

What are these pros and cons of coaching? How does a balance sheet show the good things and the bad? There are many important positive values in coaching that may make the negative aspects unimportant. The intrinsic rewards far outweigh the materialistic rewards, but each individual must make that decision. One coach's "plus" may be another coach's "minus." As this balance sheet is studied, only the fledgling candidate can decide how to value or place the positives and negatives.

Positive (+)	*Negative (−)*
Praise	Criticism
Accomplishments	Long hours
Salary supplement	Small hourly wage
Community contacts	Booster pressure
On-the-street recognition	Little privacy
Career advancement	Poor job security
Success	Limited success
Immersion in work	Other work suffers
Player growth	Hard work
Appreciation	Lack of colleague understanding
Respect	Disrespect
Network of peers (coaches)	Limited family life
Satisfaction	Dissatisfaction
Influence on players	Little player dedication
Immediate feedback	Community reaction
Always busy, needed	High stress level

This simple list of good and bad points involved in a coaching career does not contain all the aspects to be considered, but it may provide a device to use in considering a life's work. It is possible to make up a list that is individually designed. Any method that permits the comparison of the advantages and disadvantages of any job is or can be useful.

Also to be considered are the many tasks that are a part of a specific sport. A look at the long list of assignments, shown in Figure 5-1, undertaken by a swimming team coach can give one a pretty good idea of what the job entails.

SHOULD YOU COACH?

After considering the positive and negative aspects of a coaching career, it is advisable to take the quiz shown in Figure 5-2. It contains most of the items mentioned in the previous chapters, and it could be useful in making a decision. Two points are awarded for a "yes" answer, one point is awarded for a "maybe" or neutral answer, and zero points are awarded for a "no" answer. The possible total score is 100 points.

Summer
1. Order all equipment and supplies
2. Write requisitions
3. Ditto information sheets for the season
4. Attend coaching clinics
5. Send letters to opposing coaches confirming meet dates

Fall
1. Meet with the squad members for coming season
2. Hand out information for coming season
3. Confirm that all swimmers and divers have medical forms

Season
1. Organize daily practices and have the number of sessions necessary for the size of the team
2. Call opposing coaches a week in advance to confirm meets
3. Be sure that all forms necessary are signed and turned in prior to practice
4. Get eligibility list turned in
5. Check eligibility of the swimmers weekly
6. Decide who is swimming in which events each week and post the information
7. Get equipment (kickboards, etc.) out and ready for each practice session
8. Turn in a list of swimmers to be excused for meets
9. Fill out "back to class" excuses for swimmers who have missed classes
10. Arrange transportation
    a. Requisition buses
    b. Arrange for parent transportation when needed
    c. Requisition, pick up, and drive vans to away meets
11. Publicity
    a. Write articles for local papers
    b. Arrange for team pictures for school publications and local papers
    c. Arrange for pictures for the KSHSAA (activities association) when requested
    d. Arrange for publicity in school publications

(continued)

Figure 5-1 Swimming coach's duties

12. Meets
    a. Set up the required equipment (lane ropes, etc.) necessary to run a meet
    b. Get swimmers' cards ready for meet
    c. Arrange for timers and scorers for each home meet
    d. Clean up the pool and put away equipment after a home meet
    e. Clean up the locker room after each home meet
13. Diving
    a. Be sure that practice is organized and all safety precautions are taken
    b. Get diving judges for each home meet and away meets
    c. Arrange for an announcer for home meets
    d. Arrange for a diving scorer for home meets
    e. Fill out diving sheets for each meet and be sure that the correct dives are listed
    f. Get diving equipment ready for home meets
14. Invitational and League Meets
    a. Send invitations to schools
    b. Have meet sanctioned with KSHSAA
    c. Arrange for adult helpers for the meet
    d. Type and ditto heat sheets
    e. Type and send results to opposing coaches
    f. Have coaches meeting
    g. Order awards for the meet
    h. Set up for the meet (extra time needed for meets where there are several schools present)
15. Arrange for the national anthem to be played
16. Fill out entry forms for local, invitational, league, and state meets
17. Arrange whirlpool treatment and/or supervise weight room treatment for injured athlete
18. Wash swimsuits after every meet and wash warmups four times a season
19. Repair uniforms and swimsuits
20. Assign lockers
21. Arrange for stroke judges for each home meet
22. Repair equipment during the season and arrange to have the pool clean for each home meet
23. Arrange for the use of the video tape machine, run it during practices and at meets
24. Keep the record board up-to-date
25. Be responsible for security and safety in the locker room

(continued)

Figure 5–1   Continued

> 26. Clean up the locker room after each practice
> 27. Attend Booster Club meetings
> 28. Attend coaches' meetings
> 29. Maintain a balanced budget
> 30. Prepare speeches for pep assemblies
>
> *Post-Season*
>
> 1. Get all equipment and uniforms turned in, repaired, washed, and stored
> 2. Fill out the budget forms for the season and prepare the budget for the coming year
> 3. Turn in a complete team inventory
> 4. Schedule meets for the next season
> 5. Organize the team banquet
>   a. Make arrangements for the caterer
>   b. Take care of the financial aspects of the banquet
>   c. Organize the banquet program
>   d. Turn in a list of swimmers and divers who have lettered
>   e. Sign the letter and award form for the season
>   f. Make decorations for the banquet
>   g. Have the trophies the team has won during the season lettered
>   h. Set up the banquet on "banquet night"
>   i. Compile the team scrapbook
> 6. Clean out lockers
> 7. Fill out scholarship forms for graduating seniors
> 8. Fill out All-American forms for swimmers and divers earning them
> 9. Order All-American forms if necessary

Figure 5-1 Continued

Courtesy of Carolyn Howard, Girls' Swimming Team Coach, Shawnee Mission East High School, Shawnee Mission, Kansas.

SUMMARY

Coaching can be a lifelong occupation or a pleasant, temporary avocation, but for the period of time it is pursued it can be exciting, demanding, and consuming. The role of a coach with its many facets can be, and has been, filled by people of many backgrounds with a wide variety of experiences. Some successful ones may possess a coaching sense, which is akin to an athlete being a natural. This talent may be a combination of many kinds of abilities that come together in the athletic environment and reflect the

	Yes	Maybe	No
Can You:			
1. Handle long hours of physical work			
2. Handle long hours of mental work			
3. Talk with parents of players			
4. Organize a staff			
5. Listen to players' concerns			
6. Arrange for a game			
7. Lose with composure			
8. Win graciously			
9. Set training rules			
10. Discipline players			
11. Order uniforms			
12. Write a news story			
13. Make a speech			
14. Drive a bus			
15. Prepare an equipment bid list			
16. Keep playing statistics			
17. Be a good family person			
18. Mark off fields or line floors			
19. Be a role model for the team			
20. Be away from home			
21. Demonstrate skills and techniques			
22. Live with stress			
23. Use audio-visual equipment			
Have You:			
24. An even disposition			
25. Gained new sport knowledge this week			
26. Been an assistant			
27. Good physical health			
28. Good mental health			
29. At least ten books in your sports library			
30. Been to a sports clinic this year			
Are You:			
31. An athlete			
32. Sportsmanlike			
33. Cooperative			
34. Drug free			
35. A good teacher			
36. Safety conscious			
Do You:			
37. Like young people			
38. Know complex strategy of sport			
39. Know about liability			
40. Know conditioning fundamentals			
41. Like to teach			
42. Know how to pick a team			
43. Like to win			
44. Like to win fairly			
45. Know budgeting and purchasing			
46. Know how to raise money			
47. Know current rules			
48. Like attending to details			
49. Know ten other coaches			
50. Think coaching is fun			

Scoring
A score of 100 is impossible for most ordinary, truthful people.
A score of 75-99 = YES, you will probably be a good coach.
A score of 50-74 = YES, you can learn to be a coach.
A score of 49 or less = Are you sure that you are in the right field?

Figure 5-2 Check your aptitude for coaching

idea that some coaches, like some teachers, are born, not made. This natural talent should be cultivated through education, pruned and shaped in sports, and harvested in the coaching field. Others become successful coaches through hard work, training, and determination. Whatever route is followed, a rewarding career can result.

The scores on the quiz and the balance sheet will give some clues about personal evaluation and should help in deciding if this is the life role to be pursued. If there are more "yeses" than "nos" and more "pluses" than "minuses," then a person can be well on the way to earning the right to say, "I am a coach!"

ENDNOTES

1. J. L. Stillwell, "Why Physical Education Majors Want to Coach," *Journal of Physical Education and Recreation* (November/December 1979): 80.
2. P. Maravich, "What Every Coach Must Learn," *National Federation News* (November 1985): 28.

PART 2

The Coach and the Athlete

6

Biological Considerations

CHILDREN
ADOLESCENTS
RACE
SUMMARY

Athletes are like snowflakes in that there are millions of them and no two are exactly alike. The differences are a result of biological and cultural phenomena. An individual is born with definite biological characteristics (bone structure, muscle mass, sense acuity, etc.), and, after birth, cultural aspects (family, neighborhood, school peers, experiences, etc.) enter the picture to influence life patterns.

Although society and educational institutions join hands with coaches to modify general player behavior, little can be done to alter basic, genetic physical characteristics and capacities. Developing these inherited qualities is the coach's job, and eliciting one more inch, or ace, or goal, is the result of training. This is what coaching is all about.

Genetic factors play a major role in success in sports skills, even though form in performance is an individual matter. Athletes are limited in what they can do by their biological make-up. They can only jump so far, run so fast, or exert so much force, regardless of how much time they spend in the training arena or the playing field. There are very few who come close to realizing their maximum potential. For most athletes, there is a wide gap between what they are capable of doing and what they really do. Those who come nearest to this potential are the "star" performers. A good coach will help all athletes attempt to reach their star level.

These factors play another important role in the life of an athlete: that of determining activity interests. If a boy is small, he may be interested in wrestling, where he can compete in his own weight class, rather than in playing football, where he could be matched against someone who outweighs him by one hundred pounds. A girl interested in track and field may choose the shot rather than the dashes because she is large and cannot run too fast. The choice of a sport or an event by an athlete, then, may be based on inherent abilities that can be utilized for success and reduce the chances of injury.

CHILDREN

A child is a child, not a miniature adult; the body's biological systems are immature. The rate at which each matures is an individual matter;

each has a personal timetable, and growth is a continuous but uneven process. Growth is rapid during the first 2 or 3 years of life, slows down during the middle and late childhood years, and then spurts as the adolescent years begin.

Figure 6-1 Fielding is not a simple task (Photographer: Mickey Adair)

Maturation Rate Chronological age is not an accurate indicator of physiological age. It is not unusual for differences in rate of maturity to exceed 5 years within one chronological age/year. A group of 11-year-olds may include individuals whose body cells are not at the maturity level of the average 9-year-old, while others will have maturational ages equivalent to 14 chronological years.

The rate at which children mature is closely related to their somatotype—endomorphy (being fat, having a great deal of visceral tissue), mesomorphy (being sturdy, having a muscular build), and ectomorphy (being thin, having a linear build).[1] There is no pure body build, but a person is generally more one type than the other two. During childhood, endomorphs and mesomorphs are likely to be the tallest and/or heaviest within their age group, and they tend to mature at an earlier age than do ectomorphs. They also tend to be shorter and stockier adults compared to the later-maturing ectomorphs.

Implications It is important that children grow and compete at their own pace and that precautions be taken to ensure their safety if they choose to participate. This could mean encouraging a child to move from one league to another or to change activities. A primary concern in most leagues should be mismatching, in size and/or skill.

It would be ideal to have each youth sports participant receive a thorough physical examination, including X-rays to determine skeletal growth and defects, and it would also be ideal to have a professional evaluation of the coaches to determine their qualifications to work with this group. Unfortunately, this ideal rarely exists; therefore, the coach on the scene makes recommendations about both the children and the program.

These coaches must remember that strength and motor skills are developmental and often do not keep pace with height and weight. Size does not necessarily mean that the child is strong and skilled. Both strength and skill can be developed, of course, but too much emphasis on strength-requiring activities or complex motor performance can harm still-growing bones.

All children need an opportunity to learn how to play and to refine social and physical skills. To ensure that children have these opportunities, coaches and league officials should:

1. Encourage parents to have the child examined by a physician who is knowledgeable about children and sports.
2. Provide a wide range of sports and vary the skill level and intensity of competition.
3. Use, and encourage parents to use, good judgment in counseling children into appropriate activities.
4. Provide proper equipment and safe facilities.
5. Stress enjoyment and skill development, not winning.
6. Narrow age group ranges within each grouping, have a 2-year span rather than a 3-year span.
7. Allow players to be moved either up or down within the league.

8. Place children in groups of similar size and ability.
9. Employ fitness and skills tests specific to the sport.
10. Use appropriate routines to keep children in shape for the activity and allow time for recovery from injury or illness before playing again.

Motor Development

At age 6, the age at which some children begin to play in organized leagues, a child's general motor control has matured to the extent that many patterns of movement are well defined. Basic skills necessary for successful play are usually apparent in unrefined forms. A child may be able to perform basic locomotor skills (running, skipping, jumping, etc.), but not those skills that require coordination between the eyes and limbs (throwing, catching, hitting, kicking), as these are slower to develop. However, as children of the same age have different levels of motor skill development, and different opportunities to learn to perform, only a limited number of very young children possess high levels of skill for their age. These mature pre-schoolers participate in organized athletics that require basic skills but are usually deficient in refined skills and should not be considered the norm for children of that age.

As children mature, acquired motor traits become more established into individualized movement behaviors. They become more efficient and can perform previously attempted skills with greater success and ease; skills acquired earlier continue to be perfected. Ability increases, along with the development of the fitness components of strength and endurance. Such development allows more complex tasks to be performed. In the last stage of childhood, the prepubescent period, children emulate many of the activities played by adults; they are concerned about playing well and can perform many sports skills proficiently.

Implications

Most young children are not ready for competition organized by adults. They need opportunities and activities in which they can develop and improve basic skills, but not external pressure to perform beyond their developmental abilities. When children do begin to play forms of adult games, modifications will be necessary. If players cannot throw too far, the diamond can be made smaller; if they have difficulty tracking a moving object, a batting tee can be used; if they do not have the strength to swing a bat, smaller ones are available. It is not necessary to play football with the same size ball the pros use. The basketball court or the soccer field does not have to be regulation size. Nothing is "holy" about the games the big people play, but the games should not be modified to the degree that skill is not a requirement. Placing too many people on a team, having the net too low, or making too few or too many rules can spoil the game for almost everyone.

Sports offerings should be based on children's needs and level of development. Activities that lead the participant to a higher level of action are best from a developmental standpoint.

Physiological Aspects

Because of their immature body systems, children are definitely physiologically handicapped compared to adolescents and adults. They need time to grow. Their cardiovascular systems are inferior for several rea-

Figure 6-2 A batting tee is helpful (Photographer: Mickey Adair)

sons. Children's maximal oxygen uptake is not as high as might be expected from body size. The amount of hemoglobin (oxygen transporter in the body) is relatively low when compared with that of adults. Cardiac output has been found to be lower in children; however, a more rapid heart rate partly compensates for this difference.[2] Allowing for body size, 8- to 10-year-old children's cardiovascular systems can supply only approximately three-fourths as much of the oxygen needed for their working muscles as 16- to 18-year-olds'. Research does indicate that young children respond favorably to endurance-type activity, and cardiologists generally agree that the "normal" heart of a growing child is able to respond to the demands of strenuous exercise with no evidence that this organ is damaged by stress. It is not known, though, what the long-range impact will be.

The number of muscle cells in a muscle group is probably established well before the individual reaches the age of one year. The proportion between fast twitch fibers (white) and slow twitch fibers (red) is also a question of genetics and not possible to modify by training.[3] Three factors appear to affect the muscular strength of maturing children: increased size of the anatomical dimensions, results of aging itself, and sexual maturity. Between the ages of 6 and 20, four-fifths of the strength development occurs.[4] Children adapt to a lower level of strength utilization than adults do and, in all probability, will not be as strong as their appearances suggest. Their bodies' ability to handle stress of heavy exercise will not be as great as those of more mature individuals.

One's skeletal system is a dynamic structure like any of the other organic systems; structure changes as new cells are formed and old ones are carried away. A child's skeletal system undergoes rapid changes as it matures. The bones are growing, getting longer and denser, but not always at the same pace as the other systems (such as the muscular). This immature system is vulnerable to irreparable injury. The growing ends of the long bones (epiphyses or growth plates) are particularly susceptible to continuous heavy pressure, sudden wrenching, and blows. During the early stages of an injury to these areas, the symptoms of pain (tenderness over the epiphyses), reduction of the range of motion, and occasional muscle spasms may not be acute. Coaches must be alert to minor complaints of joint discomfort.

The temperature mechanism is very sensitive to stress. Heat from energy developed by working muscles must be dispelled if physical exercise is to continue. Some of this heat is lost through exhalation, but most is lost through the skin. In heavy exercise bouts, the blood flow to the skin increases, which helps dissipate heat through conduction and radiation. Heat is also dissipated through evaporation (sweating); when the temperature is high and the humidity is low, it is lost primarily by this method.

Implications

The "optimal" amount of physical activity for a child is not known; it still remains one of the medical secrets of the world. It is recognized, however, that a child can receive physiological benefits (improved cardiovascular system, decreased body fat, increased strength, etc.) from being physically active. Young participants, particularly those in strenuous activity, should be screened by medical personnel prior to taking part, and all need to be coached by knowledgeable individuals who follow correct training procedures.

Most childhood injuries—cuts and bruises—occur in activities with a significant chance of collision. Childrens' sports injuries, in general, usually result from an impact, repeated stress to a particular area, or great physical demands and physiological stress. Excessive repetitive strain to elbows can result in bone and joint abnormalities. The shock of running regularly on a hard surface can result in stress fractures in the spine, legs, or feet. Severe growth plate injuries can disrupt growth and become a chronic crippling injury if left undetected. Activities that involve falling, jumping, landing; repeated throwing motions; heavy weight lifting; and weight bearing of long duration should be performed with great caution.[5]

Many injuries will be avoided if a coach will not teach "dirty tricks" to the young participants. It is not ethical or legal to throw at someone. Children have been seriously injured, and there have been instances of death, from being hit on the head or upper trunk by a wildly thrown ball. Encouraging players to make throws of this type could result in a long injury list. Cardiac contusions as well as abdominal and neck injuries have resulted from spearing in a football game. Highly skilled athletes will not find it necessary to resort to such tactics—an elbow here, a knee there, a stick between the feet. If youngsters are taught to use their bodies and minds efficiently and safely, and to play by the rules (some of which are unwritten), they can be outstanding participants and relatively free of injuries.

Conditioning is a safety factor as well as a basis for playing success. Child athletes should do sustained stretching exercises, as being flexible is as important for them as for an adult. Well-conditioned athletes have stronger bones that, as a result, are less easily broken. Children should be conditioned to play a game at the level it demands, but they do not need to be in the same top-level condition as collegiate or professional stars are before participating. There is a danger of spending so much time getting the body ready to play that there is little or no time to spend developing motor skills.

When working in areas that demand endurance-type activities, children should be allowed to quit when they say they are tired. They may need to be encouraged to continue, but it is better to stop too soon than too late, as there have been cases of cardiac arrest in children. There will be those who must be told to stop—their color changes drastically (too red or too white), they are unable to talk because they are trying to catch their breath, or they become dizzy or lightheaded. Young runners need to set a well-balanced training program and limit hard workouts to a maximum of three times a week. Girls should be urged to avoid specializing in distance running before puberty; intensive training may delay puberty unduly and cause an iron deficiency.

Children should not engage in heavy exercise in hot, humid conditions because their temperature mechanisms are sensitive to stress. There is a high probability of some suffering hypothermia (heat stroke, heat exhaustion, muscle cramps). Heat exhaustion is the most common and least dangerous form of heat prostration. Symptoms include profuse sweating, cold and clammy skin, pale face, nausea, headache, weak and fast pulse, shallow breathing, and feeling faint. Heat stroke is a far more serious type of heat prostration. Symptoms include dizziness, dry skin (no sweating), flushed skin (may turn gray), strong and fast pulse, labored breathing, and high temperature. A doctor is needed to treat the victim, but first-aid procedures call for cooling the body in the quickest possible way and placing the child in a semi-reclining position. Treatment for both conditions must be immediate. The body must be cooled in the quickest way possible and the services of a physician obtained.

The best action is to prevent rather than cure the condition. Players should be encouraged to keep body contents of magnesium and potassium high by eating such foods as tomatoes, watermelon, carrots, and bananas, and to wear loose-fitting practice clothing. Cotton materials are preferred because nylon materials retain heat. Athletes need to drink fluids before, during, and after activity sessions. Water is a good, inexpensive liquid that can be readily available. Athletes must be encouraged to drink (thirst is not an accurate indicator of need) and given time to replenish body fluids.

Gender Differences

What are the differences between a boy and a girl before the onset of puberty? Obviously there are some, but not as many as some people believe. More dissimilarities, other than the basic sex characteristics, can be found within each sex rather than between the two.

At birth, girls tend to be slightly shorter and lighter than their male counterparts, but these differences soon disappear. During their childhood years there are no significant differences in their heights and weights. Girls mature faster; at age 6 their body cells are about a year nearer maturity than those of boys at that age, and at age 12 or 13 they are two biological years ahead. On the average, girls reach puberty at the age of 12 or 13, about two years before boys. This additional 2-year span of growth seems to provide boys with considerable height and strength advantage.

Sex differences in muscle, bone, and fat are small at birth but become more distinct as age advances. The characteristic differences in body shape and size begin to appear at puberty. Boys surpass girls in height and weight as their skeletal systems become larger and denser and their muscular systems continue to develop.

Even though there are relatively few biological differences, boys generally score higher on many performance tests. The American Alliance for Health, Physical Education, Recreation and Dance (AAHPERD) Health Related Fitness Tests scores indicate that 10-, 11-, and 12-year-old boys are slightly stronger and have more endurance than do girls of the same age.[6] Girls are more flexible and have a higher percent body fat. The results of the National Children and Youth Fitness Study revealed basically the same differences.[7] Also, it has been found that 3-, 4-, 5-, and 6-year-old boys are better at selected throwing, jumping, and running skills than are girls of the same age.[8] It is not known whether these differences are based entirely on developmental characteristics, or whether social pressures and expectations for girls have limited their activity, resulting in lower scores.

Figure 6–3   Children enjoy competing (Courtesy of Miami Dade Community College, South Campus, Miami, Florida)

Implications   There is no reason, on the basis of being female, why girls cannot participate in sports and develop a high degree of skill. Many would like to have a better opportunity to participate with other girls and/or boys. Boys and girls can play with or against one another; the primary concern is that the group be performance-matched and size-matched. Mismatching occurs too often both in groups composed of only one sex and in groups made up of both boys and girls. Peers can help one improve playing skills and also play a major role in determining future life patterns. Research has shown that girls who play mostly with boys or in coed groups are more likely to be sports participants when they become women.[9] When girls have the same expectations and experiences that boys do, the performance gap will narrow.

ADOLESCENTS

The entry into the adolescent years is not a sudden, single event, but part of a gradually unfolding process that starts at the beginning of an individual's life. Puberty, the point in life at which sexual maturity begins, is marked by well-defined changes in secondary sex characteristics and functions.

Adolescence marks a period in the lives of many females at which their interest in certain sports wanes and their performance levels stabilize or decrease. For most boys the opposite is true as their physical skills continue to improve and their interest in participation remains high. This phenomenon is the result of cultural rather than biological factors. The individual who is biologically "normal" is capable of meeting the ordinary demands of physical exercise, athletic training, and competitive sports.

Growth Rate

In general, youngsters begin their growth spurt about two years before puberty; the rate slows down after puberty. No one knows when growth really ceases, but girls reach full height at about nineteen years and boys approximately two years later.[10] In both sexes there are early and late maturers; the rate of growth is an individual process.

During adolescence, height increases approximately 25 percent and body weight 100 percent. Girls may be somewhat larger than boys when young teenagers. In both sexes the extremities and neck grow faster than the head and trunk; many appear to become "all arms and legs."

Implications

Because growth is so rapid, skill level may not keep pace with height. Looks can be very deceiving; a 6-foot 13-year-old may have the height for basketball, but not the coordination. A coach must be patient because the young athlete will need help in developing basic motor skills as well as those specifically needed for the sport. The youth may look like an adult but is not.

There will be a variety of sizes in a try-out group. Coaches will have late maturers interested in being a member of either the junior or the senior high school squads. It pays a coach to look closely at potential development.

A safety concern still remains for children's play—that of having injuries as a result of small players participating in contact sports with larger individuals. Ability grouping and weight classes remain viable methods for arranging competition, but it may not always be possible. Having a 100-pounder and a 150-pounder with high-level basic motor skills compete against each other is not equitable; it is difficult to compensate for that 50-pound difference. Performance matching is also important, and having several teams in one sport (that is, varsity, junior varsity, ninth grade) gives the young athlete an opportunity to play and develop. If skill or size groupings are not available, perhaps individuals need to be counseled into an activity suited to their size as well as basic abilities.

Body Build and Composition

It is evident that all males are not built alike, that females vary in body structure, and that the typical female is not built like the typical male. These characteristic differences in body build and composition appear at puberty. Boys grow into men who, on the norm, are taller and heavier than women. The male skeleton becomes stronger and denser; the boy will become a man with broader shoulders and a greater chest girth than the woman's. The width of his other bones will be, on the average, 10 percent greater with girth measurements at the abdomen and thigh equal to hers.[11,12]

The hormone estrogen promotes the accumulation of fat in the female, predominantly in the breasts and lower portion of the body. The androgen hormones are responsible for the mature male possessing a greater lean body weight, but he does have subcutaneous fat that is carried predominantly in the abdominal and upper trunk areas of his body. Men have a tendency to be fat above the belt, women below the belt. The average female has about seven more pounds of subcutaneous fat than does the average male; the typical 21-year-old has 25.73 percent body fat whereas her male counterpart has 14.56 percent body fat.[13,14]

Other differences between the two sexes begin to appear. Most females have lower centers of gravity, and some have bones that fit into rather deep grooves at the joints, resulting in conditions such as "knock knees" or pronounced hyperextension of the elbow. Males usually have longer limbs and bigger hands and feet; their total bone structure is larger than that of females. There are differences within each sex; all male adolescents will not be equal in size, nor will females. Even though there is a broad range of differences within each sex, males do seem to have the advantage over females in athletic performance.

Implications Adolescents have not reached their full growth, but their body structure is one of the many factors contributing to success in the world of sport. Variations in body configuration are related to the efficiency and effectiveness of performance in sport activities. The tall person may find success in basketball or swimming but have little success in soccer; there long levers will be difficult to manipulate, and a high center of gravity will make abrupt changes of direction more difficult. The short, light individual with powerful shoulders may never make the football team but could become an outstanding gymnast. The "skinny kid" might become a state class distance runner. Once the sport has been determined, body build also contributes to assignment to positions within a sport. Size and shape could help determine whether or not to be a first baseman or shortstop, setter or spiker, offensive lineman or defensive back, sprinter or distance runner, freestyler or backstroker, goalie or center forward.

The average adolescent male with broad shoulders, relatively slimmer hips, bigger hands, and greater height has many advantages over the average female. Girls may have better balance because of a lower center of gravity, but this can interfere with high jumping. Short arms can be a disadvantage in striking, throwing, or reaching to make a catch. Small hands make it difficult to catch a ball, spike a volleyball, or grip equipment, and a hyperextended elbow can make archery a painful sport.

Coaches must know about and be aware of variations in body build and composition between and among each gender group as well as growth and behavior anomalies for all young people; and they should be prepared to confer with parents and players if they observe marked deviations from the norm. Such newly recognized problems as Marfan's Syndrome (characterized by extreme height, arms long in relation to height, and long, tapering fingers), which is associated with a weakness in connective tissue that may lead to heart problems, should be looked for. Coaches see postural conditions such as lordosis and scoliosis, and they note chronic pathologies (anorexia nervosa and bulimia). The pathologies may be observed in those who are trying to keep their weight down for an activity (such as track or gymnastics). An extreme low percent of body fat is the common observable symptom for both. The anorexic does not eat, while the bulimic has an abnormal hunger and the tendency to purge after eating. These individuals need professional help.

The coach cannot do anything about the athlete's basic body build, but planned training programs can help the athlete achieve at the maximum level allowed by inherited body characteristics. Keeping up with the times and knowing what is needed for the athlete to produce more effectively for a particular sport are imperative. Careless planning could result in too-lean basketball players or swimmers or too-fat weight lifters. Helping players choose a sport or a position in which they can be successful is very important, but it is also important not to limit access to an activity just because of size or conformation. Motivation and drive, combined with practice, strength, and endurance, can overcome some size limitations. Young athletes should be advised about, but not limited in, their options.

Cardiovascular Endurance

Adolescents have a great capacity for work, but the amount they can do is limited to a major degree by their cardiovascular systems. As with other physiological systems, this one is conditioned to meet the demands placed on it. Endurance training over an extended period of time results in changes that will make the system more efficient.

There is a gradual increase in oxygen uptake through the adolescent years. From the age of 13, males increase their maximal aerobic power at a higher rate than females.[15] In general, a female has a smaller stroke volume (the amount of blood pumped into the aorta with each heart beat) than does a male for an equivalent submaximal level of work, partially because of her smaller heart and body size.[16] However, she can compensate to a degree for this difference by exercising to increase cardiac output. Both trained and untrained females have less total blood volume, hemoglobin, and red blood cells than do comparable males. They also have smaller thoracic vital capacities (volume of air moved through the lungs), but there is no difference in maximum heart rate between males and females.[17]

Studies have shown that young individuals respond to training by showing improved performance, as do adults. Physically well-trained individuals at any age have, on the average, a greater percentage of lean body mass, higher oxygen uptake, and higher maximal cardiac output than do untrained persons.[18]

Implications

If cardiovascular endurance is a requirement for a sport, specific training programs for athletes must be designed. Overloading, placing more than a normal demand on the system over a period of time, will increase its capabilities.

Males usually reach a higher level of this aspect of physical fitness than females do, but with training the gap can be narrowed. The capacity of female teenage distance runners has been shown to be 63.24 ml/kg. min.$^{-1}$ compared to the male runners' 70.3.[19,20] Males and females can follow the same kinds of training programs, but all programs should be established on an individual basis. Both sexes are capable of competing in sports, but if cardiovascular endurance is a primary consideration, men will probably have an advantage because of sex-linked physiological factors.

A young woman's disadvantage in endurance activities is not as great as it is in those that require strength and speed. However, many females may be further handicapped in these activities because they have more dead weight to move around, and so much of their weight is concentrated in the lower trunk and thighs.

Muscular Development

Generally speaking, males have greater muscle mass than females do because of higher levels of testosterone, which stimulates muscle growth. By age 13 most boys begin to show a marked increase in muscularity. Most females will not and cannot develop muscle bulk along with strength. An average young woman of 16 has only about two-thirds as much strength as a young man does.[21] Males have a definite advantage in upper body strength (arms, shoulder, trunk) with strength values 30 to 50 percent higher than females'. However, strength in the legs is nearly identical between the sexes.[22] Males also have an additional plus factor beyond their strength advantage. They have longer bones, which provide longer levers with which to apply their strength, which produces greater force. The average male will be able to run faster, jump higher, throw farther, move greater weight, and hit farther than the average female can.

In the late 1970s and early 1980s numerous women discovered the sport of weight training or body building and are developing well-defined musculature by following a rigid physical activity and diet program. For most, though, strength training will develop strength but will not result in major gains in muscle bulk because of the lack of testosterone. Too, the programs for the typical female are not designed to produce muscle bulk.

The development of the muscles—strength, power, and endurance—is an integral part of training programs. Adolescents are capable of developing these to a higher level than children are; improved muscular development and improved coordination are a result of both experience and maturation of the central nervous system.

Implications

Coaches must be knowledgeable about the requirements of each sport, able to design team development programs as well as an individual program for each athlete, and aware of current training methods as new information is being processed daily. The establishment of exercise programs of proper intensity, duration, and frequency to help the athlete develop potential and avoid injury is vital both for the participant and the sport. Males and females follow the same specific and general weight training procedures; commonly, females use lighter weight increments.

Females may compete with or against males, but, in general, they will have better success competing within their own sex. A female could hold her own if all that was needed was agility, balance, body coordination, and flexibility, but most sports combine these factors with strength, power, and endurance. In many instances it is not a matter of who is more highly skilled, but who is bigger and stronger. The coach should also consider the fact that when the factors contributing to success in sports are not too well balanced among the participants, whether they are male or female, mismatching can be hazardous to safety.

Temperature Regulation

Sweating provides the major mechanism for heat reduction in order for cooling to take place through evaporation. As one sweats, important electrolytes, which are necessary for proper muscular function, are lost; therefore, differences in sweat loss can be of serious concern in maintaining proper body fluid and electrolyte balance. Being active for extended periods of time in high temperature conditions can result in athletes' losing 6 to 8 percent of their body weight in fluids.

Training increases the amount of sweat that one produces and lowers the level of exertion at which one begins to perspire. Females generally sweat less than males do, possibly because estrogen inhibits sweating to a degree; thus, they may be more vulnerable to heat stress.[23] Also, there is the disadvantage of having more subcutaneous fat, which can act as a blanket in inhibiting heat diffusion. However, well-trained women's cooling capacity improves as they increase their VO_2 max levels and percentage of lean body mass. Some people of both sexes—such as the obese, poorly conditioned, diabetic, or recently ill—have great difficulty working in high temperature conditions.

The mechanisms that work against heat reduction can be advantageous in situations requiring heat retention. Thus, fat layers that inhibit heat reduction are advantageous in long-distance swimming events, winter activities, or any events with low temperature environments. Males require greater caloric expenditures to maintain normal body temperature than do women in the same activities.

Implications

Body temperature must be maintained within a normal range because extremely high temperatures, especially if accompanied by high humidity, or extremely low temperatures could result in permanent physiological damage or death. The active athlete must sweat, and the sweat must evaporate if the temperature is to remain relatively constant. The rate of evaporation is affected by the environmental temperature and humidity; high humidity does not allow the sweat to evaporate.

The coach ought to provide as safe an environment as possible. Workouts should be scheduled under the most favorable conditions, at least until the athletes become acclimated to the conditions. Practicing early and late rather than in the heat of the day in summer may be the best schedule. Long practice sessions in hot, humid conditions can lead to a malfunction of the athlete's temperature-regulating mechanism and should be avoided. Heat stroke and heat exhaustion are frequently observed in football players during the August practice sessions. The effects of heat and humidity on the players are compounded by the uniforms they wear to prevent injury. Clothing deters heat loss. During hot weather it is better for athletes to practice in light-colored and lightweight clothing, in as brief a uniform as possible, and work into activity routines gradually.

Replacing body fluids can also prevent many problems of heat stress. Athletes who are to practice for extended periods of time—30 minutes or longer—in hot, humid temperatures should drink a quart of water before beginning the session and a cup of water every 10 to 15 minutes during the session.[24] Players' thirst mechanisms cannot be relied on to make them ask for water because by the time an athlete becomes thirsty, dehydration may already be a problem. During high-intensity exercise of 85 minutes or less, water appears to be the best fluid to drink.[25] In activities of longer duration a sugar supplement may be necessary; fructose is a better substrate than glucose.

When activities are conducted in cold temperatures, it is essential that players be fully and warmly clothed. Body temperature can be maintained in cold weather if the athlete continues to be active and wears proper clothing, which has layers to be removed or added as the weather and activity require. The feet, hands, ears, and head should be covered as well as the rest of the body. A great amount of heat can escape from uncovered areas, and the extremities could suffer from frostbite if not protected.

Coaches should use preventive measures to avoid heat and cold problems. They need also to have emergency plans for heat and sunstroke as well as for chilling and frostbite; these can occur in practices and contests in spite of all the precautions.

Gynecological Considerations

The effect that participation in athletics has upon the female reproductive system has been a primary concern since the beginning of women's participation in athletic events. Girls and women have not always been encouraged, nor given the opportunity, to participate in sports. They have been discouraged from participating in events that might "jar" the pelvic area, involve much body contact, or require the cardiovascular system to be fully utilized.

The uterus was thought to be highly vulnerable to injury. This was serious in itself, but particularly for later life, especially regarding childbearing. However, there have been few injuries to the female reproductive organs, as they are much better protected, being internal, than are the males'. The breasts are vulnerable, but serious injury to this area is extremely rare.

Another primary area of concern evolves around the menstrual cycle. Both sexes are subject to hormonal fluctuations that may be manifested in different ways, such as having "low" days, but shortage of the hormone progesterone in a female results in a more visible sign—the menstrual flow. This is one part of a cycle that begins at puberty and ends at menopause. These two stages occur at no set age but vary with the individual. Usually a girl will enter the pubescent period while in middle school (age 11, 12, or 13), but it may be earlier or later. A woman enters menopause somewhere around the age of 50, but, as it is with the beginning, the end can be several years before or later. Normally a woman will menstruate 4 to 6 days at 20- to 30-day intervals, but this also varies with the individual.

Should female athletes avoid exercise and competition during this period of the cycle? Probably not. All females are not the same, even though normal biochemical changes do occur in the body preceding and during the actual bleeding. Much attention has been given to premenstrual syndrome (PMS), a little-understood combination of physiological and psychological symptoms varying widely among women. Symptoms that can appear at this time are pain (cramps, headache, joint pain, muscle pain, low back pain), nausea, protruding abdomen, enlarged and tender breasts, acne, increased congestion in the pelvic area, decreased flexibility in the lower back, weight gain, and lowered threshold for pain. Behavior mood changes include increased depression, irritability, tenseness, and lethargy. The shortage of progesterone also results in a drop in blood sugar, an imbalance of sodium and potassium in and around the cells, and excessive water retention.

Many females have none (or at least they are not aware of any) of the symptoms; some have a few of the symptoms; others may find themselves exhibiting all of them. Dysmenorrhea, painful menstruation, is not normal and can be caused by either functional or structural disorders. Studies show that this is less common in female athletes than in average female nonathletes who do not exercise regularly. Athletes tend to avoid, ignore, or get over many of the symptoms, perhaps because they are in better physical condition. Individual variability is so great that no general rule can be made about participation.

Female athletes are more prone to secondary amenorrhea (cessation of menstrual flow for at least 4 months) than are nonathletic females. This condition has been associated with low percent body fat in athletes who participate in endurance activities—running, swimming, dancing, rowing. What is the ideal percent body fat for an athlete? There is not one but carrying less fat requires less energy and is more efficient up to a point. Being too lean may lead to extreme fatigue which, of course, impairs efficiency and increases the likelihood of harming the body. A summary of research related to female runners reports that 12 to 14 percent body fat is appropriate for most top competitive runners. The percent would rise with age (a runner in her thirties might efficiently carry 22 percent body fat) as one's tissue changes as one gets older.[26]

Other variables associated with amenorrhea include a vegetarian diet and a high altitude environment.[27] Amenorrheic athletes may be at risk of decreased bone mineral content and iron. This condition associated with physical training appears to be rapidly reversible once training is discontinued; however, little information about the long-range effect is now available.[28]

Implications

The menstrual cycle, unique to the female, should not interfere with training or performance. A large majority of gynecologists place no restrictions on women's daily routine so that they can participate in vigorous activity and intensive sports competition during all phases of the cycle.

The Committee on the Medical Aspects of Sports of the American Medical Association has indicated that exercises can improve regulation of the menstrual cycle. Female athletes, following active sports involvement of international caliber, have experienced greater ease of delivery and more complication-free pregnancies than recorded for a normal but less physically active group.[29]

Limitations are generally unnecessary for the healthy, well-trained woman; the healthy, untrained woman can also continue her normal physical activities. Women have broken records at various stages of their cycle, performed below their average standards, and executed skills at their usual performance levels during their period, so no conclusions can be made about performing. Those who experience no difficulty may be allowed to continue their training and performance routines. Those who have difficulty should not be forced into routines; it may be necessary to make some sort of provision for them, such as a lighter workout or a different type of workout.

Even though the female continues to participate, a few bad effects could affect performance. Discomfort may throw timing off in a gymnastics routine; water retention may add several pounds (sometimes as much as five extra pounds) to body weight, making it more difficult to jump or run. It is possible to endanger a performance by the power of suggestion; positive thoughts, not negative ones, need to be engrained in the player's mind. Menstruation is a normal event and should be treated as one.

Physiological and psychological problems associated with the menstrual cycle, whether they are called dysmenorrhea or PMS, need to be alleviated. Functional causes such as poor posture, lack of rest, improper diet, lack of flexibility in the lower trunk, or wearing restrictive clothing may be handled by the individual. A physician should deal with problems that persist or are severe. If medication or food supplements are needed, only a physician should prescribe. In regard to amenorrhea, the coach should be well aware of the athlete's general condition and training regimen and adjust the program to meet the total needs of the participant. The athlete should see a physician if menses do not resume when training is discontinued or if the condition exists for longer than a year.

RACE

In the United States, the overwhelming majority of the athletes participating in competitive athletics are either black or white; there are few other racial groups represented. The apparent dominance of blacks in some sports or events, as well as the seeming dominance of whites in others, has raised questions about the possibility of genetic differences between the two groups.

Biological Factors

Are there really biological characteristics that result in an overwhelming majority of swimmers, golfers, tennis players, hockey team members, gymnasts, and lacrosse athletes (to name a few) being white? Prior to the 1980s, one might have thought so after watching various sports activities on television. If one were a black male, he could box; be a sprinter or hurdler; play basketball, football, and baseball; and perform the running long jump and the triple jump. A black female could be a standout performer in selected track and field events and basketball but did not fare too well in other sports.

Blacks have been the subject of much research, but little evidence for any organic differences between blacks and whites has been ascribed. Differences within groups far exceed any differences between the two races. Attempts have been made to explain black athletic superiority by race-linked physical and physiological characteristics. Studies have shown that blacks have longer limbs, shorter trunks, less body fat, more slender hips, wider calf bones, more tendons and less muscle, greater arm circumference, and more muscle fibers for speed and power than do whites. Generally these studies were conducted with a select group of blacks, and to generalize the findings to the black population as a whole constitutes an error.[30]

Even if there were some patterns of genetic differences among representative samples of blacks and whites, this would be a very poor basis for generalizations. Success in sports is certainly related to physical traits, but not to just one or two; cognitive and affective characteristics also enter the picture. One might come up with a theoretical description of a sprinter, but there would then need to be an explanation of why sprinters come in a variety of shapes and sizes—tall and slender, short and stocky, tall and muscular, long legged, short legged. There are also exceptions that do not fit theoretical descriptions or racial frameworks. When African blacks won distance races in the Olympics and other notable games, the idea that they did not have the lung capacity to run long distances was dispelled.

Within each race, as well as among the races, there are common body builds as well as other physiological and anatomical characteristics. The chances are that the greater differences in conformation—height, weight, leg length, shoulder width—are important, but it is difficult, if not impossible, to tie these to race. Also, the classic conformation of races is changing, and present-day members are generally bigger and stronger than those of past generations. Improved nutrition, health services, and training procedures have contributed to these changes.

Implications

Coaches must avoid stereotyping athletes by race. The evidence that one racial group can perform in one event better than another can is not conclusive; coaches should select the athlete whose skill and condition will get the job done.

It will be wise to treat players as individuals, evaluate their talents, and form teams or squads on actual, not perceived, ability. No coach can permit prejudice or ignorance to get in the way of a successful player, team, or season.

Experience Factors

As there is little, if any, evidence of organic differences between blacks and whites, perhaps it is experiences (nurture) that lead blacks into and keep them in sports. Those who participate in physical activity and find

Biological Considerations   83

Figure 6–4   Skill is not determined by the color of one's skin (Courtesy of The Florida State University. Photographer: Ryals Lee)

that they are good will continue to play as they mature. Who does not prefer to work at something that one does do well, that gives recognition and social status, and that may be a means to attend a college or university? In addition, sports abound with role models who have "made it" in terms of megadollars and notoriety.

Some sports, such as track and field and basketball, seem to attract a major number of young black males and females, while individual sports like tennis and golf are chosen by white youth. This has been attributed to socioeconomic status and opportunity. Many whites can afford to pay country club fees while blacks have basketball hoops on every playground and limited space for courts and courses.

A practice in the past has been to assign black males to team positions associated with physical speed, physical quickness, and high achievement motivation. On a football team they were running backs, wide receivers, and defensive backs. They were outfielders on the baseball team. Black women seemed to follow this same pattern as the sports programs for females grew rapidly in the 1970s. On basketball teams they were front-line players, not playmakers; on the volleyball teams they were spikers, not setters.[31] This practice appears to be diminishing as blacks are participating successfully in a wider variety of sports and are not automatically assigned to a specific position.

Implications

Although there appear to be cultural differences in positions played or sports participated in by members of various races, these can be attributed to experience and opportunity, not to race or inherited characteristics. Coaches will be well advised to seek and develop talent for all positions and for all sports.

As integration in schools and communities continues to provide more equitable opportunities and experiences for children and youth of all races, the tendency to ascribe characteristics to one group or another should disappear. Real ability needs to become the criterion for selection and participation.

SUMMARY

When dealing with athletes of any age, sex, or race, coaches need to consider their individual and group characteristics. They must remember that children grow, develop, and function differently from adolescents, and that adolescents are not fully-matured adults. Males and females have different performance levels and abilities, but some of these differences may be as great within a sex as between sexes; therefore, only general conclusions can be drawn about ability. There also are as great within-race as between-race differences, so no coaching decisions should be made on race alone.

It is absolutely essential for coaches to be knowledgeable about human physiology if they are to design training programs that follow guidelines based on facts and not fiction. This knowledge will not only help young athletes reach their potential, but also will guard against injury. Actual, not perceived, ability should be the basis for all player training and selection, and for all coaching.

ENDNOTES

1. G. L. Rarick and V. Seefeldt, "Characteristics of the Young Athlete," in *Youth Sports Guide for Coaches and Parents*, ed. J. R. Thomas (Washington, D.C.: AAHPER, 1977), pp. 24–43.
2. P. Åstrand, "The Child in Sport and Physical Activity—Physiology," in *Child in Sport and Physical Activity*, ed. J. G. Albinson and G. M. Andrew (Baltimore: University Park Press, 1976), pp. 19–33.

3. P. D. Gollnick, R. B. Armstrong, C. W. Saubert, IV, K. Piehl, and B. Saltin, "Enzyme Activity and Fiber Composition in Skeletal Muscle of Untrained and Trained Men," *Journal of Applied Physiology* 33 (1972): 312.
4. P. Åstrand and K. Rodahl, *Textbook of Work Physiology*, 2nd ed. (New York: McGraw-Hill, 1977), pp. 176–189.
5. D. D. Arnheim, *Modern Principles of Athletic Training* (St. Louis: Times Mirror/Mosby College Publishing, 1985), p. 108.
6. *Lifetime Health Related Physical Fitness Test Manual* (Reston, Va.: AAHPER, 1980), pp. 23–35.
7. J. G. Ross, C. O. Dotson, G. G. Gilbert, and S. J. Katz, "New Standards for Fitness Measurement," *Journal of Physical Education, Recreation and Dance* (January 1985): NCYFS 20.
8. A. M. Morris, J. M. Williams, A. E. Atwater, and J. H. Wilmore, "Age and Sex Differences in Motor Performance of 3 Through 6 Year Old Children," *Research Quarterly for Exercise and Sport* 53 (1982): 214.
9. *Headway, The Women's Sports Foundation Newsletter* (San Francisco: Winter 1985–86), p. 1.
10. L. J. Stone and J. Church, *Childhood and Adolescence: A Psychology of the Growing Person,* 3rd ed. (New York: Random House, 1973), p. 422.
11. J. H. Wilmore and A. R. Behnke, "An Anthropometric Estimation of Body Density and Lean Body Weight in Young Women," *American Journal of Clinical Nutrition* 23 (1970): 267.
12. J. H. Wilmore and A. R. Behnke, "An Anthropometric Estimation of Body Density and Lean Body Weight in Young Men," *Journal of Applied Physiology* 27 (1969): 25.
13. R. M. Malina and G. L. Rarick, "Growth Physique and Motor Performance," in *Physical Activity Human Growth and Development,* ed. G. L. Rarick (New York: Academic Press, 1973).
14. Wilmore and Behnke, "An Anthropometric Estimation of Body Density."
15. Åstrand, "The Child in Sport and Physical Activity—Physiology."
16. Åstrand and Rodahl, *Textbook of Work Physiology.*
17. Åstrand, "The Child in Sport and Physical Activity—Physiology."
18. B. R. Londeree and M. L. Moeschberger, "Effects of Age and Other Factors on Maximum Heart Rate," *Research Quarterly for Exercise and Sport* 55 (1984): 318.
19. E. Burke and F. C. Bush, "Physiological and Anthropometric Assessment of Successful Teenage Distance Runners," *Research Quarterly* 50 (1979): 180.
20. D. L. Costill and E. Winrow, "Maximal Oxygen Uptake Among Marathon Runners," *Archives of Physical Medicine and Rehabilitation* 5 (1970): 317.
21. D. R. Lamb, *Physiology of Exercise: Responses and Adaptations* (New York: Macmillan, 1978), p. 228.
22. J. H. Wilmore, "The Female Athlete," *The Journal of School Health* (April 1977): 227.
23. Lamb, *Physiology of Exercise,* p. 225.
24. D. L. Costill, "Water and Electrolytes," in *Ergogenic Aids and Muscular Performance,* ed. W. P. Morgan (New York: Academic Press, 1972), pp. 293–320.
25. R. G. McMurray, J. R. Wilson, and B. Kitchell, "The Effects of Fructose and Glucose on High Intensity Endurance Performance," *Research Quarterly for Exercise and Sport* 54 (1983): 156.
26. B. Hasselbring, "Are You Running Too Thin?" *Women's Sports & Fitness* (December 1986): 10.
27. K. A. Carberg, "A Survey of Menstrual Function in Athletes," *European Journal of Applied Physiology and Occupational Physiology* 51 (1983): 211.

28. J. M. Stager, "Reversibility of Amenorrhea in Athletes," *Sports Medicine* 1 (1984): 337.
29. R. W. Corbitt and associates, "Female Athletes," *Journal of Physical Education and Recreation* (January 1975): 45.
30. H. Edwards, *Sociology of Sport* (Homewood, Ill.: Dorsey Press, 1973), p. 193.
31. M. D. Murphy, "The Involvement of Blacks in Women's Athletics in Member Institutions of the Association of Intercollegiate Athletics for Women," Ph.D. dissertation, The Florida State University, 1980.

7

Meeting the Athlete

PREPARATION
THE MEETING
SUMMARY

Coaching is not a seasonal activity. Soccer or tennis matches may be played in the fall, but the coach begins "coaching" long before the first match and will end long after the final one. More often than not, the season is never-ending, and the higher a coach moves up the hierarchy, the greater are the time demands. Recreational leagues are more seasonal than interscholastic leagues, which are more seasonal than intercollegiate leagues. For many coaches, though, the season really begins when they meet prospective team members for the first time. The tone and stage of the upcoming season are set at this first meeting of the "new" year.

PREPARATION

Total preparation for any phase of the season is very important. Primary in preparation, of course, is making contact with all former and prospective team members. For many coaches this creates few problems, as they have kept players in a summer program or else the season begins during the school year. Others will make initial contact with potential athletes by utilizing a variety of communication modes. Prior to making these contacts, a meeting time has to be established and a meeting area reserved. There is nothing wrong with making several contacts with an individual, but there must be no variation in the information that is being given; all details should be made final prior to the first announcement.

Notification

Many coaches have no need to advertise, while others will use different methods to ensure a full house at the first team meeting. Each school, each principal, and each athletic director may have a particular procedure to follow in disseminating information to potential or actual team members, and a coach's method should be approved by the administrators. The first step, particularly for a new coach, is to match last year's files with this year's enrollment to determine who may be returning. Files are a good source for addresses and phone numbers of former athletes who should be contacted. Coaches of feeder schools are usually pleased to give names of students who are transferring to the school, and physical education teachers at all levels may recommend students. Personal contact with these potential new players can be very helpful. Announcements placed in the school and local papers, given on radio and television stations, posted on school bulletin boards and in favorite hangouts, and reported on the school public-address system reach many prospective participants. Most coaches want to inform as many people as possible that the season is about to begin. "Beating the bushes or sidewalks" for players can have a big payoff for a coach and team.

Announcements Whether one is an agency volunteer or a school coach, the clarity of the first meeting announcement is important. All the vital information must be included in the notice—date, day, beginning and ending times, location, and what the individual is to bring. The head and assistant coaches' names and phone numbers need to be listed in case there are questions to be answered about the program or schedule, or in case there is a need for transportation after school.

Time When scheduling this first assembly for the squad, a coach must consider customs of the community. The time/date should not conflict with religious meetings, important events for the community, school functions, or state and national holidays. Coaches of most school teams can assume that an after-school meeting is appropriate; but in a school where most students are transported by school buses, an activity period may be more appropriate.

This meeting must be scheduled well ahead of the season, before scheduled practices begin. Practice times are too valuable to miss. There may be a need for alternate meeting plans should some situation interfere.

Facility Securing an appropriate meeting site is important. Coaches can make a mistake by assuming that a room is available and failing to make proper arrangements well in advance. Someone has to make sure that there are enough chairs, blackboards, and other furniture to meet the expected needs. Lighting, cooling/heating, and key systems have to be checked; nothing can be left to chance. Having an easily located and accessible meeting room is vitally important. All planning will go for naught if prospective players cannot find where the meeting is being held.

THE MEETING

Once arrangements for the meeting place are made and all interested persons have been notified, procedures for the meeting are established. As first impressions can be very important, coaches should make every effort to have this first gathering proceed to a successful conclusion. The tempo

> For all JUNIORS and SENIORS WHO PLAN TO PLAY TENNIS FOR THE LANCER TEAM.
>
> This is to let you know that TENNIS PRACTICE will be starting on THURSDAY, AUGUST 14
>
> We will have two practices on that day (come to either one) on the Lancer courts.
>
> 8:00–10:00 A.M.
> or
> 10:00–Noon
>
> On Friday, August 15, we will have the same practice schedule. You may come to either one. When school starts we will have three sessions each day:
>
> 6:15–7:30 A.M. For those who prefer to practice early or who have something to do after school
>
> 2:10–3:30 P.M. For seniors who are on an early dismissal schedule
>
> 3:30–5:00 P.M. For those who have not attended an earlier practice
>
> Have your MEDICAL FORM, signed by both the DOCTOR and your PARENTS. DO NOT come without this completed form.
>
> August 18 through August 22 we will be running a tennis tournament. You will sign up for this tournament when you come on August 14 or 15. If you cannot attend practice on these days, check in any morning at 8:00 A.M. on August 18–22 and I will put you in the tournament. This tournament will determine your groupings.
>
> NOTE: If you have not completed your SUMMER TENNIS TOURNAMENT schedule, do not come out for practice. It does not matter what kind of tournament it is, you cannot practice for the team and still be playing in a tournament. However, I would appreciate it if you would let me know that you plan to play tennis for East and that you are playing in a tournament so I will know that you will be at practice as soon as the summer season ends.
>
> You may practice in your own practice clothing and you will need your own racket, shoes, and socks.
>
> If you have not been playing this summer, get your racket out and hit a few balls. I will see you on Thursday, August 14, at 8:00 or 10:00 A.M. on the Lancer courts.
>
> C. Howard
> Tennis Coach
> Shawnee Mission East High School
> Office phone 813-2107

Figure 7-1 Tennis team tryouts

Courtesy of Carolyn Howard, Tennis Coach, Shawnee Mission East High School, Shawnee Mission, Kansas.

for the entire season is being set at this occasion; the routine and style a coach intends to follow all year will be established.

Meetings begin on time. The coaching staff must be at the meeting site early to check on the facility and to set an example of promptness. Too much delay makes it evident that being on time is not expected.

Coaches set the social stage by dressing appropriately. Frequently, a school coach will wear something other than the typical coaching attire. Being well groomed can increase an individual's own self-confidence and the confidence of the players in the coach. A player/coach of a community softball team has a different role to play and can be more relaxed in dress.

Introductions are the first order of business. The head coach, if a new one, could be introduced by the principal or athletic director. Most coaches, however, elect to introduce themselves and then their staff. School coaches usually tell the players how to refer to them and the assistants—Coach, Miss Smith, Mr. Bob, Dr. Jones. First names or nicknames should be avoided. Some coaches want to move to a more informal relationship with the players later, which is easy to do, but it will be difficult to move from informal to formal if that seems necessary. The nonschool league coach will not have this problem with age peers, but may need to consider an appropriate title when dealing with children.

If the meeting must be conducted in an outside area, there are special problems to consider. Distractions such as extreme weather conditions (sun, cold, wind), band practice, traffic, admiring students, litter-strewn fields, or cheerleaders are to be avoided if possible. There should be nothing to distract players from the business at hand.

It is a good idea to make arrangements for an alternate meeting site. Some unforeseen incident can make the first choice unusable.

Equipment

All materials must be prepared well ahead. Personal data sheets, playbooks, rule sheets, and the like may have to be typed and photocopied by a coach unless there happens to be secretarial assistance available. The amount of materials needed can be estimated; it is better to have too many copies than too few. Pencils or pens may have to be supplied if players are expected to complete forms.

Projectors or VCRs have to be reserved unless the athletic department has its own, and even then it is wise to have one set aside. Films or slides (whatever is to be shown) should be ordered, received, and previewed by the coaching staff. Extra bulbs, adaptor plugs, and a projectionist may be needed. All details must be taken care of prior to the meeting. Many coaches prepare checklists of what is to be taken care of and by whom. Items may be checked off by the head coach as each task is completed.

Agenda

Players who receive an agenda for the meeting, either in a handout or on the blackboard, may be more attentive and interested because they will have a basic idea of what is coming. The head coach, if a leadership role is being set, may choose to give a brief overview of the program and a short résumé of his or her experience relating to coaching. Players are also interested in the assistants' experiences; each can deliver a few brief statements, or the head coach can include these along with the introductions. This needs to be selective information; intimate details of one's life are irrelevant. The primary thing is to let the players know that they are in good hands in a sport situation that will be very vital in their lives.

Responsibilities, as well as the authority, of assistant coaches, managers, trainers, and the like, have to be made known. Players must be made aware of the importance of each coach to the team. Unless this is done, many players may assume that the head coach is the only authority figure.

A major item on the agenda will be the players' orientation to the program. They should be presented with a year-long overview of what they are expected to do throughout the entire season. Pre-season plans, the game schedule, and post-season plans should be outlined in brief but sufficient detail. Players like to know what to expect, and a coach should present a realistic preview of what lies ahead.

If the past season is mentioned, only positive terms are to be used. The season may have been a disaster and the coach fired, but there is no place for derogatory remarks. The present is built on the past, and the coach will build a future on that foundation.

Goals and Objectives

This is the time to define goals and objectives so that players will be aware of those set (for individuals and for the team as a whole) by the coaching staff, and individual goals can be viewed against the background of group goals. Coaches may have very personal and private goals (such as wishing to have 25 new players try out, desiring to get through the first game without appearing too stupid, or hoping to avoid being sued), but it is not necessary to share these with the team.

A coach will be expected to make a public statement, perhaps to be released later, about what the team will be aiming for during the season. These goals need to be realistic and reachable but not too easily gained. After considering the returnees, schedule, staff, opponents, and the total situation, the coach should be able to make a realistic educated guess about what is possible. For some teams a realistic goal would be to have full squads appear for a meet; it may be all that can be expected. For others an 80 percent win record could be appropriate. A few take a matter-of-fact aim for the city, state, or national championship. Nothing is impossible, but there might be a few things that are highly improbable. Some coaches are eternal optimists and speak of the team's chances in glowing terms; others are naturally pessimistic and play down team potential. A wise coach may take a position somewhere in the middle, a balance of the two; reachable goals, mixed with luck, might stretch to even higher goals. The coach should expect the players to give just a little more effort than it is believed they can produce, because if nothing is asked for, nothing may be received.

It might be appropriate to have goals/objectives posted in the meeting area. When prospective players arrive they will see, *"Gopher High Will Be Number One"* or *"The Rattlers Will Strike First."* Others may be printed on cards and given to players to post in their rooms. They will see *"I Will Give 110 Percent Effort"* or *"We Are The Best"* the first thing every morning and the last thing every night.

Personal Data Coaches may have a wealth of information about returning players from last year's team; but, in order to update records for these players and to begin records for others, they often require players to complete a personal data form. This needs to be designed to fit a particular situation; only information pertinent to the player and activity should be sought. It is a rare player who enjoys completing forms, so short and simple ones are usually best. Clear language and good grammar are also important. Members of the English department are often generous with their knowledge and time and will help staff of other departments with their writing when asked.

It is assumed that the prospective athletes can read and write well enough to give the information requested. If they are youngsters, parents may be asked to complete the forms because children may not have access to the information needed. If they are high school students or adults who cannot read, someone may need to read the questions aloud and record their answers. Each item should be explained even though complete instructions may accompany the form. If the forms are completed and returned at the first meeting, the coach will have one less item to worry about. If the forms are to be returned later, they must be collected; otherwise the players may assume that the information is not important and forget about them. It is a good idea for a coach to have a list for each player and check off items, such as the data form (Figure 7-2), as they are completed and returned.

Some players may give false information. There are those who do not want the truth known, others do this to see the coach's reaction, and others do not know the correct answers. Those players who are ashamed or afraid to tell the truth believe that lies will make them sound like all others on the team, especially if their background is not like their peers'. It is not much fun to be different—especially when one is poor and/or a member of a minority group. All information may be accepted as given, or spot checks can be made against records or by talking with selected people. Players should know that the information has a useful purpose but that it has nothing, or very little, to do with player selection. Coaches use this information to help understand the player; it may assist with motivational strategies and utlizing special talent, or there may be items that would be useful in helping players in their personal lives.

In order to conform with the Buckley Amendment, each player should give permission for the school to release information about himself or herself, including permission for pictures to be published. The statement, which is often included in the eligibility form, must be signed by the parent or guardian unless the athlete is of legal age, and even then it is advisable.

Team Standards (Rules) Rules and standards should be discussed at the first meeting before the season really begins. The players need to know behavior expectations early because they may have to adjust their life styles, decide how to beat the system, or quit.

94 The Coach and the Athlete

```
             SPORT _____

Name _____ Preferred name _____ Date _____
Age _____  Birthdate _____ Religious preference _____
Home address _____ Phone number _____
Parents' (Father) _____ Occupation _____
         (Mother) _____ Occupation _____
         (Guardian—name and relation) _____
         Occupation _____
Brothers and sisters (names and ages) _____
_____

Educational goals _____
Occupational goals _____
Personal goals _____
Present job _____ Weekly income/allowance _____
School subjects taking _____
Favorite sport to play _____ To watch _____
Previous experience in (sport) _____
_____

Previous experience in other sports _____
_____

Goals for (sport) _____
_____

Extracurricular activities (in school) _____
_____ (out of school) _____
_____

Offices held _____
Hobbies _____
Girl (boy) friend's name _____ Grade _____
Why participating in this sport _____
_____

Sports heroes/heroines _____
Favorite subject _____ Favorite teacher _____
Sports relatives (father, mother, sister, brother, aunt, uncle,
cousin) played _____
_____

Coach's personal note _____
_____
```

Figure 7–2   Personal data form

If there are no team rules, they should know this. There may be only one rule to discuss, "You are on your own and may set your own standards until the team or your play begins to suffer." If a coach elects to establish team standards (and some are usually necessary for the sake of order and cohesion), they should be for that particular team in that particular situation. Copies, such as shown in Figure 7–3, need to be distributed to players at the first meeting.

WHEAT RIDGE VOLLEYBALL

1985

Welcome to the 1985 volleyball season! Volleyball begins the thirteenth year of competition in Jefferson County and at the state level will hold the eleventh state tournament. Ten of the eleven state championship teams have been Jefferson County teams. In 1984, first, second, and third place went to Jefferson County teams.

Wheat Ridge High School will be hosting the first round of the state tournament this year. Four teams will represent our league and we *will* be one of them. Our theme this year is "Aim for a star" and one of those stars is the state tournament. The season is highly competitive and short, so our practice time is very valuable. Players and parents must be willing to make sacrifices in order for our program to be successful.

Rules and Regulations

The following rules are set up by the county, school and coaches for the good of the team and the individual.

A. Maintain scholarship eligibility as set forth by Jefferson County and Wheat Ridge.
B. Absolute adherence to the training rule contract.
C. Dedication to the Wheat Ridge volleyball program. Volleyball must be your number one sport during the entire fall season.
D. Practice
  1. All members are expected to be in attendance for the duration of all practice sessions.
  2. Team members must contact the head coach if an emergency should arise and she cannot attend or must arrive late to practice. Please schedule doctor and dentist appointments at times other than scheduled practices.
  3. Penalty for lateness to practice:
    a. 1–5 minutes late: 2 sets of stairs for every minute.
    b. Over 5 minutes late you *do not* attend practice.
    c. Two unexcused absences you are dismissed from the team.
E. Sophomore and Junior Varsity team members are expected to be at all varsity games. You are to remain on the gym floor until the varsity team has finished their warm-up. Various duties will be given to members of these teams. Failure to take part in these duties will result in a suspension of a game.
F. Game Days
  1. All members are expected to ride the school bus to and from games held away from Wheat Ridge.
  2. Look sharp on game days! No faded jeans or sloppy dress!

Figure 7-3 Team standards

Courtesy of Mary G. Anderson, Head Volleyball Coach, Wheat Ridge Senior High School, Wheat Ridge, Colorado.

Eligibility

A player's eligibility is the ultimate responsibility of the coach. Coaches have to be able to quote verbatim the eligibility rules of the agency governing play, and so should the players. In school leagues several factors are involved in eligibility: number of years of participation, transfer regulations, residence of the player and his or her family, grade point average, number of courses/hours passed last year or last term, courses enrolled in at the present time, year in school, amateur/professional status. In nonschool leagues the requirements for team membership are less stringent. Players must be aware of whatever the regulations are and accept responsibility for being eligible or "legal." An entire season can stand or fall on this factor.

The school coach must require the players to bring in a copy of their birth certificate. These should not be kept, but the school may have a copy made for the student's file, to verify age, and then return it to the athlete. These should already be on file for returning players.

Student athletes should be informed if a grade check will be made with each of their teachers at some point during the term. They are responsible for their academic eligibility status, but the coach is the one who may pay the highest price for playing an ineligible player. The athlete may not play that sport again that year, or ever, but the coach may lose a position, and the team, as well as the school, may be penalized.

Clearance Forms

Generally, three clearance forms are required: physical examination, notarized statement from the parent or guardian to allow the player admission to a hospital if they cannot be reached, and proof of medical insurance. These records should be placed in the individual player's file where they can be easily reached in case of emergencies.

At the first session the players must be told that physical examinations are required prior to participation in practice. Examination forms are to be completed by the player's family physician or by a local doctor who may volunteer to examine the squad members. If exams are to be given en masse, players need to be told the day, date, time, and place. It may be feasible to have players sign up for specific times. If players go to their own physicians to have the examination completed, they also have to be aware of the due date.

A coach hopes and prays that no player will have to go to the hospital, but provisions have to be made "just in case." There will be times, especially on out-of-town trips, when the parents or guardians cannot be reached immediately. Permission granted prior to an accident may help avoid serious complications.

Players generally are given an option in regard to medical insurance—either have a policy with the family or get one through the athletic department. They may do both, but one or the other is required. The cost of school insurance and the coverage are presented to the squad members, and they are told to discuss these with their parents. Parents (or the player if he or she is self-supporting and of legal age) should be requested to make a written statement concerning their choice.

Another clearance form often requested is written permission from the parent or guardian allowing the youth to play. It may be a simple form merely stating that the parents or guardian grant permission, or it may be a more elaborate form stating rules that the player is expected to follow. The parents or guardian are then asked if they understand the conditions involved in participation and, after knowing these, do they still grant permission. See Chapter 19.

There has to be a deadline for returning all forms if athletes were not asked to bring them to the meeting. They need to be informed, orally and in writing, of the consequences for not meeting the deadlines. In non-school leagues or with adults, and in some states where 18 is the legal age, the completion of some forms may not be necessary. It is important, however, to have a medical exam, proof of insurance, and parent or spouse permission for hospitalization or surgery.

Other Agenda Items

The financial situation must be explained. Players should know how much the season is going to cost them in dollars and cents. They need to be aware of what they must buy, for example, shoes, a racket, nose clips, warm-ups, practice clothes, and so on. All expenses that may face the player (the cost of the medical exam, cost of insurance, meals for out-of-town trips) should be discussed. If players will be expected to raise money, the amount and methods are items to be considered.

Team selection methods (discussed in Chapter 8), when it will be done, and the criteria for selection have a prominent place on the agenda. If there is one set of policies governing participation in qualifying meets and another set that applies to championship competition, players deserve to know. The more objective these criteria can be, the better for all.

The award system, the types and criteria to be used, needs to be explained. It may be too soon to elect captains, but policies regarding the selection can be discussed. The coach may appoint a captain (it may be wise to appoint two) at the beginning of the season. It may be a senior member, one who established a leadership position in the past season, or one who is not objectionable to anyone. Other coaches appoint a captain for each contest, one who earned the right in practice, or all players may be given the opportunity. Many times the team members select the captain(s)—at the beginning of the season, for each contest, sometime during the season, or after the final meet. However it is to be done, responsibilities need to be specified, the position recognized as an important and honored one, and the selection process outlined in detail.

Additional information to be covered by handouts and discussions may concern practice schedules, playing schedules, travel regulations, locker room procedures, uniform assignments, care of facilities, and similar matters. Players need an opportunity to ask questions. Perhaps the returning athletes who have lettered would like to give a few "onward and upward" words to bring the meeting to a close. If the coach believes that the team members are reluctant either to ask questions or to comment spontaneously, he or she may ask or "prime" a few players, in advance of the meeting, to participate in the discussion.

This first meeting does not have to be all business. Many coaches combine it with a watermelon feast, hamburger fry, or a picnic. They believe that a social is a good way for players to get to know one another before the work begins, and it also affords an opportunity for the coaches and players to interact.

SUMMARY

This first gathering of players that marks the beginning of a new season can be an auspicious occasion. The climate, tone, or style for the year can be established and necessary business can be accomplished.

The coach should organize this meeting well, present all pertinent information, collect or arrange to collect all necessary forms, establish team procedures, and become established as the leader. It needs to be as short as possible, and, when the work is over, it could turn into a social affair.

Systematic planning makes a meeting productive, satisfying to players and coaches alike, and a useful occasion rather than something to avoid. The old adage is true, "Well begun, half done."

8

Selecting the Athlete

SIZE OF THE SQUAD
UNSTRUCTURED SELECTION
STRUCTURED SELECTION
INFORMING THE PLAYERS
SUMMARY

There can be no game without players. There does not have to be a coach but there must be players, and a coach's success depends on them. The team's achievements have their base in the skill, character, and condition of the athletes, so the selection of a team may be the most important and most difficult task of the season.

Since situations vary widely, a coach will need to adapt a system for each particular circumstance. Several systems may be utilized before one is found that is suitable, and then it may work well with certain groups but not with others. There is no right, wrong, or foolproof method, but a good coach develops a "sense" for discovering the talented athlete, or potentially talented one, who is willing to put in the hard work needed to become a great game player.

Many coaches do not seem to mind judging whether or not a player is good enough to make the squad, but others find this a most complex and distasteful task. There are players at the extreme ends of the continuum—some "winners" who leave no doubt about their abilities and interest and some "losers" who do not have the basic qualities. It is the players in between that give the coaches ulcers because they invariably select one who should have been cut and cut one who should have been retained. There is always the possibility that injuries, illnesses, or players quitting will deplete the squad. It is also possible that a potentially good player will be turned off by not being kept on the squad and will never play again.

Is it really fair not to cut a player? Will a coach be doing individuals a favor by keeping them on the squad when the chances of their playing are almost nonexistent? Staying on the squad can be very time consuming for the participant, and this time could possibly be put to more profitable use—working, studying, participating in another sport, or taking part in another activity.

SIZE OF THE SQUAD

The size of the squad will vary with individual situations. Primary consideration has to be given to the number on the sports team, rules accompanying the sport, and the type of play involved. Soccer teams field 11 players, as do most football teams, but they do not need to carry as large a squad; football games have free substitution, specialists, and more injuries than soccer does. Golf squads operate well with few participants, but track teams need to carry many members.

Another factor to consider is the extent of the funding. This would determine such things as the number of coaches assigned to the sport, available equipment, schedule of contests, the number of teams in the sport, as well as the number of players on the squad. The total number of players competing for positions, as well as their skill levels and ages or classifications, are contributing elements. If there are many freshmen with potential trying out, they may be retained in order to maintain their interest and develop their skills. Senior marginal squad members, with the same levels of skill as these freshmen, are often cut if the squad size is a concern.

The number of available uniforms, spaces for practice, number of lockers, and the amount of equipment will often force the coach to make decisions about selection. All these considerations are crucial for players to participate in the activity fully.

There are situations and schools where all players can remain "out" for a sport. Junior varsity teams, "B" teams, and others can be formed to take care of everyone; and, if other schools in the area have similar teams, scheduling will not be a problem. There are definite advantages to having several teams. The first, and most important, is that more individuals have an opportunity to take part in the program. Also, more parental support will be available, and players may maintain a higher level of motivation as they work to "move up" the hierarchy or to avoid "moving down." Another point to consider is that athletes need playing experience; participation in JV games is preparation for next year. A disadvantage may be that players feel pressured and uncertain if their team positions are threatened. Another disadvantage is that coaches may not have the time to spend on fairly evaluating a large number of players. Too, large numbers could have an adverse effect on unity among coaches as well as players and would definitely increase the expenses and overload the facilities.

UNSTRUCTURED SELECTION

On some occasions the determination of the number of players on a team is the result of a policy, philosophy, or circumstance not expected by the coach. The effect of this unstructured selection process is different from a planned or structured process.

No-Cut Policy   There are times when a no-cut policy will be in effect; this may be the administration's or the coach's policy. In some leagues, generally those established for younger players, the rule is that "all who want to play become members of a team." In some instances, players are assigned to teams on the basis of ability (varsity, junior varsity) or on the basis of grade level (seventh-grade team, eighth-grade team). If the administration's policy is that all stay and all play, the idea is to build interest and skill in a sport.

More often, the decision to cut rests with the coach rather than with the administration. There are coaches whose experience and common sense tell them that most players will be needed sooner or later—not in scheduled contests but in practice, not this season but next season, not at the beginning of the season but after it is well under way. There are those coaches whose basic philosophical belief is that sport is for everyone. If prospective athletes care enough to work to make the squad, then there is a place for them. Coaches who have this philosophy may choose to work with younger players, in a junior high/middle school or youth athletic league, where winning is important but the total development of the individual takes precedence.

For some coaches the decision may be easier if the sport is able to utilize all who care to participate. Football and track and field could do this, but tennis and golf could not. Some squads may be so small that coaches must think of recruiting rather than cutting. It is difficult to field an 11-player football team with an 18-player squad, or a strong swimming team with only 6 out for competition.

Self-Cut Policy

Some coaches do not cut players but let the players cut themselves. Practices may be too demanding for some; the early hours of the two-a-days may not be worth the effort. Running long distances, up and down stairs, and suicide drills in hot humid weather with few water breaks can eliminate all but those who really want to play. For some individuals the practices are dehumanizing; they elect to quit rather than to play. A coach may think that a player is going to quit, so the player is dropped. In this way a coach can say, "I have not had a player quit on me yet."

A coach must be prepared to make decisions concerning those who quit and then elect to try again. Players should not be going and coming at will, but it may be wise to leave an opening for those who would like to return, if not this season, then next year. Taking time to talk with one who chooses to leave may offer options for both coach and player while giving information that could be helpful to the coach.

Recruiting

Occasionally the coach's selection is limited because the tryout group is small in number, or those who are considered to be the better athletes are not among the prospects. Coaches who want or need additional team members must go after them; the method will vary with the coach and with the situation. There is an indirect approach in which the coach attempts to get a message to the potential players through the parents, girlfriend (boyfriend), peer group, an influential community member, or a former star athlete. These persons are asked to talk with the individuals and encourage them to be a team member. It may be that a coach of another sport, one in which the athlete is participating, stands in the way. This coach may be approached and an attempt made to work out some sort of agreement so that the athlete may participate in both activities. The sport environment could be made more attractive to some individuals. Such things as a good playing schedule, well-organized practices, favorable publicity, and special events may entice additional players.

Of course, a coach can always talk with the sought-after individuals. The potential athletes may have felt that they simply were not skilled enough to compete, or perhaps they needed the added encouragement of being asked to join the team.

There are those coaches who promise everything from a starting berth to a college scholarship. Although this may be considered unethical and unfair, they will allow some individuals special privileges; general team rules will not apply. The coach may choose this extreme route or may simply talk with the individual about the advantages of participation.

Whatever the method, it should be employed only after deep thought and careful planning. The coach's job may be on the line, but the price to pay to get an athlete could be extremely high.

STRUCTURED SELECTION

If the plan is to select players, a certain sequence or structure has to be established, and the decision on what is to be measured should be made. Then the coach must design drills and situations in which players can be judged fairly, and develop a method of scoring so that valid performance information can be used in evaluation. Players ought to be informed of the selection process, including the time frame, at the beginning of the season; it is a mistake to let the process be a surprise.

Objective Selection

Some attributes or skills can be objectively measured in simulated or drill situations, but using these nongame situations is not always functional because they are quite different from contest conditions. Unfortunately, it is seldom possible to rate in a "real contest" before selections must be made, so the drills need to be as gamelike as a coach can make them. Other attributes having specific application to the sport may also be measured, such as speed, endurance, or strength.

Skill

One thing is certain—the player must have fundamental skills. How are these measured? First, a question should be answered. "What do I want to measure and why these?" The major physical elements and basic skills required will vary with the sport. All sports do not make the same demands on the participants, so the important aspects for each sport must be isolated. Major physical elements may be assessed by giving tests: How fast can she run a mile? How far can he swim in 15 minutes? How high can she jump? How much dead weight can he lift? What is her speed in the 40-yard dash? How quickly can he maneuver through an obstacle course? How many sit-ups can she do in a minute? These general performance tests should have special application to the sport; a coach does not need to gather unnecessary data.

Skills specific to the sport can be assessed by administering skills tests: How far can he throw the ball? How well does she serve? How accurate is his free throw shooting? How accurate is her putting? The drawback to this type of testing is that a player may pass a test but fail when playing the game. There are always those who will not pass some of the skill tests but still be very good game players. Performance of skills outside the contest situation is not always an accurate indicator of an athlete's playing ability, so these tests should be just one of several selection criteria.

A third way to evaluate skill level is by keeping performance charts. Records of the goals scored, goals prevented, tackles made, batting averages, driving distances, serving accuracy, and so on, are frequently kept of performances in practice. Scrimmages are a vital part of practices, and records of individual performances could and should be kept over a sufficiently long period of time to get a player's profile. Intra-squad games are good proving grounds for grading players' performances. "Jamborees" with other teams in the area can also offer all players the opportunity to display their talents; these place the team members in very realistic contest settings. It can be helpful for outsiders, other coaches, or former players to assist with the evaluations.

Coaches of individual sports may have less difficulty selecting squads. Time trials, challenge matches, ladder tournaments, swim-offs, and so on, can be held to determine the better performers. These are useful ways not only of selecting a team but also of determining who will participate in upcoming matches or meets.

Whatever the methods, all players deserve to be given a fair and equal chance. Tryouts need to be long enough to allow all players an opportunity to be seen by the coach and with equal time for participation in intra-squad games. Proof of equitable opportunity, good records, can help a coach if a legal issue arises.

Other Factors   What else should be considered in addition to performance? Body build is vitally important to any sport. A basketball coach may take a 6-foot, 6-inch aspirant before a 5-foot, 10-inch hopeful, but neither gymnasts nor soccer players need height. Specific positions in football call for bulk, while a swimmer could use big hands and feet, and height. Coaches usually consider height and weight and conformation in their selection process.

Additional factors that must be considered are age of the player, year in school, and experience. Most coaches will select a younger player, in a lower grade in school but of equal ability, over an older player. They speculate that there is time to develop the younger player and that he or she will be of more use to the squad for a longer time. However, age can mean experience and maturity of skill. If the individuals have played before, their previous coaches can furnish needed details, but the new coach should see them work before making the final judgment. The former coach could have overestimated or underestimated the usefulness of the player.

A coach should make sure that the players selected will be available for practices and games. If a player works, has difficulty with transportation, or is unsure of parental permission to play, problems will arise.

Answers to questions such as the following should be known before selections are finalized: Will their religion and sport practices conflict? Will they be taking a vacation in the middle of the season? Are they participating in another sport? Are they eligible to play? Are they likely to remain so? Do they live in the correct district as established by the governing agency? Are their ages correct and their grades high enough?

Subjective Evaluation

The factors that "are in the eye of the beholder" are equally as important as those measured objectively, but they are more difficult to evaluate. The personality traits, behavioral characteristics, personal character, and attitude that determine how an individual will react to coaching, adversity, and competition could be more important than a player's physical attributes.

Personality Traits

Attempts to determine personality traits or profiles unique to the top athlete have resulted in disagreement among researchers. Coaches, though, seem to know what is needed as they look for those who are willing to make great sacrifices to achieve success. They would like their players to be coachable, self-disciplined, enthusiastic, dedicated, determined, mentally tough, adaptable, compatible, and proud. How can these traits be measured? Experienced coaches observe players' actions on and off the field of play; generally, they are concerned with what happens during practice times because this is similar to the "real thing." Observation is a very good evaluative tool, and most veteran coaches are keen observers. Even though personality traits may be difficult to define, coaches recognize them in a player.

There are personality tests available, but they may be time consuming and difficult to interpret, telling a coach very little. Few coaches use these tests, and those who do enlist the aid of an experienced individual to administer, score, and interpret the test and results. If such a test is given, it should be administered at the beginning of the season and used to help give a coach a more objective view of the participant. The information derived ought to be used in a constructive manner to motivate, guide, and counsel the athlete.

Coaches do not always agree on which personality traits are important or valuable. Some say, "I will take heart, desire, and determination over size, ability, and speed." Others say, "They do not have to be good, just determined," or, "I can teach a girl with a good attitude a lot of skill in three weeks but I cannot change a girl with good skill and a bad attitude as quickly." There are others who say, "I want the skilled; those who can do the job get the call. I can teach the rest—how to act, sportsmanship, attitude," or "I do not care how they act, just so they can play the game," or "Each player has the chance to prove himself in practice and is rewarded for his guts and determination by becoming a member of the team. However, that doesn't mean that he will get to play in the game." Some coaches maintain, "A coach cannot be purely objective and base player selection on skill and talent alone. There are outstanding players who are not good team members and are disruptive influences. Get rid of them."

Personal Traits

The legislation permitting access to student records by students and their parents has caused a reduction in the personal information available about a student. The anecdotal records, reports, and comments that were once filed in the permanent folder now appear only rarely; therefore, school records are of limited value in gaining knowledge of players' personal traits or characteristic behaviors.

Coaches need and want to know about the personal lives and personal traits of their prospective team members; however, they must seek other sources of information. Talking with teachers, fellow coaches, parents, members of the community, and other students can provide answers to some questions. Often, coaches can learn a great deal just by watching and listening. They must be aware of what is happening in the world of the athletes.

Even though all the information received is not fully usable in the selection process, it may be important in dealing with student athletes to know about their lives and actions. Answers can be found to such questions as: What sort of reputation does the player have? Is he or she reported to be a troublemaker, a drug user, unstable, unmanageable, lazy, a truant? Is the player a good student, reliable, stable, cooperative, hardworking, and a good sport?

If it appears worth the effort to select a troubled or troublesome player for a squad, either for the player's sake or the team's sake, the coach should not assume that the player will become trouble-free simply by joining the team. Not all wayward players can be changed, and sometimes their behavior can adversely influence other team members. It will take time and effort on the coach's part to deal with a difficult player, and it may or may not turn out that it is worth the effort.

Coaches can record behaviors in practices that would reflect attitudes and personality characteristics, but this is very time consuming. If players' actions are observed and recorded, the records should cover all phases of practices over a period of time. A simple checklist of questions, such as the one that follows, can be devised quickly for specific situations.

1. Is the player willing to repeat techniques over and over with the same degree of enthusiasm?
2. Is the player first on the field and the last one to leave?
3. Is the player on time for practice?
4. Is the player dressed in the required uniform?
5. Does the player listen and appear to do as instructed?
6. Is the player a leader in other areas?
7. Is the player a complainer?
8. Does the player have frequent alibis or explanations for mistakes?
9. Does the player take care of uniforms and equipment?
10. Does the player have a neat appearance?
11. Does the player appear to have fun but not at the expense of teammates?

Figure 8-1 Players' practice behaviors are indicative of game behaviors (Courtesy of Rickards High School, Tallahassee, Florida. Photographer: Mickey Adair)

12. Does the player build up rather than tear down teammates?
13. Does the player run to the huddle, to get in line, to take a turn, on and off the field?
14. Does the player appear to be injury prone?
15. Does the player appear to fit into the group?

Teams are like families. There is a place for almost every kind of individual, but, as in families, there are certain traits that seem characteristic. In the selection process, coaches will want to consider the values in having a diverse group. Some coaches want only one kind of player, but others prefer a mixture of types and consider the single type team too homogeneous or bland for their tastes.

Peer Evaluations

In some situations coaches permit players to evaluate their teammates. If this method is used, the process must be clearly explained and a list of the criteria and/or rating scales to be used supplied. Players may be asked to rank their teammates in order of importance to the team. They do not rank themselves, but they do sign the evaluation sheet. Having them give the rationale for their first and last choices can be very informative. The evaluations need to take place more than once; perhaps the rating could be done after each of the first three weeks of practice. This means work for head coaches as they and/or their assistant coaches should tally the results. Whatever schedule is used, time must be allowed for the players to perform and be observed in varying situations, and time must be allowed for the coaches to read the evaluations and observe the players again. It is very probable that a coach may miss something important that a player has picked up.

INFORMING THE PLAYERS

Different methods are used to inform the players of who is on the final squad list. A few coaches seat the players before or after practice and read the names of those who are to remain on the team. Others post a list of those who made the team, with players' names listed alphabetically or in order of choice.

There are those coaches who prepare a list but hand it to the players on the last day of open practice. If several people evaluate, the players are often given these results without the names of the evaluators. If a number of coaches are involved, they may be assigned a number; then all that the player may see is a coach's number matched with the player's rating.

A time-consuming method, but one that some coaches prefer to use, is to call the players into the office and talk with each individually. Players are told whether or not they made the squad, why or why not, and are given words of encouragement or discouragement. Other coaches ask those individuals who did not make the squad to come to the office a week after the final cut. This gives everyone a chance to recover before the final conversation.

Whatever the method, it should be devised with the players' welfare in mind. There is no easy or simple way to inform a player that he or she did not make the squad, but all coaches should try to be humanistic in this difficult situation.

Coaches must also be prepared to talk with the individuals' parents or guardians. Many do not contact a coach to ask, "Why wasn't my child selected?" but there are those who may. They will phone and/or come by the coach's office or home immediately after hearing the news. Their approaches will vary from calm to stormy. Coaches must be ready to back up their decisions with objective data; there needs to be sound reasoning for eliminating an individual. If possible, the parents (guardians) should be handled gently, firmly, fairly, and quickly. A coach cannot afford to react in anger, fear, or frustration.

SUMMARY

The success of the entire season rests with the coach's ability to select a group of players whose talents, personalities, and qualities can be melded and molded into a team. Physical prowess alone is not enough to overcome unsatisfactory personal characteristics. Personal charm cannot substitute for lack of skill or poor condition.

No matter what the philosophy of the organization is or what the coach's favorite method of selection may be, the bottom line is the make-up and quality of the final squad. The best method will be the one that selects the player who "can do and will do."

A team must be composed of skilled, fit, cooperative, enthusiastic, loyal players. Skill can be evaluated objectively, as can physical condition, but the personal qualities that make or break a player and/or team are more difficult to assess. Coaches should use every possible source to learn about their players and then select very carefully.

9

Teaching the Athlete

TEACHING/COACHING/LEARNING
SUMMARY

Generally, the primary objective of a coach is to win; to win means to develop winning players. Players must perform at a high level in a contest. Their performances will be the result of two factors: game skill (physical and mental) and motivation. A player who is motivated but not too skilled may perform well; however, the performance level would be much higher if he or she possessed both attributes.

Coaches are there to help the players develop skill, to motivate those who are not self-disciplined, and to assist those who are. This is easier said than done, as coaches work with a widely divergent group of individuals. These players will not process information in the same way or at the same rate, develop physical skills equally, nor respond in a like manner to the same motivational techniques.

Which is more important—skill level or motivational level? Many coaches believe that the game is at least 75 percent "heart" (drive, determination, desire to do well) and 25 percent skill. The chances are that the higher the level of play—National Basketball Association as opposed to the Biddy Basketball League—the more important the skill becomes. However, regardless of the level, the player has to want to play before he or she can realize playing capabilities in a contest. "I don't know what makes a player want to play; they walk out there sometimes and just can't play," said Tom Landry, coach of the Dallas Cowboys.[1]

TEACHING/COACHING/LEARNING

It is difficult, if not impossible, to separate coaching from teaching. Ask coaches what they are going to do to prepare for the next match and many will answer, "Teach, teach, teach." Bertha Frank Teague, one of three female members of the National Basketball Hall of Fame and the "winningest" high school coach in the United States (her girls' basketball teams in Byng, Oklahoma, won 90 percent of their games played in a 43-year span), said, "To be a good coach, you must first learn to be a good teacher."[2] John Thompson, respected coach of the Georgetown University men's basketball team, calls the gymnasium his "classroom."

Coaches as teachers have to be knowledgeable about learning principles. Many veteran coaches have relied on the trial-and-error method, but could have been more effective sooner if they had known earlier what they know now. There is not one best method of teaching—methods should be based on what is being taught, by whom, to whom, under what conditions, and for what purpose.

Whatever the coach wants the players to learn, it must be planned. Skill development, behavior modification, and cognitive development must be a part of a master plan, if they are to be used. Players' performances tell something about the effectiveness of teaching methods; however, it should be remembered that learning and performance are not the same thing. Learning has taken place if actions are changed on a more or less permanent basis, but levels of performance may vary from game to game after a skill is learned.

An individual's success in sports is determined to a major degree by three basic factors: genetics, motivation, and experience. There are few natural athletes, but *genetic* factors do play a primary role. Most human behavior is learned, but development is dependent upon the interaction between inherited and environmental factors.

The individual must be continuously *motivated*. Athletes must have reasons to keep working and doing; otherwise, skill will not be developed or refined. Past *experiences* and intensive practice of motor skills in a variety of sports, or in physical activities that have developed basic movement patterns or skills, will serve as an extremely strong base on which to build more advanced sports skills. The coach should not have to go back to lesson one to teach basics if the player is experienced and has advanced to a higher level.

There are many principles of learning based on research in the laboratory and in the field. Results of research studies, and the application of this knowledge, could be of invaluable help to coaches and to the players with whom they work. The summaries in this chapter of such research are designed to help a coach understand basic principles and concepts of the teaching/coaching/learning process as they apply to the player, to teaching, to practice, and to performance.

The Player

Understanding players, how they develop and how they perform, is fundamental to the coaching process. Coaches must learn to recognize physical, psychological, and skill differences in and between the players in order to use the variety of talent and ability found in the team. All coaches must determine the differences in performance so that each individual player can be used to the best advantage for the person and for the team.

Physical Differences

It is obvious that players vary in their structure, body type, and sex. These differences may not influence learning, but they can have a great effect on performance.

Body type or body build contributes to success in specific sports activities, but its use as sole means of predicting success in a specific sport is limited. Height could contribute to the success of a volleyball spiker, but it is not as important to the setter. Bulk would be an asset to a football lineman, but not to a free safety. Generally, distance runners are "lean"; throwing event athletes are not. Tennis players come in all shapes and sizes, but they might be better if they had a predominantly mesomorphic body build rather than an endomorphic one. There are exceptions to the norm, however. There are athletes like "Spud" Webb, a 5'6" professional basketball player who won the 1986 National Basketball Association slam-dunk contest. Also, the perception of the desired body build for a particular sport changes. Mary Lou Retton, the star gymnast of the 1984 Olympics, did not have the physical conformation of Nadia Comaneci, the diminutive gymnast and star of the 1976 Olympics. Coaches should not be too quick to categorize players simply by their physical make-up but take the time to study their performance and their motivation. In this age of specialization of sport roles, there ought to be a place for almost everyone who truly wants to play.

Sex differences are apparent at an early age even though the skill development potential for most boys and girls is relatively equal. Preschool boys are found to be superior to pre-school girls in the skills of speed running, long jumping, and throwing; 6-year-old girls have better balance.[3] After adolescence, strength and height differences make for performance differences in men and women, and cultural pressures are stronger for both sexes. It should be noted, however, that physiological and psychological differences between male and female world-class athletes are minimal.

Psychological Differences

Just as players differ in physical characteristics, so do they differ psychologically. They vary in intelligence level, rate of learning, emotional state, motivational response, and levels of aspiration. Each of these variables can affect both learning and performance; therefore, they are important for coaches to know and understand.

Intelligence level (IQ) does not correlate highly with skill level, but the highly skilled player with the high IQ should learn quickly and may be more adept at positions such as quarterback on the football team or setter on the volleyball team. Coaches will probably have a mixed group, as most teachers do, but the learning ability of the athlete will determine how fast to present material and how complex it may be. All good athletes, regardless of their sport, have to be intelligent enough to make judgments in play. Some coaches suggest not mixing two intellectual extremes, the very high with the very low, in groups that have to work detailed patterns of play together. Either a relatively "slow" group or a relatively "fast" group might get better results. However, IQ is not the only measure of intelligence; there are other types that are very important, such as game sense, people sense, and common sense.

Emotional state varies with the individual and is of primary concern to a coach. The highly emotional, highly anxious, tense player may need to be calmed, while others who appear to be easygoing and low key may need to be aroused. Emotional states influence learning as well as performance. Each individual has an optimal arousal level, a level at which he or she operates most effectively. Good coaches make a concerted effort to know this level and to know how to alter approaches to gain the desired state in practice and at contest time. Refer to page 128 for more detail.

Level of aspiration, based on past successes and failures, is a primary determinant of an individual's success or failure. Those who set high goals and have reasonable success will have higher achievement. Success breeds success; if the players are able to reach goals, they will raise their levels of aspiration. Players who fail will lower them. One who favorably completes an endeavor will generally continue to be motivated. Coaches should help players set high but reachable goals; the swimmer may never be Olympic material, but he or she could win an event in a state meet. Players need to be encouraged to set immediate and intermediate goals and then to set higher sights when those are accomplished.

Motivational level depends on the needs, goals, and values of each player; when a player's goals and payoffs are congruent with the team's, a high level of motivation can be maintained. Players must be highly motivated to endure long hours of practice for a brief time of performance; they must really want to do it. Coaches who make it possible for all team members to see the personal, as well as the team, benefit for cooperative behavior and hard work will usually field winners.

Rate of learning varies with the individual. Early success does not always indicate later achievement. A "fast starter" in junior high may improve rapidly, then seem to get worse before the skill level seems to stabilize. Another in the same age group may progress very slowly at first but keep improving and be a so-called late bloomer. Coaches have missed working with a potentially outstanding athlete by cutting or neglecting one that could not get it all together, while building a team around another young athlete who looked like a future Heisman trophy winner but peaked early and never improved.

Critical learning periods are apparent. Children can perform complex skills quite early; for instance, a baby can swim in a fashion before the age of 1 year. If some skills are not introduced by a certain age, the delay can be detrimental to the individual trying to learn a skill. It can be very difficult to teach a teenager to throw, a 20-year-old gymnastic skills, or an adult to ride a bicycle. One is never too old to learn, but age can have some adverse effects on learning motor skills. The degree and rate of success depends on earlier experiences and their relationships to skills being currently taught.

Skill Differences

There are skill differences, just as there are physical and psychological differences; and, although skilled performance is dependent on these two factors, it also is an area to be studied and understood by itself. The coach will need to recognize and understand developmental stages of performance, variances in skill ability, and differences in acceptable form. Doing it differently is not necessarily incorrect; it might be a technical breakthrough.

Developmental levels of players are important because unless they are ready physically, mentally, and emotionally, they cannot learn to perform. Players are handicapped if the abilities necessary for performing skills are not developed; children may remember the components of a skill but not be physically capable of putting these together to produce a successful performance. If locomotor skills are not at an effective level, there is no way the individual can learn to play any sport. If the hand-eye coordination has not been developed, a player cannot catch or hit balls successfully. Those with limited coordination will have greater difficulty performing many basic sport skills; those who cannot process complex information will have difficulty remembering which way to run on a specific play pattern; and those who cannot handle the emotions involved in playing and being with people are not ready to play some games.

Skill level will vary widely within a group. Players do not come to practice with the same degrees of skill. Some will have never played before, while others will have a high level of skills specific to the activity. Evaluating abilities to determine the skill levels of players is necessary so that practices and strategies can be planned. Coaches must teach different ability groups differently. Physical activity, rather than lecture, should be emphasized in the early stages of learning a skill, but advanced players can profit from extensive verbal instructions and can analyze details. It is difficult to keep beginners interested for long periods of time, while advanced players can concentrate for lengthy sessions. The coach may find it easier to keep players of mixed skill levels functioning better by dividing practice sessions into a series of short periods or by grouping the squad by ability.

Form is an individual matter in that there is no one absolute way to perform a skill, but there are mechanical principles that should be applied and classic styles to which most players conform. Each individual has a characteristic way of moving that may be most efficient for him or her, and a good coach will consider this in attempting to correct performance. Successful performance—shorter times, greater distances, more points—is the ultimate goal, so coaches must seek efficient movement patterns for each individual player and not be limited by traditional ways of playing. Before the 1960s no one seriously considered using the "Fosbury Flop" form in the high jump or the two-handed backhand in tennis. The two-handed underhand free throw shot is now being used by a negligible number of basketball players, but early in the game it was the only shot. Soccer style place-kicking in football was unheard of in the 1950s, but it became the style in the 1970s. If a player is highly successful, perhaps the coach could ruin a good thing by trying to make him or her conform to a basic pattern.

Teaching Skills Coaches must learn how to teach. This means that the coach has to set the stage, provide a proper learning environment, provide instructional materials, present information or activities to be learned in such a manner that players can learn them, and give feedback on performance. Coaches teach and coach; players learn and perform. The productive situation occurs when players learn what coaches want them to learn and when both

116 *The Coach and the Athlete*

groups have common understandings about how to do it. Coaches, then, must understand the need for appropriate environment or learning place, for appropriate methods of instruction, and for appropriate feedback or critiques on performance. Perhaps the essence of coaching is being able to recognize weak performance, diagnose the difficulty, and suggest a better way.

Learning Environment

The learning environment—gymnasium, field, pool, court—should be conducive to learning. It is important that the performing area is safe, clean, dry, and warm (or cool) and that the equipment is in good repair and in appropriate supply. Player learning and performance can be impaired if these are not taken care of. Refer to page 132 for additional information. No one learns well when attention is diverted from skill to hazard or when the equipment is not suitable for the skill level. The safest areas and best equipment are priorities. It is also difficult for a player not to be diverted if there are visual or auditory distractions. If outside, the coach should try to teach in an area away from the street, traffic, and visitors. If inside, the intercom should be turned off, nonplayers kept out of the area, and the temperature maintained at an optimal level. The coach's task is to ensure that the player's attention is focused on the skill being taught.

Figure 9-1 Make sure that instructions are understood (Courtesy of Miami Dade Community College, South Campus, Miami, Florida)

Methods of Instruction

There are many styles and methods of teaching, but generally the teaching of skills follows a basic pattern. This general pattern follows accepted motor learning theory.

First, the *lesson* is introduced. A coach tells the players the order of the day by talking with them or by posting the information on the bulletin board. They are given "the picture."

Second, the *skill* is presented. If it is unfamiliar, the players may not understand it until they see the entire action, nor may they comprehend why and how the skill is performed. Steps to be followed in skill teaching are as follows:

1. Introduce the skill. Define it and relate its importance to individual and team success.
2. Teach logically and sequentially; move from the simple to the complex. Provide only essential details. The first and last bits of information will probably be remembered longer, so keep the discussion short.
3. Demonstrate the desired action. Have a coach or player illustrate the correct way. Movies, slides, still pictures, and diagrams are also effective illustrators. Demonstrate the action several times to provide views from various angles.
4. Use simple, accurate language. Do not take it for granted that players understand what is said. If "hold the man on base" is taken literally, both opponents and umpires will be unhappy.
5. Encourage players to ask questions and do not assume that they understand if no questions are asked. Stimulate interaction by asking a player to verbalize what has just been taught or to teach the skill to a teammate, but, to avoid embarrassing anyone, be certain to call on highly skilled or proficient players.

Third, the players will need to *practice* the skill as quickly as possible; participation ought to take the greater portion of the session. It is better to place emphasis on the correct action performed than on mistakes made, and on the right way rather than the wrong way. Players need to receive feedback and to be reinforced. All players should be watched by a coach; it is poor teaching technique to notice only a few. It is also poor teaching technique to vent anger on those who are not doing well, unless they are obviously goofing off or unless they respond positively to anger. If a coach becomes angry with athletes because they are not intelligent, do not understand, are confused, and/or are frightened, the result will usually be deteriorating performances. If the athlete is not intelligent, the instructions may need to be made less complex. Often another demonstration will help or an assistant might physically move the player through the action until a feel for it is developed. Players can be asked to repeat what they heard and perhaps then the missing cue will be found. If athletes are frightened, they need to be calmed. There may be times when it is better to forget the instructions and concentrate on the player. Reassurance and encouragement get very good results. Assignments to practice on one's own may be useful.

The fourth component is *evaluation*, a never-ending process. Players' actions must be observed throughout each session, day after day. Not only does every athlete want and need to be noticed (some will continue to make errors just to get attention), but they also need to be rated. Drills to ascertain level of attainment should be devised. There should be a time in each session to discuss the successes and failures and the good and bad points of the day, allowing players an opportunity to contribute to the teaching/coaching/learning process. The evaluation period can be held on the field or in the dressing room, and can serve as a cooling-off period, a togetherness time, an opportunity for reaffirmation, and a critique session.

Cues and Aids

The use of cues and aids is indispensable in skill teaching/learning. As players receive sensory input in a variety of ways, coaches must determine the process that each uses, although there are general principles for sensory reception and processing. Visual and auditory cues are always helpful, but they are especially effective when the skill is a new one. Physical manipulation—actually moving the body part through the range of movement—works very well with those who learn kinesthetically or are slow learners. Training devices, such as flutter boards and spike-its, can be helpful when used in gamelike situations. However, misuse of teaching devices—such as moving a body part beyond its safe range of motion or presenting inaccurate cues or feedback—can be a deterrent to skill development and may cause injury.

Visual cues should be used extensively; approximately 80 percent of all learning utilizes one's visual sense. Bulletin boards, diagrams, photographs, video tapes, slides, movies, loop films, and people are excellent teaching/coaching aids. Players make their own visual cues simply by watching a place kicker send the ball through the uprights, a volleyball player spike the ball, a high jumper approach the bar, or a swimmer execute a turn.

Auditory aids have a more limited use. Players can listen to instructions, a tape, records, or a sound track, but they do not remember information they hear as well as information they see. The "crack" of the bat tells of a solid hit, the "roar" of the crowd signals success, the "sound" made by a driver hitting a golf ball correctly says that it was a good hit, but these are usually heard after the fact. Music is often used to soothe or arouse players; this has not been proved effective, but if coach and players think it helps, then it does.

Verbal cues are also good teaching/learning aids. Each sport has its own colorful language to describe appropriate action that is frequently used to communicate an idea to players. If the player is having difficulty getting the glove low on ground balls, a coach may say, "Take dirt." If they want runners to stay low over a hurdle, they tell them to "bite the hurdle." One "slings" a discus, "puts" a shot, and "swings through" a ball. Every coach has a vocabulary for a particular sport.

Feedback Being aware of the situation—getting feedback—plays a major role in skill learning. Not only is it a motivation, but the athlete should use the information to make necessary adjustments in the execution of the technique. How would it be to play a game and never know how well you did—never to know whether or not the ball went into the cup, whether the skill was performed correctly, or if you contributed to the success of the team? A player gets feedback through the senses, but the coach must also give information; players need to know what the coach sees in their performances. The coach observes practice and play, comments on the good and the bad, and talks to the scrub as well as the star. Refer to page 136 for more detail.

Kinesthetic feedback is valuable. A golfer knows that the shot was a good one without watching the flight of the ball; the swimmer knows that the turn was poorly executed without being told. They get feedback from the "way it feels"; this tells them that they executed the skills well if they had previously learned what "good" feels like. Moving a player physically through an action can help establish the proper feel.

Game and practice films are often used. The art of filming depends on a good camera person to film what a coach wants. If a program cannot afford to have an entire game filmed, aides must know exactly what the coach wants filmed; it should not be left to their discretion unless they

Figure 9-2   Participants need to know how they performed (Courtesy of Maclay School, Inc., Tallahassee, Florida. Photographer: Mickey Adair)

are very experienced and have worked with the coach previously. Video taping is frequently done because it is relatively inexpensive and the equipment is often available through the school system. Coaches should preview the film and make notes on the well-executed movements, as well as on those poorly executed, before the players view it. Generally, the film is then shown to the team as a group, but a coach may want to emphasize certain sections for a specific individual or group.

Summaries of the contests can be very useful to team members—for instance times, distances, heights, tackles, blocked shots, assists, and goals. These statistics, kept by assistants during a contest, reinforce what the coach says and what films reveal. They can be very effective substitutes for films.

Practice

Repeating an activity, or attempting to perform it, is practice. This repetition is necessary for learning a motor skill or activity. Practice does not make perfect, as the old adage would have one believe, but it does make permanent whatever is repeated. Repeating an activity beyond the time necessary to learn it originally is called overlearning, and it is this overlearning that results in automatic movement patterns. When skills become automatic and need not be consciously thought about, the player can attend to strategy, and high-level and exciting sports can result.

Coaches will need to consider many things in planning practices, but all the mechanical details considered will be useless unless basic understandings about practice and learning theory are also involved in the planning. They must know about suitable length and frequency of practice periods, about appropriate practice conditions, and about the appropriate condition of the players if their precious minutes or hours are to be most productive. Refer to page 134 for more information.

Length and Frequency

The length, frequency, and amount of practice sessions will vary according to the sport, the skill level of the players, the interest and the attention span of the players, and the rules of the league or other sponsoring organization. A coach will have to consider all these in planning.

Short, frequent practice periods seem to be best for young or novice players, or for mastery of new skills. If a player does not have sufficient stamina, strength, or endurance to perform the task, it is wise to practice just to the fatigue level when efficiency begins to decline. This is good not only for learning but also for avoiding injuries that can result from undue fatigue. If, because of short attention span, a young player is unable to focus on the task at hand for a long period of time, then the coach must resort to short exposures to one activity and provide a variety of things to do.

Longer practice periods can be productive when players are in good physical condition, when they have learned basic skills, and when their interest level or interest span permits it. Many coaches believe that long practices are always necessary, regardless of age or stage of the player. This is a fallacy; in fact, excessive practice, in length or frequency, can be counterproductive. There are some coaches who can make a 3-hour practice seem short, while others can make an hour session an eternity.

Figure 9-3   Drills can be used to improve playing skills and fitness levels (Photographer: Mickey Adair)

Many coaches separate activities needed for conditioning and those needed to develop skill; others combine the two as they use drills that condition and develop technique (such as repeatedly running planned plays involving several players). Long practice sessions whose major purpose is increasing strength and endurance can promote physical conditioning, but both the learning and performance of skill may decline when fatigue sets in. If a coach has little control over scheduled practice times, new skills should be taught at the beginning of the session, when players are fresh, and the later portion reserved for conditioning.

Two-a-day practices, scheduled at the beginning of the season by many coaches, enable them to use short instructional periods frequently and also have time for conditioning. However practices are scheduled, they ought to be purposeful—players should know what they will be doing, the objectives to be reached, and the time frame. This information, mixed with good drills, can help make a practice session appear to be brief. Practices do not need to drag on until the athletes are bored, disgruntled, and losing their enthusiasm, even if skill mastery seems limited at the moment. There has to be time for repeatedly executing a skill; otherwise, few players will learn it. If time should be limited, even with two-a-days or three-a-days, it is better to stay with simple or basic patterns and perhaps add a variation later in the season. A team will have greater success when members execute some techniques very well than when they execute a multitude of techniques poorly.

Gamelike Conditions

Once players have learned a skill or strategy, they need to practice it under simulated or gamelike conditions. Drills having the appearance or characteristics of a real event ought to be provided. Hitting a tennis ball thrown by a machine is not the same as hitting one returned by an opponent. Shooting a basket while being guarded by someone who does not want the team to score is quite different from a set shot drill that leaves the player unguarded. Practicing in a quiet, sterile atmosphere is very unlike performing before a group of verbal spectators. The quiet environment and stationary drills are needed; but, when sufficient skill is developed, the coach needs to move into gamelike scrimmages. To prepare for competition, each athlete, as well as the team as a whole, must practice every conceivable contest situation. This also shows players where they are weak and how and why they need to practice.

Mental Practice

Mental practice (imagery) is as essential as physical practice is. Mentally seeing oneself performing a skill as it should be done—from beginning to end—can be a very effective tool. First, the athlete must have a clear picture of the correct way to execute the movement and have the "feel" of it. Experienced and highly skilled players will find this easy to do as they already have the "picture." Beginners may find it rather difficult to do and have to combine mental practice with physical practice. Suggested skills are these:

1. Focus on the skill. (mental)
2. Get into ready position. (physical)
3. Verbalize the execution. (mental)
4. Execute the skill. (physical)
5. Assess the result. (mental)

Keeping the practice positive is a must. For example, the hitter should see the hole between first and second base, not the defensive players. Mental practice can be used when players do not have access to the court or field, when they are home thinking about the event, or just prior to the contest. This focus on activity, seeing one's self in the "mind's eye," is in essence, a practice session. Another advantage in this simulated activity is gaining familiarity with an imagined situation. If the athlete can envision walking to the free throw line, hearing the crowd roar as the referee hands the ball, sense the feeling of bouncing the ball, and see the ball arch into the basket, then perhaps the real situation will be more familiar and the task easier to perform.

Reinforcement

Just as in teaching appropriate behavior, coaches use reinforcing stimuli, positive and/or negative, to elicit skilled performances. A common pattern is to give positive reinforcers for acceptable work and negative reinforcers for unacceptable actions. Either technique can be very effective, but in many situations the positive approach may produce better results. Some coaches, not understanding the power of positive reinforcement, use the negative approach almost exclusively. A coach must make a deliberate choice about the basic style of reinforcement and coaching behavior to be demonstrated. This means that coaches must evaluate what they now do. Refer to page 138 for additional information.

Positive reinforcement, often referred to as the reward system, ranges from receiving praise, gifts, and playing time (extrinsic), to achieving a goal (intrinsic). Generally, success is a better reinforcer than failure, and players will continue to work, practice, and train if believing that they are moving toward a goal. Reinforcing positively does not mean that all actions of the players are accepted. Positive criticism is necessary for skill and playing improvement, and coaches have a duty to evaluate performance so as to improve it.

Negative reinforcement is sometimes considered to be the same as punishment, but it can be any form of unpleasant response. Negative reinforcers can be extrinsic (being yelled at, benched, denied a privilege) or intrinsic (disappointment when a goal is missed). Coaches can make players know that they have failed to meet a standard, or players can punish themselves for a poor performance. It is evident that such actions are effective. Few players will be late to practice if it means running the bleachers for 30 minutes or adding another hour to tennis practice. Some players are accustomed to, and respond only to, negative reinforcement; they may, along with some coaches, consider the use of positive reinforcement or lack of negative reinforcement as weakness. Other players, however, are turned away from sports by "tough guy" behavior on the coach's part. Constant criticism, like constant praise, can lose its effectiveness. Whatever form the reinforcement takes, it must never be harmful or degrading. Physical abuse administered by some coaches is not only detrimental to learning and potentially dangerous for the player but is illegal as well.

Transfer of Skill

Being good in one sport provides no guarantee of having a high skill level in another sport, and coaches should not expect unlike skills to transfer to another situation. Basic abilities and conditions, such as agility, stamina, coordination, strength, and good sense, make it possible for a player to adapt to a new game; but such abilities and conditions do not ensure it. An outstanding basketball player may not be a volleyball star until learning new skills, but the ability to jump is basic to both sports and therefore useful in the change from one to the other. A highly skilled trampolinist could have great difficulty learning to swim, but he or she may become a great diver because of the similarity of the moves in both.

When there are similar actions or requirements in sports and the coach wants the player to move from one to another, or even from one position or skill to another in the same sport, the coach must be careful to point out the similarities. It should not be assumed that players will grasp similar concepts easily. Sometimes all that is required is a remark such as, "Remember how you performed the smash in tennis? Well, the spike is something like it." On another occasion it may be necessary to describe the skill or manipulate the player through the action in order for the athlete to get the "feel."

The transfer or understandings of skills may become more important within a sport than between sports, as there are fewer and fewer multi-sport athletes. Younger players can still enjoy the pleasure that participation in a variety of sports can bring, but older athletes must begin to specialize in many instances. As youth sport becomes more like professional sport, seasons lengthen, practices become more numerous, and conditioning is a year-round business. The ability to grasp similarities in skill and strategy will still be important, however, and coaches should develop this understanding in their players to as great a degree as possible.

SUMMARY

There is a very close relationship between teaching, coaching, and learning. A coach's position is to understand the processes involved in these areas and to elicit high levels of skill and game performance from players. Principles of teaching and learning must be applied if players' time and talents are to be effectively utilized.

Recognizing that there are physical, psychological, and skill differences among the squad members, coaches should help players get the most from their basic abilities. Squad members will have different body builds, vary in psychological make-up, and have assorted levels of skill. A coach will look for certain characteristics—height in basketball players, long legs for the high jumpers, and intelligence for all—but should remember that many factors contribute to the making of a star athlete.

Coaches are responsible for players' learning and performance; therefore, they must establish good teaching/learning situations and make careful plans for their "lessons." Players must have practice time to refine their skills and must receive feedback on their performances. The proof of the effectiveness of both players' and coaches' work is found in the contest. This is where all the hard work pays off.

ENDNOTES

1. "Landry, Grant Blast Schedule," *Tallahassee Democrat*, 6 October 1979, p. 28, Football Extra.
2. B. F. Teague, *Basketball for Girls* (New York: Ronald Press, 1962), p. ii.
3. A. M. Morris, J. M. Williams, A. E. Atwater, and J. H. Wilmore, "Age and Sex Differences in Motor Performance of 3 Through 6 Year Old Children," *Research Quarterly for Exercise and Sport* 53 (1982): 214.

10

Motivating the Athlete

MOTIVATIONAL PLANNING
MOTIVATIONAL APPROACHES
SUMMARY

Motivation—that something prompting an individual to act in a certain way—is an abstract part of learning and performance. It cannot be seen, heard, tasted, touched, or smelled; however, everyone knows that it is present because its resultant behavior is seen. Motivation is responsible for:

1. Selection and preference for some activity.
2. Persistence at the activity.
3. Intensity and vigor of performance.
4. Adequacy of performance relative to standards.[1]

Motivating the athlete involves more than giving words of encouragement or discouragement, a pat on the shoulder, or a kick in the seat. Good coaches know what to do. Many have a "feeling" for doing the right thing at the right time, others have learned by trial and error, many keep current with research in the area and apply motivational theories, and there are those who use all three methods. All realize that the results of their motivational efforts depend on the participant and the situation; they know their athletes as well as they can and they establish a purpose that is important to all concerned.

It would be ideal, and remarkable, if each athlete interacted with the coach and the team in the same positive way. Most are motivated to participate, or they would not be attending practices, but they are individuals and react to their situations in different ways. Persistence, effort, and performance standards will vary for each team member as well as for a group. A coach has to know techniques for getting the individual and the squad "up" for practices, games, and tournaments. Unfortunately, no one has yet come up with a magic elixir to bottle and sell to coaches needing a formula to lift a player and/or team beyond, or even to, their real ability levels.

MOTIVATIONAL PLANNING

Nothing is going to work for all coaches with all players all the time. Most coaches are pleased if the techniques motivate most of the players most of the time. Being aware of some motivational methods may help avoid unnecessary mistakes. Planning the approach very carefully and thoroughly before putting it into effect should result in a more effective program.

Know Yourself, Be Yourself

Each coach has to develop a philosophy about motivation and have confidence in it. Personality and style must complement an individual's philosophy. Each must think through personal goals and values and not attempt to be someone else.

Many new coaches attempt to follow in the paths of their former coaches or one with whom they have worked, heard speak, or read about. They can learn from these others but cannot be these others; what is successful for one may be failure for another because each is a unique individual. If coaches are loud, they should be loud; if they are positive reinforcers, they should award the pluses; if they believe that practices need to be fun, they should plan with this in mind; if they believe that effort wins gold stars, they should make the awards. Players recognize a fake front very quickly; they can see the real "coach." However, coaches who believe that they can behave as they please may find that acceptance does not always come just because they are being their "real" selves. Actions must be tempered with solid judgment and knowledge.

Know Results of Current Research

"What's new?" Coaches should know. Motivation is not the easiest area to study, but researchers, both pure and applied, are continually adding to the knowledge of the subject. It is impossible, or perhaps not wise, to make definite statements about motivation; but, considering what has been reported, there is reason to be confident of the following:

1. An athlete will not learn nor perform well in situations unless motivated to do so.
2. The motivation may come from within (intrinsic); the athlete is taking part because of the pleasure derived from the activity. The motivation may come from without (extrinsic); the athlete is participating because "material" rewards may be forthcoming.
    a. Intrinsic motivation is usually stronger and longer lasting than extrinsic motivation. Those who work by themselves or with the group and know that no external reward is in the offing will persist in their efforts.
    b. A fine line lies between intrinsic and extrinsic motivation, and it is difficult to know where one stops and the other begins.
    c. Children usually play for the joy of it, but if prizes and awards are given, extrinsic motivators will usually become more important.
    d. Giving extrinsic motivators to those already intrinsically motivated generally does not increase motivation.
3. There are many ways to motivate, and each person responds differently because all are not motivated in the same way to the same degree.

a. Reinforcement is vital and most respond better to positive reinforcement; however, there are those who respond more favorably to negative reinforcement.
b. Success does not always increase motivation. There are those who are motivated by failure.
4. Knowledge of results—to know the time, the height, the number of points scored—is important.
5. Feedback—to be aware of the situation, whether or not the movement is correctly executed—is important.
6. Higher motivation may impede progress in complex tasks. There is a point, called optimal arousal, at which one performs best.
    a. If arousal or stress level goes past an individually determined optimum, performance deteriorates.
    b. Performances (i.e., weight lifting, marathon running) requiring great strength, endurance, and courage are usually increased by high arousal levels.
    c. Performances (i.e., volleyball, tennis) requiring clear thinking, precise movements, fine coordination, and peripheral vision are generally hindered by too high arousal levels.
    d. Some positions in some sports (i.e., defensive linemen in football) require higher levels of arousal than other positions (i.e., center, quarterback).
7. The athletes' level of aspiration—their goals—may serve as a strong motivator if these guidelines are followed.
    a. Set realistic, challenging but attainable, long- and short-range goals.
    b. Set measurable goals.
    c. Confirm the goal by writing it or making a public statement before team members or a video camera.
    d. Have coaches serve as facilitators by providing examples of goals and helping the athlete be realistic.[2]
8. Incentive motivation—what keeps the young athlete continually making an effort—is vitally important.
    a. Affiliation (making friends) and excellence (doing something very well) are the two strongest and most consistent incentive conditions.
    b. Stress incentives (seeking excitement) rank third, and aggression (intimidating others) and independence incentives (doing things without others' help) fall farther down in the rankings.
    c. The same incentives basically motivate children regardless of their age, sport, sex, or culture.[3]

Analyze the Situation

The sport and the athletes are two considerations to be analyzed by the coach trying to understand how athletes are or can be motivated. It is essential to know both if a motivational plan is to be made that could result in a successful season.

In analyzing the sport, coaches will consider such aspects as its complexity, appeal, community or cultural value, time demands, and physical requirements. In analyzing the athletes, aspects to be examined include age, skill level, personality, sports experience, and cultural background.

The Sport

When considering motivation, coaches need to determine why their sport is attractive or appealing to athletes and why some players prefer one activity to another. There must be great value in the eyes of the participants or they will not subject themselves to the demands of a sport. If participation and/or performance decline, a coach will look for reasons why the activity no longer attracts athletes to play.

There are cycles in the popularity of sports; a sport may gain or lose acceptance or priority with the public and players alike. For males, basketball is "the" sport in some schools, but football occupies the number one position in others. For females, swimming is the queen of sports in sections of the country, but in other areas volleyball may be the popular activity. Occasionally a new sport will appear on the scene; soccer gained great acceptance by Americans in the 1970s.

Figure 10-1 A great game (Courtesy of Miami Dade Community College, North Campus, Miami, Florida. Photographer: Bob Bailey)

All sports are demanding of the participant's time, but some, such as swimming, have excessive demands. Members of swim teams not only have two-a-day workouts the year round but also have an early practice time of 5:30 A.M. Yet, thousands of young people stay with these programs for many years. What is so appealing? The coach? The opportunity to compete? A place for everyone? The hope of being a world class swimmer? An acceptance by the American culture? Addiction to activity is part of the motivation.

Some sports that are new to players, if not to the athletic scene, may seem complex and must be introduced at the participants' level. Skilled performers are often embarrassed or uncomfortable if they cannot immediately do well in a new activity. There are athletes who refuse to continue in a game like volleyball—which is unlike the traditional trio of football, basketball, and baseball—unless they can be quickly instructed or coached to some level of personal success.

Spectator interest can be another motivating factor. Large, enthusiastic crowds can encourage athletes to play well. Players want the social and community recognition that can come when the team is successful and the community values that success. Until that time arrives, the coach can help the situation by scheduling contests when it is possible for fans, at least parents, to attend. Having free admittance to the contest will also encourage some people to attend.

The Athlete

If coaches hope to motivate their players, it is essential that they know the athletes well—what interests them and what demands their attention, as well as routine information such as age, height, weight, grade, and family background. As suggested earlier in this book, there are many sources of information in the school or agency and from peers and parents. However, the major source is the athlete. If the coach is considered an important person in the player's life, then the athlete is more likely to share concerns, dreams, and hopes.

It will help to know why athletes are participating. Ninety-one percent of the high school athletes responding to a questionnaire from the Iowa High School Athletic Association reported that they participated in organized athletics because they wanted to. The top three positive values gained through participation were teamwork and cooperation with peers, a lot of fun, and pride.[4] Unfortunately, in organized athletics some do not play just for the love of the sport. Parental pressure is often present, as is peer pressure. Players may be trying for a college scholarship. The Personal Data Form (discussed in Chapter 7) should give insight into their reasons. If a player's original motivational force is removed, then it may be necessary for a coach to provide a prop or some additional reason for participation. If the motivational force is increased, it may be necessary to "curb" the player so that he or she will not burn out too soon. Being cognizant of individual personalities can also be helpful. As mentioned in Chapter 8, the results of a personality test may suggest the athletes' personality traits and give the coach an idea about their strong and weak points. If athletes need to develop more self-confidence, the coach can help them set short and attainable goals; they need to do something to make them feel good about themselves. If they seem to have a limited sense of responsibility, it may be that they need an opportunity to develop this trait.

Home environment can be very important. A player who comes from a background that offers material possessions may be motivated by praise, while one who has had few material possessions may work hard for a steak dinner. Motivation has to be individualized for the best results.

Players' basic needs must be satisfied before they can concentrate on a game. Some may come to school or to practice without having sufficient food to permit them to do their work. They need to be fed before they can respond to elaborate motivational techniques. Others may come from socially deprived backgrounds and thus feel insecure, inadequate, or afraid. Before they can respond or produce fully, they must feel they are a part of the team. Players whose basic biological and social needs are met are better prepared to play and to react to coaching and teaching.

Players participate in activities that have meaning and value (a payoff) for them. When coaches know players' goals, when players know coaches' goals, and when these two sets of goals are congruent or similar, then a team can move in one direction. Motivation consists of finding out what athletes really want to do and become and then helping them use sport to do it.

Athletics do not permit players to be separated or insulated from their actions or their environment, so, in this real world, there is an opportunity to move up the ladder of personal development. A point for coaches to remember is that players do not come to them with lives like blank sheets. Their team members are always pushed by their past, held by the present, and pulled by the future.

Be Aware of Personal Actions

It is a mistake to teach (preach) one thing and do something else. Coaches should not say, "Let your teammates know how they are doing; talk to them," while failing to give a word of praise. Players should not be told that they must stay calm and cool while the coach rants and raves. Are players being asked to be prompt, well organized, and prepared while coaches are not expected to follow these patterns? A coach's actions speak loudly and clearly; they are motivators.

Analyze the Results

Analysis of program, players, and results should be an ongoing process beginning when preparation for the season gets underway and ending only when it is time for the next season. If the techniques are successful, the action can be continued. If they are unsuccessful, changes in approach need to be initiated. A coach should not insist that a plan is good and practicable when it is obviously not. How will one know that the techniques are working? If goals and objectives are being met, then it is working. Players will be at practice on time, dressed, and anxious to play. They will try to do as the coach says, there will be few squabbles, and contest anxiety levels will be at the right height. But, of course, all techniques will not work; there are no perfect people, practices, or contests. Coaches must attempt to observe their motivational methods and results as objectively as possible.

MOTIVATIONAL APPROACHES

It is very difficult for many coaches to say exactly what they use to motivate their players and teams. The list of successful approaches is long. Ask the experienced ones what they do and the replies are, "Use anything that stays within the rules of the team and the laws of the land." "Do anything and everything." "Use anything that will play on an athlete's psychology and emotional feelings." "It just depends; individual sports are more self-motivating." "Do not like to use gimmicks." "Develop pride in self, school, and sport."

Coaches are willing to share their ideas, however, and the sections that follow contain recommendations from many coaches in the field. These ideas represent actual procedures that have been followed. Some may seem contradictory, but this is because coaches use different approaches to similar situations or similar approaches to different situations.

What a coach does is important, but of equal importance is when it is done. Timing is the key; there is a critical time to act or to use an approach, and one's "gut" feeling may be the best timing device of all. A pat on the back at the right time is better than a hug too early or too late. A few select words at the right moment can do much more than a long speech at the wrong time.

Regardless of the approach used, certain conditions must be present. If players are to be effectively and significantly motivated, they must:

1. Feel unique or special in some way.
2. Be handled on a personal level.
3. Clearly understand and agree with team goals.[5]

Facilities and Equipment

Motivation through facilities and equipment is one sure way to inspire many of the team members. Coaches and players can work together to create an environment that will help develop a sense of pride in one's self, the team, and team unity. It can bring recognition to individuals as well as to the team and school, create safe and secure conditions, and encourage players to achieve. Suggestions from coaches in the field include the following:

1. Have stylish, well-fitting uniforms.
2. Use good safe equipment (i.e., balls, mats, head gear, nets, backstops).
3. Keep facilities/equipment in good repair (i.e., mend broken fences, repair the bleacher seats, sew the rip in the ball bag, fill the holes in the infield, replace the grip on the hockey stick).
4. Make liberal use of school colors (i.e., paint fences, lockers, locker rooms, benches).
5. Improve the locker room area.
   a. Have a separate locker room if possible.

b. Assign team lockers in one area, if there are not separate rooms.
   c. Paint the lockers, or the trim, in school colors.
   d. Place player's name and an action picture on the locker.
   e. Carpet the room (a business in town may donate one).
   f. Put in a refrigerator (an old one will do), paint it the school colors; paste a picture of the school mascot on it, and fill it with oranges or lemonade. (Ask players to pay for what they take. Place a cup inside for the money, or assign team members the responsibility of collecting money and buying supplies.)
   g. Have a large bulletin board placed where it can be easily seen by the players. Keep it covered with interesting, informative, and up-to-date material.
   h. Have a record board. Think of many events to record in order to have many players recognized.
   i. Post signs and slogans on doors, walls, bulletin boards. Get the art department to help design these. Do not use too many or they will be ignored. Change them frequently.
   j. Provide music. Have a central system or let the players furnish the music: the distance people may select this week, the sprinters the next.
   k. Keep the area clean. Assign the team this responsibility.
6. Conduct home meets, contests in an impressive manner (i.e., have the clocks in working order, the nets set at the right height and tension, the field lined, an announcer who knows what is going on).
7. Travel in the best possible style.
   a. Paint a logo on school bus or van (school art department may help).
   b. Have travel uniforms (home economics department could assist).
   c. Use individual travel bags that are emblazoned with the school logo (one set could be used by several teams during the year).

Recognition

Players enjoy being noticed and having their accomplishments recognized. A coach does this in practice, before or after a contest, and on the playground; however, having others recognize these feats is a strong motivator. Innumerable coaches have used innumerable approaches; these are just a few of the possible ideas:

1. Establish a "Wall of Fame" where players who were outstanding in the most recent contest will be recognized. Place it on a wall in the hall corridor, gymnasium, cafeteria, or foyer.
2. Get names in the newspapers, on the radio, on television. Attempt to get recognition for all players, not just the "stars."

3. Have announcements read on the school's public-address system before and after contests.
4. Set up a picture-taking day. Post pictures in central parts of the building. Have them available for publicity through the media.
5. Have a town business honor the player of the week.
6. Establish a "Reach Your Goal" club. Anyone who reaches a preestablished goal (a difficult one) gets his or her name printed in the "goal" book.
7. Have a pre-season booklet with pictures of team members, data about each one, information about the coaches, and the schedule. (Merchants may sponsor a page.)
8. End the season with a banquet and recognize outstanding contributions of players. (An all-sports one is good, but one for a single sport may be better.)

Practice

Good, well-planned practices are great motivators. These daily sessions are conducted to develop a player's skills, mental and physical, and improve levels of conditioning. Unfortunately, putting in the time does not guarantee that one learns; motivation is also a necessary ingredient. The coach should manipulate the environmental variables to establish a good learning situation. This is done in many ways.

1. Start and end sessions on time.
2. Have well-planned, useful practices.
3. Make practices enjoyable; this does not mean that they have to be "fun," but they can be.
4. Use a variety of drills.
5. Include some type of scrimmage in each practice.
6. Keep the practice active—do the lecturing and discussing in the dressing room before and after being on the practice field.
7. Post the day's, week's, and season's schedules.
8. Play with the athletes; be personally involved in some but not all of the drills. (This is not feasible in all sports.)
9. Direct attention from failure; look at the present and future.
10. Set goals for the day, for the week, for the season.
11. Have competitive events—ladder tournaments, two-on-two, dribble races, challenge matches.
12. Give positive verbal encouragement.
13. Do not go all-out in pre-season work with full-scale scrimmages, the best equipment, official officials, the new uniforms. Save something special for the season's opener.
14. Be an enthusiastic coach.
15. Prepare the players mentally and physically.
16. Give the players a day off.
17. Play some other type of game/sport one day; break the routine.
18. Work with all the players.

Figure 10-2 Players enjoy gamelike scrimmages (Courtesy of Maclay School, Inc., Tallahassee, Florida. Photographer: Mickey Adair)

Player Involvement

The game is for the participants. If this is true, they should be involved in the program in ways other than as players on the field. Most are capable of assuming responsibilities; if they have a major role in the planning and execution of the team's as well as their own actions, they will possibly be more strongly oriented to team goals. Players can be involved in several ways.

1. Establish a player council to give the players a voice in policies, and allow them to contribute to the over-all program.
2. Allow players to evaluate coaches at the end of the season.
3. Work with players to set individual and team goals.
4. Have each player state his or her goals (intentions) before the squad members and coaches. Keep a record of these statements and remind the players of their intentions as the season progresses.
5. Graphically chart with the team what the season will be in terms of challenges.
6. Have players lead the warm-up drills; change leaders each day so that all get a turn.
7. Encourage players to assume responsibility for preparing themselves mentally and physically for a match.
8. Get player input regarding uniform style.

Personal Touch

Good coaches have a "personal touch" when it comes to working with the players. Each player is important, has a special role on the team, and should be recognized as an individual. A coach will find ways to let individuals know that they are a cut above the ordinary. In return, the coach will often get a better all-around player.

1. Send a birthday card to each player.
2. Grade everyone, not just the top players, on game films.
3. Be firm, fair, and friendly to all.
4. Visit with the parents/guardians.
5. Set a good example.
6. Keep in touch during the off-season by letter or phone, or call a meeting.
7. Find a place on the team for all who want to play.
8. Be available to help the player at times other than the practice or contest.
9. Recognize success in areas other than athletics (i.e., the lead in the school play, membership in honor clubs, reporter for the school paper).
10. Attend events in which the player is taking part (i.e., special awards ceremony, fashion show, another sport contest).
11. Recognize the players' birthdays by placing a sign that reads "Athlete of the Day" and posting the names of the players with birthdays on the date.
12. Show respect for each player.
13. Know each player's name and use it.
14. Give each player some one-to-one time; ask a question and hear the answer.

Feedback

If players' performances are to improve, they must receive information about their performances. This type of feedback reinforces behavior and serves as a motivator. Many techniques can be used to inform a player if he or she is performing well, reaching a goal, failing to reach a goal, doing better or worse than teammates.

1. Film the game, review the films, and then meet with the players individually or in groups (i.e., special teams, sprinters, defensive players).
2. Use video playback during practice.
3. Utilize statistics; compute batting averages, earned run averages, fielding percentages.
4. Evaluate weekly performances of all and talk with each player.
5. Keep close contact during practice and games; tell the players what they are doing right/wrong, need to do.
6. Treat each athlete as an individual; give individuals reports on their performances, not always in comparative terms.
7. Be exact with the information; say, "Lengthen your stride six inches," not "You made a poor pass."
8. Keep the information simple; do not bombard the player with unnecessary information.

Motivating the Athlete 137

Figure 10-3 Be specific with information (Courtesy of Rickards High School, Tallahassee, Florida. Photographer: Mickey Adair)

Reinforcement

Coaches must approve of properly executed acts or disapprove of improperly executed ones if they are to mold a player's performance. Giving fair treatment to all players is very important. Inconsistency can produce confusion, distrust, and jealousy, so the pleasure or the pain should be distributed equally. There should be no difference in expectations, insofar as regulations are concerned, between the best player and the last one on the bench, or the opening game and the play-off contest. Sport is a place to learn and practice fair play; coaches set the example. Whatever has been decided as an appropriate reward or punishment needs to be awarded as soon as is practical and with an even hand.

1. Look for actions to reinforce; do not take things for granted.
2. Use praise; comment favorably on well-executed actions.
3. Give a surprise, like a watermelon break, if a practice goes well.
4. Reinforce immediately; reward the effort as well as the results.
5. Punish the entire team for one player's mistakes.
6. Brag about the good things, but don't do this on every play or action because it will lose its effectiveness.
7. Tell them the good points and what needs to be changed or corrected. Be encouraging.
8. Let the players know that they can contribute to the team; each is important.
9. Threaten the players with extra sprints, a lengthened practice, removal from a game, or demotion, and follow through when the situation demands.
10. Raise voice to emphasize a point.

Preparing for the Game

One of the most important, and yet most difficult, tasks is to motivate players for a game. A coach should not wait until the hour or the day of the match, but should begin to get the athletes "up for the game" as soon as the last one has ended. It is a mistake to look too far ahead to a future match and overlook a present one; this is a good way to lose unexpectedly. There are coaches who go to almost any extreme to arouse their squads—throw chairs, yell and scream, grab players and shake them, break windows, ram their fists through walls—but most are successful in using much lower key approaches.

1. Have a good game plan; prepare the players well in advance.
2. Use a positive approach and expect good things to happen.
3. Play music to get them "in the mood."
4. Talk before a game. Use a pep talk, give them an inspired message, read a poem, dedicate the contest to someone, challenge them, tell them an anecdote, give them a personal challenge, threaten them.
5. Bring out new uniforms for the key game.

Motivating the Athlete **139**

Figure 10-4 Have the players ready for action (Courtesy of Miami Dade Community College-North, Miami, Florida. Photographer: Bob Bailey)

6. Have team members wear school colors on the day of the game.
7. Enter the field as a unit and have a hot-shot warm-up.
8. Show records of those who preceded them.
9. Give each player a T-shirt that says "We are the best" or "We can do it."
10. Ask a former player, team leader, popular coach, or community leader to give a strong spirit talk.
11. Tell them a derogatory remark supposedly made by another team.
12. Show films, good ones, of what they have done and how well they have played.
13. Use a scheduled game against a bigger opponent as a challenge; instill a fierce desire in the underdog to defeat the larger, more formidable opponent.
14. Be under control; the coach sets the mood, and if he or she gets too uptight and irrational, the team will too.
15. Make promises and keep them; if the team wins or plays well, they get a day off.

16. Have the team sit quietly and think about themselves, about their individual performance, and how it fits into the team concept.

Awards/ Rewards

Like everyone else, players enjoy receiving awards/rewards. "Effort should bring something in return" is a statement made in the American culture. "If I do this, what is it worth?" is the question asked by many athletes. Awards come in many forms—verbal praise, a pat on the back, a short practice period, a trip to a college game, food—but many players like something permanent to show for their "job well done."

1. Award letters, sweaters, or jackets.
2. Award a school blanket with the player's name on it to the 3- or 4-year letterperson.
3. Give trophies/plaques for special honors.
4. Give a T-shirt to the player the team selects as the player of the week.
5. Award a decal, a star, or the school logo for outstanding play in a game. The coaches set the criteria, and the award is placed on the helmet.
6. Have the best players each week on the traveling squad.
7. Take top performers to the top meets.
8. Give the top performers the best equipment.
9. Award a steak dinner for making a lay-up in a game with the nondominant hand from the nondominant side of the basket.
10. Place pictures of the outstanding players of the week in a downtown business establishment.
11. Assign seniors and letterpersons their choice of lockers, uniform numbers, seats on the bus.

Rituals

Sporting events are filled with rituals; captains meet in the center of the playing area for a coin toss, "The Star-Spangled Banner" is played, and teams dress in school colors. Teams have rituals, too. Old ones are discarded and new ones are established, but the rituals remain to serve as motivators.

1. Have the same player lead the team onto the court for each game.
2. Meet with players in the locker room before the game and join hands as the team members repeat the Lord's Prayer.
3. Meet under the goal posts on the home field after each game.
4. Eat lunch together on the day of the contest.
5. Use the same types of warm-up drills prior to each match.
6. Have players carry their helmets at all times on away trips.
7. Wear school colors on the day of the game.
8. Wear some piece of the uniform, usually the jersey, the day of the game.
9. Have team members establish a new ritual that has a unique part of the past.

Pride

It is important for a player to have pride—a high opinion of one's own worth and position, and of the team, the school, and the community. Pride is an internal motivator that is not innate but must be developed. The state or feeling of being proud can be a very strong, enduring influence on an athlete's performance. Those who believe in themselves and what they are doing will put much more effort into the cause.

1. Give each player a T-shirt that says, "_____ is a member of the lacrosse team."
2. Have the team's captains help design the uniforms.
3. Invite a former athlete back to work with the squad.
4. Give responsibilities to the seniors to see that the work gets done.
5. Remind the team of the school's winning tradition.
6. Invite a well-known athlete or coach from a college or pro team to talk with the squad.
7. Recognize the worth of each player.
8. Work to make the team and members known to the school and community through pep assemblies, publicity in the local media, services to the community.
9. Expect the coaching staff to show pride in themselves and their work and to be proud of the team and individual players.
10. Give all players an opportunity to be somebody.
11. Be a coach who sets an example of "what sports are all about."

Team Togetherness

The statement "There is no I in team" is a sort of paradox because a coach is attempting to develop an individual's self-esteem while asking him or her to be secondary to the total team. It may be expecting too much of players to ask them to like all the others, but it would help if they did try to understand one another and to have mutual respect. Generally, teams with compatible members and common goals have greater success than do teams with members in constant turmoil.

1. Treat all players, the sub to the star, the same.
2. Stay together at certain events.
3. Attend church together.
4. Dress alike for certain occasions.
5. Meet at someone's house for dinner the night before the game.
6. Develop a positive image by being disciplined, well dressed, and well prepared.
7. Set team goals and be proud of reaching them.
8. Have players knowledgeable about responsibilities of positions other than their own—put the point guard under the basket a few times.
9. Have team representatives meet regularly with the coaching staff.

10. Develop pride within the subunits—give them recognition with a name like "the fangs" or the "sub squad."
11. Have the players know something about one another.
12. Make seat assignments on the bus and change seating arrangements frequently.
13. Assign a senior member of the squad as a buddy to a younger member.
14. Utilize as many players in a game as you possibly can—emphasize that all are a vital part of the team.
15. Have player and coach "get-togethers."
16. Have a coaching staff that works well together.

Gimmicks

Using a gimmick to motivate does not mean that one must resort to trickery. A coach uses many tactics; often something new, different, or unusual in an approach pushes the right button in the player. Coaches are always seeking new ways to develop the drive and desire in players, and "little things can mean a lot." Innumerable ones are used.

1. Over the door to the dressing room post a one-word message: "Determination," "Pride," "Win."
2. Have a living mascot—a student dressed as the team emblem.
3. Quietly post signs in the yards (or hallways of apartments) of the players: "A Murfreesboro Rattler lives here."
4. Hand the athletes a note wrapped around a wooden match at the end of practice with instructions to light the match and read the note at 10:00 P.M. Write a joke, a message, a challenge.
5. Hand out pencils with the team's schedule on them.
6. Sell suckers with "Tribe Pride" printed on the stick.
7. Post signs to establish a desirable mental state:
"*Believe* that it is possible to win."
"*Respect* the Tigers' capabilities."
"*Believe* that you must put forth an all-out effort."
"*Be anxious* in regard to the outcome."
"*Be up* for the game."
"*Be determined* to make this a peak performance."
"*Be determined* to put the team above personal gain."
8. Support players in a unique endeavor. (Some football players have their heads shaved, and coaches may also agree to do this.)

Slogans

Many coaches are convinced that slogans and sayings are motivational aids. They post these in their gyms, in locker rooms, over stadium entrances, and in their offices, quoting them frequently. Some are so well known that their authors are immediately identifiable, such as the quote attributed to Vince Lombardi, "Winning isn't everything, it is the only thing." There are many others.

1. "Neither success nor failure is final."
2. "The difficult I expect you to do immediately, the impossible may take a little longer."
3. "You are accountable for your behavior."
4. "Championships do not just happen, they are earned."
5. "Teamwork is everything."
6. "When the going gets tough the tough get going."
7. "The gate to excellence is surrounded by a sea of sweat."
8. "It is not the size of the dog in the fight but the size of fight in the dog."
9. "The only way to win is to work at it."
10. "If everybody does not want it, nobody gets it."
11. "To be average is to be the lowest of the good and the best of the bad. Who wants to be average!"

A Change in Routine

Frequently, a team gets in a slump or hits a dry spell. Players go stale, the zip is gone, and the entire program seems "snake bit." This is the time to make a change in routine, in program, or in direction. It often turns out that a simple alteration in procedure can spark a group or bring a team back to its former style of operation. Coaches should not hesitate to do something different.

1. Give them an unexpected day off.
2. Utilize new and different drills in practice.
3. Rearrange the week's practice schedule.
4. Develop a new pre-game routine.
5. Arrange an all-out pep rally prior to the contest.
6. Get different styles of uniforms.
7. Change the color combinations of the uniforms.
8. Change the schedule if possible; play some different teams or reschedule current opponents on different dates.
9. Keep the same symbol but change the image—Sammy Seminole to Savage Sam, a perched eagle to one preparing to attack, a coiled snake to a striking one.

Team Supporters

All teams have a following of fans, a group of boosters, a loyal band of parents and friends who support them in many ways, both financially and psychologically. Not only do they serve the team as scorers, timers, drivers, cooks, and chaperones, they also serve as motivators for the players. These loyal fans need to be thanked for their efforts and encouraged to continue their support. Many ideas have been proposed and used. Some of the more useful ones are listed.

1. Have coaches visible in the community—join service and civic organizations.
2. Develop a good team reputation by having the members be on their best behavior on trips and in town.
3. Have an assembly program in the feeder schools; get the young ones interested.

Figure 10-5 Having fan support is a great motivator (Courtesy of Florida State University, Tallahassee, Florida. Photographer: Barry Mittman)

4. Perform at halftime of another event.
5. Encourage the Recreation Department, Girls' Club, YMCA, to start a sports program and offer to set up coaching clinics.
6. Be available and make an effort to speak to civic groups.
7. Have free nights for parents, for the fans.

8. Invite parents, girlfriends, boyfriends, representatives of the local media to come to a "picture" day or some special practice day.
9. If the sport is a new one to the area, invite people to an "explanation" meeting—explain and demonstrate the equipment, uniforms, rules.
10. Have an appreciation night for the principal.
11. Have a Parents' Night. Every mother gets a flower and the father gets a miniature ball with their child's name on it. Introduce the parents before the contest and have the cheerleaders escort them to a special seating area.
12. Invite parents to a special event, such as the awards banquet, and give them special recognition.
13. Have a "thank you" note printed in the local paper.
14. Arrange for boosters to accompany the team on out-of-town trips.

During Play

Once the game begins, what can a coach do that might make a difference between winning or losing, having a team member play well or poorly, and developing team cohesiveness or team disarray? Obviously, adjustments in team strategy and play of an individual can be made, but more is needed. The players must be motivated "to do the best they can." Regardless of the conditions, a coach's actions and words can make a difference.

1. Maintain self-control; act rather than react.
2. Recognize a successful action or extreme effort.
3. Use punishment sparingly and in a corrective way; do not punish young athletes for making errors in a game.
4. Give encouraging messages—with words, pats on the back, eye contact, body position.
5. Give players another chance; do not "pull" them for a mistake or two.
6. Use substitutes at times other than when the game is obviously won or lost.
7. Create no situations that might embarrass players or place them in a "no win" position.

Half Time

A problem facing all coaches is motivating the team or players at a break in the action. So many variables are involved that it is difficult to pinpoint a specific action that should be undertaken. Is the team or individual player the favorite or the underdog, ahead or behind, down or up, angry or complacent? Whatever the situation, the action generally takes the form of a "pep" talk, a game strategy adjustment, or a combination of both. The content and length of the message depend on the nature of the team or individual player and the events that have taken place in the game. Coaches should plan ahead by thinking through possible circumstances and making plan #1 and plan #2 for each speech.

1. Use a chalkboard to illustrate the adjustments; players can see much better than they can hear.
2. Emphasize what they did correctly; find something to reinforce, regardless of the contest score.
3. First, get their attention—slam a door shut, kick a bucket, or jump upon a desk or table.
4. Have complete silence when they come into the locker room; they need time to think about past actions.
5. Focus their attention on the upcoming play; the end-of-the-game score is what counts.
6. Get excited. If the team is to get excited, the coach leads the way. Be calm. If the team is to be calm, the coach needs to set an example.
7. Talk coherently—be clear and concise; make a point and then move to the next one.
8. Encourage and instruct rather than demand.
9. Work on individuals; try to get them to spark the team.
10. Define responsibilities so that team members will avoid blaming each other.
11. Give them a fight talk and/or chewing out if they have been playing below par.
12. Use an emotional appeal—win for the player who is hurt, the former player, the spectators who traveled all the way to see them.
13. Tell them what they really need to know just before they return to the playing area so that they will feel confident as they return to the action.

SUMMARY

Coaches need to be psychologists, as well as teachers, as players' performances may be dependent more on their motivation to play than on their skill. When coaches know their sport and the players well, then they can determine how to ensure that the team, as well as individual players, will perform to their maximum.

There are many ways to focus attention on the game, on the quality of play, and on anticipated success. Each coach must develop a system of motivational procedures and "gimmicks" that seem to work for each squad. These procedures may vary as the make-up of a team changes from year to year or as community interest declines or grows, but they are invaluable and must be a part of each coach's expertise or "bag of tricks."

ENDNOTES

1. R. N. Singer, "The Motivation in Sport," *International Journal of Sport Psychology 8* (1977): 1.

2. R. S. Weinberg, "Motivating Athletes Through Goal Setting," *Journal of Physical Education, Recreation and Dance* (November/December 1982): 46.
3. R. B. Alderman, "Strategies for Motivating Young Athletes," in *Sports Psychology: An Analysis of Athletic Behavior,* ed. W. F. Staub (Ithaca, N.Y.: Movement Publications, 1978), pp. 49–61.
4. "Athletic Participation: Students Give Their Views," *National Federation News* (April 1985): 4.
5. T. A. Tutko and J. W. Richards, *Psychology of Coaching* (Allyn and Bacon, 1971), p. 125.

11

Developing Appropriate Behavior

**DISCIPLINE
PLANNING PROCEDURES
SUMMARY**

Many coaches attempt to shape team members into a preconceived model of behavior. There is no one behavior style in the United States that can be followed without alteration because styles change with the section of the country, size of community, sport, coach, ethnic background of the population, age of the participant, and sponsoring agency.

The coach has the ultimate responsibility in determining what expected player behaviors will be and how control is to be maintained or these behaviors elicited. Individual participants may be expected to display a set of characteristic behaviors for a particular sport environment even though they may be permitted some variance in personal or subgroup actions. Coaches must be aware of all the factors in their situations before deciding what actions are to be strengthened, tolerated, ignored, or repressed.

A young person just out of college on a first job may find that even the small 5-year age difference between teacher/coach and student/athlete provides entirely different patterns of behavior from those accepted or expected so recently. It is not that players cannot or will not be disciplined or directed, but methods of discipline or modifying behavior may have to be changed to fit the situation or the person. A coach must understand how to deal with individuals and their individual needs, and must recognize that individuals make groups, not vice versa. Appropriate standards for both group and individual behavior should not conflict but should be congruent with the coach's and team's goals.

DISCIPLINE

Discipline, the setting of limitations, is necessary if a collection of individuals is to become a team. The degree of control necessary will vary with players; hence, there can be no single or standard approach. It is almost impossible to truly know another person, but one can learn many things about others by making a concerted effort. A coach will have to know the players—as well as it is possible under the circumstances—in order to determine how to work with them in the area of discipline.

Basic Areas

The primary area of a sport that requires disciplined behavior from players is concerned with preparation for play. Players must be physically, mentally, and emotionally prepared to participate if they, and the team as a whole, are to play well.

Another area that many coaches concern themselves with is team image. They believe that players who will accept the responsibility of representing a team, and elect to modify their behavior accordingly, contribute to team success as well as to their own.

Physically Ready

A player must be ready to play well over an extended period of time. The degree of strength and endurance needed will vary with each activity and with the age and experience of the participant, but these two capacities have to be maintained for high levels of performance and for the player and team safety. Conditioning is hard work, and not fun for many people, so a coach will have to use extrinsic motivational techniques to encourage those who lack the self-discipline to work at being physically ready.

Mentally Ready

An athlete needs to be mentally ready to play. Game plans and strategies have to be learned. This requires that the player be able to absorb information in the "chalk talks" and practice drills, as well as study and do homework when out of the direct control of the coach. There is a large cognitive and intellectual area in athletics; the "dumb jocks" image, one that has prevailed for many years, is neither accurate nor kind. Learning assignments, defenses, plays, and strategies demands strict attention to the mastery of a lot of information.

Emotionally Ready

A team member also has to be emotionally ready to play and to continue to play under control. Ideally, players can use self-control to manage their behavior, but coaches must often impose strict external discipline so that athletes do not lose control. It is not sporting for a player to have a temper tantrum and stamp his or her feet like a spoiled child. It is not acceptable for a player to speak offensively to an official. It is not acceptable for one player to strike another. The generation of highly emotional states is considered to be a motivation factor by many coaches, but this can increase the likelihood of players losing emotional control and blowing their assignments or even being thrown out of a game. There is an efficient emotional level for all the team members; they need help finding it.

Acceptable Image

A final aspect of discipline, that of creating or presenting an acceptable image, may be the most difficult. The coach and the team are in the public eye, with greater public notice and scrutiny the higher up the competitive ladder they are. In a sense, coaches and athletes belong to the public; and the coach, the acknowledged leader who represents the school, club, department, or league as well as the team, answers for the players' actions both on the field and off. A positive public image requires that all players follow social customs in the community, especially when recognizable as a part of a team.

Coaches will need to consider the effectiveness of having team members dress in a specific way for an event. Neat-appearing athletes look good to the community. They may also be on their better behavior if they feel that they can be identified.

Players need to learn that community approval is a necessary part of the athletic scene and that each player represents every other player, the coach, and the school or league. Good behavior reaps dividends; poor behavior hurts the entire program.

Developing a Code

Many coaches develop, define, or refine a code of behavior for themselves and their teams. Sometimes this code is fully thought through, and sometimes it is just a feeling of good or bad; but it is always there. Good coaches spend time determining what they expect from themselves, their staff, and the players, and what they will accept in deviations from that standard.

Step One

The first step in developing a code of behavior is to study one's own personal values. What is absolutely necessary and important? What are the ways of behaving that will be required from the players as they follow a conditioning routine, as they learn strategy, as they exhibit strong feelings, and as they live their lives? Next, the coach needs to decide what items in the code are desirable but do not require absolute conformity, things believed in and preferred but not worth creating a hassle over.

A good example of this was the great controversy in the 1960s and 1970s over the hair length for young men. No one since Samson has had his strength or endurance altered by growing or cutting hair, but many coaches felt such personal affront over long hair that they caused themselves ulcers and drove fine athletes away from a sport in which they could compete. Hair length is an emotional item, not a rational one (unless a health/safety factor is involved), and disagreements over it are wasteful in the teaching/coaching/learning process.

Nondebatable items in the code will reflect coaches' ethical and moral standards, as well as their professional training and judgment. Myth, hearsay, prejudice, and unexamined tradition are not sound bases for a code of behavior. Coaches who spend enough time to determine what they believe and what they know can say with some confidence, "Here I stand."

Step Two

The next step is to consider the players and their levels of personal development and ability to be self-directing. Expectations for players to follow a code of behavior should allow for strengths and weaknesses in this area. Some players will need no external discipline as they will accept standards and will be able to behave acceptably without coercion or supervision. Many will try to do as the coach wishes but will need supervision and some control. These are either too young and inexperienced to be self-directing or too personally immature to operate without a little supervision. There is a third group that has no self-control. This last group should be assisted to become at least partially self-directing, or the coach's energies will be dissipated in trying to bring them into conformity.

The large majority of players will fall into the middle group. Although they are capable, at any age, of making many sound, objective judgments, they may not choose to (and may really prefer to have the coach assume this responsibility for them). They can then say, "I have to do this or the coach will not let me play," which may relieve peer group pressure. A coach's requirements for behavior make it easier for players to know how to act; and, by checking up, a coach makes it easier for them to conform.

Step Three   Finally, coaches should take a look at the particular sport and its requirements. Some are convinced that it is more important to exert control over team sport players than over individual sport participants because the letdown by a team player affects the entire team, thus the outcome of the game for many people. They state that individual participants can let down and be responsible only for their own play, although this may affect a team total in golf, tennis, swimming, or gymnastics.

Team sports require close cooperation and coordination of many players. One individual in poor condition, upset, or unaware of strategy can disrupt an entire team. Team sports also require full squads for practice and games; if the goalie or the point guard or the spiker is not there, the entire team and the contest suffer.

Finalizing   When coaches have developed their code of behavior, their set of requirements or rules and regulations for their players, they then have to consider whether these are for the good of the players, the good of the team, or the good of the coach. Ideally, everyone should be considered; but in the ultimate showdown among team, player, and the coach, it will have to be decided who or what is valued most. In the final analysis, the coach's true set of values will shine through, and one who has considered a reasoned decision before the occasion for a quick judgment occurs is fortunate. What is helpful is to weigh all elements and then attempt to decide how to behave before having to face a controversy and the possibility of losing one's self-control.

Rule Making   After establishing a basic code of behavior as a guide, the coach then needs to consider what rules and regulations might be necessary and the degree to which the staff and players will participate in the rules-making process. A generally effective procedure has been to let players and assistant coaches participate as fully as possible in establishing specific rules, as this increases the players' feeling of ownership and decreases the need for their being constantly supervised. If athletes are personally committed to rules, they will be more willing to abide by them.

Coaches should not consider participation by players in setting rules and regulations to be a sign of inadequacy. Power and strength do not necessarily diminish with player input; in fact, they may increase as players come to understand and share in rules development.

Assistant coaches' input is also important and valuable, as enforcement will be their task and their experience can lead to sound policy decisions. The role of assistant coaches in establishing and carrying out rules should be made very clear. All coaches need authority as well as responsibility.

As rules are established, several questions must be answered. Are they necessary? Are they enforceable? Are they fair? Will there be exceptions or must everyone follow the letter rather than the spirit of the rule? What are the penalties? Full discussion of these questions prior to the start of a season can prevent many problems and make the solving of others easier.

Rule Criteria   Is the rule necessary? What is needed to make the player/team successful? Is it essential that the players do not drink, smoke, use drugs; that they go to bed at a certain hour and eat the right foods; that they stay away from certain people and places? The rule should be relevant to the sport as well as for the good of the individual player.

Is the rule enforceable? Can a player be made to wear short hair, go to church each Sunday, not frequent bars? If the rule is "Be in bed by 11:00 P.M.," how can this be checked? Making rules and then wearing blinders can do much more harm than good.

Is the rule fair? Is it fair to have special practices at odd times when many of the players work or have difficulty arranging for transportation? Is it fair to request that the players wear special clothes for specific events when they may not own appropriate clothing and cannot afford to buy them? Is it fair to require that they enroll in certain courses because the instructor is lenient and will not require athletes to study? Is it fair to ask the individual to sacrifice for the good of the team when it may cost money, injury, pride, or grades?

Exceptions   The chances are that some, if not all, of the rules will be broken. When this happens, will there be exceptions to the rule? Will it be situational or will it apply to the star and scrub alike, to a child of the rich as well as to the child of the poor, for a nonconference contest and a conference one, to all ethnic groups equally? It is very difficult not to show favoritism among players, but a coach should not discriminate. To say that to discipline a player would hurt the team may be a poor excuse. Avoiding facing a disciplinary issue when there will be repercussions from the parents, administrators, or team supporters may be an immediate easy way out, but it may cost the players, team, and coach later. Unfortunately, when a coach's job is on the line, based on whether the big event is won or lost, there may be a great temptation to bend the rules and violate established policy. To bend or not to bend a rule can be a great ethical dilemma of a coach for which there is no easy answer.

To say that there will be no situational variances could be just as bad as having too many. Is the problem of players being late to practice because their parents did not get them to the gymnasium the same as being late because the practice gear was forgotten and left behind? Is not being in bed by 10:00 P.M. because the movie had not ended the same as failing to do so because the parents would not let the youth into the house? Not only are there two sides to a situation, the right way and the wrong way, but there may also be a shaded area between the two. A coach should get all details, not be "conned" by the players, and be reasonable.

Penalties

What happens when the rules are broken? Generally, the athlete who breaks a rule pays a penalty; and, more often than not, a negative reinforcer is used. The pattern for most coaches seems to be to disregard players who keep the rules and punish the players who break the rules. Whatever pattern is followed, the coach should keep in mind, and let the player know, that the punishment is for the act, or the failure to act, not for the individual.

Will the team be informed of disciplinary measures as they are informed of the rules? If they are not told, the coach can always "pull something out of a hat," and this is not a wise procedure. Players prefer to be told what to expect if a rule is broken. To be told not to be late for a trip without being told that they will be left behind can create bad feelings toward the coach. To surprise everyone by making all team members run an extra mile when one player is late can be a very poor move psychologically. Three lists could be prepared—one of rules, one of the purposes, and one of what will happen if a rule is broken. None should be kept a secret nor made up as the season progresses.

When should a player be penalized for the offense? Grudges have no place in any part of a game. An experienced coach will not bring up last week's problem to add to the current ones, and will not punish a player today for something that happened days ago. To be effective, the penalty must be awarded as soon after the infraction as possible. If the penalty is not to participate in a contest, the action should not be delayed; the player ought to be kept out of an immediate contest, not the one that is held weeks after the incident. If the penalty for not running the play correctly is 5 laps, it is best to enforce the penalty while the mistake is fresh on the player's mind. If laps are accumulated, a player could eventually owe 100 miles and never get the debt paid.

Will the penalty complement the rule? Most players will do their penance (if they do not, they might not be on the team tomorrow), but they will understand more fully making a payment equal to the error of their ways. The penalty imposed should be based on the act, not on the individual involved. Personal biases of a coach must not alter the penalty, either in severity or leniency. Coaches often come up with two classifications of rules: major and minor. Major penalties are imposed—sitting out a game or tournament, being off the team for a month, being off the team permanently—for breaking major rules. The breaking of minor rules calls for minor penalties—running 5 laps, running the bleachers, not starting a game.

PLANNING PROCEDURES

As in the business and academic worlds, plans in the coaching world must be systematically formulated. However, the process should not be made final until the material (personnel) and the product (goals and objectives) are known. Once coaches know these, they can work through a hierarchy of procedures. Completing each before moving to the next is essential because each depends on the previous one. Procedures should be made final only after careful study and thought and a record made of these determinations. This is necessary in order to avoid conflict and confusion between the coaches and administrators, among the members of the coaching staff, between the coaches and the players, among the players, and between the coaches and parents.

Some experienced coaches may follow procedures that are already in their minds, others may simply use what someone else has set up, and there are those who look for assistance. Until a personal set has been developed, the following may serve as a guide:

1. Determine and list environments (gyms, fields, locker rooms) where players are to be controlled.
2. Determine and list three sets of behaviors—acceptable, unacceptable, and neutral—for the team members in these environments.
3. Determine and list the reinforcers, positive and/or negative, for these behaviors.
4. Determine the control variables:
   a. When is the behavior to be exhibited?
   b. When will the reinforcers be administered?
   c. How and by whom will the reinforcers be administered?
5. Inform the team members of behaviors, reinforcers, and control variables.
6. Evaluate the effects.

Environments When and where will the athlete's behavior be controlled? It is impossible, and should not be necessary, to manage every facet of the player's life; however, it will be essential to have rules governing actions in some situations. Practice sessions and contests must have regulations if objectives are to be accomplished. Other areas such as the athlete's home life, leisure time activities, school time, and work pursuits are not easily controlled and may or may not be the coach's business.

Behaviors The head coach, or someone whose judgment is valued, must decide which behaviors contribute to the teaching/coaching/learning situation and enhance the team's success, which will detract or disrupt, and which are necessary in a social sense but will have no effect on player or team success. There are no standard lists; each behavior selected as appropriate should be specific to a particular situation. What is acceptable to one coach may be of no consequence to another and unacceptable to a third. Contents of the lists will vary with the coach, sport, and community.

An important point to consider is whether or not the actions can be judged. Some behaviors are more easily evaluated than others—being on time for a practice can be objectively measured, but putting forth total effort calls for some subjective evaluation. The list should not be so extensive that it results in too much time being spent on checking actions.

Whatever behaviors are placed on the list must be as explicitly defined as possible. A statement such as "Do nothing to embarrass yourself, the team, or school" is vague. "Attend each practice and contest" is a more explicit statement, as is "Be on time and ready for every practice and contest by being fully dressed, equipped, and on the field no later than the stated time."

Acceptable Behavior

What behaviors are acceptable for the players, the team, and the coaches in the previously selected situations? What actions are really necessary for the good of the player and the team? It may be wise to make a list of items concerned with each area of activity, with acceptable behaviors named for each. Examples for the practice environment are:

1. Attendance: Attend all practices unless you are excused by the head coach prior to the session. Proven player illness or injury and a family emergency will be accepted as legitimate excuses.
2. Locker Room: Keep the area clean and neat by:
   a. Showing respect for other's property by not marking on surfaces and not damaging benches, plumbing, facilities, and lockers
   b. Keeping clothes not being worn in your locker
   c. Placing used uniforms in the designated area
   d. Placing used towels in the designated area
   e. Returning all equipment to the correct bins
   f. Using facilities for the purposes for which they were designed.
3. Promptness: Be fully dressed in the proper uniform for the day in the assigned area no later than the stated time.
4. Effort: Try as hard as possible; do not "loaf"; always be ready to take your turn; run instead of walk.
5. Teamwork: Help your teammates; do not be a ball-hog or a show-off; cooperate with coaches; follow instructions.

Unacceptable Behaviors

Unacceptable behaviors could be the direct opposite of those that are acceptable—cutting practices, being late to meetings, showing disrespect to a coach—but the list should also contain different items. For example:

1. Locker Room: Taking items belonging to another individual.
2. Attendance: Missing more than 1 session each week and more than 5 times during the pre-season and competitive season.

The list of unacceptable behaviors could also be under an item not listed in the acceptable category. For example:

Conduct: Displaying unsportsmanlike actions during a practice or game by:

1. Slamming equipment to the ground.
2. Hitting a teammate, coach, manager, or trainer.
3. Using foul language.
4. Making obscene gestures.
5. Verbally degrading a teammate, coach, official, manager, trainer, or fan.
6. Throwing a temper tantrum.

Neutral Behaviors

Neutral behaviors are those about which the coach has no firm policy. If the act is omitted from the two previous lists, one would assume that it is "neutral"; however, what may be a neutral action at the beginning of the season may become acceptable or unacceptable later. Circumstances may make it necessary to reclassify the behavior, so lists may be composed but are not always "cast in concrete." Examples of neutral behavior include:

1. Dating.
2. Working at jobs that have no time conflict with classes, practices, or contests.
3. Wearing hair any length.
4. Dressing in whatever is stylish.
5. Taking an active part in other school activities.
6. Being a member of another sports team.
7. Choosing one's own friends.

Reinforcers

Behaviors need to be reinforced, either positively or negatively, to elicit desired actions from players. Praise, success, and rewards can keep a player working long and hard for a goal. Punishment, criticism, and threats can make a player work hard for the time being. Coaches often use a mixture of both to accomplish goals and to develop or strengthen desired behavior patterns.

Once the list of behaviors has been determined, reinforcers that seem appropriate for each should be selected. The head coach will have to decide whether to reward acceptable action, or whether to assume that appropriate behavior is the norm and to punish unacceptable actions.

Cultural Influences

Among cultural influences, there are two that exert very strong pressure on athletes and whose approval or disapproval must constantly be considered—peers and family. Peer groups can, through approving or disapproving a player's actions, make that player conform to or ignore stipulations. A girlfriend or boyfriend can often "out influence" a coach. Family agreement or disagreement with team rules can be just as influential in supporting or undermining authority. When rules are in line with family ideals or peer values, a coach will have less difficulty in having team members toe the line. If the rules are not congruent, both coaches and players are placed in a difficult situation. Requests need to be reasonable so that both peers and family can join coaches in reinforcing the rules.

A coach must also be reasonable with players when they are already feeling hindered by their home situations. Some players must work to support themselves and their families, so to punish a player for not being able to focus totally on a team is wrong. It is much better to supply praise for doing the right thing and then to help such athletes find a better, different, nonconflicting job. Many players have to attend to children after school, either their own or younger brothers and sisters. These young people need encouragement rather than discouragement and a helping hand instead of a knock. A positive, hopeful attitude about their lives can free players to perform well and be better citizens and students.

Players whose peers encourage the use of drugs may rapidly change their behavior when the new peer group of team members supports avoidance of all harmful substances. Positive support of positive behavior is very powerful.

The Approach   Currently, the consensus among psychologists and educators is that it is better to use a positive rather than a negative approach. A reward lets an individual know that the act was right, while punishment only tells one that the act was wrong but not what was right. An encouraging word, a touch, a wink are positive reinforcers. Material rewards—those who come out every day get a suit and become a member of the team, those who work hard in practice will get to play in the game, or those who swim the required number of laps each day for one week get a small surprise like an apple—can also be very influential positive reinforcers.

Yelling, threatening, or hitting are very strong negative reinforcers. Many coaches use these negative reinforcers with players who act in an unacceptable manner, but often the players become angry, confused, or embarrassed and may rebel against the system. Punishments administered by coaches include: "If they are late for practice, they run a lap for each minute they are late; if they miss a practice without having a legitimate excuse, they swim an extra hour the next day; if they do not attend classes the day of the game, they do not play that day; if they goof off in practice, they get no water break; if they come dressed inappropriately for travel, they stay home; if they are caught drinking beer during the season, they are off the team; if they are late for practice, all team members must run the bleachers."

Many coaches appear to be concerned with what players should not do rather than with what they should do. Although the reverse of the coin may be more effective, whatever is determined to be correct for the group has to be reinforced. If the behavior is on the coach's list, then it is important enough for attention and enforcement. If a coach finds that it is not so important, then it ought to be placed in the neutral category. It can be more trouble than it is worth to keep ordinary, unimportant actions on a "must do" list.

Control Variables   As coaches plan their control methods or procedures, they will need to consider when to expect certain actions to occur, when to administer the reinforcers, and who will be involved in the process. Considering these in advance of any occasion requiring action can help a coach deal with whatever may occur.

Situation — Explicit expectations of the squad members must be given. Athletes must know: Are the regulations in force all year or just during the playing season? Are certain actions expected on game days only or on all school days? Are there different expectations for practice on the day before a game, on trips, on the night before a match? Should they behave differently in practice than in a game? Must they associate only with team members at certain times? Rules need to be clear to avoid misunderstanding and disharmony.

When — Not only should a coach make clear the occasions when certain actions are expected but also when reinforcers will be administered. In sports the result of a player's action is public. There is immediate knowledge of results when the ball enters the goal or does not, when the runner is the fastest or the slowest. The closer the feedback is to the action, the quicker a corrected performance can occur. This is also true in the behavioral realm; the closer the reinforcement is to the action, the more likely it is that the reinforcement (reward, lack of reward, punishment) will be effective. It does not take much to offer positive reinforcement or support. An arm around the shoulder, a smile, or a thumbs-up signal will do the job. Negative reinforcement includes benching the player, scowling, or giving verbal criticism. Occasionally, reinforcement must be delayed. Examples of the acceptable use of delayed reinforcement are requiring a player to attend all pre-season workouts before receiving a uniform, or running 500 miles to get a T-shirt. It could be necessary to wait until a game is scheduled to omit a player from the starting line-up for an infraction of a practice procedure.

Reinforcement given too late or too frequently may lose its effectiveness. Late awards or praise will not be as meaningful. Punishments that are late may be for almost-forgotten events and may arrive after intervening praise. An athlete will often ignore constant criticism or nagging, but he or she will usually listen to an occasional correction. Constant approval, whether or not earned, will also reduce the capacity to hear and believe, while a pat on the back in recognition of real accomplishment can be very supportive.

Who — Who is to reinforce? Do all coaches reward as well as punish? Coaches who have responsibilities need the authority to support their positions. If behaviors and reinforcers have been predetermined, there should be few problems resulting from having different people administer the rewards and punishments.

What role will the team members play? Some coaches prefer to keep "official" reinforcement out of the hands of players, while others encourage them to take an active part. Peer pressure is a powerful reinforcer, and there are times when this reward or punishment can exert a strong influence. It may be more meaningful if teammates decide on and apply a reinforcer for unsportsmanlike conduct or for stealing another player's gear. The reward may be more special if team members select a teammate as the "hustler" of the week or the game captain. Coaches who allow team members, either the entire squad or a representative group, to apply

Inform the Team Members

reinforcers must keep control over their actions and allow them to operate within established guidelines. Teammates are as capable of doling out punishment or negative reinforcement as they are in recognizing superior performance with positive reinforcement.

Prospective athletes and current team members should be given a list of expected behaviors and potential reinforcers at the initial meeting of the year. They need to know what actions are expected and what happens if they do not live up to these expectations. Most would like to please the coaching staff and are interested in knowing the actions that will gain approval.

Coaches' statements of expected behavior will never be identical, but most will be similar. These lists of expectations should be clearly written so that there can be no misunderstandings. An example of a coach's list is shown on page 95.

Evaluate

Evaluation must be a continuous process, not something that is done only at the end of the season. After the decisions of what to do and how to do it have been made and the action has begun, then it becomes necessary to check their effectiveness. Coaches will want to look at the expectations at several points throughout the year. Many situations will be obvious while others will be more subtle, but an alert coaching staff will be aware of how they and the squad members are behaving and performing under a variety of conditions. Simple checklists are sometimes used in evaluation.

1. Am I being fair and consistent?
2. Are the players responding and behaving consistently?
3. Are the players continually behaving in an acceptable manner?
4. How are players responding to specific positive reinforcement?
5. How are players responding to specific negative reinforcement?
6. What player behaviors are affecting the situation positively?
7. What player behaviors are affecting the situation negatively?

When the coaching staff has determined the answers to these questions, then new plans can be made, old ones modified, or the present practice continued. A coach who really focuses on a team and its actions and interactions can improve the quality of life of players and also move nearer to a winning season.

SUMMARY

Behaviors are learned. Head coaches have to decide whether or not to attempt overtly to modify players' behaviors by establishing and enforcing rules. If the decision is, "Yes, there will be rules," then systematic planning specific to the situation should begin. Decisions concerning the environments to be controlled, expected behaviors, control variables, communication procedures, and evaluation need to be made. These decisions may be made by the head coach, coaching staff, and/or athletes; however, the final plans will reflect the head coach's philosophy and the standards of the school and community. These two considerations need close attention before plans are made final.

12

Life Management Concerns

DRUGS
STRESS
EDUCATION
SUMMARY

Increasingly, all educators and workers with young people are concerned about damaging and destructive behavior that appears to exist in society today and that is increasingly attractive to youth. Schools and other agencies that work with children have begun to take a pro-active rather than a re-active role in trying to protect young people's health and personalities from dangers that appear intriguing and adult. Coaches, as individuals with great influence over their players and other youth, must play an increasingly strong role in protecting players from themselves and from devastating influences both inside and outside the school or agency community.

Learning to "manage one's own life" rationally and productively is a never-ending process that has to begin at a very early age. Among many things, children have to say "no" to drugs, deal with the stresses of growing up, and master both fundamental and advanced academic skills. Because they have direct access to those who are athletes and deal with these concerns every day, coaches are front-line personnel in the war to save children and youth from excesses and actions that will harm them. They must assist their players to manage their lives successfully.

DRUGS

Studies, as well as ordinary observation, indicate that the use of drugs, including alcohol and tobacco, is prevalent among students. A survey of over 15,000 members of the senior high class of 1986 revealed that 50.9 percent had smoked marijuana, 23.4 percent had used illegal stimulants, 16.9 percent had tried cocaine, and 10.4 percent had used sedatives at least once. Just over 65 percent had drunk alcohol and 29.6 percent had smoked a cigarette within 30 days of completing the survey.[1] Being a team member does not disqualify one from being a drug user, and chemical abuse is as common among athletes as in any other group. The National Federation of High School Associations has made a firm commitment to enter the field of chemical use prevention and has sponsored workshops for coaches and players conducted by the Chemical Health Resource Center and the Hazeldon-Cork Sports Education Program.[2] School districts also provide clinics to help faculty recognize symptoms of, and behaviors related to, drug use and abuse; to give guidelines for dealing with those with drug problems; and to establish policy for all students and staff.

There are those who believe that athletes are "All American" types who would not use drugs or engage in harmful behavior, but a high school soccer coach, who is also a drug abuse counselor, says: "Any coach who doesn't think he has drugs on his team is crazy. He is either naive or ignoring it."[3] The fact is that drug abuse by children and youth is quite common and is a serious national concern.

Coaches' Concerns

Few coaches place winning above a player's health or well-being. Because they care about their players, they are disturbed when they discover that team members are not only breaking training but are also actually doing harm to themselves.

Alcohol and Tobacco

As alcohol and tobacco are the drugs most used by students, a coach can assume that this is also occurring among team members. These drugs, also commonly used by adults, are deadly and habit forming. Alcohol abuse can reduce academic, athletic, and work performance; ruin a person's health, and be a killer on the highway. The smoking of tobacco has been proved to be a cause of heart and lung disease, and chewing or dipping tobacco can lead to cancers and other mouth disorders. Besides causing health problems, smoking can interfere with athletic performance. The use of alcohol and tobacco by players cannot be permitted. A serious concern and conflict for the coach can arise if he or she drinks, smokes, chews, or dips; however, concern for the players must override personal preferences.

Performance Enhancing Drugs

Another problem and concern for coaches is the use of drugs to improve or extend a player's ability to perform athletic feats. Anabolic steroids and human growth hormones (HGH) are being seen more and more in very young athletes who want something to make them bigger and stronger. These drugs can disrupt hormonal balances and be harmful to the still-developing bodies of boys and girls. Even though a growth and weight spurt might be observed, the side effects are not worth the risks involved. It is known that the serious, and even fatal, effects of this group of drugs are more common when begun at an early age.[4] The use of steroids has been linked to liver damage, heart disease, hypertension, acne, baldness, atrophy of the testes, and aggressive and psychotic behavior in males. In females they tend to cause secondary sex characteristics such as excessive and abnormal hair distribution and deepening of the voice as well as clitoral enlargement. The most obvious and dangerous sign of the use of HGH is acromegaly, a group of characteristics known as the Frankenstein look. Coaches must be aware of any use of these drugs and

Figure 12-1 Play well without using performance enhancing drugs (Courtesy Malvern High School, Malvern, Arkansas. Photographer: Susan Scantlin)

vehemently discourage administration by parents, players, unauthorized physicians, or anyone else. Above all, a coach must never prescribe or administer these drugs.

Stimulants are also considered to be in the performance enhancing group. Amphetamines, caffeine, and ephedrine are central nervous system "uppers" that result in impairment of motor function even though the player may think that he or she is performing well. They are used to increase alertness, to decrease pain and fatigue, to improve the ability to perform simple tasks, and to suppress the appetite. The performer, not feeling fatigue, may push past the point of pain to the point of injury to the muscular and skeletal systems. Although circulation and respiration are speeded up, there is no benefit to the skeletal muscles, and stresses already on the body are compounded. These drugs do not really enhance performance, and they do cause harm to the user.[5]

Mood Enhancing Drugs

Many people, including young athletes, take drugs to "feel good." Alcohol and tobacco are among these but are not as immediately dangerous as marijuana, cocaine, heroin, lysergic acid diethylamide (LSD), polychlorinated byphenyl (PCB), and barbiturates. Marijuana is, after alcohol, the substance most abused by youth and has damaging effects on both academic and athletic performance that can last four to six weeks after use. Major effects from use include heat stress syndrome, impairment of coordination, slowed reaction time, memory loss, and prolonged learning time. There is also an antimotivational syndrome characterized by a decline in mental and physical performance, difficulty in concentrating, impaired memory, and loss of memory.[6] There is no gain, only loss, in the use of "pot."

Cocaine, reported in one study to be the most prevalent street drug after marijuana,[7] in its powdered, freebased form, as well as in its more dangerous "crack" form, can be deadly. Because it is becoming cheaper, youngsters can more readily afford it; therefore, coaches can expect to find it among the players. Cocaine use has many warning signs. It produces instant euphoria and feelings of competence, but consistent use leads to irritability and paranoid ideas and can result in convulsions and death. It is extremely addictive with an overwhelming compulsion to continue use as long as possible. Medical problems include, among others, deterioration of health, loss of energy, seizures or convulsions, constant sniffles, heart palpitations, and lack of interest in health or hygiene. Psychiatric problems include anxiety, irritability, depression, panic, delusions, loss of interest in friends, loss of memory, blackouts, and thoughts of suicide.[8] It is ironic that all these horrors are derived from something that is taken to feel good. Coaches must watch for, and be aware of, these symptoms if their players are to be saved and salvaged.

Other mood enhancing drugs—heroin, LSD, PCP among them—are also addicting and can lead to delusions, convulsions, and death. They appear not to be as readily available as marijuana and cocaine but are just as destructive to personality, performance, and health. There is nothing of value in any of these; no one wins, everyone loses.

Coaches' Actions

Knowing the effects of drug use on players can be a terrible concern for a coach, but being able to do something about it can help alleviate that concern and improve the lives of players and the program. Mental health agencies have prepared lists of characteristics of chemical drug abusers, the Drug Enforcement Administration (DEA) has published steps coaches can take, and school districts have established policies and guidelines for coaches and players. Generally, the characteristics of the abuses, the rules for coaches, and school policies apply to all drugs.

Be a Role Model

Foremost among the actions a coach must take is to be a drug-free role model, a good example, a "do as I do" person. Many coaches use alcohol and tobacco, which are licit drugs, but it may be necessary to give up drinking, smoking, and/or chewing. A coach who is concerned about the athletes must avoid these and other drugs. If individuals cannot give up personal drugs, they should consider choosing another profession where one's actions are not important to anyone's life.

Not only must coaches be passive role models but they must also be active examples in that they do not give drugs to players either to enhance performance or mood, that they keep drugs away from players, and keep players in drug-free environments. They have to decrease, not increase, problems.

Recognize Abuse

Many local mental health agencies will assist coaches in their efforts to recognize players with drug problems and offer assistance to both players and coaches in meeting those problems. Personnel will conduct workshops as well as provide information such as "sketching out" the abusive adolescent. An abuser stays up late and sleeps late, becomes a "different" person, changes friends, isolates self from family, exhibits hostility, "explodes" with little provocation, gets expelled from school, does not perform to academic ability, is dishonest and steals, is abusive, has been caught with drugs before, and is labeled a "burnout" by peers.[9] Two or three of these characteristics might be found in almost any young person, but the continued exhibiting of most of them is a danger sign that must be recognized. Anyone who works with young people in a setting like a school or agency, where there is regular contact with them, can recognize these changes and start action for remediation or rehabilitation.

Some school districts have started testing all their athletes for drug use, although it is not yet recommended by the National Federation. Drug testing by universities and professional teams is now an established procedure and is generally considered effective in determining previous use of most illicit drugs.

Take Action

The DEA has listed what coaches can do to help keep players and schools drug free. The list includes calling captains together to discuss the situation, talking with athletes as a group, enforcing all training rules and school regulations, conferring with parents about problems and about signing pledge cards, investigating violations and taking immediate action, confronting the athlete (in private), advising about legal penalties, and establishing a plan for working with athletes.[10]

Some school districts establish policies similar to these and add policies of their own. One district requires coaches to meet with parents to discuss options open to players violating drug policies: either to be suspended from the team or to seek assistance from the substance abuse specialist.[11] Another district requires athletes and parents to sign a drug-free pledge in which they acknowledge that a violation of drug policy will result in immediate suspension. (See Figure 12-2.)

The most important action a coach can take may be to help players learn to say "NO" and to avoid drugs altogether. It may be necessary to extend efforts into the elementary schools, as it appears that very young children are being introduced to the drugs. It is said that elementary children do things to make them feel older, that middle school youth do things to be accepted, and that high school students do things to have a good time. If this is so, then methods other than drug abuse must be found to satisfy needs. Some suggestions are these:

1. Expect good behavior; set up and enforce rules.
2. Teach resistance skills; practice saying "NO."

JEFFERSON COUNTY SCHOOLS

TRAINING RULE CONTRACT

The Jefferson County Schools have established certain training rules by which the young men and women who participate in the interscholastic program are expected to abide. To eliminate any misunderstanding about the rules and regulations, please *READ* them below, *SIGN* and *RETURN* the form to the school.

1. The use or possession of drugs or alcoholic beverages in any form will not be tolerated regardless of quantity. Any days of suspension as a consequence of violation of the R-1 Drug/Alcohol Policy shall be applied toward suspensions as a result of this training rule contract.

    a. The first violation of the above rule means suspension from all athletics for fifteen days from the beginning of the competitive season (inclusive of Saturdays).
    b. The second violation will result in a 60 competitive day suspension from all athletics.
    c. The third violation will result in an athlete being suspended from athletics for one calendar year.

2. The use of tobacco in any form is prohibited.
    The first violation will result in a one contest suspension if there are ten or less total contests in that sport. For sports with more than ten contests, the consequence shall be a two contest suspension. Further violations will result in doubling the original amount of the penalty for the first violation.

3. Observance of all training rules involving smoking and the use or possession of alcohol or drugs is a responsibility of the athlete.

4. Athletes are expected to conduct themselves in a commendable manner at all times in the school, the classroom, during athletic contests toward opponents, officials and spectators. The use of profane language is not acceptable and will not be tolerated.

Athletes who violate this contract *MUST* attend all practices but may not dress in team uniform or compete in any scrimmage or interschool competitions.

This contract is in effect from the signing date for one calendar year and needs to be renewed at least annually.

AS THE PARENT OF _____ I have read the above rules
(Athlete's Name)
and I understand that my son/daughter will be governed by these training rules as an athlete in the Jefferson County athletic program.

SIGNED _____
(Parent or Guardian)

SIGNED _____
(Athlete)

DATE _____

Figure 12-2   School drug policy

Courtesy of Alice Barron, Coordinator of Athletics, Jefferson County Schools, Lakewood, Colorado.

3. Use peer leaders; identify and recruit role models.
4. Focus on immediate concerns such as social acceptance instead of long-range ones like good health.
5. Obtain public commitments to a drug-free life—spoken, written, or on video tape.
6. Provide attractive alternatives; set up social as well as athletic programs that are attractive.

Anyone can see that the role of a coach in helping players or students stay drug free is difficult but rewarding. If there is to be a productive, healthy generation, coaches must be at the head of the line of action.

STRESS

It seems that society places either real or perceived pressures on children and youth that cause them emotional and physical difficulties and that lead them to find sometimes inappropriate and dangerous solutions to their problems. Families, peers, schools, and coaches may all contribute to pressures for success, popularity, and athletic prowess that are beyond the capability of the individual at that time.

Coaches' Concerns

Stress is not necessarily bad; one's body, and life, would not function without continuous input or stressors. The dangerous stress—distress—is what is commonly accepted as stress; this additional pressure, which is usually more psychological than physiological for young people, is the destructive kind. Everyone needs some stress to function at optimum levels, but too much stress can be ruinous. Helping people find the proper balance is imperative.

Families

The expectations of a player's, or student's, family can either make or break his or her self-confidence and self-concept; and it is confidence, poise, and a feeling of self-worth that help one face the world and succeed in it. Being able to perform well can assist in stress reduction.

Parents usually want only what is best for their child, but often their ideal for that child is unrealistic and tied up with parental goals rather than the youth's goals. Some are frustrated athletes themselves who want to gain glory from their child's performances. Others push their children well beyond usual expectations and even to injury and permanent physical and emotional damage.

Besides physical stress, there is the psychological stress involved in not being up to parents' expectations and in being berated for poor play. One need only watch a Little League game to observe the psychological pressure that some parents place on their children to perform beyond their developmental capabilities. If children are made to feel like failures, they will assume that they are failures—that they are no good and are not valued by the family.

Many players come from families with parents who are obviously unhappy or going through a divorce, while others come from one-parent homes where there is always a struggle to pay the bills. Both situations can be very stressful. Some may come from neglectful and abusive families who damage them physically and psychologically. Coaches must remember that family pressures are primary stressors in one's life.

Peers

Most young people want to be like, and be liked by, all other young people. The peer group, either the one the youth is in or wants to be in, can place enormous pressure on an individual. There are imagined values that young people feel they must meet—clear skin, good teeth, slim/trim bodies, designer clothes, well-styled hair, and great social poise. As most are not able to meet these standards either developmentally or economically or through heredity, there is much general depression about it. Not being popular, however that is defined, can create anxiety and frustration and lead to withdrawal and isolation. Being the "odd person out" is a terrible thing in a young person's life.

Athletes usually make up a significant group that is looked up to, or at least recognized, by their schoolmates. Even though they may be in a status position, they still have the insecurities of their peers with the added pressure of being highly visible on campus and in the community.

Academic

All students are faced with higher standards for promotion and graduation and with more frustration and anxiety because of this. Those who do not care about an education or who could slip by without studying are now faced with demands for academic performance that they are not equipped to meet.

A new stress factor for some athletes is meeting standards for admission to a college or university. Prior to the mid-1980s many knew that there were institutions of higher learning that would admit a star athlete without regard to high school academic accomplishments. Now the pressure is on to satisfy higher scholastic standards required by the National Collegiate Athletic Association.

Pressure to Win

There is definitely pressure to win in the minds of Iowa high school athletes, 66 percent of whom said that they put the pressure on themselves. Other pressures came from coaches (22 percent), the community (14 percent), and parents (4 percent).[12] One might wonder why they place this pressure on themselves and might assume that it was to please themselves, to please someone else, to gain fame and recognition, or to be a recipient of an athletic scholarship from a major university. When they were asked about negative reactions to athletic participation, their top replies were:

1. Too much time away from studies.
2. Expected to be better than others because of being an athlete.
3. Too much pressure to win.

Pressure from the coach comes in different ways. In response to what they liked least about their coaches, the Iowa students replied:

1. My coach thinks his/her sport should be my whole life.
2. My coach expects me to practice and compete the year around.
3. My coach thinks a loss makes him/her look bad.[13]

Suicide

Coaches must be concerned that suicide is a leading cause of death among young people. There is no doubt that children have problems that they cannot handle. Between 1973 and 1980, there was a 53 percent increase in referrals to a child psychiatric service, with 18 percent of all referrals being suicidal in 1984.[14] This situation has reached epidemic proportions in some cities and schools, and other agencies, have established task forces to attempt to bring relief to tormented children before it is too late. Florida, for example, requires all teachers to assume a responsibility for suicide prevention.

Not all depressed young people are suicidal, but not all seemingly cheerful ones are indeed happy. In the 1986 National Collegiate Athletic Association Outdoor Track and Field Championships an international class athlete, a pre-med major with superior grades, apparently tried to kill herself by jumping off a bridge. She was described as a classic over-achiever whose personal standards were so high she felt she had failed herself or someone else. Once one reaches the top, it becomes extremely difficult to stay there or to go higher.

There appears to be a sequence of events leading up to suicide attempts, three identifiable stages.[15] First, there is a long-standing history of problems from childhood to early adolescence primarily involving social and family instability. The second stage begins with adolescence and involves an escalation of problems and acute behavioral changes. The final stage involves a total breakdown of social relationships or failure situations. It is also reported that many suicidal attempters were not in school at the time of the attempt because of truancy or expulsion. Peer relations have suffered, social ties have been cut, the child has few friends, and there is no one to talk with about problems. There may be such acute dependency needs that peers are threatened and ultimately reject the individual.

Coaches' Actions

Coaches can, and should, play a major role in helping athletes reduce or avoid pressure. Being skillful imparters of knowledge and guidance and deliberate reducers of stress are both tasks and roles that can and must be assumed. Avoiding being a cause of serious anxiety or pressure is a serious undertaking.

Be a Communicator

Being a good communicator is an essential ingredient of success when one is dealing with athletes and parents. A coach would do well to follow these guidelines:

1. Have credibility.
2. Have a positive approach.
3. Send verbal messages high in information.
4. Communicate with consistency.
5. Learn how to listen.
6. Improve nonverbal messages.[16]

Frequently one's speech contains three messages—what was said, what the listener heard, and what the speaker meant to say. Coaches must be careful to convey clear, exact information because many problems begin with misunderstanding and misinterpretation, with simple situations becoming anxiety-producing issues. A coach has an obligation to "talk straight" to the team members and parents and to do so with kindness and compassion.

Honesty is fundamental to credible communication. When a statement is given, a promise is made, or a confidence is shared, there should be absolute reliability in the coach's integrity and goodwill. Trust, faith, and a warm relationship are stress reducers.

Coaches need to listen to athletes, to hear what they say. They can prevent stress, or at least alleviate it, by doing such simple things as listening without interrupting, asking questions to clarify a point, and showing respect for what is said. Body language—nonverbal communication—bombards team members with messages. They are aware of the coach's tone of voice, the look in his eyes, the way she holds her hands, the position of his body, the look on her face as they hear words they really do not want to hear. Nonverbal messages soften the blow of verbal ones and let the player know that the coach really cares. Knowing this may make the difference between something being understood and accepted or something becoming a traumatic situation.

Consistently providing accurate information, ranging from course requirements for graduation to how team members will be selected, is only one of a coach's responsibilities. Being a friend and listening post and offering commonsense answers to troubled youth is another opportunity to improve the life of a young person.

Be a Stress Reducer

Coaches must be aware that they create much anxiety with their demeanor, their expectations, and their practice, travel, and contest schedules and that this situation can be altered. Physical and emotional stress can be relieved by having sensible practices, reasonable schedules, and proper training procedures. Fear is also a stressor and should not be used as a motivator. Positive reinforcement can help in pressure reduction.

The player should be assisted in establishing challenging but attainable goals and asked to share in setting goals. Determining measurable, intermediate objectives will give players an opportunity for more immediate success and perhaps improve their self-concept.

With few exceptions, developing a "oneness" concept for a team is one of a coach's goals because it can be a primary determiner of how well a season goes. It can also give individual team members stability in their lives—to belong to a group is very important. Because interdependence among players does not come naturally, coaches have to be alert for situations or individuals—leaders, catalysts, loners, dividers—that can make or break a team or player. Care must be taken not to permit ethnic, religious, sexual, or handicapped jokes, comments, or slurs. Constructive behavior is a key to building successful teams and individuals.

Peers, other than team members, can also participate in supportive behavior. If coaches and other faculty both exemplify or model sound stress-reducing behaviors, and offer direct instruction about useful and acceptable stress reduction activity to athletes and nonathletes, peer influence may be valuable.

The family of an athlete can be a part of the stress reduction solution. Coaches may have to point out the pressures that they are placing on their children, as many are unaware of their actions. It may be necessary to help a parent understand the limits of a child's abilities or priorities. If the family needs assistance in reducing tension at home (which in turn places added stress on a child), the coach might find community organizations or agencies that can help.

In suicide attempts, threats, or possibilities, coaches have an obligation to provide as much personal support as possible and also to get the athlete professional help immediately. If the developmental stages of suicide are observed, the coach, the coaching staff, and the entire school or agency must be mobilized to combat it.

EDUCATION

Many students—athletes and nonathletes—who possess minimal academic skills graduate from high schools. Nonathletes may go unnoticed, but frequently athletes are referred to as "dumb jocks," and jokes about their ignorance and illiteracy are told.

It does not seem reasonable to use the dumb jock title after one recalls that an athlete became president of the United States, one currently sits on the United States Supreme Court bench, and several command a million dollars a year for playing a game. Too many, though, have not met with success in the classroom and, as a result, have found themselves unable to lead productive lives following graduation. What has happened? It is difficult to point to any one factor, but it is evident that some are "graduating" from high schools as uneducated individuals.

Coaches' Concerns

Coaches must be concerned about this academic problem that is a social issue and may become a legal one if education is a right and not a privilege. The primary immediate concern is that athletes also be students who are taking full advantage of the educational opportunities offered at the school. A second concern, which may be primary to many coaches, is that the players be academically eligible to participate in extracurricular activities. A third concern of most coaches is that athletes "make it" after graduating from high school, either continuing their formal education, entering the work force, or contributing to society in some positive way.

Academic Achievement

Teachers are expected to have various competencies, one of them being the ability to develop students' academic skills. A difficult task at best, this is almost an impossibility when students have no interest in learning. Some athletes fall in this group and are among those who shuffle along from one grade to the next even though they may be only functionally literate. Often, teachers expect very little or nothing from these students and pass them to avoid having them in class for two years in a row. Or they may be softhearted and pass the students just to be nice. Occasionally, a coach talks the teacher into making exceptions so that the failing grade will become a passing one. There are also times when a grade on a transcript gets changed by some mysterious force. If these situations exist, athletes will have little incentive to be students, especially if their coach does not push for academic achievement.

Many forces are gathering to "clean up" this academic farce. Not only are states requiring higher academic standards for promotion and graduation but are also enacting more stringent academic requirements for participation in extracurricular activities. Texas legislators led the way when they passed a law (the so-called no pass, no play rule) that prohibits high school students from participating in extracurricular activities if they do not pass all courses with a 70 percent or higher score. Other states followed suit in making standards for participation tougher, and some high school associations and individual school districts established standards above those set by governing bodies.

The regulations have a profound effect on students and teams. Some coaches fear that the requirements hurt slow learners, and some principals fear that students will seek only easy courses after the basic requirements are satisfied. Coaches and schools are concerned because many athletes are ineligible. In some cases it is not possible to field a team of superior players, and in other instances it is not possible to field a team at all. The short-range effects may be temporarily damaging to teams, but the long-range effects will be beneficial to all concerned.

The National Collegiate Athletic Association gave a major boost to high school academics with the passage of Proposition 48, a bylaw requiring high school students to take a specified course load, maintain a certain grade point average, and/or achieve a stated score on the SAT or ACT tests before entering competitive athletic programs in Division I schools. These requirements, phased in over a three-year period, began with the 1986 graduating high school seniors, and many athletes felt its impact. Thirty percent of both the football players and basketball players (male) on the *Parade* magazine All-American teams failed to qualify to compete in their freshman seasons.[17] At least 397 male athletes (224 football players, 120 basketball players, and 53 who played other sports) who were awarded athletic scholarships in 1986 were ineligible to compete in their freshman year.[18] Fifteen of the nation's top 50 high school male basketball players could not play.

After Graduation

What happens after high school graduation day? Graduates go in many directions. Many continue their formal education, some immediately join the work force, and others enlist in the armed forces. A few drift around to see the country, some hang around the park or local gathering place, and there are those who end up in the state correctional institution. There are so many good things and bad things that can happen to players that assistance is essential; sometimes a coach is the person available to give advice and support.

If, as happens in some instances, players have never had to make decisions for themselves or to be responsible for their actions because a coach was there to "take care of everything" for them, then they are at a disadvantage in the real world. Operating in a sheltered environment may do little to prepare them for life after "glory days" have ended. "Where do I go from here?" is a question asked by many high school graduates, athletes included. If they are to have productive and satisfying lives, then they must be well educated in academic, economic, and social skills. Coaches may be able to help in all three areas.

Coaches' Actions

What responsibilities do coaches have toward their athletes' educational development? They should assume a large share because they are well aware of players' potentials, problems, difficulties, and special skills, and they are in a position to help. Coaches must take action both for the players' sakes and for the good of the athletic program.

Be a Role Model

As for all athletic and personal, as well as academic, endeavors, coaches must serve as role models and present the image of an educated person. They should speak well, write well, exhibit pleasure and excitement in reading and learning, and demonstrate a high regard for education.

Most coaches are scholars of their games, keep up with all new developments, and collect extensive sports libraries. They should also keep up with local, state, and national events and read more than the sports pages. Most are educated, with at least one college degree, and thus are examples of those who choose to continue their education past high school.

If coaches are also teachers, their classes should be more than "roll out the ball and play games," as it does not take an educated person to do this. They may find it necessary to dress in something other than coaching attire on occasion and to take an active part in school programs, political action groups, and community affairs. To be seen in various roles and to be known as a well-rounded individual rather than a "jock" will be a positive influence.

Be an Educator

All coaches are teachers, whether employed by the school system or not; thus, as educators, they should be concerned with the full development of their charges, not just with one subject or one sport. The goals of education and the policies and procedures that are established for education apply to all programs and all personnel. Coaches are obligated to carry out these policies to meet these goals.

A positive interest in a student's education can be exhibited by encouraging good study habits, providing assistance with lessons, and promoting regular class attendance. Coaches should boost the value of academic skills and not permit students to do less than their best. They should get their players remedial help for basic academic skills as soon as, and as often as, necessary and encourage them in their learning tasks.

As educators concerned with players' academic accomplishments, coaches should arrange for good learning environments. This requires practice and game schedules that do not interfere with class schedules, study time, or opportunities for sufficient rest. An emerging pattern is one of assigning an assistant coach to act as an academic advisor. The coach's duties include making sure that athletes take the required courses, attend classes, and arrange a reasonable class schedule. Too, they monitor the athletes' academic progress and encourage them to take the ACT or SAT as soon as possible. A few coaches are now substituting a study hall for a practice period (Thursday before a football game scheduled for Friday) to ensure some supervised schoolwork.

Academic integrity is an important possession of an educator, and coaches have their integrity questioned more often than most faculty members do. Resisting the temptation to cheat, they must be a positive force for honesty and trustworthiness. The idea of learning by doing, doing one's own work, has to supported. There must be no attempt to induce other faculty to lower academic standards for their players. Grades on transcripts are recorded "in concrete" as far as a coach is concerned; there must be no tampering.

Coaches are to assist in providing educational opportunities for the athletes, not to do the work for them. Part of one's education is to develop self-discipline and to assume responsibility for one's own actions. Coaches can, and should, do only so much; then it must be left to the athlete to follow through with the work. Coaches serve as resource persons and facilitators.

Be a Career Starter

Many athletes need help with their careers, in finding jobs and/or in continuing their formal education. Too few have connections that are frequently necessary for entering the work force or an institution of higher learning. Coaches know their players and the people in the community; the people in the community know the coaches. It seems logical that coaches become employment agents, matching prospective employers with athletes who are prospective employees or, at least, arranging interviews. The athletes may need additional assistance with such things as what to wear, what questions to ask, what information the employer will ask, and the like. If coaches cannot supply this information, then athletes should be referred to someone who can.

There is a need for coaches to know about colleges and universities, particularly their academic programs, athletic programs, and coaching staffs. It may be convenient for them to visit campuses to talk with selected personnel and look over the facilities or to talk with current and former students, specifically athletes. Bulletins, fliers, and catalogs are available, and having these on file could be useful for prospective students. Most athletes will seek their coach's advice about continuing their education, and the coach should be able to help them although the final choice must be made by the player and the parents. In talking with the athletes, both they and the coach may find it helpful if the coach follows these suggestions:

1. Encourage better athletes to attend summer sports camps where they can be seen by college coaches.
2. Stress the importance of selecting a college for reasons other than the reputation of the athletic program.
    a. The programs and degrees offered.
    b. The size of the institution. Is the population of some dormitories larger than the home town's, or is it too small?
    c. The caliber of competition. Is the individual likely to do well?
    d. The location of the college. Will the parents be able to see the games, will it be too expensive for the athlete to come home occasionally, or is the campus isolated or in the city?
    e. The total cost of an education. What will be the expenses above the amount of a scholarship?
    f. The stability of the coaching staff. Is the head coach moving up or down or out?
    g. The percentage of athletes that graduate.
3. Suggest that several levels of colleges be considered, particularly if the athlete is not sure of his or her capabilities.
4. Encourage the athlete to consider carefully and narrow the choices to a few as soon as possible.
5. Encourage athletes to visit campuses to look over the environment and talk with different people.
6. Leave the decision making to the athlete and the parents.[19]

SUMMARY

Athletes have to learn to manage their own lives, and coaches should help them. This is a duty that must be performed.

Drug abuse has entered homes, schools, and playgrounds; a stressful society is taking its toll of youth; suicide is growing among young people and presents a terrible waste of talent and potential; and pressures for improved academic performance have increased. Coaches have an obligation to combat drug abuse, to reduce stressors, to watch for signs of acute personal distress, and to encourage athletes to study and graduate.

The coaches' actions in helping players learn life management skills are to be a good role model, to care about their team members, and to encourage them to develop physically, emotionally, and academically. It is imperative that young people are led to believe that they can "overcome" and "become."

ENDNOTES

1. "Drug Use By High School Seniors," *Drugs and Drug Abuse Newsletter* (January/February 1987): 11.
2. "Workshops Benefit More Than 12,000," *National Federation News* (January 1986): 17.
3. R. Dennis, "Drugs in School: Sobering Issue for Prep Athletes," *Florida Times Union* (January 19, 1986): C-3.
4. R. T. Bergman, "Drug Abuse: An Ever Growing Problem," reprinted from "The First Aider, Cramer Products, Inc." in *National Federation News* (April 1985): 27.
5. Ibid.
6. Ibid.
7. "Express Emotions Through Alcohol," *Drugs and Drug Abuse Newsletter* (December 1985): 113.
8. M. Gold, "1-800-COCAINE," Pamphlet (Delray, Fla.: Florida Medical Board for 1-800-Cocaine).
9. M. J. McCarthy, "General Sketch of the Chemically Abusive Adolescent," unpublished document, Apalachee Community Mental Health Services, Tallahassee, Florida.
10. "What Coaches Can Do," pamphlet *For Coaches Only* cited in *National Federation News* (April 1985): 29.
11. "Drug and Alcohol Guidelines," *Policy Guidelines for Student Activities in Leon County, Florida* (1985): 74.
12. "Athletic Participation: Students Give Their Views," *National Federation News* (April 1985): 4.
13. Ibid.
14. M. Shaffi, J. R. Whittinghill, D. C. Dolen, V. D. Pearson, A. Derrick, and S. Carrigan, "Psychological Reconstruction of Completed Suicide in Childhood and Adolescence," in *Suicide in the Young,* ed. H. S. Sudak, A. B. Ford, and N. B. Rushforth (Boston: John Wright and P.S.G. Inc., 1984), pp. 271–294.
15. D. Anderson, "Diagnosis and Prediction of Suicide Risk Among Adolescents," in *Self Destructive Behavior in Children and Adolescents*, ed. C. F. Wells and I. R. Stuart (New York: Van Nostrand and Reinhold Co., 1981), pp. 45–47.
16. R. Martens, R. W. Christina, J. S. Hower, and B. Sharkey, *Coaching Young Athletes* (Champaign, Ill.: Human Kinetics Publishers, 1981): p. 29.
17. "Rule 48 Leaves Holes," *Tallahassee Democrat,* (August 13, 1986): C-2.

18. K. Mulligan, "Prop Outs," *Tallahassee Democrat* (August 24, 1986): F-1.
19. R. J. Sabock, "Recruiting," *Journal of Physical Education, Recreation and Dance* (August 1985): 26.

PART 3

The Coach as an Administrator

13

Fiscal Management

FINANCING
THE BUDGET
SUMMARY

Coaches cannot afford to focus solely on their athletes and the team's win-loss records, nor can they limit their knowledge and skill to the X's and O's of coaching a sport. Some of the most critical, frustrating, and difficult problems that a coach encounters, irrespective of sport or agency, occur in the area of fiscal management. Economic conditions, government legislation, and public attitude may result in a lack of financial support that threatens the existence of an athletic program or a specific team. Problems resulting from lack of funding are compounded by coaches' lack of knowledge and skill in getting additional support in the form of money or gifts-in-kind, in managing funds, and in dealing with budgets.

FINANCING

With the trend of reduced government spending, the continual threat of inflation, and an unstable economy for many businesses and families, supporters of public and private schools resist efforts to increase taxes, tuitions, or donations that fund an agency. When funding fails to keep up with inflation or increased costs caused by other reasons, supplemental revenue must be obtained. Few athletic teams have been self-supporting even though coaches' salaries, utilities, and cost of support personnel (such as custodians) are generally paid for by a school's general fund. A common practice has been for one or two high revenue sports to generate sufficient funds to cover the entire athletic budget for equipment and travel expenses. However, if revenue-producing sports can support only themselves and if taxpayers fight to cut taxation or to place their dollars in something other than athletics, it becomes imperative for a coach to seek additional sources of support.

Factors Affecting the Cost

Predicting the cost of running an athletic program is hazardous but necessary. All an administrator can do is be cognizant of the economic situation, project high, and hope that the program will be able to operate in the black. The factors that will primarily determine whether the pro-

Economic Conditions

jected budget will be sufficient—national, state, and local economies; energy supplies and cost; demands of federal legislation—are all out of the coach's control; however, they should be of primary interest.

The state of the economy cannot be separated from anything that is tied to money, athletic programs included. Sources of funds for all budget items—travel, officials, salaries, equipment, utilities, insurance—are affected by the financial plight of a particular region or the nation as a whole. Inflation has a direct effect on the cost of operations; the dollar does not go as far as it did! If the numbers of unemployed increase, the funds that individuals have to spend on extras are reduced, thereby hurting gate receipts and booster contributions. Also, the closing of a business or plant will sharply affect the tax base of a small or moderate-size community. The trend toward conservative fiscal policies at all levels of government has affected all school activities and has a particular impact on athletics.

Energy

Now, as always, energy is a critical concern. It is closely tied to the economy and, therefore, contributes to problems that have just been discussed. Energy, the lack of it or the cost of it, creates special fiscal problems that must be given serious thought and consideration. The prices paid for energy—particularly in the forms of gas, electricity, and petroleum-based products—deplete a budget rapidly. Oil prices may drop and travel become less expensive, or the cost of electricity and products manufactured from petroleum may remain high. Whatever the situation, coaches must make budget decisions with energy in mind. In the following chapters, more will be said about special considerations that should be given to this issue when making decisions about equipment, scheduling, and transportation.

Federal Legislation

The legislation that created financial problems in many schools in the 1970s was Title IX of the Education Amendments of 1972, which was finally effective in 1978. It mandated that no individual shall be discriminated against on the basis of sex in any educational institution receiving federal funds in any form. The *Grove City College (PA)* v. *Bell* ruling by the United States Supreme Court in February 1984 eliminated most of the strength of this 1970s legislation, so currently, Title IX prohibits sex discrimination in specific programs and activities receiving direct benefit of federal funds. There is strong support from various groups and individuals for Congress to approve legislation that will restore Title IX to its original institution-wide strength.

Another law that caused financial problems in schools is Public Law 94-142, also effective in 1978, which requires no discrimination on the basis of handicapping conditions, and provides that students should be placed and allowed to perform in the least restrictive environment. It does not require interscholastic athletic programs for handicapped students, but it does require that they be permitted to participate in as advanced programs as their skills will take them. Individual rules committees of the National Federation of State High School Associations revised rules of several sports so as to accommodate athletes with handicapping conditions. Also, facilities and equipment were altered. For example, the Illinois State High School Athletic Association experimented with a light located on the side of the track and synchronized with the starter's gun to allow a more equitable start for deaf and hard-of-hearing runners.[1]

In an attempt to decrease the federal deficit, there is continual proposal of bills to control spending and redefine the tax structure. The primary one of note in the mid-80s was the Gramm-Rudman Bill, designed to balance the national budget by 1991. When such bills are passed, it can mean a cut in fund allocation for education, which, in turn, lessens financial support for extracurricular activities.

Public Attitude

The desire for a comprehensive sports program by an agency must be matched by the community's desire to support this program adequately. As the public becomes more concerned with what their tax dollars are funding and with the need for higher academic standards, athletics become less important to many. Nevertheless, the interest in athletics remains high, even though the 1985 report of the National Federation of State High School Associations indicated a slight decrease in the number of participants in high school athletics between 1980 and 1985. Male participation decreased by 4 percent, while female participation decreased by 5 percent. No comparison can be made between these data and the 1977–78 report (the year of peak participation in high school athletics) since the federation changed the method of collecting data. Male participation in high school athletics still approximately doubles female participation.

The 1985 report also indicated a slight decrease in the number of state championships that were sponsored by state associations. However, all schools do not field teams in all sports, as it is not financially feasible when many of the sports are non-revenue producing and depend on the community for additional support. The coach and athletic department must work so that there will be no poor cousins, as participants in the so-called "minor sports" should expect to travel, eat, sleep, have quality equipment, and receive the same type of award as do athletes who participate in "major sports."

Sources of Revenue

The potential sources of revenue are as endless as the imagination of the coach, athletic director, or individual placed in charge of increasing funding. Each community supports programs differently, but it seems to be an exception rather than a rule when they are totally financed by tax money. Even when gate receipts and other revenue are added to a tax allocation, only a few of the most successful programs meet their financial needs.

One who is, or desires to be, a coach must be ready to be a financial wizard. Coaches must not only raise funds but must also be able to estimate rather accurately the amount of expected revenue (see Figure 13–1). Common sources of the expected revenue are discussed in the following pages.

```
Activity _____        Head Coach _____
Academic Year _____           Date Filed _____


1. Gate Receipts
      Season Tickets      _____ @ _____ = _____
      Single Contest      _____ @ _____ = _____
      Invitational Event  _____ @ _____ = _____
                                                            Total (1) _____
2. Concessions
     Food
       Popcorn                                          _____
       Peanuts                                          _____
       Cold Drinks                                      _____
       Coffee                                           _____
       Hotdogs                                          _____
       Programs          _____ @ _____ = _____
                                                            Total (2) _____
3. Fund-Raising Projects
       Auction                                          _____
       Bingo Night                                      _____
                                                            Total (3) _____
4. Community Support
       Booster Donations                                _____
       Advertisements                                   _____
                                                            Total (4) _____
5. Miscellaneous
                                                            Total (5) _____

                                                   Grand Total  _____
```

Figure 13-1   Estimated revenue

Schools' General Budget Allocations

Funds from general allocations supply the major share of athletic dollars, whether the school is private or public or whether the money comes from taxes, private donations, or church boards. The percent of athletic support from the school budget varies from school to school, but some funding is essential. Many school districts believe that athletics are as much a part of the educational program as are English, science, and mathematics, and should be funded in the same way. At the other end of the spectrum are the schools that provide very little funding of athletic programs. Somewhere in the middle are school districts that provide each high school minimum funding for equipment, officials, transportation of students, fees, travel costs for coaches, and catastrophic insurance for participants for all sports (boys and girls) except football.

It is often heard that athletic programs are self-supporting, but such statements are not true. Individuals making such comments have given little thought or consideration to the actual cost of athletics and to where funds come from. When expenditures from general allocations are analyzed, it can be seen that thousands of dollars are spent for salaries, buildings, fields, and operating costs, and that programs would not exist without this basic funding.

Salary supplements for coaching seldom come out of gate receipts. These supplements, or coaching salaries, are usually paid from the district salary budget and are not charged against the athletic budget or the school's general fund.

Facilities, such as gymnasiums and fields, may require the largest expenditure from bonds, taxes, or the school's general account. This is not charged to the athletic account. The funds for original construction of such facilities are usually received from school bonds and are used for instruction as well as for athletics. In some schools, special funds are set aside for additional new construction (such as scoreboards, press boxes, film rooms, weight rooms), but often these are gifts from boosters or friends.

Maintenance cost for the upkeep of facilities is generally paid from the school's maintenance budget. This maintenance may also include the preparation and cleanup required for a contest. It is not unusual, however, for the school to charge the athletic budget a set fee or a percentage of the gate receipts to cover such custodial costs and maintenance services. Some schools absorb the cost of utilities; others will charge the athletic budget a utilities fee for contests but not for practice time. These utilities costs alone reach an impressive figure over a year's time.

Seed money consists of funds that are often allocated to new schools, to old schools to upgrade their programs, or to those that are going to initiate a new program, to allow the purchase of new equipment. This was a frequent occurrence with the girls' athletic programs in the 1970s as innumerable groups needed one-time allocations to get the sports started. In some districts this money is loaned and must be paid back from future revenues, while other districts ask no repayment. These funds may come from local tax dollars or from a special tax levied (by the school district) on each ticket sold for an athletic contest. An example of a special tax levy would be a 10 cent charge for every ticket sold, the money going into a seed money replacement account.

Transportation is also subsidized by many school districts. Athletic teams frequently make use of school buses or vans, with the athletic budget charged only for the driver's salary and fuel. In some instances, not even these expenses are charged to athletics.

Gate Receipts

This source of revenue is not very dependable, and setting expenditures based on estimated gate receipts should be done in a very conservative manner. If the sport is having a good season, the weather is favorable, or the community is very supportive, gate receipts may be high. However, one bad night in terms of weather, a series of losses, or the lack of community interest can cause gate receipts to fall far short of estimations. A labor strike or other crises within the economy occurring during a season could also affect income from this source. Gate receipts generally are an important source of revenue and are used in a variety of ways, depending on the school. In some instances the entire operating budget must be covered by ticket sales. Others require revenue sports to generate their budget while the school provides nonrevenue sports with money. Still other schools will approve a budget that meets the needs of the program; then, if the gate receipts of the revenue sports do not generate sufficient funds, the school will provide the difference from a contingency fund. The latter method appears to be based on the soundest educational philosophy.

Ticket sales and the price of tickets should be determined by the market value of the product or what the target population will pay to see a sports event. Regardless of how much money is needed, it makes no sense to charge more (or less) than fans are willing to pay. Athletic departments have many "publics" to be concerned about. Students, working adults in the community, retired persons, military personnel, special interest groups, and so on, need to be considered. Tickets for children and senior citizens are frequently priced lower than those for other citizens. Group rates are sometimes available to scout troops, families, church youth, and local civic organizations. The population needs to be surveyed before a final decision on the price of a ticket is made.

Annual all-sports tickets that provide reduced price admission to all sports events are sold by many schools. These are made available to students as well as to adults. The sale of these tickets combines the advantage of having funds early and of having fewer ticket-selling campaigns. Receipts are allocated by a formula based on the price of the ticket.

Season tickets provide a guaranteed income and operating cash at the beginning of the season. If the athletic account is at a critical level, money generated by early season ticket sales could make a significant contribution to a balanced account. Many individuals buy season tickets, knowing that they will attend only a few events, just to give financial support to the school. Some businesses buy season tickets to give their customers or to show their support for the program. They are pleased to display a certificate stating, *"We Support the Lions—Season Ticket Purchaser."* There are other advantages to season ticket purchasers: the average price per contest is usually reduced, perhaps 20 percent; they do not have to stand in lines; they are often provided with the best reserved seats in the stands and have reserved parking places; and, in a few schools, they have a special lounge.

Season ticket sales campaigns must be well organized if they are to succeed. Any plan should include several major points:

1. Advertise at the beginning of the sales effort. Support of the communication media is necessary to help publicize the campaign. Posters, fliers, and banners need to be placed throughout the community where large numbers of people are likely to see them. Announcements made at school gatherings, civic club meetings, and other appropriate group functions will convey the message.

2. Make it convenient for the fan to buy a ticket. Identify numerous locations in the community, in addition to the school, where purchases can be made. These sites must be carefully located so that fans can get to them conveniently and quickly. Store owners or managers are frequently very willing to permit their establishments to be used as a ticket outlet.
3. Mobilize team supporters to help with the campaign. Many communities have successfully used the booster club to conduct sales. Set goals that are attainable, but allow for the possibility of exceeding the target and give recognition awards to the top sales group or individuals.

Booster Organizations

More and more schools are turning to booster clubs as an organizational alternative for supplementing the athletic program's revenues, and those schools have found that this is much more efficient than having each coach or team attempt a money-raising project. The value of such groups to the total operation is important to any sports team. Chapter 23 contains information regarding such support groups.

Special Projects

Large amounts of money are raised by athletes, parents, and coaches in many different types of projects. These are the same type used by the boosters, but projects may not be as successful because of the available manpower that a community-wide organization can provide. A few of the more common projects are:

1. Selling door-to-door in the community, as well as at school, such items as candy, nuts, fruit, donuts, theater tickets. (See Figure 13-2.)
2. Staffing concession stands at school lunch hours, before and after classes, for special functions, at community and county events.
3. Working at group projects such as washing cars, picking and selling fruits/vegetables, collecting materials that can be recycled, organizing an all-sports carnival.
4. Organizing celebrity tournaments, tournaments for area sports teams, garage sales, pancake breakfasts, fish dinners, sports camps.
5. Placing vending machines in the school.
6. Sponsoring jog-a-thons, swim-a-thons, volleyball-serving contests, free-throw contests.
7. Holding raffles, bingo parties, work days, auctions.
8. Hosting a "roast" of a local celebrity; sponsoring a concert of local artists.
9. Selling novelty items such as T-shirts, pennants, caps, bumper stickers.

There are also many commercial fund-raising companies that will come to the school, organize, and help run a fund-raising project. Schools that utilize the help of such companies usually make considerably more

STUDENT FUND RAISING PERMISSION CARD

LCS — Leon County Schools

EVENT _____

DATE _____ TIME _____

SPONSOR _____

EMERGENCY PHONE NUMBER AND CONTACT PERSON

_____

_____

Your child, _____, has voluntarily chosen to participate in the above fund raising activity. This event has been approved by the Principal, with the understanding that the following guidelines will be observed:

1. The "buddy system" will be used.
2. No "after dark" door to door sales.
3. Student will detach and wear the I.D. card found at the bottom of this form (must be visible).
4. Students will not enter any residence.
5. The "sale" may only take place during the above date and time.

Parent/Guardian's signature

_____ date _____

- -

LCS — Leon County Schools

DATE _____

TIME _____

STUDENT'S NAME _____

SCHOOL _____

CLUB _____

EMERGENCY PHONE NUMBER AND PERSON TO CONTACT _____

This student is involved in a school approved/fund raising activity. We would appreciate your support.

Figure 13-2   Special project identification card

Courtesy of Jeff Dukes, Director of Student Activities, Leon County School District, Tallahassee, Florida.

money than do those who run their own projects. The school administration must be careful when scheduling and coordinating fund-raising projects. Proper spacing of the dates of each event in relation to what segment of the community will be affected is essential to avoid duplication of effort and to assure each organization a successful fund-raising endeavor. In terms of time, effort, and the cost to produce a single project, it may be better to have teams (whether all in one school or in several schools) sponsor one big fund-raising project each year.

Money raised from these types of activities usually is deposited in the school's activity fund, athletic fund, or similar internal account, with the sport for which the money was raised credited with the deposit. Normally, school districts do not permit school organizations to open individual banking accounts.

Advertisements

Merchants and businesses can be a valuable source of revenue through a well-planned program of advertisement selling. If the athletic department conducts a strong public relations program with the business segment of the community, their support will be forthcoming—both financially and politically. Advertisements in game programs, on scoreboards, on outfield fences, on the backs of tickets, or on season schedules can generate considerable revenue. Another item that helps to promote the athletic program is the small wallet-sized schedule card. Businesses will often print these free of charge if their advertisement can go on one side; however, a school cannot expect local businesspeople to buy advertising if they were ignored when it came time to purchase equipment and supplies sold by the local dealers. This is not to say that schools must buy only from local merchants, but they should be given the opportunity to bid on the school's supplies and equipment needs.

Planning and organizing for an ad campaign is usually a task for the coach or the athletic director. Some coaches tackle this task alone, but a clever one will involve the staff and team supporters. Sometimes parents or booster clubs can assist with this planning. This eases the burden on the coach and at the same time provides interested people in the community an opportunity to become involved in the program in a tangible way. People will be more likely to contribute to a program if they have been a part of the action and can identify with its success.

Prospective advertisers may be identified by contacting booster club members, parents, and other school personnel. Some of the advertisers may very well be members of the boosters. When names are provided, an appointment must be made to meet with the individual responsible for advertisement. This person should know who the coach is and the purpose of the meeting. The coach should clearly state the time and day of the appointment, as any misunderstanding with a busy executive may turn off a "live prospect." All appointments must be kept.

Soliciting funds, though not easy for some coaches, is an essential task. A well-organized "game plan" is a necessary first step. Campaigns should be conducted in a businesslike manner. The coach has to do homework in order to know something about the business and the businessperson that will be promoted through the sports program. One way to interest a person in the school's program is by being interested in the concerns of the business. The coach, like any salesperson in the business world, must be well prepared to make a presentation to the manager, owner, or executive in charge of advertisement. Coaches should be knowledgeable about what they are trying to sell. Ideas concerning layout, size, costs, location in the program or on the fence, or other related information are essential. One should dress appropriately and be prepared to make the best impression possible. Many businesses buy ads only as a service to the school or athletic program; but, in doing so, they like to be shown the courtesy that a respected person and member of the business community should command.

Student Activity Fees

Many schools assess each student a basic fee at the beginning of the year. The money generated by this fee is used to support all student activities, including athletics. The funds are deposited into a single account and then allocated to eligible organizations by some predetermined formula.

Advantages of this approach are fourfold. The first is that all club and sport organizations in the school will have minimum funding at the beginning of the year. Another advantage is that the amount of money generated can easily and fairly accurately be determined, since it is based on enrollment, which can usually be predicted within a few students. The third advantage is similar to that of the season tickets. Students do not have to stand in line, and they pay a reduced rate. The advantage for the athletic program is that every student paying the fee will not attend every athletic event, so many nonspectators are still contributing to the financial support of the program.

Disadvantages of instituting the student fee program include community opposition. Many parents feel that the student activity fee is just another form of taxation with which to finance the school. These parents feel that schools are free and public, provided by law, and already paid for through taxes. They oppose any additional charges. Another disadvantage of the standard fee is the plight of the student whose parents cannot afford the fee, especially parents who may have a large number of children in school. If this plan is instituted in a school, there must be alternative plans ready for the student who is unable to pay. The student may possibly work at the school to earn the fee card, or be granted the fee card following procedures and guidelines that are used in the free or reduced price lunch program.

Participation Fees

In a small percentage of schools, athletes pay a user fee; it costs to be a member of a team. Fees vary from school to school. A student may pay as little as $5 or as much as $50 for the privilege of being an "athlete," with the fees usually being deposited in the school's general fund or in the general athletic account. Typically, adjustments are made for students from the same family, those who participate in more than one sport, and those who cannot afford to pay.

Anyone considering the implementation of a fee system must take care to ensure its legality. Charging for participating in a public school function may be in violation of laws in some states.

Other Internal Sources

The sources of revenue that have already been discussed provide the most dollars, but there are other sources within the school or organization that may be very lucrative and contribute a great deal to the athletic program. Coaches are always looking for new or unique ways to raise money, but there are several activities that have proved to be consistent suppliers of revenue.

Concessions at sporting events are excellent revenue sources. Many schools will permit sport groups, particularly nonrevenue-producing sports, to operate concessions at events that attract large numbers of people. At some schools, clubs or organizations must bid for the concessions, while at other schools each organization that is interested is given the concessions on a rotating basis. A school may assign the concessions to the junior class, who use the profits to pay for the prom. At other schools the concessions are treated like gate receipts, the sole property of the athletic department. If this is permitted, coaches having the supervisory responsibility must organize it as a business operation. Those who look for a good profit margin set up a system of careful checks and balances regarding the handling of money and control of supplies. They cater to the interests and tastes of the clientele and order with care to ensure that what is ordered is what will sell, resulting in a reasonably high profit. Many concessionnaires do not stock a great variety of items and will sell only those items on which they can make at least a 50 percent profit.

Program sales can also be profitable, as they generally contain advertisements that pay for the printing. The decisions about who is permitted to operate the program sales concession is generally handled in the same manner as are concessions. If athletes are permitted to sell programs, the money may go to the general athletic account or may be assigned to the sport whose athletes sell the programs. In either case the operation should be conducted in a businesslike manner. Work teams established with team leaders can help ensure organization and adequate coverage of the crowd. A system for inventory and fiscal control must be established so that all workers know who is responsible. As with concessions, an accurate accounting system is a must if profits are to be realized. The school usually has an established policy concerning the handling of money by student organizations, but, as supervisor, the coach is ultimately responsible for the total program.

Towel fees are assessed at many schools. Students in physical education and athletics are required to pay a fee by the term, by the sport, or for the entire year. If these schools have their own towels and laundry equipment, rather than having towels supplied by a commercial company, sizable profits can be realized. These fees are usually credited to a laundry account, and at regular intervals the excess funds that are available, after laundry expenses have been paid out and the towel inventory replenished, are usually split and transferred into the physical education and athletic accounts. A great deal of work goes into towel service in relation to financial returns. Unless an accurate towel checkout system is used, inventories can and will be lost; it does not take many towels to account for a semester's profit. Coaches will also have to do much of the laundry to eliminate the costs of labor that could consume the majority of the profits. The use of student managers could help eliminate some of the pressure on the coaches. In rare instances booster clubs provide volunteers to help with this project.

Lock and locker fees work in the same way as the towel fee does but are probably more common than the towel service. Some schools will place lock and locker fees into the school's general fund, and all that athletics can realize from the fee is a supply of locks and sufficient locker space for the athletic teams.

Vending machines are managed by the athletic department in many schools, with the profits contributing to the support of the athletic programs. Carefully placed machines can yield considerable profit. State and federal legislation governing school lunch programs may prohibit the machines from containing carbonated beverages and candy, but many other items, such as fruit, fruit juices, milk, nuts, and sugar-free gum, may be sold. One who is patient, efficient, and honest should be placed in charge, as keeping the machines well stocked is a never-ending task; and handling money and students is a very time-consuming, mentally taxing process.

THE BUDGET

As inflation decreases the buying power of the athletic dollar, careful and wise planning becomes extremely important. The budget is the essential element in prudent fiscal management. It must be reflective of program goals and objectives, long-term as well as immediate, and should show the priorities of the program. With funding for athletics at most schools failing to keep pace with increasing costs, with the need to split the community's sports dollars between men's and women's sports, and with the increased criticism of athletics that is occurring in some areas, placing the athletic program on a solid financial foundation is essential. The coach of each sport must be actively involved in developing the total athletic budget and must make sure that each program is accountable.

Types of Budgets

Two types of budgets concern a coach: long-range and short-range. The long-range budget will be for more than a year and could be as long as 10 to 15 years, with the average length from 3 to 5 years. This budget will reflect long-term needs and goals of the athletic program. Such items as maintenance, renovations, and new structures may appear on the long-range budget but may not show up on a budget for a specific year. If a conscientious job is done with the long-range plan, many maintenance or equipment emergencies will not occur. In estimating the receipts and expenses over several years, coaches must be very careful. Because of the energy problem and inflation, even three-year projections are a guess. This still does not eliminate the value of the long-range budget.

The short-term or annual budget reflects what is needed to operate the sport or total program for one fiscal year. For schools, the fiscal year generally runs from July 1 to June 30; however, it is becoming more popular to have the fiscal year run from the beginning of school in the fall to the beginning of the next school year, such as September 1 to August 31. It is also possible to find schools whose fiscal year will run the same as the calendar year.

The budget is a record of estimated and requested expenses. Once approved, it serves as a guide against misuse of the athletic funds; it will ensure that money is spent on priority items and not on coaches' fancies. This budget, along with those of all other departments in the school, is used to establish the school's total budget.

A budget is typically composed of four sections, with the first section generally reserved for a statement of philosophy, goals, and objectives. The second section should be an overview, showing expenditures and receipts by broad categories. This section is a summary of the third section and should be arranged so that a person can look quickly to see if the proposed budget is balanced, or if equal funding is planned. Section three is the portion containing the itemized expenses of each team and the detailed lists of projected receipts. The athletic director usually requires coaches to develop this type of budget for their specific sport. The last section contains supporting materials, such as team schedules.

Contemporary coaches use a computer to facilitate budget preparation and management. Nearly all schools have microcomputers that faculty members may use; if one can read, follow directions, and type (a hunt-and-peck method is sufficient), he or she can use them. Software exists that will place inventories, past budgets, projected revenues, expenses, and the like, at a coach's fingertips.

Budget Preparation

Techniques used to develop the annual and long-range budgets are the same; the scope of consideration may be a little different. The long-range budget may contain more capital outlay items and more items that deal with maintenance and renovation, whereas the annual budget will contain mostly supply items, plus a few maintenance or renovation items that will occur during the upcoming year. Most school budgets contain three types of expenditures: capital outlay, expense, and maintenance. Capital outlay is expenditures for items that will last for some time (such as weight machines, mats, goals, lockers). Expense items are those related to travel, uniforms, salaries, and other expendable items (such as balls, bats, trainer's supplies). School maintenance budgets could provide additional funds for athletics, as some schools will permit the renovation of equipment to be paid out of the general maintenance budget.

The actual form and content of a budget that a coach must turn in will vary from school to school, depending on local demands. Some administrators will require the coach to list resources needed with details and justifications. Other administrators will provide a form that requires extensive listing in detail of items requested, almost to the point of counting paper clips. Most coaches hope for a middle-of-the-road approach. The budget document should contain enough detail to provide essential information needed to operate the program and show at a glance the planned expenditures and receipts. Figure 13–3 shows a sample form that might be used in constructing a budget. This particular

Activity _____   Head Coach _____

Category 1. Transportation

TO: A _____ mi. rd. trip @ _____ = _____
    B _____ mi. rd. trip @ _____ = _____
    C _____ mi. rd. trip @ _____ = _____
    D _____ mi. rd. trip @ _____ = _____
    E _____ mi. rd. trip @ _____ = _____
    F _____ mi. rd. trip @ _____ = _____
    G _____ mi. rd. trip @ _____ = _____
    H _____ mi. rd. trip @ _____ = _____
    I _____ mi. rd. trip @ _____ = _____
    J _____ mi. rd. trip @ _____ = _____

                                          Total (1) _____

Category 2. Scouting

TO: A _____ mi. rd. trip @ _____ = _____
    B _____ mi. rd. trip @ _____ = _____
    C _____ mi. rd. trip @ _____ = _____
    D _____ mi. rd. trip @ _____ = _____
    E _____ mi. rd. trip @ _____ = _____
    F _____ mi. rd. trip @ _____ = _____
    G _____ mi. rd. trip @ _____ = _____
    H _____ mi. rd. trip @ _____ = _____
    I _____ mi. rd. trip @ _____ = _____
    J _____ mi. rd. trip @ _____ = _____

                                          Total (2) _____

Category 3. Meals

Event: _____
      Breakfast _____ Lunch _____ Dinner _____ = _____
Event: _____
      Breakfast _____ Lunch _____ Dinner _____ = _____
Event: _____
      Breakfast _____ Lunch _____ Dinner _____ = _____
Event: _____
      Breakfast _____ Lunch _____ Dinner _____ = _____

                                          Total (3) _____

Category 4. Motels (indicate room rate per day)

Event: _____
    _____ Rooms for _____ nights = _____
Event: _____
    _____ Rooms for _____ nights = _____
Event: _____
    _____ Rooms for _____ nights = _____

                                          Total (4) _____

(continued)

Figure 13-3   Worksheet: proposed athletic budget for 19 ____ to ____

Category 5. New Equipment
   Quantity   Item Description   Unit Price   Extension

                                                              Total (5) _____

Category 6. Medical Supplies
   Quantity   Item Description   Unit Price   Extension

                                                              Total (6) _____

Category 7. Workers
  Name:
  Task:
  Rate/Total:

  Name:
  Task:
  Rate/Total:

  Name:
  Task:
  Rate/Total:

                                                              Total (7) _____

Category 8. Security
    _____ Games @ _____

                                                              Total (8) _____

Category 9. Officials
    _____ Games @ _____

                                                              Total (9) _____

Category 10. Guarantees
  School _____ Amount _____
  School _____ Amount _____
  School _____ Amount _____
  School _____ Amount _____

                                                             Total (10) _____

Category 11. Printing
   Quantity   Description   Unit Price   Extension

                                                              Total (11) _____

(continued)

Figure 13–3   Continued

Category 12. Awards
   Type   Estimated Number   Unit Price   Extension

                                           Total (12) _____

Category 13. Miscellaneous Office Expense
   Quantity   Item Description   Unit Price   Extension

                                           Total (13) _____

Category 14. Film Program: Film and Processing
   _____ Rolls @ _____ + Processing _____ = _____
   Transportation/Mailing _____ Rolls @ _____ = _____

                                           Total (14) _____

Category 15. Equipment Repairs
   Quantity   Item Description   Unit Price   Extension

                                           Total (15) _____

Category 16. Entry Fee
   Approximate Date   Event   Fee Amount

                                           Total (16) _____

Category 17. Tickets
   Season   _____ Rolls @ _____ = _____
   Single Event   _____ Rolls @ _____ = _____
   Tournament   _____ Rolls @ _____ = _____
                                           Total (17) _____

Category 18. Tournaments—Host
   A. Officials   _____
   B. Score Keeper   _____
   C. Clock Operator   _____
   D. Tournament Mgr.   _____
   E. Janitorial Service _____
   F. Awards   _____
   G. Other (specify)   _____
                                           Total (18) _____

Category 19. Other (please specify)

                                           Total (19) _____
                                      Grand Total (1–19) _____

Figure 13-3   Continued

form, providing for a moderate amount of detail, is also flexible enough to be used by all sports in the program. Such an approach would be beneficial for the athletic director with all the information from all the sports in the same format.

Pre-Planning Tasks

Prior to the actual development of the budget, several tasks should be completed. An inventory of supplies, equipment, and facilities must be conducted. The coach ought to carefully check the condition of these items to help develop the long-range budget. The second task involves a study of previous budgets and dealers' bids. This will reveal what items have consistently been ordered, which dealer offers the most competitive prices, and the length of time that it may require to receive the order. Another reason for studying previous budgets is to determine differences between budgeted expenses and actual expenses. This information may be used in developing the long-range budget. The fourth task that a coach needs to do is make a conservative estimate of expected revenue. It can be beneficial to study the budgets of other schools comparable in size and level of competition.

Expenses

Having covered the pre-planning items, the coach is ready to begin listing expense items in a systematic way. This type of approach will reduce the chance of overlooking items that should be included in the budget. Expenses will vary depending on the sport, but such items as equipment, game expenses, maintenance cost, membership fees, staff inservice training, printing costs, and salaries should be considered.

Need for a Balanced Budget

Whether or not a coach needs to develop a balanced budget depends on how funding of the sport occurs. If a sport has to be self-supporting, the expenses must not exceed the revenue. If, however, only the total athletic budget needs to be balanced, the coach of a specific sport may be able to turn in a budget that is not balanced (or one that may not show any income, such as for cross-country or golf). Those who must balance the income with the outgo have to be good predictors of potential revenues and projected expenses. Historical information will be very helpful in predicting income. By projecting the type of season the team will have (win-loss record) and then looking at records of comparable past years, a coach can get a pretty good idea of future income. Schedules, though, are not always similar. More than one coach has overpredicted simply because of a schedule change that added or eliminated a team that was a good draw. If a sport is supposed to be self-supporting, boosters will often guarantee a set amount of money or fund-raising projects may need to be written into the budget in order to balance receipts and expenses. Fortunately for coaches, few sports at the high school level are expected to be completely self-supporting.

Cost Analysis

The information that can be obtained from a cost analysis can be very helpful to a coach preparing a budget. In sports, cost analysis is usually used to determine the per player cost of the sport. This figure is obtained by dividing the number of athletes involved in the sport into the projected expenditures. A more sophisticated analysis could show the per player cost of each item, such as salaries, equipment, and travel. A set of cost analysis figures is very helpful in determining the equality of expenditure requests between sports—say football and volleyball. In this comparison, coaches may want to do a per player cost analysis of each item in order to identify where greater expenditure for football is actually occurring.

Finalizing the Budget

With these three sets of data in hand (income, expense, and cost analysis), the coach is ready to lay out both the annual and the long-range budgets. In the process, it is essential to take a critical look at the program. This should begin with the coach asking questions like those in, but not restricted to, the following list:

1. Will the projected revenue support the proposed expenses?
2. How does my sport compare with other sports in the school on a proportional or absolute basis?
3. Does the comparison show that I am spending too much or too little?
4. Are there gaps or inequalities in selected areas?
5. Are there games on my schedule that cost much more than the average per game cost?
6. Are purchases for equipment and supplies being conducted in the most efficient manner?
7. How effective is the inventory and control system for athletic equipment?
8. Has there been an upward or downward trend in athletic revenues?
9. Have attendance figures remained constant, gone up, or gone down? If there has been a change, what were the factors causing it?

Realistic answers to questions like the ones above will give information and direction for making changes that will establish a more reasonable and defensible budget. Coaches across the country have battled with the problem of budget and the necessity to "tighten the belt" on costs. Several approaches being used are listed below. Each should be carefully scrutinized in relation to the particular situation and sport to determine whether or not it is a practical suggestion.

1. Reduce the number of teams offered in the sport if there are several (varsity, junior varsity, freshmen).
2. Work with other coaches in the district or league to combine equipment orders to permit buying in large lots.
3. Purchase quality goods that have a longer life than less expensive items do.
4. Have athletes furnish some of their gear, such as shoes, socks, practice shorts and shirts, rackets, practice balls, golf clubs, and tights.

5. Assign responsibilities for watering grass areas and marking fields for practice and scrimmages to the coaches or student managers.
6. Reduce the number of out-of-town games when scheduling nonconference games.
7. Restrict the schedule for junior high, junior varsity, or freshmen teams to schools within the city or the shortest range possible.
8. Work with other coaches to plan contest dates and travel so that more than one team can share a bus (e.g., men's and women's track teams, tennis teams, baseball and softball teams, or whatever combination can fill a bus).
9. Eliminate or reduce meals provided on road games.
10. Reduce the number of players taken on trips.
11. Reduce the number of players on the squad.
12. Reduce the number of night contests.
13. Halt the practice of allowing players to "walk off" with uniform items.
14. Eliminate out-of-season practices (e.g., spring football or fall softball practices).
15. Share the cost of facility upkeep with another agency (e.g., the school district and recreation department share cost and responsibility).
16. Require athletes to pay a participation fee.
17. Eliminate scouting trips by sharing basic information about teams with other coaches.
18. Eliminate spending a night on the road by leaving early the day of the contest.
19. Check on alternate places to stay—the YMCA, YWCA, and tourist homes are often less expensive than motels.
20. Join a travel club to take advantage of well-planned trips and discounts.
21. Prepare meals at a campground or motel with the necessary facilities.
22. Plan activities systematically whether purchasing equipment or taking a trip.
23. Share expenses with a team from a nearby school that is traveling to the same event.
24. Ask parents and other team followers to provide transportation, to clean and repair equipment, and so on.

SUMMARY

Once the cost study has been completed, budget reconstruction efforts have been accomplished, and plans have been laid for increasing or maintaining revenue levels, the coach has a guide for the future of that sport. The product becomes an operating plan that the coach, athletic director, principal, and other appropriate personnel can study and understand.

Because fiscal management is so important for viable athletic programs, coaches must become proficient in securing operating funds, expending these wisely, and dealing with shifting economic factors. Success is measured by sound business practice and budget balancing, as well as by a winning season. The two types of success are related, as one supports and feeds on the other. Winning seasons provide financial relief, but good financial programs can lead to winning teams.

ENDNOTE

1. "High School Rule Changes Accommodate Handicapped Athletes," AAHPERD *Update* (January 1980): 4.

# 14

Purchasing Criteria

JUSTIFICATIONS FOR PURCHASING
SELECTION OF EQUIPMENT AND
   UNIFORMS
SUMMARY

Every coach must have a method of determining what equipment will be purchased. When the budget is sufficient to purchase anything needed or wanted, the decisions concerning what to buy are not difficult. Even so, regardless of a budget, a coach must be guided by certain criteria when making the final decision about which piece or brand of equipment to purchase. Two considerations of equal importance are rules requirements and safety. A team or athlete cannot compete if equipment does not meet rules specifications, and a coach should never permit an athlete to enter a practice or game without quality protective equipment. Other considerations, in order of importance, are budget, minimum amount needed, quality of equipment, and standardization.

JUSTIFICATIONS FOR PURCHASING

There are numerous reasons for equipment purchases. Three primary ones are requirements for safety of the athletes, purchases required by new rules, and the needs of the program.

Safety and Performance

As mentioned previously, the overriding criterion when purchasing equipment is the safety of the athletes. Secondary to safety is performance. Each sport will have different requirements simply because of the nature of the activity. Some will require tight-fitting uniforms, while others will require more freedom in the fit of the garments. The choice of the uniform materials should be determined by the activity and the area of the country in which the item will be used.

Freedom of Movement

Unrestricted movement in sports is extremely important for both safety and performance; it must be a top priority in selecting protective equipment and uniforms. If uniforms restrict flexibility or quickness of movement, an athlete could suffer an injury. Also, the fit of the uniform may significantly affect performance. Swimmers look for suits that will produce the least amount of resistance in the water. Gymnasts want a uniform that is close fitting, attractive, and stretchable. Uniforms for sports such as basketball and volleyball must provide freedom of movement of the arms and shoulders and not restrict the jumping actions. Athletic uniform styles change as nonsport styles change, but the requirement remains the same—freedom of movement.

Protection

There are safety and protective considerations in addition to those required by rules of the sport. Safety of athletes should be ensured by purchasing uniforms that will help avoid injuries and provide protection against environmental conditions. Volleyball players can protect their lower arms by wearing long-sleeved jerseys and protect their knees by wearing knee pads. Softball players can prevent many leg abrasions by wearing long pants instead of shorts or by wearing sliding pads. Shoes that serve particular protective functions can be bought, and long stockings help protect the lower legs. A player who is reasonably well protected from injury, and whose uniform and shoes fit comfortably, will probably perform better than one who lacks these aids.

Climate

Climate is a major consideration when buying equipment, particularly uniforms and footwear. The purchase of game and practice uniforms, shoes, warmups, and foul-weather gear must be based on the weather conditions under which the squad will practice and compete.

Temperature will influence the type, style, and amount of equipment and uniforms needed in a particular area. Athletes who play in high temperatures must have uniforms that will allow for dissipation of body heat. This normally is not a problem except in sports like football where heavy protective apparel tends to hold in body heat. Cold presents problems uniquely different from those with heat. Uniforms must not only keep the player warm but must also be light enough to allow for the dissipation of perspiration and permit the freedom of movement necessary for maximum performance. A major problem for athletes performing in cold temperature is chilling. This can occur when perspiration builds up between the body and the protective clothing. If the moisture does not evaporate and the athlete slows down (such as when a football player goes to the bench), it will cool and chill the individual. Protection for sideline players in outdoor sports in the northern regions should include parkas and blankets, and perhaps even heaters and canopies along the bench. Players in the warmer climates may need only windbreakers or light parkas. Athletes who perform indoors also need consideration. If the temperature in an arena is cool to compensate for the heat generated by the crowd, players who are not active should wear warmups.

Precipitation, as with temperature conditions, affects the type and amount of protection needed. Heavy waterproof gear, such as parkas or ponchos, may be needed to protect nonparticipants from cold rain or snow, while lightweight plastic rain gear may be sufficient protection from warm rain.

Rules Requirements

Each sport has its own specific regulations about equipment to be used and uniforms that may be worn. These usually fall into two categories: player safety and player identification. When rules are changed, a suffi-

Figure 14-1 Protective equipment must be available for practices as well as for games (Photographer: Mickey Adair)

cient lead time is generally allowed to enable schools to implement the new requirements through the normal replacement of old or worn-out items. These rules may vary from state to state, from conference to conference, and among regulatory agencies. Each coach has the responsibility of making sure that all equipment purchased will meet the rules and regulations established by the governing body.

Safety Various sports have different regulations as to shoes and cleats, pads, chest protectors, helmets, masks, gloves, and other protective items with special emphasis on the quality and/or design. Protective padding may also be required on permanent structures such as goalposts, walls in gymnasiums, and areas around the gymnastics apparatus.

Identification Rules of the sport usually require proper identification of players and teams. They specify which team can have a choice of uniform color, the location and size of numbers and names on uniforms, and the decoration that may go on a garment (such as the width of the arm bands or stripes). Most of these rules are designed to aid officials working the contest, while others are for spectator convenience.

Program Needs Program needs that justify the buying of equipment fall into three general areas: equipment needed for a new program, equipment needed to maintain the present inventory, and equipment needed to expand an existing program. These situations are interrelated and all must be considered.

New Program An experienced coach has suggested that the budget for a new program be broken into four categories.[1] The first one concerns expenses that have to be taken care of before the team can play, such as travel expenses and officials' fees. The second category involves the money spent on basic equipment for practices and contests (such as bats, balls, bases, and protective equipment). Category three consists of budgeting for uniforms, and the final category concerns the so-called luxury items, those that are nice to have but are not really essential.

If the coach is inexperienced, consulting with coaches from other schools could prove beneficial. Quantity and quality of various items can be fairly accurately projected by an experienced coach or by a novice who follows good advice. A reputable sporting goods dealer or manufacturer's representative can also provide valuable information. Equipment purchases for new programs are usually one-time allocations. When making the initial purchase, the coach should consider a long-range plan for equipment purchasing that includes replacement of items annually. Such things as uniforms, both for practice and contests, should be of such quality that one or two sets can be added each year and still match all uniforms. If the allocation for the initial purchase is limited, the coach might consider buying equipment of varying degrees of quality. This approach has two benefits in that it allows the purchase of more equipment with the allocation, and it results in a staggered replacement schedule. For example, if 15 basketballs are to be bought, a coach may choose to buy

5 top-grade balls, 5 balls of moderate quality, and 5 inexpensive ones. Each quality will have different life expectancy, requiring only the 5 inexpensive balls to be replaced the first year. At that time they should be replaced with top-quality products that have a long life expectancy.

Replacement Needs

An inventory of equipment, taken immediately following the end of the season, will indicate the replacement needs for the next season. The inventory should reveal what items are in usable condition and what items need to be repaired, renovated, or replaced; then coaches can determine the amount and type of equipment to be ordered. Returning athletes who have specific requirements for uniforms, shoes, or special protective equipment must be considered, as well as new specifications imposed by rule changes.

Program Expansion

If there are plans to enlarge a squad or to add a team or several teams, the amount of additional equipment needed must be calculated in proportion to the size of the expansion. The quantity of all items will not always need to be increased in direct proportion to the number of team members. For example, with additional volleyball teams, few additional balls need to be ordered if practice times are staggered. Expansion is not as expensive as the cost of beginning a program because equipment that can be used by all players does not have to be duplicated. Cooperative planning by all coaches involved can save money. If the expansion is in the area of junior varsity or freshmen teams, a common practice is to pass down uniforms and equipment from the varsity team. This is an acceptable way of reducing the cost of expanding the program as long as the equipment made available to those teams provides maximum protection. The appearance of uniforms and other items need not be high-quality, but the safety and protection of the athlete cannot be compromised. Football is a sport where handed-down equipment can place the young athlete in grave danger. Young athletes unskilled in football techniques and equipped with protective gear that does not fit properly are accidents waiting to happen. Any coach who condones this type of program is legally liable if someone is injured. Program expansion should be permitted only if protection and instruction can be provided the athletes.

Player Needs

When buying equipment, the coach must consider the players who will be using it. The size, age, and sex of the athlete are prime considerations even though there is some equipment that will not be affected by these. A tennis ball, a high-jump cross bar, a badminton net, and a field hockey ball are a few of the many items that will be the same regardless of the size, age, or sex of the participant.

Age and Size

These two factors provide basic guidelines for buying. The age of the athlete will determine level of competition, which may in turn determine the size, weight, or other dimensions of the piece of equipment. Size is important and should receive careful consideration. Poorly fitted uniforms, protective equipment, or shoes often lead to injury. The size or strength of athletes should also determine the type of equipment purchased. Bat size, racket weight, stick length, pad size, and the like, need to be fitted to the individual. In order to avoid extensive alterations, the coach should carefully study the manufacturer's size and measurement charts, measure the player's size accurately, and consider the growth potential of the player before ordering.

Sex

There are few differences between nonpersonal equipment requirements for men's and women's teams in the same sport. Rules that regulate the size, height, or weight of certain items may have differences related to sex, just as rules do for age differences. There are sex differences, however, in personal equipment and uniforms. Different protective equipment is required. Uniforms for men and women are not designed or sized alike. Fitting men's uniforms is not difficult because manufacturers have had experience in making men's athletic clothing. As more women require uniforms, manufacturers are increasing their efforts to meet these needs as they met the need for athletic shoes for women in the 1970s. Prior to that time, many women bought men's shoes in order to get a high-quality shoe that would last. Women who continue to do this should be careful of the fit, as men's shoes are normally constructed wider than women's shoes; wearing poorly fitted shoes decreases protection and increases irritation.

SELECTION OF EQUIPMENT AND UNIFORMS

Beginning coaches can get good advice and counsel from experienced coaches, salespeople, specialists, and faculty members. These individuals are usually willing to share their knowledge and expertise. Home economics teachers should be experts on fabric selection and care, while industrial arts faculty can advise on construction, durability, and maintenance of equipment. All assistance possible should be obtained before making final selections—errors in selection of items must be endured for the life of the equipment. Coaches must know about categories and specifications, requirements for protective gear, special considerations for uniforms, and how to make long-range purchase plans.

Categories

Equipment used in sports can be placed in four categories: developmental equipment, teaching equipment, practice equipment, and game equipment. Each type has a specific purpose, and usually only practice and game equipment are similar.

Developmental Equipment

Items in this category are often referred to as conditioning or training equipment. They include free weights, weight machines, isokinetic machines, medicine balls, jump ropes, and other exercise apparatus. Most of these items are rather expensive, usually very durable, and useful for male and female athletes in all sports. At some schools this type of equipment cannot be bought through the school budget. If this is true, then the coach must seek outside funding from boosters, parent groups, or civic organizations. These items require permanent space if they are to be used effectively. Occasionally, items that are used but in good condition can be purchased for a fair price from a local college, club, or business that is buying new equipment. Before buying secondhand items, the buyer must make sure that they are in good condition and likely to remain so for a reasonable period of time. Buying goods just because the price is right can be very expensive in the long run.

Teaching Equipment

This category includes items purchased to teach skills that are a part of sport. Examples include video tape cameras, blocking sleds, ball machines, spiking apparatus, safety belts, and rebound machines. Some of these are commercial products, and others may be built by a coach. Items that are built by a coach or someone in the school shop are generally less expensive; however, construction costs must be planned for in the budget. Used items may be purchased from a variety of sources. They must be checked for defects before being bought, and safety must not be sacrificed for the less expensive equipment. If safety cannot be guaranteed, the item should be purchased new from a dealer.

Practice Equipment

This equipment is similar to that used during a contest. It can be older, blemished, or repaired, but it should have the same playing qualities as that used in the actual game. A basketball coach or a volleyball coach should not ask players to practice with inexpensive rubber balls if leather balls are to be used for competition. The appearance of practice equipment may not matter, but its performance does. Most coaches do not buy equipment for practice unless they are starting a new program and have no used items available. A typical procedure is to use game equipment from early season games or previous years. This reinforces the need to buy good quality items that will be durable and take plenty of abuse. Coaches of team sports—where the coach may want the players to be able to change the color of their jerseys quickly—often buy some type of reversible jersey or shirt. Others prefer pinnies, vests, or slip-over jerseys. The cost of equipment in this category can be held to a minimum as long as safety is not compromised.

Game Equipment

This category is comprised of equipment used in a contest. Many sports or conferences have rules that require new balls for each game, match, or tournament. Some have set specifications concerning the quality, quantity, and, in many cases, even the brand name of the balls that must be used in conference-sponsored events. If a coach is hosting contests of this type, such items must be placed in the budget. Game uniforms are also a major consideration. Most state high school activities associations and/or conferences have established rules determining the design of the uniform that can be used, but the quality is decided by the coach. The type of material, stitching patterns, washability, and durability must be considered when buying uniforms. Shoes that will be used during the contest must be the best quality available to ensure maximum safety and performance. The shoes selected must suit the conditions under which they will be used. There is no "general" type of shoe; they are specific to the sport as well as to the playing surfaces.

Protective Equipment

It cannot be emphasized too often or too strongly that safety considerations are the primary concern when buying equipment. Nothing should come ahead of the player's welfare. Protective equipment that should be considered, depending on the sport, includes headgear, pads, shoes, gloves, and other similar items. Organizations such as the National Operating Commission for Safety in Athletic Equipment (NOCSAE) and the American Society for Testing and Materials (ASTM) F-8 Committee on Sports Equipment and Facilities, along with the National Federation of State High School Associations (NFSHSA), have worked diligently to develop safety standards for athletic equipment. A large sum should be allotted from the budget for this type of equipment, but it should be remembered that the most expensive equipment does not always afford the most protection.

Headgear

Helmets and other protective headgear come in a variety of shapes, are constructed of different materials, utilize several types of suspension systems, and can carry a multitude of colors and decorations. The primary concern when purchasing headgear is protection, while comfort and appearance follow in order of importance. Although many sports have protective headgear, there is not an official standard for headgear except for football. Football helmets are required to carry the approval of NOCSAE.

Padding

Protective paddings are made of a variety of quality materials, are designed to protect specific vulnerable areas of the body, and usually include special design features advocated by the manufacturer. Protective pads may be worn under a uniform (as in football), or over the uniform (as in hockey), while others are made to be slipped on and off frequently and easily during the contest (as the catcher's chest protector). However and whenever the padding is worn, the purpose remains the same—to protect players, both those who wear the padding and those who might come in contact with the padding. When purchasing protective equipment, a coach should concentrate on the fit, protective quality, maintenance procedures, and durability.

Shoes

Coaches must pay particular attention to the shoes of their players. Proper fit should be a major concern. Shoes that are not properly fitted will cause soreness, contribute to injuries, reduce performances, and contribute to abnormally fast wear. Athletes should not be permitted to wear shoes that are hand-me-downs. The coach must arrange, by some means, for the athlete to get a good pair of well-fitting shoes. Quality material and construction are also important for durability. If the coach needs advice, athletic shoe manufacturers' representatives or local dealers are usually more than happy to assist.

Gloves

Purchasing protective covering for the hands is also important. Baseball and softball gloves and mitts are items of considerable expense (as are those for other sports, such as ice hockey), but they will last for several seasons when given proper care. Gloves of lighter construction, such as

Figure 14–2 Helmets and pads must give maximum protection (Courtesy of Rickards High School, Tallahassee, Florida. Photographer: Mickey Adair)

those used in golf and handball, are not as expensive, but they provide less protection. All gloves should fit well and be constructed of quality material, usually leather, with as much padding as necessary and with strong stitching. The safety of the athlete, as well as the outcome of the contest, may well rest with these items.

Others

There is a variety of other types of protective equipment to be considered. Glasses guards and mouth protectors are important in preventing injuries to the eyes and mouth. Socks are also protective equipment, as they help protect the feet against blisters and other types of soreness. Athletic supporters, cups, and protective bras are included under the heading of protective equipment. Coaches must consider the need for, and the ability of the program to purchase, such items.

General Considerations for Uniform Selection

In purchasing uniforms, a coach needs to keep several things in mind, primarily the safety of the athlete. Matters that need to be considered include fit, material, decoration, color, maintenance, and cost (immediate and long-term). As stated before, it is necessary for a coach to learn as much about the items as possible (quality, durability, and cleanability) before placing an order.

Uniform Fit

The cut and fit of the uniform are extremely important because the player must be free to move efficiently and effectively. When it is possible, each player should be measured and the uniform fitted just for that individual. Frequently, however, schools buy stock sizes and then fit the squad members into the available uniforms. The development of stretchy materials has assisted coaches in making this procedure more acceptable. Most manufacturers have developed sizing charts that indicate the number of each size uniform a school should have in stock for a sport squad of a given size. These charts are based on years of experience, are fairly accurate, and are available to coaches from most retailers. In any community where there might be a particular group of students (possibly an ethnic group) that might be larger or smaller than the so-called national norms, a coach would have to modify the recommendations of the sizing charts to take the size of the local population into consideration. Players' preferences concerning the fit may be considered also. Coaches often permit an athlete to wear a uniform a size larger if the individual likes a loose-fitting one and if it does not affect the athlete's safety or performance. Women may choose to order a boy's or man's uniform, or a man may need to order a boy's uniform. A coach must do whatever seems reasonable considering safety, fit, and cost.

Maintenance

An important matter to consider in buying uniforms is the ease of their care. When at all possible—and it is possible for most sports—buy washable uniforms. Whether the school does the laundering or the players wash their own suits, uniforms need to be kept clean and good looking during the season without frequent visits to the cleaners. Dry cleaning is much too expensive for any ordinary program; materials and trim that might require it should be avoided. Uniforms that need to be ironed are also difficult to maintain. If players wash their own uniforms or take them home to be laundered, each player or parent, or both, needs to be fully informed about the proper cleaning method. Uniforms are too costly to be ruined by improper care. Purchasing uniforms that are easy to care for can also improve the sanitation situation. If they are simple to wash, players or coaches may wash them more frequently.

Cost

The cost of selected equipment will vary according to safety requirements, the need for and the planned use of equipment, its need for maintenance, and the overall budget. Coaches should select the very best quality they can afford; it will be a bargain in the long run. They should put their money into equipment that meets standards and is made of good fabrics with good workmanship. The next section of this chapter is devoted to purchasing procedures, but the consideration of cost is a major item in criteria for selection. Coaches must watch out for true bargains, not be fooled by cheap prices for cheap goods, buy on need and not on impulse, and know the true value of each item.

Special Considerations for Uniform Selection

Prior to purchasing uniforms, a coach must read the rules of the sport to ensure that policies governing uniforms are followed—such things as the numbering system, allowable decoration, and colors of home or road uniforms. There are, besides, other points to consider: each item of the uniform has its own characteristics and special uses that must be taken into account when purchases are made.

Materials

There are many fine materials on the market that look good and wear well. Each sport may have a need for a particular type of material, such as quick-drying nylon for swimming, but the same fabrics are generally used in most uniforms. Standard materials are cotton, wool, synthetics, or a combination (such as dacron and cotton, or orlon and wool). Durene is the highest-grade cotton material and, when sanforized, does not shrink. Cotton is the coolest material, but all cottons do not lend themselves to wash-and-wear. Blends of cotton and synthetics or synthetics alone are easy to maintain, requiring very little ironing.

Appearance

The appearance of a team should be important to the team and the coach. Research shows that appearance can have a psychological effect on players and opponents. If players think that they look good, they are more likely to play closer to their potential. Wearing team or school colors is a long-time tradition, and the use of color is helpful to the spectators in identifying their team. Appearance will be affected by uniform design, fit, material, and the color combination selected. Generally, it is not wise to purchase uniforms of extreme designs; a style that can be worn for several years should be selected. Durable fabrics and colors should be selected, and new materials or colors ought not to be bought until they have been thoroughly tested in a washing machine. Gaudy trimmings and fancy emblems should be avoided. The coach should go for a simple design, bright clear colors, easily readable names, and bold clear numbers. The fringe, braid, and cute emblems can be left to people who have more money than taste or sense.

Jerseys

When buying jerseys or shirts, a coach has to consider the uniqueness of the sport. Design is important; football jerseys need to accommodate shoulder pads, long-sleeved volleyball shirts should protect elbows and forearms, and bowling shirts must be cut to allow freedom of movement. Shirts and jerseys should be long enough to fit well down into pants or shorts if the sport calls for this. Armholes or sleeves need to be full cut for freedom of action; however, girls' jerseys should also be cut for modesty. Fabrics for these items are usually knits or woven fabrics with "give" or stretch to accommodate freedom of movement. Care must be taken when selecting letters or numerals. Manufacturers state that sewn-on items can negatively affect the stretchability of the fabric, leading to rips, tears, and reduced comfort. The larger the item sewn on, the more stretch the shirt will lose.

Pants and Shorts

A coach selecting these pieces of the uniform should be careful to choose heavy-duty fabrics. They may be of the same fibers as jerseys but with heavier weight and stronger construction. The wear and tear on the material is largely determined by the sport; this in turn serves as a guide in determining the fabric to be selected. Each sport has its own requirements for uniform design, safety, color, and decoration that must be considered. When buying pants or shorts, be certain that colors match the shirt colors, are well made, fit the players, and do not restrict movement. All uniform items should be purchased at one time. Color batches vary; so, when items are ordered at separate times, colors may not match.

Tunics and Kilts

The selection of these items—used primarily in girls' and women's field hockey, lacrosse, and sometimes soccer—should follow the same guidelines as for other uniform items. Wool flannel has been a traditional fabric, but other materials are now in use. Generally, woven rather than knit materials are selected. The trend is toward blends of synthetics with fibers such as wool or cotton.

Swimsuits and Tights

Swimming, wrestling, and gymnastics have special needs. Swim trunks and suits are generally of very lightweight materials that cling to the swimmer and reduce resistance. They should be of strong fabric that can resist the deteriorating effects of chlorine and sun. Wrestling tights are usually knitted blends of cotton with manmade fibers and are of heavy-duty quality to resist abrasions. Leotards and tights used by gymnasts are of a heavier knit than are swimsuits but are lighter than wrestling tights. In all cases the design of the uniform should give freedom of movement and protection with modesty.

Warmups

In a number of sports, the warmup is as much a part of the uniform as are jerseys and shorts. The decision to purchase these garments should be primarily based on the health and safety needs of the participants, with appearance and color secondary considerations. A basic design consideration is the ease with which they can be put on and taken off. Coaches do not want a player to struggle with zippers while trying to enter a game, nor do they want a player to avoid putting on a warmup after coming out because it is too much trouble. Jackets or pullovers must be large enough for free movement when worn over a uniform. It is common practice to buy a fabric jacket two sizes larger and a knit jacket one size larger than uniform size, unless the manufacturer has designed the garment to meet special requirements.

Warmup pants are made to actual waist size and will therefore correspond to uniform measurements. They are generally full cut to go over the uniform; thus, length is the major consideration. Order short sizes for those males who are 5 feet, 9 inches, and under, and long sizes for those over 6 feet. Women's sizes may be gauged a little differently, but all warmups are usually unisex items. Special care must be taken in ordering for unusually large or tall players and unusually small ones. The coach may need to solicit the assistance of the dealer and/or local tailor to secure proper fit even after the suit is special-ordered.

Thought must also be given to color and decoration. When possible, all uniforms, including warmups, should be purchased from the same company at the same time. The decorations, including team insignia and name of player, need to be in good taste and readable. Fancy scripts are difficult to read, ornate designs may fade, and the generally increased cost of these items does not improve either the general appearance of the athlete, the quality of the item, or the state of the budget.

Materials will depend on the sport. Choose heavy-fleeced fabrics for cold weather, but select lighter-weight knits for an indoor activity such as gymnastics. Waterproof and windproof materials are a must for those who play outdoors in the cold, wet seasons. The warmups can have two layers of materials, warm fabrics next to the body and weatherproof fabrics on the outside. As with all uniform items, a coach must consider quality, comfort, and durability before decoration and special color combinations.

SUMMARY

Coaches should not randomly decide what equipment is to be purchased, but must make these decisions based on specific, predetermined criteria. Safety must be the primary consideration, but rules requirements, budget, minimum amount needed, quality of equipment, and standardization are also important. Price of items cannot be a limiting factor when safety and rules requirements are being considered; however, when considering the total picture, the coach may follow this rule of thumb, "The most for the least." This includes both quality and quantity.

ENDNOTE

1. P. Adam, "Equipping a New Softball Program? Do It Right," *United States Women Coaches and Athletes* (May/June 1979): 41.

15

Purchasing Procedures

EQUIPMENT MANAGEMENT CYCLE
PURCHASING GUIDELINES
SUMMARY

Next to the athlete, the most important components of a successful sports program are supplies and equipment. A program that has an excellent inventory of quality equipment will not necessarily be successful, but it is a rare exception when a program with inadequate equipment will be able to match the competition. There are certain essentials that every team needs so that it will not be hampered in its preparation for a contest (for example, a sufficient number of basketballs for practice, adequate equipment for a weight program, or enough hurdles for proper training).

Although many coaches, taking basic items for granted, are concerned with supplies and equipment that should be termed luxuries, every team in an athletic program should have essential items before frill equipment is purchased for any sport. Weight machines and video equipment can benefit all sports and should be invested in before a specific sport is allowed to order nonessential equipment (like an extra set of game uniforms). The coach of each sport must realize that a specific sport's budget is only one of many to be integrated into a departmental budget.

An adequate supply of essential materials and equipment does not happen by chance; it occurs as the result of an organized, planned program of purchasing. Each coach must know the priority items and make a distinction between what is necessary for a program and what would be nice to have. Equipment and supplies consume a large portion of a sport's annual budget, and the successful manager/coach can stretch the budget dollars to build the equipment inventory. In the matter of purchasing items, the coach's responsibility is to buy quality and quantity for the least possible amount.

Quality is of particular importance so that all players are properly equipped and protected. Product liability suits against manufacturers and athletic programs have increased concern for the safety and performance characteristics of equipment as they relate to player success and risk. The problem of legal liability is addressed in Chapter 19.

With the increased cost of supporting a sports program, the renewed emphasis on academics, and the ever-present unstable economy, a well-planned and well-organized program for purchasing supplies and equipment is a must. In order to have such a program, the athletic director and coaches, experienced or inexperienced, have to be knowledgeable about the purchase and care of all items. It is absolutely essential for one to know what, how, where, and when to buy athletic equipment and supplies. Using a computer to assist with this process will save a coach valuable time and money.

EQUIPMENT MANAGEMENT CYCLE

Equipment management is a continuous process that can be viewed as a sequence of events, as shown in Figure 15-1. The inventory is the logical beginning for such a cycle; it is here that basic information regarding the amount and condition of equipment on hand is determined. These data, along with the determination of new equipment needs, will be used in developing the budget for the upcoming season and in placing orders for purchase and repair of equipment.

Not distinct and independent, the steps in the cycle are continuous, with some stages overlapping. For example, a coach is continually studying new equipment coming on the market and may be placing an order for some items while developing specifications to be used in bidding on others. Care and maintenance also continue year-round, but the cycle diagram does reflect the fact that equipment management can be viewed as a series of logical events.

Each of the steps will be discussed in the pages that follow with

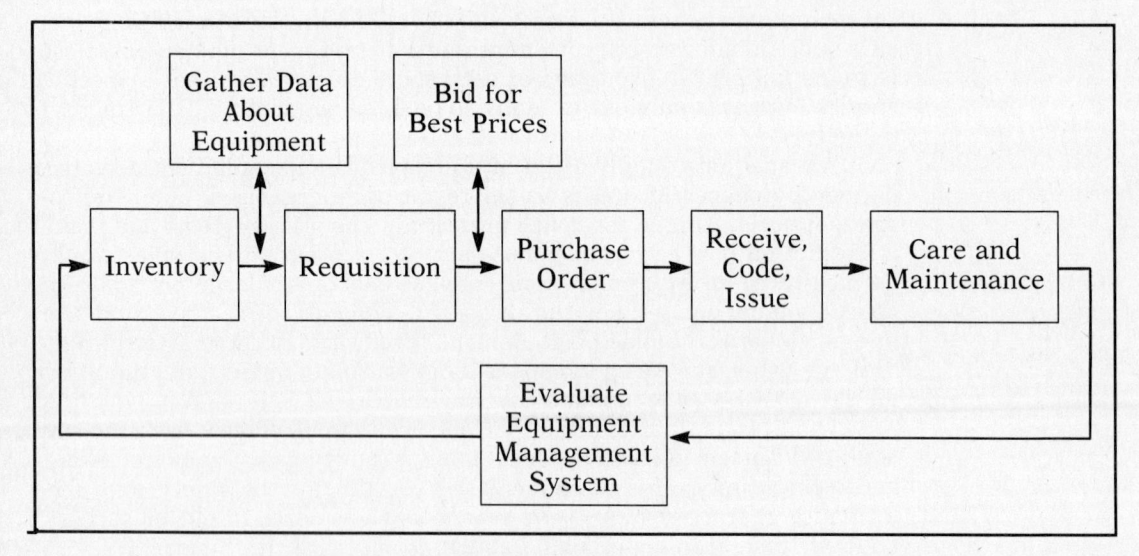

Figure 15-1   Equipment management cycle

the exception of one: evaluation of the system. Evaluation is an ongoing process, but at least annually the coach should thoroughly analyze and evaluate the management system. The inventory data in particular will reveal such important information as how much equipment has been lost or stolen, how effective (and honest) were the people assigned the responsibilities, and how effective the system was in maintenance and repair.

Inventory

A thorough inventory of the equipment on hand is essential to sound equipment management. Simply speaking, an inventory is the sorting, counting, and evaluating of the condition of all items on hand. Data from the inventory will indicate what must be purchased to operate next year's program. More specifically, the list permits the coach to determine:

1. Equipment available for use next year.
2. Items to be repaired.
3. Items to be discarded and replaced.
4. Equipment to be purchased for next season.

Another value of the inventory is showing the effectiveness of the equipment control system. Too many items unaccounted for indicates that something is wrong with either the system or the personnel involved in the control of the program. A lack of control means lost equipment and a drain on the budget.

The inventory should be conducted no less than once a year, preferably right after the end of each playing season. The coach works with the equipment manager, if there is one, to conduct the inventory to gain a better understanding of the overall equipment operation and firsthand information about equipment needs. A complete report is prepared and submitted to the athletic director, principal, and/or supervisor.

There are any number of forms that might be used in conducting an inventory. The important concern is that the coach design a form or use the standard form from the school that will give the information needed. It should be simple, yet detailed enough to give the desired data and to provide easy transfer for computer use. A sample form is shown in Figure 15-2.

New Equipment Information

If the inventory has been conducted and the needs have been identified immediately following the playing season, there is time for systematic gathering of information about the items that must be bought for the next season. This is an important step because many brands, types, and qualities of equipment exist on the market. Determining needs early allows a coach to consult with dealers about various types of equipment, to acquire and study samples and materials from manufacturers, and to read research data that may have been published about the effectiveness and durability of the product. The more information the coach has on the products needed, the wiser the decisions will be concerning selection of the equipment and uniforms that are safest, of the best quality, and lowest in price. There are a number of sources and techniques to help a

Items Used	Previous Inventory Count	Number Bought During Year	Total Number to Be Accounted For	Total Inventory (Usable Condition)	Present Inventory (Need Repairs)	Inventory Number of Articles Not Accounted For	Total Number of New to Be Needed

Close of _____ School _____ Season, 19___ (sport)

Day of Inventory _____, 19___
(month, day)

Coach _____
Athletic Director _____
Student Manager _____

Figure 15-2   Inventory of equipment

coach gather relevant information; as many of these as possible should be utilized.

    Among the best places to learn much about all the new equipment and uniforms are conventions or other gatherings of coaches, athletic directors, physical educators, or recreators. Most companies that manufacture products related to athletics set up display booths in exhibit areas so that a coach can find, in one concentrated space, all the newest things. Every booth is manned by knowledgeable staff who have brochures and catalogs available and who can answer questions and possibly take orders.

Reputable firms are eager to provide good service to their customers and will have their sales personnel visit schools to discuss equipment and supply needs. Most of the salespeople will bring with them various samples of new products coming on the market and will make available samples of special items that coaches have requested. Often, they will distribute printed materials describing test results and actual performance data for the items they sell. Some firms will routinely lend a piece of equipment or a uniform item to a customer to try out for a period of time. They are often eager to lend new items coming on the market or ones that they feel will be an improvement over current equipment. In this way items can be tested in a game situation to judge their quality and performance. The coach should be careful to avoid being "obligated" to the company that lends a piece of equipment. Knowing all the conditions concerned with the use of an item that is a temporary gift may prevent later problems.

Reading current books, magazines, and research articles in journals will keep coaches well informed of what is new on the sports market. Spending money for related published information is a smart investment, as coaches will be aware of the latest equipment and have factual data to accompany a purchase request. Some of the State High School Athletic/ Activity Associations publish useful information about equipment and supplies in their monthly bulletins. These state associations and the National Federation serve as resources and clearing houses for information about products, particularly concerning safety features.

Another valuable source of information is coaches in the area. Their experience with particular products and brands will be helpful in determining good- and poor-quality items and those that will give the greatest safety and longest life.

Requisition

With the inventory completed, the list of needs prepared, a priority order established, and wise selections made regarding the specific items needed, it is time to begin the actual purchase process. Assuming that the budget has been approved (or at least clearance to order has been given), a coach is ready to prepare the requisition. (See Figure 15-3.)

A requisition is a form on which the coach requests certain items. Actual requisition forms may differ from system to system, but the basic information asked for on the forms is essentially the same. The most frequently requested categories include a description of the item to be purchased; the cost of a single item; the quantity; total cost; and information about substitution, if acceptable. This information must be provided for each item being ordered. Coaches are cautioned to be very careful to give a detailed, clearly worded description of what they want. It is from this form that others, distant from the coaching scene, will prepare the forms for bidding or actual orders from which dealers must decide what to ship. Information provided by the coach is the only reference they will have. Poor information will lead to the wrong products or inferior items being ordered and/or shipped.

Requisitions should be prepared in an orderly fashion and neatly

SEND TO: PURCHASING DEPT. **GENERAL REQUISITION** West Central High School

INSTRUCTIONS: Prepare in triplicate. Forward first two copies to Purchasing Department. Second copy will be returned with requisition number for your file. The number assigned to this requisition should be referenced if it is necessary to contact the Purchasing Department concerning this requisition. Describe each item completely. Specify the noun first. Double space between items. When an item is for specialized use give details of how it will be used and for what purpose. Requisitions received without departmental information and/or complete item description will be returned For further information see Section 2, Subject 1.1 of the University Business Manual.

Department/Acct. No.	Object Code	Date
9999999		7/21/87

Date Required	Location for Delivery
1/15/88	West Central High School Gym

Individual's name initiating request	Telephone No.
Johnson, D. J.	555-9999

Approved for Dept.	Dean or Division Head

EMERGENCY TELEPHONE SERVICE ONLY

If emergency telephone service is necessary list the telephone number to be charged ________
Emergency telephone service must be certified by Principal Investigator or Department Head.

____
Signed by P.I. or Dept. Head

(DO NOT WRITE IN THIS SPACE)

Requisition Number ________

Date Received ________

Purchase Order Number ________

Item No.	Item Description: Give complete specifications (SPECIFY NOUN FIRST) including size, color, grade, catalog or part number and brand name.	Object Code	Quantity & Unit	Unit Price	Disc. %	Extended TOTAL	Recommended Vendor, (Complete address including zip)
1	Starter's Pistol - all steel, 7 shot, double action. P. C. 42-69		1	37.00		37.00	Express Sporting Goods, Inc. 000 First Street Denver, Colorado 80208
2	Stop Watch - standard split with memory P. C. 92-64		1	89.00		89.00	same as above
3	Batons - anodized aluminum, red, lightweight, satin finish, rounded ends, P. C. 69-4		2	2.10		4.20	same as above

DOUBLE SPACE BETWEEN THE ABOVE ITEMS

P.O. No. (1-6) | Memo No. (7-12) | (13) | Vendor No. (14-22) | Terms (23) | FOB (24) | Ship To (25) | Del. Date (26-31) | (32-33) (34-35) (36-37) Standard Statement | (38) Type

(39) Action | Bid, Cont. No., Quote (40-48) | Attn. To (49-55) | Agent (56) | Req'd by (57-63) | Avl. Bal. (64) | Req. Date (65-70) | Req. No. (71-77) | (78) Blanket P.O. | (79) Print Code | (80) Card Code

FSU Form GR 24 Rev. 2/80 **THIS SPACE FOR USE OF PURCHASING ONLY** **SEND TO: PURCHASING DEPT.**

Figure 15–3 General requisition

typed. More likely than not, the coach will prepare a rough draft, possibly a penciled copy, and give it to the office secretary for typing, since few coaches have their own secretarial service. Neat, detailed copies are required in order to keep accurate records. Appropriate specifications and dates can be stored in a computer, allowing the coach or secretary to retrieve information quickly.

To aid coaches in staying within their budgets, someone other than the coach must usually approve requisitions. Very often, they will be reviewed and approved by the athletic director, principal, or business manager. Two philosophies exist relating to the review and approval of the requisitions. Some administrators and supervisors want to approve every request themselves, regardless of the items involved. Others take the position that if an item was included in the budget and the budget was approved, then requisitions can be sent from the coach directly to the bookkeeper or finance officer, who can quickly check the budget for that coach and approve the requisition of the item(s) requested. In this situation, only requisitions of items not included in the budget would be routed through the offices of the athletic director or another administrator. The latter process provides for less administrative processing; however, it does require that detailed budgets be prepared. Coaches must be ready to participate in either system with persistence and patience and to use the computer to facilitate the process.

Bulk Purchasing and Bidding

Buying in large quantities, bulk purchasing, is a good way to decrease expenditures. When several schools combine their requests and prepare only one requisition for a hundred or more pieces of the same item, dollars will be saved. Dealers are able to offer a better price for a large volume order because of the reduced cost of handling and storage, or because of lower production and selling costs.

Once a requisition is completed and approved, it will either be processed (and a purchase order prepared) or be sent to the next appropriate person so that bid specifications can be prepared. Most organizations have set dollar limits at which purchases must go "out on bid." These limits vary widely. Requests for purchases under the set limits may be made without going through the bid process; however, many organizations will require quotations from a minimum of three firms before orders can be placed. Coaches must familiarize themselves with local policy in this regard.

Specifications

Specifications are required in all cases where bulk purchasing is done. They can be brief or detailed, depending on the item being ordered—those for tennis balls may require only a brand name, company name, and a catalog page number, whereas basketball uniform specifications will need additional information such as fabric, special tailoring details, and lettering.

Some organizations will appoint a committee of coaches to assist in preparing specifications for the items to be bid. The committee uses information from previous requisitions and consults with manufacturers and other coaches. Quite often this committee is called back to help evaluate actual bids received to ensure that specifications are being met.

Bidding

Purchasers or organizations advertise for bids through such sources as the newspapers or through direct mailing of the specifications to dealers who have requested to be notified when bids are advertised. A specified time, usually 30 to 90 days, is given for the vendor to prepare and submit bids. In the "open bid" process, a specified time on a certain day is set for the formal opening of the bids. At that time, the purchasing agent and/or the committee opens the bids to determine which ones met the specifications and which of those is the lowest bid. Under bidding regulations in most states, the lowest bidder must be awarded the contract unless there is justifiable reason for not doing so. The more common reasons for which a low bid can be refused are that the company did not bid the specifications as requested or that the company has a record of poor service or failure to perform as contracted. Once the bid has been awarded, orders can be placed.

Purchase Orders

After authorization to purchase has been given, a purchase order form is prepared and sent to the dealer. A purchase order authorizes a dealer to fill an order as requested by the purchaser. School systems typically have a standard form used by the departments in the organization, although there will be some variation in purchasing procedures from one school to another. In small systems all purchase orders may be prepared and authorized at an individual school, while larger systems may have a central purchasing office that issues the purchase orders for all items that were bid. Since budget controls are necessary to help programs stay within their budgets, the coach may find that only one person has been designated the authority to issue a purchase order. Usually this is the school's bookkeeper, and generally a senior administrator's signature is required on the purchase order before it is mailed. In some cases that person may designate the athletic director as the person to sign all athletic purchases. The information put on the purchase order is similar to that required on the requisition, and most often it is prepared from the information provided on the requisition.

A purchase order contains three very important items of information. One is the purchase order number. Most of the forms include instructions stating: "The above purchase order number *MUST* appear on the invoice." This requirement ensures that purchase orders are issued before goods are shipped, which in turn ensures that the purchase was approved by the appropriate person. A second feature is that numbers are issued *serially* (in numerical order); this helps keep track of purchases. Having the number on the invoice or billing from the dealer makes it easier for the bookkeeper to match the billing with the purchase order before payment of the bill. The third important feature is the *date* on the order. If proper purchasing procedures have been followed, the date on the order will be earlier than the date on the dealer's invoice (billing). Sometimes the date may be the same if the purchase order was processed as a quick-order request. Coaches must be careful to abide by this requirement. Although dealers know that they should not fill an order without the purchase order, invariably some will do so anyway. Coaches must protect their operation and make sure that correct procedures are followed.

Auditing

All books of state or local governmental agencies, as well as those of private organizations, are audited for proper receipt of funds, proper expenditure of funds, and proper accounting of items purchased. Auditors do not deal kindly with administrators or their agents when discrepancies appear or when equipment is not properly ordered, received, or used. Using the computer for fiscal management, purchasing procedures, and equipment management will enhance the audit process. One practice to be avoided is the delivery of goods before the items are officially ordered and approved. Impatience with a slow system may tempt a coach to order supplies in advance of approval, but this can cause serious difficulty with the vendor if, after delivery, the request is denied. Coaches who cannot follow the stipulated procedures may have their budget authority taken away from them, or they may even lose their jobs. They must also take care that there is no hint of payoff for sending business to a particular vendor or for giving a vendor some knowledge or assistance that might make a bid more acceptable. Coaches must not accept gifts from dealers, unless all coaches get the same gift, and they should use samples only for the purposes stipulated. Numerous coaches have been fired and indicted for receiving illegal payoffs.

PURCHASING GUIDELINES

Those purchasing equipment and uniforms would be wise to follow procedures, suggestions, and guidelines offered by coaches with years of experience in purchasing and in stretching the dollar. They recommend using standardized equipment and uniforms, buying over a number of years, buying competitively, buying on the basis of a known or projected need, and always utilizing an established, reputable dealer.

Standardization Uniforms and equipment should be standardized whenever possible. Standardization will allow a coach to replace items a few pieces at a time, rather than having to order a complete set of uniforms or complete inventory of a specific equipment item each year.

Uniforms The need for standardized colors and design has been previously mentioned. This permits extended use of the uniforms by many players over several years without presenting a "hand-me-down" look. It is also possible to purchase standardized sizes that will fit most players and thus maintain a stock of uniforms for the team. Tailor-made or individually fitted uniforms have a tendency to "walk off" with the players for whom they were purchased. Standardized uniform purchasing permits wider flexibility for serving a number of players at a decreased cost over a period of years. It will allow the coach to purchase only a few new suits each year—particularly useful if the budget is tight. If the coach purchases a new set every year, standardization should still be the rule. Many times a jersey is lost or damaged and needs to be replaced and, if the uniforms are fairly standard, the coach will be able to replace the item(s) quickly and at a lower cost.

Equipment For equipment of a permanent nature it is advantageous to purchase good quality from a reputable company that has been in business for a long time and is likely to be for a long time after the equipment has been purchased. The coach can rely on this type of dealer for replacements and repairs. All gymnastic equipment should be purchased from one company that can provide standard parts for the items they sell. Training equipment should be purchased from companies that have standardized and compatible components for replacement or for expansion. It may be a costly error to buy permanent and expensive equipment from a new firm for a cheaper price unless the school can get firm guarantees from somewhere or someone that the material will hold up and that the dealer or manufacturer will be around to service the equipment.

Long-Range Planning It is imperative that athletic departments plan purchases over a number of years so that budgets can be established and funds secured to cover necessary needs. Looking ahead permits the athletic director, the principal, the supervisor, and/or the public to know what coaches need and to understand and help with fund-raising attempts. There are special times to buy and particular guidelines to follow. Planning ahead makes purchasing simpler and more productive.

When to Buy Buying at the correct time is an important consideration in the management process. Coaches who place orders for their sport at the appropriate time during the year help ensure that the items will be in the equipment room and ready to be issued when the new season begins. Early ordering also gives a coach time to correct errors in delivery and to mark and code all items prior to the time they are to be used. Once practice begins, the focus can be on coaching rather than on supplies.

Time Schedule A time schedule should be established with definite guideline dates for equipment purchases. General rules of thumb would be spring sports by mid-October, fall sports by mid-February, and winter sports by mid-May. Following a routine schedule of early buying will allow the dealer and manufacturers to fill an order and ensure satisfaction of the sport's equipment needs. Figure 15-4 provides guidelines for establishing time schedules.

	Sept.	Oct.	Nov.	Dec.	Jan.	Feb.	Mar.	April	May	June	July	Aug.
Fall Sports			I	I	B	B	O		R	R		
Winter Sports	R						I	I/B	B/O	O		R
Spring Sports		R	R	R					I/B	I/B	O	O

I = Inventory equipment and supplies on hand
B = Prepare budget, gain approval
O = Place orders for needed equipment
R = Receive and code equipment and supplies

Figure 15-4   Buyer's calendar

Dealer Discounts and Closeouts

Bargains should always be considered. If coaches have planned ahead and know that the items being offered for sale are of good quality and are needed, a savings can be made; however, items should not be bought just because they are on sale. Athletic departments ought to look for legitimate discounts and closeouts and then take advantage of them. Discounts offered by reliable, trusted dealers can help both the team and the vendor.

Competitive Bidding

Whenever possible, the competitive bidding process should be used. Some schools require all items to be purchased through this process. If a school combines the needs of several teams, or if several schools combine their needs, lower prices can be obtained for goods. Competition among vendors challenges them to shave the cost to the maximum possible to get an order. A system of standardized purchases, discussed earlier, is very useful in preparing bids and securing low prices.

Where to Buy

Determining the dealer(s) from whom supplies will be purchased may be as important as knowing what to buy. Developing a "cadre" of sports equipment dealers in whom coaches have confidence and who can provide quality products at competitive prices is a valuable addition to the coaches' list of specialists on whom they can rely. As it is not possible, and perhaps not necessary, to be a specialist in all aspects of a sport, a coach needs to develop a network of sports equipment and supply dealers who are knowledgeable in their field or business. The dealer must be trustworthy and willing to work with the coach when help is needed. The latitude the coach has to pick and choose from whom to buy is governed by the size of the community, what is to be purchased, and local policies (written and unwritten) regarding the use of local or out-of-town vendors.

In large metropolitan communities, such as Chicago or Denver, there are many vendors from whom to choose. Conversely, in the small communities there may be no local dealer or only one relatively small store. If the choice is limited, one should make a concerted effort to meet the dealer to discuss available products and the team's needs. In the large community a coach can carefully shop around among the dealers to find those with whom to transact business. In a small community, some distance from a metropolitan area, the coach must look to companies willing to serve and travel to the outlying regions.

Whether the order is for $15 or $3,000 may have a bearing on the coach's freedom and choice of dealer. Generally, when small orders need to be made—perhaps because of an emergency—coaches are able to buy items from their internal accounts following emergency purchase ordering procedures. Most school districts, following established local policy or state fiscal policies, will require the use of bids on large dollar purchases. The dollar level at which the requirement of a bid occurs varies from school to school.

Where established sport equipment dealers are available, the team's needs can be filled by working through these dealers. The dealer may not have all items in stock but will be able to place an order with those manufacturers who prefer to sell and ship through local dealers. There may be some specialized equipment, such as blocking sleds and gymnastics equipment, that will possibly require the coach to shop through catalogs and work directly with the manufacturers. Even in the latter case, the dealers with whom a coach regularly trades are usually more than happy to provide advice and assistance.

Local Vendors Many manufacturers and some dealers have salespeople who call on coaches and athletic departments on a regular basis. If representing reputable companies, these salespeople can provide good service, sound advice, low price, and quality products equal to or better than that of the local vendors. Manufacturers of large pieces of equipment, such as some weight machine companies, often have no local representative. Other companies, such as those specializing in uniform sales, may have not only a factory representative to assist with selection and purchase but a local dealer too. Ball manufacturers, making and selling everything from tennis balls to footballs, also utilize salespeople who call on coaches and local vendors.

These salespeople can provide information on the latest equipment, the maintenance and repair of items, guidelines for sizes and styles, and generally helpful information. Coaches often do not need to choose between local or nonlocal vendors, as both can complement each other to provide a coach with total service. A coach, local vendor, and regional vendor should combine forces to get the best materials at the best price.

Reconditioned Equipment A common practice followed by numerous professional and college teams (and by some school and agency teams) is to have equipment reconditioned rather than to purchase new items. Reputable companies make some items "as good as new" for a small percentage of the original cost. If this procedure is followed, coaches must know the company and its work because extreme care regarding safety has to be taken (for example, football helmets must carry NOCSAE approval). Quality cannot be sacrificed to save dollars.

SUMMARY

This chapter has discussed the intricacies of buying supplies and equipment. Coaches who are seeking the best for athletes will follow specified guidelines as well as general suggestions from experienced personnel in order to select quality items at a good price and to observe sound procedures in securing them. While being able to buy successfully may not rate as high in a coach's book as does developing skills and strategies, expertise in this area will save time and energy for the primary task of working with athletes and can make both tasks easier.

16

Equipment Management

RECEIVING, CONTROLLING, ISSUING
PLANNING FOR CARE AND
   MAINTENANCE
SUMMARY

Budgeting and purchasing new items are directly affected by a coach's plan for managing supplies and equipment. If the management plan contains policies that are sound and applicable to the local situation, a useful system for purchasing, receiving, controlling, storing, issuing, and maintaining all items can be developed. If, however, coaches do not keep up with what they have, or cannot maintain it in usable condition, careful planning and purchasing procedures can be nullified.

Equipment management can be greatly facilitated by using the computer and software programs available (or easily written) that will permit coaches to keep inventories readily available. Data on the amount and condition of each type of equipment, records for each athlete, and initial costs versus projected replacement costs can be stored and quickly retrieved to make the coach's job of equipment management easier and less time-consuming. Using a computer can make it easier to keep track of purchase orders, shipping invoices, and back orders and to compare bids. Additionally, the computer can enhance coordination between the business office and the athletic department, provide the administration information for all sports, and improve communication with equipment vendors.

RECEIVING, CONTROLLING, ISSUING

A well-planned and organized system for receiving, coding, storing, and issuing equipment must be developed. Otherwise, benefits gained from the hard work put into fund raising, budget construction, and the purchasing process will have been exercises in futility. One of the major problems in this area of management is the loss of items either by theft or careless handling. This loss, which can consume a large percentage of an annual budget, reduces the coach's ability to build the equipment inventory to a satisfactory level. Such loss can be traced directly to the lack of adequate policies and procedures for handling equipment. If a coach hopes to reduce loss, appropriate policies and procedures must be developed and instituted, and a secure storage area must be made available. It is a coach's responsibility to see that these regulations are carried out and that the facility remains secure.

Receiving Once the purchase order has been approved and sent to the dealer, the coach must then be concerned with receiving the shipment. This must not be handled in a haphazard manner; a well-planned, systematic procedure should be followed. Having and following an established plan will ensure the correct recording of what was received and provide a system for matching items received with items on the purchase order.

Responsibility The responsibility for processing incoming shipments will vary from school to school, but one individual should be specified as the receiving agent. Because coaches are not always available, a logical choice is the school's full-time or part-time equipment manager or business manager. The receiving agent should sign for the delivery and record the transaction to include time, date, shipping agency, manufacturer, and number of packages. Packages should be stored in a secure area and the head coach notified immediately so that he or she can open the shipment and check the contents. The business office may require the coach to sign the log acknowledging receipt of the shipment, as the ultimate responsibility of ensuring that specifications are met rests with the coach. Any discrepancies must be identified and brought to the attention of the shipper prior to the payment of the bill. This is especially important if the purchase has been made from a regional or national vendor. Careless handling can decrease the quantity or quality of equipment; this may result in the coach's having to answer to a charge of mismanagement of funds.

Procedures When a representative of the school signs for the acceptance of a shipment, that person has signed an agreement with the shipping agent, not with the equipment dealer. The only check necessary at that time is to make sure that the number of pieces that the shipping invoice indicates were to be delivered were actually delivered. Where shipments are received will also vary from school to school. It may be more convenient to receive deliveries in the storage area, but equipment is often delivered to the principal's office or central maintenance area. Someone, coaches or maintenance personnel, will then have to move all items to the athletic storage area.

Once the shipment is at the athletic department's storage area, the coach or equipment manager should locate the box that is marked "Invoice Inside" or the envelope taped to the outside. This dealer's invoice is the document used to check in the items. The invoice must be compared to the school's purchase order to see if the order numbers correspond. Discrepancies between the school's order and the dealer's invoice must be identified, with a notation made if the dealer backordered any part of the order for a later delivery.

The next step in the receiving procedure is the actual checking of each individual item. The first concern is for the quantity of the items. Does the number received match the number on the invoice? If they match, that item should be checked and initialed; if the numbers do not match, then the number of missing items should be noted on the invoice. Once all of the same item have been counted, the condition of each should be checked. Every box should be opened and each item examined. For example, balls need to be checked to make sure that they hold air, that the stitching is not broken, or that they are not blemished. Even top-quality items can be damaged—a zipper will not open, a shoe is minus cleats, a tennis racket has a broken string. Any faulty equipment found should be noted on the invoice. The coach must also make sure that substitutions have not been made. Occasionally, companies—in their zeal to fill an order or by a simple mistake—may substitute a relatively similar but cheaper item for the one ordered. Substitutions should be made only when the school's agent has given permission.

For items such as uniforms and shoes, specifications (color, size, etc.) must be verified. Uniforms may be placed on hangers and hung on the same rack. In this way it will be rather easy to see if a slightly different shade of color slipped into the shipment. Uniform sizes may also be checked at this time. As with any other item, shoes have to be carefully examined. Not only should the sizes be checked (if a dozen pairs of size 10's were ordered, there should be this exact number) but also each pair should be checked to see if in fact it is a pair and not two lefts or two rights. These mistakes could happen very easily, and quite by accident, especially if the order is being filled by a local vendor who serves the dual role of retailer and wholesaler. The coach is responsible for catching such mistakes.

Checking in equipment is a tedious but very important job. The coach should never sign the invoice or send it to the business office until every item has been verified. It is difficult to correct orders or to exchange damaged items once the bill has been paid. A coach may choose to use other staff members or student managers to help with this task. If such is the case, they should be told exactly what to look for or be assigned a specific task (such as counting and checking off the number of balls) while the head coach checks the quality. Assistance from others would decrease the length of time required to process a large order.

Controlling

After the order has been checked in and the invoice has been signed and forwarded to the proper office, the equipment is ready to be placed in inventory. The process of preparing equipment for use includes marking, coding, and entering the items on the inventory records. Once that is completed, items may be placed on the shelves, ready to be used.

Marking and Coding

The basic rule for marking equipment is to be sure that the system used will permanently identify the item in such a way that no one will be in doubt as to whom it belongs. Generally, the name or initials of the school are written, stamped, or stenciled on in indelible ink. Where ink is not appropriate, an electric marking pen, a branding iron, quick drying enamel, or decals can be used. Some marking systems prefer to place the school name in large letters in a highly visible place so that it will be more difficult for the items to be taken away by mistake.

Equipment Management **235**

The basic concern in coding is to be able to sort items out by size, type, or sport and to be able to determine the purchase date and thus the durability of the goods. The system for a single sport may be as simple as assigning a player a number and then putting that number on all uniform items. A departmental coding system is usually much more complex and is used for all equipment, not just uniforms.

One system of coding basketball uniform shorts consists of assigning a sequence of numbers for each waist size. All size 28 waists might be numbered 1 through 10, all size 30's numbered 11 through 20, and so on. Jerseys, especially game ones, are usually ordered with numbers that may serve as the identification and control number. If practice jerseys are ordered without numbers, the player's game jersey number may be placed on the neck, tail, front, and/or back of the shirt.

Items frequently exchanged, such as towels or socks, should be marked with the school's identification mark and the purchase date. A separate number is not needed for each item. Items such as socks may carry a code that would aid sorting by size. Balls and other small equipment should be marked in the same relative place. Markings should include the school's initials, the year of purchase, and the item number. An example of this system is a volleyball marked "MHS-88-1." This coding would stand for Murfreesboro High School, a 1988 year of purchase, and the inventory number of 1.

Coaches ought to mark everything that the school owns so that there will be no doubt about ownership. Once new equipment is marked and coded, it should be added to the master inventory list by type and number to provide the athletic deparment with a record of all supplies on hand.

Storing

A basic need of an efficient and effective program of equipment management is storage that permits control and allows for monitoring access. If there is a choice of areas, the room should not be next to pools, the heating unit, or spaces that are likely to flood if it rains or if there are plumbing problems. It should be a well-lighted and ventilated area with a checkout window and counter for issuing equipment in a location that permits good traffic patterns. Strong key locks, with a very limited number of keys issued, need to be used to secure doors and windows. Sometimes it is necessary to place bars or heavy wire mesh over openings and to secure doubly such popular items as warmups by locking them in storage room cabinets. Having cabinets, racks, shelves, hooks, bins, and drawers allows space to be used fully. Periodic checks for pests and mildew are necessary, and there should be no delay in taking action to clear the area of both.

Issuing

An organized and systematic plan for issuing equipment is a necessity. The coach must devise a system before the athletes report to receive items assigned to them. Whatever plan is used should fit the particular situation, the sport, school, equipment to be handled, and facilities. Regardless of specific procedures, the underlying purpose of any plan remains the same—control of equipment.

*Player
Responsibility*

The first step in issuing equipment is to inform the athletes what their responsibilities are in relation to the items checked out to them. They must realize that the items are on loan and not given as gifts. It should be very clear to all athletes what their responsibilities are if an item is lost or damaged beyond normal wear. Different schools have different policies, which may vary from reimbursing the school the price of new equipment to pro-rating the cost of the item based on age and use. Athletes must be made aware that they contribute as much to the success of the program by helping maintain the department's equipment as they do by their playing on the fields and floors of competition. A program that is annually spending its money on game jerseys, because athletes fail to return them, will not have the funds to buy items to refine the athletes' skills.

Recording

Record keeping is fundamental to any successful system of issuing equipment. Student managers can aid in the recording as items are issued. Each coach must use some type of procedure for noting which player received what piece of equipment. There are many types of forms that can be used; most are similar to the one shown in Figure 16-1.

Procedures

The number of each item should be recorded as the athlete receives it. After all items have been issued, the athlete should be asked to sign a card to verify that the equipment has been received. Signing the card not only acknowledges this fact but also helps instill the feeling of having entered an agreement. The athlete may thus feel more obligated to return the items received or to reimburse the school. Many schools will add a statement above the athlete's signature line that clearly states the school's policy concerning lost or damaged equipment. During the year, if items are exchanged, this is noted on the card. The number of the newly issued equipment should be recorded on the card and the athlete required to initial the transaction. At the end of the season, the coach or manager examines each piece of equipment and, if it is in acceptable condition, checks that item off the individual's equipment card.

When the sport season is over, each head coach is responsible for making sure that all items that were issued to players, assistant coaches, and managers are returned. It may be necessary to remind them to return the items; it may even be necessary for the coach to get them from a locker or wherever they can be located. The coach must be careful to follow correct procedures so as not to violate the student's legal rights (these are discussed in Chapter 19), but he or she must do what is necessary to clear the equipment-issuing record. No program can afford to lose even the smallest item.

PLANNING FOR CARE AND MAINTENANCE

Because no program can afford to purchase all new equipment each year, the care and maintenance of old items is extremely important. Successful maintenance programs keep each item of equipment in use for a maxi-

```
┌─────────────────────────────────────────────────────────┐
│                    Sport _____                  │
│   Name (print) _____│
│                 (Last)        (First)         (Middle)  │
│   Class _____  Homeroom Teacher _____│
│   Home Address _____  Phone Number _____ │
│   _____│
│                        Equipment Issued                 │
│                  │            │ Returned   │  Amount    │
│                  │            │ in Accept. │  Paid      │
│   Item           │ Issue No.  │ Condition  │ for Loss or│
│                  │            │            │  Damage    │
│   _____│_____│_____│_____│
│   _____│_____│_____│_____│
│   _____│_____│_____│_____│
│   _____│_____│_____│_____│
│   _____│_____│_____│_____│
│   _____│_____│_____│_____│
│   _____│_____│_____│_____│
│                                                         │
│   I have received and will be responsible for the       │
│   articles listed hereon which have been charged to me, │
│   and agree that they will not be used for any purpose  │
│   but regularly scheduled school athletics while in my  │
│   possession. I also promise to return these items when │
│   asked to do so or pay for same at face value.         │
│                                                         │
│                   Signed _____  Date _____    │
└─────────────────────────────────────────────────────────┘
```

Figure 16-1   Equipment issue

mum number of years, allowing the budget dollars to be spent on new equipment rather than on replacement items. Equipment loss can be as great from improper or insufficient cleaning, or the lack of repair, as from theft and wear. Coaches and equipment managers must be concerned with such things as mildew, rips and tears, broken laces, and splintered sticks. Good cleaning, repairing, and storing procedures are too important to be ignored.

Annual Plan   As with other aspects of coaching and program management, the care and maintenance of equipment is a continuous, ongoing operation. There are many different things that a coach must be concerned with, depending on the time of the year. Each concern is of equal importance and cannot be omitted. In order to ensure that each step is successfully completed at the correct time, the coach must develop an annual plan that can be divided into three time periods: pre-season, playing season, and post-season.

Pre-Season

As new items arrive, they must be processed (as previously discussed) and stored in the proper manner, ready for immediate use. Storage areas should be inspected to see if the temperature and humidity levels are still appropriate. This is a primary consideration when selecting or building a storage area, but periodic checks need to be made to be sure that the equipment is not ruined by changes in these two conditions.

Pre-season is the time that the coach reviews procedures for handling the laundry. If a commercial cleaner or laundry will be employed for uniforms and towels, arrangements should be made well before the season begins. The cost and schedule of when the laundry will need to be picked up and returned are issues that need to be clarified. If the school operates its own washing machines and dryers, this is the time to run a maintenance check to see if all the units work. Also, the coach should check out the student managers or the staff members who will be responsible for operating these machines to make sure that they know how to operate them. Regardless of how the laundry is handled—commercial cleaner or school machines—the coach must make sure that those who will take care of the laundry are aware of the manufacturer's directions.

If the school relies on the parents of the players to help keep uniforms clean, letters containing proper instructions should be sent to these people. The general information to be included in this letter includes caution about the use of bleach, hot water, and drying when cleaning each item. If players have to do their own laundry, they should be given a copy of this letter.

This is also the time when the coach checks through all equipment to be certain that it is ready to be issued. There should be no repair or maintenance needs at this time if proper care was given during the post-season period. Each year, though, there are usually a few items that were overlooked and may require repair before being used.

Playing Season

The playing season may be divided into three sections: practices, home contests, and road contests. Each presents different concerns related to the care and maintenance of equipment, and it is helpful to establish routine procedures for each. Using student managers can be very helpful, especially if many athletes are involved in the sport or if a great deal of equipment is involved. Players can also assist, but they must be informed of their responsibilities.

Practice sessions require players, student managers, and coaches to perform specified duties. Players must make sure that uniforms and shoes are hung properly or placed in the correct area to ensure that they will dry before the next day's practice; they should not expect coaches and managers to do this for them. Athletes should report any tears or damages that may have occurred that day; managers also need to check equipment for any damage that may have happened during practice. They should make sure that all equipment is returned to the proper area. Balls, rackets, ball machines, or whatever items are used must be placed in the storage areas. Coaches, or one specific coach, should be responsible for verifying that equipment has been taken care of according to established procedures.

Home contests require the same procedures as practices do. Uniforms are hung to dry in order to prevent damage. Before washing and cleaning, each item is carefully checked for rips, tears, snags, frayed areas, or heavily stained spots so that they can be taken care of prior to the next contest. The equipment is checked in, inspected for damage, and then placed in its proper space. Equipment is not stored until it is repaired and cleaned. Usually one person has the responsibility for uniforms and equipment; however, the coach has the ultimate responsibility and should make routine checks to ensure that things are in order.

Road contests demand special procedures because then it is not possible to follow normal routines. Uniforms and equipment should be checked for damages before being packed. The individual who is packing should count each item to make sure that all items are accounted for prior to leaving for home. If players pack and carry their own uniforms, they are responsible for checking uniforms for any damage. If the team returns home immediately, the uniforms must be unpacked and hung to dry as soon as players arrive at the gymnasium or field house. The equipment is stored in its proper place at this time. Once the team has returned to its home facilities, normal home game procedures can be followed. Particular care must be taken on road trips not to leave jackets, balls, shoes, gloves, and such items behind when the team leaves for home, or to permit damp and soiled uniforms to stay in these conditions for a lengthy period of time.

Extended trips require additional equipment care. If the team is on a long road trip, players must be instructed on the proper care of their uniforms. If all team uniforms are packed in an equipment trunk, the manager will be responsible for the care of the items. The host school's laundry facilities or a coin-operated laundry may be used to keep the uniforms in proper condition. It is more feasible to have two or three people doing this job than to have each player doing his or her own laundry. Although maintaining equipment on these trips is not as difficult as caring for uniforms, all items must still be checked in and repaired, if possible, or taken out of service. Awkward-sized equipment, such as vaulting poles, must have its special place on the team bus or in the motel. As for home contests and short trips, the coach has the final responsibility for the safety, maintenance, and storage of all items.

Post-Season   The period immediately following the competitive season is the most important time of year for repairing, cleaning, and storing equipment. This is the time to inspect all items carefully and to classify them as to handling procedures—repaired, discarded, or stored in present condition. Inspection for damage to uniforms should take place before cleaning; notes then pinned to each item indicating specific problems will help whoever is doing the final cleaning process. The coach or managers may be able to do some repairs, or the services of the school's home economics department may be enlisted. In some communities there may be groups, such as senior citizens, who will be pleased to assist in a repair project. After garments have been mended and cleaned they are ready to be stored. They should be packed in heavy cartons, treated for moths and other insects, tightly sealed, and stored in a cool, dry area. A list placed on the outside of the container specifying items, number, and sizes will help to locate items when preparations are made for a new season.

Equipment should be processed in the same manner and either discarded, repaired, or stored. All pieces should be repaired, cleaned, oiled, waxed, and so on, according to the manufacturer's directions. Many manufacturers will repair or renovate equipment, and items that are sent immediately following the season can be returned before being needed. Once all these tasks have been completed, the coach is ready to close the books on one season and begin to think about the next.

Care of Uniforms

The general care of uniforms has been discussed, but there are particular considerations. In carrying out proper procedures, coaches will assist in the health care of players, lengthen the lifetime of the uniform, and demonstrate good management.

Clean

Cleaning of all uniform items, either by washing or dry cleaning, is necessary to increase their usefulness, to maintain good appearance, and to follow good health practices. Avoiding infections, both self-generated and player-to-player, is a primary concern of all coaches and a basic reason for cleanliness. Germs and fungi thrive in hot, humid, dirty environments, which describe many locker rooms despite the staff's best efforts. Improperly cleaned and stored uniforms will add to the conditions conducive to germ production. Irritations, infections, and sickness among the team members are likely unless the coach provides the necessary conditions and follows prescribed procedures. When cleaning uniforms, the responsible individual should follow manufacturer's instructions that are usually placed on a label attached to the garment. More complete instructions may be obtained from dealers or by writing directly to the manufacturer.

Repair

Uniforms usually need the attention of a good seamstress or tailor when rips, snags, broken straps, missing buttons, or broken zippers appear. There may be a parent, staff member, student, or player who has the skills necessary to make needed repairs. Whoever a coach can hire, or find to volunteer, should be available on a regular basis to mend the damaged items immediately. Unmended snags can develop into greater rips and tears that make a garment unusable. Heavy fabrics that cannot be mended on a heavy-duty domestic machine may be sent to a shoe repair shop.

On some occasions, if the decoration on the garment is not too elaborate, faded uniforms can be redyed either commercially or in the team washing machine. This can provide additional use and extend the life of items that are structurally sound but unattractive. Coaches must know exactly what they are doing before they undertake this task; otherwise, they could ruin a machine as well as the uniforms.

Schedule A regular schedule for care ought to be established so that players, coaches, and managers can function harmoniously. If there is a limited number of washing machines and there are several teams playing during a single season, there has to be a coordinated program that will allow all teams' uniforms to get cleaned when needed. If players are responsible for their own garments, they must know when and how often these need to be cleaned as well as the recommended procedures.

Care of Equipment Daily attention should be given to each piece of equipment such as protective gear, balls, sticks, pads, goals, and teaching aids. In order to preserve the life of each item and to ensure the safety of the athlete, routine inspection and care has to be given all equipment. Manufacturer's instructions should accompany each item as it is received, and these should be followed. Coaches who are not sure of how to clean and repair selected pieces should contact the manufacturer or dealer to obtain the information.

On some large pieces of equipment, screws and bolts need to be kept tight and must be replaced immediately if broken or lost. Rust spots should be sanded and paint applied. Wooden items may have to be sanded to rid them of splinters. One thing is certain—it is much easier and less expensive to make minor repairs than major ones.

SUMMARY

Managing equipment and uniforms so as to get the most and the safest use possible is another responsibility of the coach. This second part of the process that begins with buying equipment must be well executed if the team is to get full value for the money expended. The lucky (or smart) coach will have a good, responsible, well-trained equipment manager to assist in the process. It is difficult to coach on the field and simultaneously keep track of all phases of equipment management. Many coaches manage to fill both roles, however, and all must know how to do everything if only to be sure that an assistant is performing properly.

Taking good care of equipment permits the coach to spend limited funds wisely. If uniforms can last an additional year, funds usually spent on uniforms may be spent for something else. If tennis rackets are taken care of, nets and balls can be bought. If towels are issued carefully, a large replacement order will not need to be made every year. The ability to manage equipment is not a gift, it is a learned skill; but in these days of tight money and reduced revenues, it is a skill that the coach must learn. If the budget is cut, the coach must know how to get and keep the most for every dollar.

17

Schedule Planning

PLANNING THE SCHEDULE
RULES FOR SCHEDULE PLANNING
SPECIAL SITUATIONS
CONTRACTING GUIDELINES
SUMMARY

The culmination of all the hard work that goes into sports activities is the contest itself. Players practice day after day, coaches put in many hours of planning the program and conducting practices, and parents and staff contribute hours of work to support the program. All this effort is directed toward "the game." Therefore, planning the schedule of contests must not be a haphazard effort; indeed, it is a vital task of a coach.

Regardless of the process used, there is a need for cooperation among all school personnel, especially coaches of other sports. Every effort should be made for "give and take," when setting dates and times for events, to ensure fair and maximum use of facilities. Coaches are, however, limited in what they can do, primarily by the rules of the State High School Associations.

PLANNING THE SCHEDULE

Preparing a good schedule is not a last-minute, short-term process; rather, it is a year-long one. This is true for any sport, but particularly important for sports that share facilities and coaches. With the increased number of sport teams and the need to coordinate facilities and transportation, using the computer to develop the school's master activities schedule is essential. This is especially so when individual coaches, and not athletic directors, have been delegated scheduling responsibilities. The master schedule with school holidays, major functions, test days, and so on, should be programmed into the computer at the end of the school year; and each coach could add tentative dates, then confirmed dates, as the scheduling process continues. A coach could then have all teams' schedules for the next year within easy reach while talking with another coach or school administrator, seeing immediately if it is possible to coordinate travel with another team or if a bus is available. Software programs that can easily be adapted for the scheduling function are accessible. A coach will quickly discover that using the computer for scheduling will prevent problems, save valuable time, and reduce expenses.

Figure 17-1 The game is the thing (Courtesy of The Florida State University, Tallahassee, Florida. Photographer: Deborah Thomas)

Time Frame

There has been a trend to schedule contests only one year ahead, as coaches have found that long-term commitments can create problems. This is especially true in rapid growth areas in which new schools open each year. Many schools, however, still attempt to schedule two-year home and home games with traditional rivals. Some high school associations prohibit contracting for contests more than three years in advance.

Every effort should be made to complete all schedules for the upcoming year before the current school year ends, and many school districts will not allow a coach to leave in June until the next year's schedule is completed, submitted, and approved. It is wise to set the schedule for the fall sports long before June, but the spring sports schedules may be completed in the fall. The rule of thumb should be to schedule at least one complete season (fall, winter, spring) ahead of a sport's season. Coaches will often explore options for dates for the next season with the opposing coach before leaving the contest site. Scheduling is also discussed at coaches' meetings, tournament gatherings, and similar situations where coaches convene.

Academic Considerations

Coaches at all levels must be concerned about the academic success of their athletes and are obligated to provide educationally sound schedules. Public outcry for academic reform in athletics, resulting in increased graduation requirements and standards, "no pass, no play" laws, and the National Collegiate Athletic Association's Proposition 48 [Bylaw 5-(1)-(j)] demands this. Contests and practices must be scheduled to cause as few class absences as possible, and they should not conflict with test days, examinations, or other academic activity. It is imperative that boys and girls receive equal consideration when schedules are made so that no one group practices or competes consistently at an undesirable time.

To the extent possible, long-distance road games on school nights should be avoided for both boys and girls, varsity and junior varsity. The result of such trips can be a sleepy group of players and student fans trying to pay attention in class the next day. Faculty and parents do not approve of an extended schedule that causes missed classes and inattentive students.

A slight change in the time of the day that the contest is to be played—perhaps as little as 30 minutes—could decrease missed class time as well as increase sleep or rest time. If long trips must be made, it may be necessary to spend the night in the opponent's area and return home the next day. This can become a lesson in history, geography, or art, as being in a different locale affords players an opportunity to see and do things that many athletes have missed. Some players have never stayed in a motel, eaten in a restaurant, visited the state capital, shopped in a department store, or seen an ocean. Many high school athletes have not traveled farther than 50 blocks away from home.

It should be remembered that athletics are for athletes, not coaches, and that the program must be planned for their best interests. As youth sports becomes increasingly like the pros, coaches must guard against the tendency to forget the original purpose, which is to give each player an opportunity to perform well. Schedules must reflect concern for the player by not being in conflict with or detracting from academic life.

Equitable Competition

When scheduling games, the coach must consider the caliber of competition as well as the school size. Coaches should not be lured into scheduling games with teams that are far superior to their team in talent and number of quality players simply for large guarantees. Coaches also should not permit personal feelings about an opponent or coach to cause them to issue a challenge simply to satisfy an ego or personal pride. Contests should not be scheduled if the sole reason is to "beat" that particular opponent. Contests ought to be scheduled on the basis of potential equitable competition, equal sizes of the players, equitable number of players per squad, and with the safety and welfare of all participants in mind.

Scheduling teams that will create a mismatch of skills is humiliating for players with little ability. Occasionally, a team blossoms overnight into a surprising champion, and suddenly all their scheduled opponents are outclassed; however, this is a "Cinderella" occasion and not a planned consequence. Coaches must be careful not to schedule their teams deliberately into situations in which both players and coaches know that they will be badly beaten.

Teams sometimes feel that they must play those better than they are in order to gain experience playing good competition. This is a legitimate reason for overmatching and acceptable where it is arranged to ensure the weaker team a competitive game that will not endanger the team members' safety.

Mismatching is not only damaging psychologically, it can also be damaging physically. Coaches should never willingly or deliberately permit smaller, lighter, inexperienced players to compete in a contact sport with players who are larger, heavier, more experienced, and vastly superior. Age groups or height and weight classifications are considerations in scheduling. Age group swimming and track programs have built-in safeguards for participants, and weight classifications for boxing, wrestling, and recreation league football ensure equality in competition. In these sports, meets or contests involve athletes who compete only at their proper level.

Factors Affecting Scheduling

In developing the schedule, a coach must consider policies and recommendations that could affect when or where games can be scheduled. Whether or not such constraints exist should be carefully checked out before a coach begins to make contacts with possible opponents.

Most state athletic/activity associations have certain regulations relating to games to be played. Some of the more common ones relate to:

1. The number of games that can be played in a season.
2. The dates for beginning and ending a season of play.
3. The distance a team can travel.
4. Interstate competition.
5. Association member versus nonmember schools.
6. Post-season competition.

National Federation of State High School Associations (NFSHSA)

This organization recommends certain procedures for the scheduling of contests. Though the Federation's rules are recommendations, they gain strength through the commitments of the state association to abide by them. Two regulations of particular importance require a team to seek the Federation's sanction for (1) dual contests, meets, and tournaments requiring more than 600 miles round-trip travel, and (2) interstate meets involving four teams from three or more states. The Federation does not permit national championships.

Local Organizations

Policies imposed by school boards, school district athletic councils, and individual schools can affect the efforts of the coach to prepare a schedule. These may restrict the distance that teams can travel, limit the number of classes that may be missed, require that more than one sport team travel together on trips, deal with overnight trips, involve budget consideration, and so on.

Conference Policies

Schools that have joined conferences or leagues may have additional regulations. There may be restrictions in the conference bylaws regarding such things as the number of conference teams to be played, length of seasons, tournaments, or play-offs. In some conferences the coaches are responsible for establishing the schedule within the conference guidelines; in other leagues and conferences, the schedule is prepared by the conference officials. Schools generally are permitted to submit pertinent data for consideration that might affect the placement of game dates, such as special holidays, school functions, testing dates, commencement, and other school-related activities. Other than consideration for the special dates, the decisions on game dates and sites are made by the person charged with preparation of schedules for the conference.

Environmental Conditions

Conditions such as weather and density of population must also be analyzed. A team in a sparsely populated area of Alaska will have more difficulty developing schedules than will a team in the densely populated areas of New York or California. Teams in some areas may not have to travel farther than 10 to 15 miles on any trip to have a complete schedule, while teams in less populated regions will travel 100 or more miles for a contest numerous times each season. Teams in states having extreme weather conditions—snow, ice, heavy rainfall—must be more concerned with travel conditions than do those in states with milder climates. In some areas, teams need to be prepared to spend a night in the field house or by the side of the highway. Emergency procedures must be planned for extreme weather conditions.

Community Traditions

Local community traditions and mores affect scheduling. Sunday play may be prohibited or limited to nonchurch hours. Special holidays, festivals, and other community events often dictate dates when contests cannot be held or dates when the school facilities will be committed to the community, thereby forcing the coach to schedule a road contest if one is to be scheduled. Ethnic and national feeling within and among local communities still may govern the teams that can be scheduled. A careful study of these potential conflicts must be made.

Other Community Teams

The presence of college teams or professional teams in a community or nearby location will also influence scheduling. Occasionally, the same facilities are used by teams of all levels, creating a mechanical scheduling problem. More serious is the problem of competing with other teams for fan support. It is not a good idea to schedule a game that would be in direct competition with more attractive teams or programs. Schools may need to improve the quality of their competition to attract fans, eliminating the "easy" teams that are played to puff up the win-loss record.

Rivalries

As rivalries mount, competition stress increases; in innumerable communities, the adult or out-of-school population becomes so caught up in the rivalry that contests have to be rescheduled to avoid serious conflicts, including riots. Many contests are played in the afternoon to deter attendance by older youths and adults. In some instances, contests are played with no spectators at undesignated sites unknown even to the players before boarding the bus. Healthy rivalries can do a great deal to help an athletic program, but unhealthy ones can destroy it. Coaches must take a major share of the responsibility for controlling rivalries so that all possible benefits will be gained from the program.

Energy Use

Scheduling can be affected more by an energy crisis than for any other single reason. The cost of transportation increased at a phenomenal rate in the 1970s, fluctuated in the 1980s, and may increase in the 1990s. Schools that must travel extended distances to compete may find it difficult to pay travel costs for maintaining schedules; thus, they must consider restrictions on travel to help hold down expenses. Some measures that have been successful are:

1. Limiting the distance that may be traveled.
2. Limiting the size of the travel squad.
3. Requiring several teams to travel on the same bus.
4. Restricting the junior high and junior varsity teams' schedule.
5. Playing more than one contest on each road trip.
6. Eliminating trips by having telephone meets for sports such as swimming.

The energy situation could also affect the time of day that a contest is played. Football may once again become an afternoon event for high schools, just as some colleges/universities have returned to playing day games to reduce the tremendous cost of lighting a field. In cold environments, afternoon basketball games may be played to reduce heating costs during nonschool hours. Eliminating night contests could save thousands of dollars for a school; however, the athletic department's income could also be reduced because many fans would not be free to attend day games. It is impossible to predict how the energy problem will affect athletic programs in the future, but any coach who does not consider possible alternatives in scheduling may be caught standing in an empty arena.

RULES FOR SCHEDULE PLANNING

A coach successful in building a good schedule, both present and future, must have carefully calculated the team's potential strengths and weaknesses season after season. How many seniors, juniors, sophomores are on the squad? Will the team be strong at the beginning of the season, or will it need some competition to allow the development of the needed depth and experience? How coaches answer questions such as these determines how successful they are at matching team abilities with a schedule. If a successful season is judged on the win-loss record, scheduling is important. Many successful coaches have been credited with having a winning season because they are not only good teachers of sports skills but shrewd schedule planners as well. However, a successful record is not the only criterion when planning a schedule. Some coaches are concerned with providing the squad members with the best experiences possible, experiences that will permit all team members to develop their maximum potential. It may be simple to build some "laughers" into a schedule that will assure a successful win-loss record, but it can be more difficult to develop a competitive schedule that benefits all concerned.

Game Balance

The proper balance of different types of games does not mean just an equal number of home and away contests. It also includes consideration of conference and nonconference teams and traditional rivals or nonrivals.

Home and Away Contests

To the extent possible, coaches should attempt to schedule an equal number of home and away games. In this way they will be assured of having a sufficient number of home contests to satisfy students and to provide good hometown support. Schedules that become heavy with away games should be avoided. Balanced schedules are helpful to the athletes because they reduce the amount of time away from home and school, thus reducing class absences. The "home court" advantage is also sought, as players seem to do better at "home," in a familiar place with supportive spectators. Generally, athletes are happier to play on their own grounds.

There are, though, exceptions to this rule. A team that does not draw large crowds, even for home games, because of community attitudes or sparseness of population, needs to schedule additional away games, especially with schools that draw big crowds. In exchange for this consideration, a guarantee can be negotiated. Since most high schools that play home and home do not split the gate, any guarantee from a school that draws big crowds would provide a better financial return than playing before empty stands at home. For example, a coach may say, "We will play you twice at your home arena for a 50-50 percentage split of the gate receipts after expenses." Both schools benefit financially. The school that offered to give up the home arena advantage makes more money than it would by playing at home in front of a small crowd that may not even cover the costs of the game. The host school can receive the same income from two games as from one home game without having to expend funds on traveling and while keeping the home site advantage.

Traditional Rivals

The coach will want to weigh carefully the time during the season when arch rivals are played. Game strategy, as well as crowd appeal, are important factors. The smart coach knows that all involved players, coaches, and fans look forward to the "big victory" of the season. The team should "peak" for these contests, with players psychologically ready to give their top performance. A team is better prepared to play such a game during the latter part of the season, but the selected opponent will also be better prepared at that time. Seasons are often judged on whether or not a team defeats the arch rival. Playing these opponents too early in the season or too close together can leave the balance of the season somewhat flat in terms of interest. It is best to place these contests somewhere after the midpoint of the season, preceded by an open date or a very weak opponent.

Conference and Nonconference Contests

The formation of conferences and leagues has contributed a great deal to creating interest in games other than one or two normally played against the arch rival. The challenge of winning the conference crown helps place a value on more than winning or losing a single contest. A coach or conference planner should attempt to distribute these games throughout the schedule to ensure a season of high-interest games. Most leagues and conferences have rules regarding the number of conference and nonconference contests that may be played if that team is to compete for the championship. Where this is required, the coach knows the balance permitted and schedules accordingly. Other conferences, because of the number of schools who are members, require each school to play all members.

When considering balance between conference and nonconference games, the coach is not always looking for an equal number of games, but rather a balance of games over the season. Some coaches do not want to play nonconference games once conference play has begun. This is particularly true if participation in league play-offs is determined on season play.

Classification Considerations

A schedule should be filled with teams that are comparable in size and talent. If a team is located in a sparsely populated region containing few schools and the travel budget is tight, contests with larger or smaller schools may be necessary. If a smaller school must be scheduled, the coach should look for one that has a good team that particular year. If a larger school must be scheduled, the coach should pick one that is a little weak. The more equal the teams, the more exciting the match beween contestants becomes. A coach that attempts to build a schedule of "patsies" in order to win does not help the team, even though the record looks good. In contact sports, the safety of the squad members and the players of the opposing squad must be an equal consideration. To know that one has a large, powerful, talented squad and then purposely schedule a smaller, less skilled team is not a credit to the integrity of a coach. Such match-ups often result in unnecessary injuries to the smaller squad and tend to build a poor reputation for that coach. Unfortunately, there are some coaches who are more interested in their win-loss record than in building solid, competitive teams with good safety records.

If tournaments or play-offs are part of the season, it is quite likely that the lack of equitable competition will eventually catch up with a team. States that have instituted play-off systems leading to state championships have corrected this problem to some extent. Schools may actually be penalized in earning points necessary to qualify for their district or regional play-off if they play teams in a lower classification.

Opponents with Good Fan Support

Building a schedule with colorful teams that have good home crowd followings ensures more excitement at home contests and increases the probability of higher gate receipts. Many schools enjoy support by their students and their community adults. Their followers will travel to distant games in large numbers to back their teams. The more teams of this type a coach can place on the schedule, the more exciting and profitable the season will be, both in revenues and in fan support.

Multiple Scheduling of Contests

Travel is a major budget item. One method of reducing travel costs is to have more than one team travel in the same bus. In order to make this possible, the coaches of all of the sports competing during the same season have to coordinate their schedules. Boys' and girls' teams in the same sport, such as basketball, could schedule road contests with the same opponents for the same day. This would allow two teams to travel for the cost of one.

Another alternative would be scheduling a common opponent for several boys' and girls' teams. Boys' and girls' golf and tennis teams could travel with the softball or baseball teams, or boys' and girls' track and field teams may share the same bus. Any system that reduces the total bus miles charged to the athletic budget provides savings. Many sports have traditionally played doubleheaders or tournament contests; baseball, volleyball, and softball are typical examples. Tournaments in particular permit a large number of games at one site, yet decrease transportation game costs and increase competitive opportunities.

Scheduling boys' and girls' team games on the same afternoon or evening also can reduce other costs, such as utilities. Scheduling both teams for the same evening might lead to more interest in the contest, since fans could watch both groups perform. In many states, boys and girls now play in back-to-back contests in basketball. Usually girls play the "preliminary" game, but in some locations, such as areas of Iowa, boys may play the opening game of this doubleheader. Swimming, track and field, tennis, golf, and gymnastics all lend themselves to joint scheduling and transportation. Junior varsity games and "B" squad games could also be scheduled in this fashion.

Such coordination of scheduling may also make it easier to contract for officials and more convenient for team followers to attend games. Parents can see both sons and daughters play in one trip. Cooperative planning by the entire athletic department makes the whole program operate more smoothly.

There are drawbacks to this type of joint scheduling. Junior varsity or junior high teams may not be able to play as frequently as they would if there was a "boys' night" and a "girls' night." One way that coaches may solve this problem is by having the junior varsity teams play alternately, the girls before each odd-numbered varsity contest and the boys prior to each even-numbered one. Another drawback may be the loss of revenue. Two teams that draw large crowds—thus making money—should not be scheduled together. A revenue sport needs to be scheduled with a nonrevenue sport or with a sport that would generate less revenue than it would cost if traveling alone.

SPECIAL SITUATIONS

The general guidelines discussed thus far are important for every coach to keep in mind when trying to build a schedule. There are, however, several scheduling situations that should be discussed individually, even though all the other considerations also apply to these situations. Attempting to schedule contests at a coaches' meeting, trying to complete a partial schedule, or planning the schedule for a winning season are special problems that every coach may need to consider at some point in a coaching career.

Scheduling at a Coaches' Meeting

The following material is adapted from information given by experienced coaches discussing actions typically taken by coaches as a group at a conference meeting.

1. Agree on the number of season games or matches.
2. Identify schools willing to play contests.
3. Assign a number to each school playing contests. These schools receive a number by lot with number one getting the first choice of an opponent. The team with number two would choose an opponent second, and so on until all teams had opponents. If there are six contests, there will be six rounds for choosing opponents.
4. Prepare a master schedule of contests, including date and home team. The home team can indicate time and place later.
5. Agree on when the nonconference contests will be played.
6. Determine number of contests required for district play to meet association guidelines.
7. Assign a district chairperson to moderate the selection rounds and to place agreed-on contests on the master schedule.
8. Designate the athletic director or coach of each home team as the one who will name the time and place of each contest, and give that information to the opponents and to the conference officials.
9. Sign contracts according to the coaches' agreements.

Completing a Partial Schedule

Not all coaches are required to have their schedules completed by June or by the end of the school year. This may create problems for a new coach if a partial schedule is inherited while most schools have their schedule fairly well filled or completed. Occasionally, too, even well-laid plans get upset or cancelled. This also requires a coach to attempt to fill a suddenly incomplete schedule after other schools have filled theirs.

As soon as it is learned that there is an open date, the coach must begin contacting potential opponents. The telephone is the best method of contact as it will allow discussion about possible dates or alternatives. If the mail is used, too much time may be lost and a schedule may not be filled. A coach who has been on the job for at least one year will have an idea of teams that would make good attractive opponents, based on the considerations previously mentioned in this chapter. If none of the teams on the list of potentials can be scheduled, a coach can still ask each contacted coach to suggest an opponent for the open date; and the "good ol' coaches" network can be used to spread the word that a valid opponent is needed.

Coaches must attempt to keep scheduling guidelines in mind when trying to fill open dates, but they may not be able to be very selective when considering factors such as distance, level of competition, or crowd attraction. However, a coach should not accept a contest for the sake of having a full schedule. Scheduling any old game may be more detrimental to a team than having an open date.

If time permits, the school can advertise in the Coaches Association's and/or the Activities Association's bulletins. Many newspapers will advertise open dates on the sports pages. The basic trick is to keep contacting people until a representative schedule is developed that will be beneficial to the team.

Scheduling for a Winning Season

It has been said that a good schedule would be a 15-50-35 schedule. This means scheduling 15 percent of the contests against strong opponents that can be beaten with a maximum effort combined with a slight off-night for the opponents. Fifty percent of the games are scheduled with opponents that offer fairly equal competition, and the remaining 35 percent of the schedule is filled with opponents that offer no real threat. If one of these last opponents were to win, it would be a major upset. Coaches try to schedule weak opponents prior to each of the strong opponents and prior to any arch rival that falls into the 50 percent group. Also, it could help to play several easy opponents at the very beginning of the schedule. This will permit a team to get off to a winning start and build confidence. However, in such sports as football where a team may play only 7 to 10 games, the schedule has room for one strong opponent and a couple of weak ones. In football, conference games often dominate or completely fill the schedule.

If advancement to the state play-offs is determined in post-season tournament play, coaches may want to try a scheduling pattern used successfully by a few basketball coaches. Highly ranked teams are scheduled early to give players needed game experience with top players and tough teams. Then, tournament play at the end of the season may appear to be easier for the team members, as they have seen "the best" while developing their own potential. The win-loss record is still important, but getting to, and possibly winning, the final round is more so.

Any coach who can consistently win the scheduling game can have a winning season year after year, even with less than superior material. A coach must evaluate incoming material, evaluate opponents' material, and then pick and choose to try to arrange a schedule that will produce a 70 percent season. There may be seasons when a coach will shoot for 100 percent, or be satisfied with 50 percent, but good scheduling can keep a team around a 70 percent winning record over the long haul. Although the required list of opponents may be large, there is always room for a little maneuvering and experienced coaches use that flexible space to the best advantage. The entire process of scheduling is designed to arrange for competitive experiences for a team and to attempt to arrange for more winning experiences than losing ones.

CONTRACTING GUIDELINES

Coaching a team is a business operation, and all aspects of the program must be managed in the same fashion as a successful business is. Coaches must be very knowledgeable about contracts and the procedures for contracting games.

Game contracts are more like formal agreements than legally binding business contracts. Considering, however, that once a contract is signed, many dollars and a great number of people are committed to ensure the proper conduct of the contracted contest, the importance of the agreement becomes more significant. Programs are prepared; tickets are printed; arrangements are made for advertisements; work schedules are set for such people as officials, ticket sellers, and security personnel; and many other management details must be taken care of. Such arrangements and/or commitments often require payment in advance for goods provided. In addition, other teams prepare their schedules based on the contracted agreements. Schools violating or breaking contracts can be reprimanded by their state associations, fined, forced to pay forfeiture fees, and quite possibly sued for breach of contract to recover expenses incurred. It is obvious that the "formal agreement" between two schools must be taken seriously and negotiated in good faith.

Most state activity/athletic associations have recognized the importance of this aspect of athletic management by incorporating specific regulations in their bylaws. Contracts for all contests are required of member schools of the association; and, in some states, uniform contract forms issued by the association are another requirement. Although contract forms themselves may be simple, they may make reference to state association guidelines and permit entry of financial agreements. Coaches must be aware of all guidelines, verify all financial agreements, and, if necessary, add statements and materials for clarity.

Between Competent Parties

Contracts must be made between competent parties. In one application of this rule, those negotiating the contract must have authority to negotiate the contract in the first place. A history teacher having no relationship with the athletic program or administration of the school has no authority to negotiate an athletic contract between two schools. Authority for contracting and signing contracts in a school is assigned to the principal and athletic director or coach of the sport; therefore, contracts for contestants must be negotiated by principals or authorized staff of the two schools.

The second application of the term refers to the parties being of sound mind. A contract is not valid when one party is determined to be legally insane.

Mutual Assent

Contracts must be based on mutual assent, commonly referred to as a "meeting of the minds." It is assumed in a contract that the parties to the contract—the two principals and athletic staff—understand and agree to all the terms specified in the contract. They should understand what is "promised."

All parties should initial the list of conditions, which may extend to the reverse side of the document or an attached sheet. It is this extended list that must be initialed and dated by the official signers of the contract. Any change in the contract must be initialed by all parties who originally signed the document. An exception to this would be if one of the signers is no longer with the school. In such a case, the newly appointed person would initial for the original signer.

Valid Considerations

Contracts must contain valid considerations. In general contract terms, valid considerations may take many forms. It may be in the form of a promise to do or not to do something. A valid consideration is usually in the form of an offer of money or of money's worth. A consideration involves both parties to a contract; this means that each party is giving or promising something to each other. In game contracts, a consideration would be one school team agreeing to play a contest with another school, or one school agreeing to pay a fixed amount as a guarantee to the other.

Special conditions regarding the contest or contest conditions should be clearly stated in the contract. Guarantees, game starting times, selection of officials, and special equipment to be provided the visiting team are examples of such conditions to include. If several schools in a community use a common community facility (such as a gymnasium, stadium, pool, field, or court), it is a good practice to include in the contract such designations as home/visiting team locker room assignments, home team benches, ends of the court or field, and similar considerations. Other stipulations that might be included are these:

1. The length of contest, such as length of quarters or innings to be played.
2. The list or order of events.
3. Weigh-in provisions in wrestling.
4. Number of complimentary tickets.
5. Color of jerseys or uniforms to be worn.
6. Ticket information such as price, reserved seats, and advance sales.
7. Special ground rules or playing area adjustments that do not conform to regular rules specifications.

Clarity

Contracts must be sufficiently clear to be enforceable. Terms that are vague, indefinite, and uncertain should be avoided. Some terms frowned upon in game contracts include "the going rate," "corresponding date," and "to be agreed on at a later date." The more details that schools agree on and include in the written contract, the more easily potential disagreements can be avoided or resolved. There can be little debate over the contract that has complete details of prior agreements, written and signed.

Legality

Contracts must not be of such nature as to be prohibited by the statutes or common law. They must not propose to contract a matter that goes against public policy, is prohibited because it is illegal or immoral, or is based on doubtful outcomes. An agreement that conspires to break the law is invalid.

Coaches do not enter into a contract to play a contest on a day or time that violates a city ordinance, school district policy, or state athletic association regulation. Nor do they agree to avoid paying taxes on ticket sales if such is required, or to use nonregistered game officials if they are required in that sport. These are illegal acts or are against public, district, or other agency policy having some regulatory influence over athletics. A sample contract form is shown in Figure 17-2.

Minnesota State High School League
GAME CONTRACT

September 10, 19 85

We, the undersigned, mutually agree to schedule and play the following game:

Varsity Football	October 17, 19 86
Type of game	Date of game
Welcome H. S. Athletic Field	7:30 P. M.
Place or site of game	Time of game

We further agree that the rules of the Minnesota State High School League shall be a part of the contract, and the following financial agreement shall likewise be a part thereof:

X *Larry Puhrman*   X *Elken Goulson*
Signature of Supt., Principal or (A.D.)   Signature of Supt., Principal or (A.D.)

Welcome High School   Trimont High School
High School   High School

The League recommends that the home school extend to the visiting school the **courtesy of approving or rejecting the officials assigned for the game. Once the officials are assigned, their decisions must be adhered to even though erroneous.**

(Original)

Figure 17-2   Game contract (Courtesy of the Minnesota State High School League, Anoka, Minnesota)

Other Information

There are other types of information that some administrators and coaches have included in the contract primarily as a courtesy to the visiting team. Items have included:

1. Location of dressing facilities.
2. Direction to the contest site.
3. Time and distance from visitor's location.
4. Any other details thought to be of possible help to the coach or principal.

Although not legal considerations, these are helpful pieces of information to help athletic contests run smoothly. They are especially important for the first games between two opponents who are strangers to each other's territory. Above all, they are courteous and hospitable gestures to guests.

SUMMARY

This chapter has presented material about preparing and planning a schedule and contracting for contests. Coaches should be aware that the success of their season can depend on their ability to arrange games or matches that are against suitable opponents and that also meet conference regulations. There are methods of scheduling that make this job easier and team success more probable. Building a schedule and contracting games are business operations. The coach signs a business agreement between two or more schools, and staff are hired, brochures and programs are printed, concessions agreements are arranged, security is contracted, and many other game management details are arranged for on the basis of that agreement. There are some who believe that the winning coach is the accomplished schedule-making coach. Novices should study the techniques of their seniors and the guidelines offered here to master the fine art of scheduling.

18

Contest Management

PRE-SEASON
PRE-CONTEST
CONTEST
POST-CONTEST
SUMMARY

Athletics may be considered educational or recreational, but the management of contests, regardless of the setting, is a business activity. The planning, organization, and execution of details related to conducting a sport event demand the same detailed attention as does any other business. Although all sports events require planning and correct execution of these plans, those that attract large crowds will demand greater effort by a coach and/or administrative staff than do those that attract few or no fans.

A contest is a major public relations activity. Good management can increase support for the team and the school, both in the amount of money and the number of fans. Well-laid plans that are carried out in a professional manner will make positive impressions on all who attend a contest, as people involved with any group (parents, supervisors, principals, or sponsors) do not want to be associated with a poorly organized program. Good management procedures will help in ways other than just improved public relations. Efficiently managed contests tend to enhance the play of the participants and to improve the conduct of the spectators. Also, if there are few or no problems encountered just before game time, the coach is free to concentrate on the game plan.

In some schools, and for some sports, many of the details may be handled by members of an administrative staff, but for other sports and other schools the burden falls on the coaches. They must perform these administrative tasks in addition to innumerable coaching duties. These administrative duties can be viewed in four stages: pre-season, pre-contest, contest, post-contest. The event will dictate the type and amount of work required.

PRE-SEASON

Planning for what lies ahead is a must. Past records and talks with experienced people can help decide what has to be done and the most efficient, effective way to proceed. A coach should make a checklist, marking off items as they are taken care of. No list is ever all-encompassing but usually includes such duties as making business arrangements, handling the publicity, preparing the equipment and facilities, and working with support groups, as well as coaching the team.

Business Arrangements

Sports seasons are business ventures with each contest just one part of the total agreement. Planning for, making, and spending funds are major concerns of all coaches.

Contest Contracts

These should be negotiated and signed at least six months prior to the date that the contest is to be played. A rule of thumb in scheduling is to complete contracts, and have them signed by both parties, in the winter or spring for fall and early winter sports, and in the spring or early fall for late winter and spring sports.

Officials

In some states the state associations assign officials to work all high school games. In these states, all that a coach has to do is to submit a completed schedule to the proper office. That office will send signed copies of the officials' contracts or a list of officials who have been assigned to work the game. In areas where coaches secure officials themselves, it is essential to contract for all contests early because the good ones will be signed quickly. Even though a sport such as tennis or track may not require registered officials, there is still a need for qualified ones. It is a poorly run event when a coach has to go into the stands to ask spectators to serve as officials so that the action can begin.

There are officials' associations that assign their members to contests in their jurisdiction if a coach contracts with them. In other locales, teams of officials work together with a coach who contracts with a group rather than with individuals. Lists of officials are frequently published by the state associations. Whichever method is used, an official's contract should be completed, just as is done with a game contract. A sample contract form is shown in Figure 18–1.

A coach must also arrange for support officials such as scorers, timers, and judges. These are often volunteers and may be parents, teachers, mature students, and community members. It will simplify matters if the same volunteers help throughout the season. Specific instructions as to rules, duties, date and time of contest, directions to the site, things unique to the situation (for example, equipment that will be furnished), the community area, and financial arrangements are given to all well ahead of the scheduled event.

Concessions

Ideally, selling food and drink is an item that coaches will not have to plan for and supervise, but they must make sure that someone or some group is in charge of this for the coming season. Booster clubs, school groups, or parents' groups are usually pleased to help with this money-making project. A month or two prior to the opening contest, the coach will need to check with the person in charge to begin completing details. If there is no one, someone has to be found. Determining goods to be sold, establishing an order system, obtaining and repairing equipment, contracting with soft-drink and vending companies, selecting and train-

CONTRACT FOR GAME OFFICIAL
MINNESOTA STATE HIGH SCHOOL LEAGUE

The undersigned herewith agree to the following assignment and terms for officiating, and that the same may be cancelled only by mutual written consent: Void if not returned in ten days.

Date of Game	Time of Game	Type of Game FB	BB		Contending Schools
December 20, 1987	6:30 PM		X		Sherburn at Welcome

Financial Agreement: Fee: $ 95.00 Mileage: $ Total: $ 95.00

*Other Conditions:

Two registered officials

FOR SCHOOL OFFICIAL:

I herewith certify that I have been authorized to enter into this agreement:

Larry Puhrman
Signature

Welcome High School
School

Athletic Director
Position

December 6, 1987
Date of Approval

****FOR THE GAME OFFICIAL:**

I herewith certify that I am a registered official with the Minnesota State High School League for the current year, and that my membership card number is: 7194

Bill Hinrichs
Signature

608 SO PRAIRIE FAIRMONT, MINNESOTA
Address

12/8/87
Date of Approval

*If the designated registered official is requested to furnish an assistant, or assistants, indicate this. It is mutually agreed that all assistants must likewise be registered officials.

**List name, address, and membership card number of assistant (or assistants) on reverse side, if contract provides for same. (Make out in duplicate; one copy to be retained by the school, the other to be retained by the official.)

Figure 18–1 Game official's contract (Courtesy of the Minnesota State High School League, Anoka, Minnesota)

ing personnel, deciding methods of getting the products to the potential customers, and establishing a banking system are items that require attention.

Tickets

If a team performs before a paying audience, the coach may be responsible for planning ticket sales. Items to be planned for include prices, printing, sales campaign, single game sales, sellers and takers, and methods of handling funds before, during, and after the game. Even though a coach does not have to handle all these assignments personally, it is his or her responsibility to see that someone has taken care of all details. The season depends in part on the financial success of ticket sales, so this aspect of pre-season planning is not to be taken lightly.

Publicity and Public Relations

Good public relations will get the team in the public's eye and keep it there. Methods vary, so all situations should be evaluated and the best available ideas put into action. Typical ways include utilizing the media, placing posters in strategic places, and making speeches to various groups.

Media

The sports staff of area newspapers, radio stations, and television stations are important people to know. A coach should communicate with them to determine procedures for reporting the news and to invite them to the team's events. It is to a coach's advantage to be knowledgeable about the news media's operations. If coaches expect the media to know their product, then they need to know the media's product. They should read the newspaper, listen to the radio station, and watch television programs. Names and phone numbers of the media personnel placed on the inside cover of the team's scorebook can help a coach make quick contact with the media following a game.

Posters

Season schedules can be printed on billfold-sized cards (these are given to individuals in the area) and on large posters (these are placed in prominent places in the area). They need to be printed early to encourage season ticket sales. Local businesses often pay for the printing in order to have their names associated with the team or just to support the school program. School colors add a nice touch; if other colors are used, those associated with arch rivals should be avoided. Handprinted single-game announcements are relatively inexpensive to prepare and can reach a large segment of the community. These are often circulated by athletes, cheerleaders, or pep club members. In many communities, announcements are placed on standards at street intersections.

Speeches

The coach must be ready to talk to area groups. The athletic department should make it known that members of the coaching staff are available to talk to various organizations. Head coaches cannot afford to be backward about being forward. They should request a place on groups' meeting schedules, write an informative speech (if a person is not a good speaker, a slide presentation can be effective), and get the proper clothes ready for the speaking circuit. Most groups prefer to hear the head coach, but, if there are overlaps in the schedule, assistants or team captains are appropriate substitutes. Head coaches need to keep an updated appointment calendar to make sure that all speaking engagements are fulfilled.

Security

Security is the responsibility of the home team. If necessary, security must be provided to game officials, visiting team members and coaches, and spectators. Officials need a dressing area separate from the team's dressing room and the coach's office, preferably one that provides total security. In some situations, security may need to be provided for officials and the visiting team as they leave the playing area and as they leave the community.

The attendance of uniformed law enforcement personnel at large gatherings is required by law in many communities so it is necessary to provide a season's schedule, with notations about special dates, to the proper authorities well ahead of the opening date. If security personnel are to be employed by a school for events such as homecoming and contests with traditional rivals, contractual agreements should be signed long before the event takes place. Although outside security officers may be present, it is usually better to have monitors who are school personnel to handle questions and problems while the crowd is under control. Whatever the arrangement, a total security package needs to be designed to prevent problems in the arena as well as in the parking lot and surrounding areas.

Equipment and Facilities

There are items that can be taken care of just prior to the opening whistle, but equipment and facilities are not two of them. Support personnel may be doing most of the work, but it is the coach's ultimate responsibility to see that everything is ready.

Equipment

Pre-season preparation includes ordering uniforms and equipment in time to receive and issue them properly before practice begins. Orders should be placed sufficiently early to allow extra time for delays and errors. Specific procedures are outlined in Chapters 15 and 16.

Player Eligibility

The coach is totally responsible for player eligibility and must make sure that an athlete who is not eligible does not participate in a contest. State association and league rules pertaining to eligibility must be studied and understood, as they vary from state to state and from league to league in terms of who is eligible to play and when and how eligibility reports are to be made. If a report is due no later than one month before the season opener, the coach must see that the deadline is met.

Pre-Game and Half-Time Activities

There is more to an athletic event than the contest itself. Pre-game rituals and half-time entertainment are a vital part of a total show. The team does not produce these shows, but those who do must work closely with the coach long before the opening whistle blows. In some schools, coaches must arrange for these activities; in other schools, they will have no input, and in still others will be asked for advice. Whatever the situation, the coach will need to coordinate with the director of game entertainment (such as band director, drill team sponsor, principal) concerning the time sequences and patterns that the team will follow coming onto the field or floor and returning to the field house or locker room. This coordination process will help ensure that all events proceed smoothly and end on a positive note.

Pre-Game Ceremony

This ritual varies with the locale. Local customs should be studied before final decisions are made. For most contests that have any sort of ceremony, it is traditional to have the national anthem played as the flag is raised. A school band often provides the music, but who raises the flag—the ROTC unit, a scout group, members of a local veterans' organization, a school group? There may be a very good local singer who would be pleased to lead the singing of the anthem, or a school choral group is usually delighted when asked to perform. It may be a very good public relations move to give different groups an opportunity to play roles in the production.

In many towns and cities invocations are given as frequently as the national anthem is played. Members of the local ministerial association will usually accept this assignment; however, the school may prefer to ask a student or faculty member to direct this part of the program. Regardless of whether it is the national anthem or an invocation, or both, what the team does during this time is always noticed by the public. Right or wrong, the public often judges the program's ethical or moral standards by the manner in which the athletes and coaches conduct themselves during this time. A coach should instruct the athletes, as well as the coaching staff, as to the expectations and their responsibilities as representatives of the athletic program and the school.

Sometimes a coach or program director may want to put some zip into the opening events to attract fans. There may be a parachute club in the area whose members would accept the challenge of landing on a field surrounded by spectators. Local Shriners generally have an act to delight young and old alike. At times talent from elementary schools is utilized; this gives the children a type of introduction to the high school and may also introduce their parents to the athletic program.

Half-Time Activity

If a sport has an intermission or a long break in the playing time, the spot can often be filled with entertaining activities. Typically, the school band and/or drill team will perform in this spot. With any group there has to be coordination of effort far enough in advance to allow the performers to practice under "gamelike" conditions. Is there a theme to be followed? How much time will they have? What sort of surface will they be working on? Will any type of equipment be allowed on the playing surface? Answers to such questions as these are needed long before performance time.

Cheerleaders

Coaches must work closely with cheerleaders and their advisor, who may also report to the athletic director. They may make decisions as to whether or not the group will be cheerleaders (lead the cheers) or entertainers, the style of uniforms to be worn, the type of cheers to be used, and when to cheer at an event. Cheering at a wrestling match is not like cheering at a football game, which is not like cheering at a volleyball match.

What cheers are appropriate? The total group should decide this before someone makes a drastic mistake. A coach should recommend cheers that are positive and not derogatory to the opponents. They may prefer cheers that incite the crowd to be very noisy. Cheering patterns are set for the season long before it begins; cheerleaders usually practice as much as teams do and have their own pre-season workouts.

Travel arrangements to the away games must be coordinated between coaches and sponsors. Some cheerleaders are permitted to ride on the bus with the team, while others are not allowed near the players until after the game. School policy has to be followed.

Medical Supervision

Athletic injuries and treatment must be planned for, and the host school must be prepared for any eventuality. More injuries occur in contact sports than in noncontact ones (some gymnastic events are exceptions to this statement); therefore, coaches for these sports must arrange for medical supervision whenever their teams play. Many states and conferences require the presence of a physician and/or ambulance crew at such contests as football. All coaches should make arrangements for appropriate medical services for practices and contests. They must plan for incidences of injuries and illnesses, especially emergency ones. This may mean having a van without passenger seats at the field, knowing the quickest route to the hospital, sending the season's schedule to the hospital or team physician, and/or making arrangements for medical personnel, other than a physician, to work with the team.

Spectator injury and illness must also be planned for, with written guidelines formulated and posted. As the manager of a facility in which a contest is held, the coach has the responsibility to protect and warn spectators about foreseeable hazards and harm. Warning may include signs and barricades; proper protection includes proper medical response.[1]

PRE-CONTEST

The day of the game arrives. If the coach has planned well and accomplished the pre-season tasks, game day will pose few problems; however, inexperienced coaches should not be surprised and dismayed if something does go wrong. Murphy's Law, "if something can go wrong, it will," applies to athletic events. There are many items to be attended to by the coach or some other responsible individual at the time of the contest, even though they may have received attention earlier in the season. There are also some things that cannot be done until immediately before game time. Experienced coaches anticipate eventualities and try to be prepared for almost anything; the key to success is planning, and the key to planning is anticipation.

Home Team

The home team carries the greater responsibility. Coaches manage and coordinate the entire affair. Of course, one criterion for good management is to have good support personnel to get things done. Assigning capable individuals to key positions and giving them responsibilities with power to carry through is a mark of a smart manager.

Equipment

Responsibility for getting equipment to the right place at the right time and having it in order lies with the team manager. The coach's responsibility is to make sure that the managers know what is required, when it is needed, where it is to be placed—and to get it there. A complete list, prepared and provided to the managers, will be invaluable. Items will vary with the sport and the type of facilities available. For a dual swimming meet, the list would include such items as:

1. Officials. Guns, blanks, official rule book, diving judges' cards, score sheets, towels, timers, whistles, tables and chairs, sharpened pencils.
2. Pool Area. Starting blocks, false start line, lane markers, scoreboard, loudspeaker.

3. Swimmers. Responsible for own suits, caps, plugs, towels, warmups or robes.
4. Incidentals. First-aid kit.

Facilities Coaches "pray" for good maintenance personnel and/or volunteer help from students, faculty, and parents to assist in preparing a facility for the upcoming action. For a soccer match the field will have to be mowed and lined, the goals checked for flaws, and the area (field and spectator area) cleaned. Lights need to be checked for night matches and entrance gates prepared to handle spectator traffic. The amount of work needed to be done depends on the sport and the facility to be used. Well-organized coaches have a list of things that have to be taken care of, and they arrange for the work to be completed on time, even if they have to become directly involved.

Officials Whether a classroom or an office, a private meeting area must be made available to the officials. A student manager should be assigned to meet them and familiarize them with the site. This is especially important if the officials are new to the area. If they are to be officiating a game between particularly strong rivals, or if there have been incidents of violence in the area, an assigned escort can provide security. If they are to be paid that day or evening, their checks (no cash) must be ready at intermission or immediately following the game.

Security This aspect may consist of protecting a team's valuables, officials after a game, fans in the stands, fans outside the playing area, coaches from the fans, participants from fans, participants from their opponents, facilities and equipment, and vehicles in the parking lot. Coaches have to know their particular situation and plan accordingly. Providing security on a large scale will involve working with the local law enforcement agencies and the school's administrative supervisor. Sometimes law officers are called in to patrol the area to prevent or solve problems, but at other times school personnel can serve as the security force.

Guests Parents, members of the press, members of the school board, former players, booster club members, and other prominent citizens are guests at one time or another. A list of names needs to be given to the parking lot supervisor, gate attendant, ushers, and public announcer. The school can arrange to have a guest tag sent to the individual or given at the entrance and can provide special parking places and seats. Guests may also receive special recognition during the contest.

Visiting Team Visiting teams are guests of the host school. Coaches and players should show courtesies to guests and remember that next year, or next week, they will probably be the visitors. A student manager or a dependable student should be assigned to meet and acquaint the visiting team with the area, particularly their dressing room and the route to the playing arena. The manager also needs to check to see if the visitors have special needs, such as a supply of drinking water, towels, or a piece of equipment, and then remain available for any services requested.

Contest Management   267

The host school arranges for visitors to dress privately, secure their belongings, shower after the game, and leave the area without being molested. There needs to be enough space to have the substitutes seated in a section protected from overzealous fans or extreme environmental conditions. The visiting team should also be made aware of the arrangements for medical emergencies.

Visiting fans are guests, too, and should be treated as such. Usually they prefer to sit together to unite their cheering efforts; however, hometown fans get the choice seats if the sections are assigned. If the seating is on a first-come, first-served basis, the visiting team should be made aware of the arrangement.

Medical Personnel

If medical personnel are to attend athletic contests, the coach or a designated person should verify that they have arrived. Availability of the ambulance service should be checked also. If no medical service is at hand, then the alternative plan worked out prior to the season goes into effect.

Media Personnel

The coach must make sure that reporters, newscasters, and photographers are recognized and allowed to come into the activity area free of charge. Special press passes signifying certain privileges may be given out early in the season; this eliminates the need for giving a list to the gate attendant for each contest. Someone who knows the players and the game plan may be assigned to give the media personnel assistance. Lineups, player numbers, information about particular players, or team information should be ready for use.

Support Personnel

Ticket sellers and takers, ushers, program vendors, concessionaires, and traffic (parking) directors need to be in their areas at preassigned times. A check has to be made to assure that members of this group are in position and ready to work well before game time.

Ticket sellers should be in their booths at least an hour before play begins. Arrangements may be made for them to pick up tickets and change money at some point, or these items may be dropped off at the booth. Previous ticket transactions and the price of each ticket can give an idea about how much money, and in what denominations, will be needed in each booth.

Ticket takers must be able to handle a variety of situations, including the problems of gate crashers. They will need a list of guests, as they usually have strict orders to keep all who do not have a ticket out of the playing area. Their only piece of equipment may be a hole punch to mark a ticket as used, but they could also have a container for ticket stubs to be used for counting purposes.

Program vendors should be assigned stations before the first fan arrives; they should have programs in their hands and change in their pockets. They may wear change aprons to make the sales more efficiently. If the facility is located in a crime area, the host school will generally use male vendors, assign them to work in pairs, and instruct them to turn in their money frequently.

Ushers are not often needed, but, if they are used, they need to be briefed on the seat assignments. It could be of additional help if some of them were first aiders who could lend assistance in emergency situations. Service clubs are often looking for projects, and one of these groups may serve in this capacity.

Concessionaires' objectives are to make money and to provide a service to the fans. Personnel and supplies have to be in the concession stand as the spectators begin to arrive. If no one else has assumed the responsibility, the coach will see that food, drink, and ice are on hand; equipment is working properly; prices are posted; change is available; and enough salespersons are working.

Traffic directors may be supplied by the school, community, and/or county. Personnel can direct traffic to and from the playing arena, help with the parking, or be available for emergencies. Whatever their assigned duties, they must be at the site before the ticket booths open. For important games, fans will arrive much earlier than usual.

Ceremonial personnel need to arrive well before the ceremonies are scheduled to begin, as they may need to practice their routine in the arena or on the field. The honor guard's efforts must be coordinated with the band or the group providing the music so they know when to begin the ceremonies and their working time frame. Band directors, drill team sponsors, and pep club advisors also need to be informed of the amount of time allotted for the pre-game and half-time activities and of what is expected of them at the end of playing time. These special groups will require assigned seating, since they usually work together during the contest. The visiting team's special groups are also accorded special seating privileges.

Special Facilities

Benches or chairs for athletes must be arranged in an area apart from the crowd. The public address system has to be checked out; restrooms will need to be cleaned, equipped, and functioning; and scoreboards must be placed in good working order. Usually, individuals are assigned to do these tasks; but, if they have not done a thorough job, the coach will have to lend a helping hand.

Home and Visiting Teams

Certain items must be taken care of by the coach regardless of whether the team is at home or on the road. Game contracts must be kept close at hand and team eligibility lists made accessible. Line-ups should be readied before game time; rules regarding these vary with the sport. Special situations, including ground rules, should be discussed by the coaches and the officials.

If a game contract calls for a financial guarantee, then the contracted guarantee, usually a check, is sometimes given to the visiting team prior to the contest, at half-time, or at the end of the game. However, it is a common practice to mail the check later, after the game's financial statement has been prepared.

Visiting Team

The duties of the visiting team are not unimportant, just different and fewer in number. There are always last-minute details to receive attention.

Contest Management 269

Transportation   The car, van, or bus may have been reserved for months, but nothing is a sure thing. The transportation needs to be on hand, in good running order, and with a reliable driver in the seat waiting for the squad members. Unreliable vehicles and drivers can endanger the lives of the players and coaches. They can also create problems if the team does not arrive in time to play. A breakdown will cost money in repairs, extra meals, and additional lodging. A coach may not be a mechanic, but an eyeball check of tires, windshield wipers, lights, gas gauge, and horn can be very revealing even to a novice.

Equipment   The team's equipment has to be available wherever the team plays. A coach's responsibility is to make a list of everything that will be needed and to give the list to a team manager in time to get everything packed and on the bus. Responsibility for everything concerning equipment usually stays with the manager until it has been returned to the home equipment room. If the team arrives at the game site minus a piece of equipment, the home team's coach or manager may be able to help. If they cannot or will not assist, a staff member can be sent into the community to search for it or a reasonable and safe substitute.

    A well-equipped first-aid kit is an essential piece of travel equipment. If a team is fortunate enough to have an athletic trainer, that person will take care of the details; however, even if the team has a physician traveling with them, the coach still may need to pack a trainer's kit.

Money   No coach wants to be without money when a team travels. One never knows when cash or a charge card will be needed for vehicle repair, an emergency illness, an injury, or a piece of equipment. Other things a team might need, such as lockers and showers, should be provided by the home team, but it cannot be assumed that all home teams will, or can, provide good accommodations for their visitors. The situation should be known prior to the team's leaving home so that team members will know whether or not to dress at home and travel in their uniforms, to take towels to use during the contest and after showering, or to take blankets to keep warm because the swimming pool is outside.

CONTEST

By the time the contest is ready to begin, the nongame details should be complete. Coaches have to be involved with the actual coaching of the team, so ongoing activities are handled by individuals who were assigned, were hired, or volunteered to do the duty. When the contest begins, all else does not cease, but a coach cannot worry about activities other than those directly involved with the game itself.

    During the game, facilities (lockers, fields, and parking lots) continue to be supervised, and members of the press corps continue to be given courteous treatment. Emergency personnel are on hand, equipment is watched closely, the fans are assisted by ushers, concession wares are sold, the band plays, and the pep group cheers. If these and other activities are being supervised by competent individuals, the coach's problems will be limited to those concerned with team play.

Coach/Player Schedule A sample of pre-game, game, and post-game schedule for coaches and players can be seen in Figure 18-2. These schedules should be planned, oftentimes to the minute, so that all items and situations are taken care of.

POST-CONTEST

It would be nice for a coach to be able to leave immediately after the final gun, but that does not happen. Post-game activities have to be completed without delay. Some of these details are team related while others are game related.

Home Team Although a whistle may signal the end of playing time, the event is not over for the coach. Coaches usually want to speak to the visiting coach, talk with their team, meet or contact members of the press, acknowledge the guests, complete business arrangements with the officials, confer with assistant coaches, check in equipment, secure the facilities, and deposit money in the bank. Coaches do not go home until long after the last event ends.

Visiting Team It is customary to meet the opposing coaches to shake hands and exchange a few words. Neither coach wants to linger, so this is a brief encounter. Some coaches shake hands before the contest to avoid the after-game formalities. The team manager who was assigned to the visitors before the game continues to be of assistance until the team leaves the dressing room.

Athletes The squad members are the coach's primary concern. They and the coach(es) usually have a meeting scheduled immediately following the contest. The first item of business is to check each player for injuries. Players should be asked for their input about their condition, but a coach and/or trainer should also check.

After a quick check for injuries, it is time to discuss the contest, the pros and cons, the team's efforts, and individual efforts. Procedures vary with coaching philosophies, but some coaches ask the players to talk about the game first, then the coaching staff responds. Other coaches speak first and then the players respond, while other coaches do all the talking. The "lessons" in the win or loss are to be used as a base for future contests, particularly the one facing the team within the next few days. A coach may analyze the overall play, the success of the game plan, the

Players
1. Evening/night before the game
   a. The team will get together for dinner and a movie or
   b. The team will meet at a coach's house for hamburgers and discuss last minute game plans.
2. Day of the game (8:00 P.M. kickoff time)
   a. Attend school as usual
   b. Eat lunch together at school
      1) Will bring a brown bag lunch and meet at the field or
      2) Will make special arrangements for eating in the cafeteria
   c. After school
      1) Go home and rest; eat suggested pre-game meal (about 4:00 P.M.) or
      2) Report to gymnasium area to eat a specially prepared meal (meet at 4:00 P.M.)
   d. Prepare for the game
      1) Players needing to be taped report to specified area at 5:15 P.M.
      2) Players not requiring taping report at 6:15 P.M.
      3) Begin to suit up at 6:30
      4) Prepare to leave the dressing room at 7:15 to be on the field for warmup drills at 7:20
      5) Return to locker room at about 7:45 for last minute discussion and to take care of personal matters
      6) Captains leave for the field at 7:50 to 7:53; other players leave at 7:55.

Coaches
1. Evening/night before the game
   a. Make a last check of game plan, depth charts, equipment, coaching assignments, etc.
   b. Meet with players if planned.
2. Day of game
   a. Teach classes as usual
   b. Check out game management details (early afternoon)
   c. Double check coaching assignments (early afternoon)
   d. Check to make sure that all materials are ready to be taken to the field (early afternoon)
   e. Report to the locker room at 5:00 P.M. to assume assignments (i.e., taping, field set-up, press box check, equipment)
   f. Hold final meetings with players by special groups
   g. Move on to the field for warmups at 7:15
   h. Return to the locker room for a final briefing at about 7:45
   i. Take the field for the game at 7:55.

Halftime Organization
1. Coaches/players (15-minute break divided into five periods)
   a. Period I. Players leave the field and return to the locker room in 1½ minutes
   b. Period II. Players sit quietly, sip liquids, take care of themselves, consult with the trainer while the coaches meet to discuss adjustments and game plans for 4 minutes
   c. Period III. Coaches meet with groups to discuss adjustments for 5 minutes
   d. Period IV. Head coach takes over with full squad to review the first half, compliment good play, indicate errors, reinforce second-half adjustments, and make motivating comments
   e. Period V. Players return to the field of play in 1½ minutes.

After the Game
1. Players
   a. Return to locker room immediately to talk with coaches
   b. Report injuries and bruises
   c. Hang uniforms in assigned area
   d. Shower and dress
   e. Gather all personal belongings and leave for home.
2. Coaches
   a. Return to locker room for post-game comments
   b. Check injuries and bruises
   c. Make necessary contacts with the news media
   d. Check to see that all equipment is stored
   e. Check to see that area is cleared of people and items
   f. Secure area
   g. Have a get-together with coaching staff and spouses or leave for home.

Figure 18–2   Game preparation

role each individual played, and the standout plays—both good and poor. It can be important to discuss the opponent's efforts, especially if they are on the schedule for a return game.

News Media

Player and game records are compiled for school records and awards and for the sports reporters. An immediate concern is getting a summary to members of the news media. Coaches often prearrange post-contest interviews for reporters covering the game who may want to talk with staff and players. If no reporter covered the contest, then results have to be called in to the media. Coaches should observe the media's deadlines and report the results regardless of whether the team has won or lost.

Guests

A coach should make an effort to acknowledge guests. It is important that guests know that the team appreciates their being at the game and how much their continued support means. Some guests are invited into the locker room to visit with the players or to stay around to talk with the coaches later. They should have an opportunity to ask questions, provide input about the game, and feel important.

Business Transactions

The officials may be paid after the game, but generally the business transactions occur during the intermission so that they can leave the contest site quickly. Others are paid through the officials' association; in such a case, a check has to be sent there if it was not sent previously. Game guarantees, if one is involved, may also be paid to the team representative. Procedures established earlier determine when the guarantee is to be paid. Generally, it is mailed to the visiting team later in the season.

Money should be deposited immediately after the game. Ticket counts and sales need to be checked to ensure honesty of personnel and to prepare a financial statement of contest receipts. A general financial statement of ticket, program, and concession sales has to be prepared and given to a designated administrator. If this business transaction belongs to the coach, it should be handled efficiently and immediately.

Team Equipment

While the coach is talking with people, the team's managers need to be checking game equipment and returning it to the storage area. Player equipment also has to be given attention. If players happen to take care of their own, then coaches and managers will have little to do except to check the dressing area after all players have gone home. If the uniforms are to be laundered at school, then a coach or a manager has the responsibility of taking care of them. Uniforms may not be washed until the next day, but they have to be sorted and hung to dry.

Facilities and Equipment

All the equipment that made the contest possible must be secured or returned to storage areas. Fixed equipment (i.e., scoreboards, jumping pits, uneven bars, and public address systems) must also be secured. Portable equipment (chairs and tables, electronic systems for scorers and timers, down markers, and lane markers) is to be stored immediately after use. Equipment left unattended may not be found the next day. The playing area and surrounding area should be checked for lost items and people.

Lights have to be turned off, windows and rooms locked, air and heating units turned off, and buildings and fields secured. In many schools, custodians or school staff are assigned to do many of these tasks; however, if no one else has been assigned these responsibilities, a coach assumes them.

Security

All too often, close control of a crowd is needed at the end of a contest because after a win—or loss—the feelings of many fans reach an emotional high. Also, parking lots, bus stops, and nearby shops where students wait for their parents may attract individuals, without allegiance to either team, who seek to injure someone in some way. Having school personnel (and security personnel if the situation warrants this) visible in the immediate vicinity and leaving the area well lighted for at least an hour after the match ends can deter malicious actions.

Coaches

The coaching staff needs to get together to go over what happened during the contest and why. Successes and failures have to be analyzed. Information from these sessions should be utilized in the future. Many coaching staffs will wait until the next morning to meet; at that time, game films or video tapes of the games are reviewed, the game is analyzed, and the plans for the next contest are born. At many schools the coach may be the entire coaching staff, so he or she will perform these activities alone.

SUMMARY

This chapter has outlined the tasks involved in managing a contest. It has suggested what procedures need to be considered for pre-season, pre-contest, contest, and post-contest situations. Advanced planning and training of support personnel can be almost as important as advanced planning and training of athletes. Both are needed for a successful season. In some schools selected administrative personnel are assigned many of the tasks. At other schools the coach has to make all arrangements.

It might be well to repeat Murphy's Law: "If anything can go wrong, it will." Therefore, plans for everything must be made to ensure that all events connected with a contest occur successfully. It would be nice if coaches had only to coach, but their attention is continually diverted by all the details and problems associated with establishing the contest. Once those are taken care of, the game can take place and a coach can focus on skill, strategy, and trying to win.

ENDNOTE

1. C. Lloyd, "Emergency Medical Response Is a Facility Responsibility," *Athletic Business* (May 1984): 34.

19
Legal Aspects

LEGAL LIABILITY
PRODUCT LIABILITY
CIVIL RIGHTS
SUMMARY

The national trend of increased litigation continues to escalate as the number of million-dollar verdicts increased from 7 in 1970 to 401 in 1984.[1] Interscholastic and other sports programs are not immune. Court cases have involved liability suits concerning a coach's negligence, defective or ineffective products, and the violation of an individual's rights. Court actions may be brought against anyone, or any group, regardless of precautions taken. Legal problems will be a primary concern of coaches and athletic programs for as long as such programs exist. If litigation and large awards for negligence continue to increase at the present rapid rate, coaches may no longer find programs in which to work; schools and agencies may choose to discontinue them, especially if liability insurance becomes unavailable or too expensive to buy.

Prior to the 1970s the majority of parents and athletes had a hesitancy about suing, as the coach was viewed as a friend and leader of children and youth. Sovereign immunity enjoyed by the state, and therefore by the public schools, prevented many suits against school districts or school boards, and, in many states, teachers and coaches were also protected by "save harmless" laws. However, many states have relinquished this immunity, and there now appears to be little reluctance to bring legal action against a coach or school district, or at least to threaten court action.

It appears that the public is more willing to sue almost anyone because they believe that someone should pay for their injury, that the insurance company and not the defendant will pay the costs, and that there is a likelihood of receiving huge monetary awards in a jury trial. The "Seattle Decision," in which a student was awarded more than 6.0 million dollars, has set a precedent for both plaintiff and defendant. Athletic and physical education administrators in all areas of endeavor must now see that all participants are warned of the dangers in each activity, including catastrophic injuries; that proper standards of safety and treatment are met; that students participate only at their level of skill and ability; and that they are prepared for participation with sequential instruction and training.[2]

In order to prove that proper procedures were followed, it is necessary to keep a dated "paper trail" or a written record of everything planned, publicized, and accomplished. Files should contain all written procedures, all practice training schedules, injury reports, facilities checklists, and safety and medical procedures. Handouts to students are also needed. In a court of law a coach must prove proper professional behavior.[3]

LEGAL LIABILITY

In order for a coach to be held legally liable for damage incurred by an athlete, negligence must be proven. In order to prove negligence, four things must be established: (1) the coach must have owed the injured person a duty, (2) some damage must have occurred, (3) the coach must be guilty of breaking or failing to carry out the duty, and (4) the coach's wrongdoing must be established as the cause of the damage.

The standard for negligence in the case of athletic personnel would be how a prudent coach, with similar training and skills, would have acted under similar circumstances. Negligence case decisions are usually based on what is known as "common law" or professionally accepted procedures. If a coach has not followed such standards, negligence will probably be proven. Where the negligence of the coach, having the duty to act, caused the injury or damage, the injured party can recover damages from the negligent coach.

Negligence is a question of fact; it can be proven by circumstantial evidence, and it is generally tried before a jury if the case goes to court. To a great extent, it is an issue or decision determined by hindsight. It is a review of the situation, at a later time, by persons who were not there when the event(s) took place, to determine (in the case of sports) whether the injury to an athlete—physically or psychologically—was the result of negligence by another.

Guidelines for Judgment

Precisely what constitutes a negligent act is not clearly defined in law texts or the statutes. Each situation, each case is judged on its own merits, taking into consideration "common law." Several guidelines have been developed over the years evolving from cases that have been tried against teachers and coaches. These tend to provide some definition of what might be established as a negligent act or behavior.

1. Did the individual have a right or obligation to participate? An athlete is not required to participate in a sports program but does so as a matter of choice—it is a privilege accorded him or her. The athlete may have the right to join a publicly supported program if qualified, but he or she is not forced to participate. When the athlete makes the decision to participate, the assumption of risk goes with the decision. That is the assumption of normal risks of that sport, not a coach's negligence. The Seattle Decision, however, requires a coach

to make plain the dangers involved. It cannot be assumed that participants recognize danger unless specifically informed.
2. Did the coach have a duty to perform? Coaches are responsible for athletes under their supervision. They have a duty to protect the athlete from harm, which involves safety procedures, proper sequencing of instruction, and proper treatment of injuries.
3. Did an actual breach of contract occur? Coaches, like doctors, lawyers, teachers, and others, are expected to have special skills and knowledge. They are also expected to conduct themselves in a professional manner reflecting a high standard of behavior. Cases involving accident or injury often weigh heavily on the action of the coach in failing to carry out responsibilities in a manner that reflects standards of the coaching profession, or some particular skill or knowledge a coach is expected to have.
4. Did the athlete suffer bodily injury? Tort liability based on negligence must involve an injury. If an athlete can prove that physical or emotional harm occurred, the coach may be subject to a judgment of negligence in the performance of duty. If written and published policies and procedures for participation and safety are followed by coaches and participants, negligence would be difficult to prove.

Guidelines for Coaches

In order to avoid charges of negligence, coaches should consider their actions and establish guidelines for their behavior. If the following risk management guidelines, or similar ones, are followed, many difficulties can be avoided.

1. Perform responsibilities in a prudent manner.
2. Follow the guidelines established in the school district, league, and/or state for safe programs.
3. Remedy any equipment or facilities deficiencies.
4. Anticipate emergencies and prepare contingency plans.
5. Carry liability insurance with high limits and broad coverage.
6. Follow currently acceptable procedures for play and for conditioning, as well as treatment of injuries.
7. Purchase the very best equipment, with safety in mind, that the budget will allow.
8. Purchase only from reputable dealers who will stand behind the products they sell. (One might consider buying only from those dealers who are well covered with liability insurance.)
9. Contract for the services of only those equipment reconditioning companies that are certified or endorsed by an association.
10. Take extreme care in adjusting, fitting, altering, and repair-

278 *The Coach as an Administrator*

Figure 19-1 What are the inherent dangers in this activity? (Courtesy of The Florida State University, Tallahassee, Florida. Photographer: Ryals Lee)

ing equipment, particularly protective items. Establish a system of routine inspection and maintenance.
11. Establish an operational system of emergency care in the event of serious injury.
12. Use vehicles that are in safe driving condition, preferably school owned, and adult drivers with good safety records.
13. Establish a system for identifying, treating, reporting, and recording all injuries. (It is advisable to follow the advice of a lawyer in establishing these.)
14. Have the school provide or arrange for accident insurance coverage for participants in the athletic program.
15. Follow good teaching procedures; teach only those skills clearly provided for in the rules.

16. Teach skills in the proper sequence; move from the simple to the complex, from the easy to the difficult, from the basic to the advanced.
17. Closely supervise all activities.
18. Consider the size and developmental level of the participant.
19. Keep up to date by knowing about the latest research findings, equipment, teaching methods, and the like.

Coach's Defense

Generally speaking, there are three basic defenses to be used for a coach who is charged with negligent conduct.

1. Contributory Negligence. A player is contributorily negligent when he or she does something that contributes toward the injury, which if not done perhaps would have prevented the injury or made it less severe.[4]
2. Assumption of Risk. Athletes assume that there is some inherent danger in sports participation. Risks are assumed when play is within the rules and usage of the game, and when they are "normal" to the game. Recent court rulings, however, require that participants be fully informed of the risks in each activity. They can assume only those risks that they have been warned about.
3. Unavoidable Accident. There was no apparent way to prevent the injury; the cause cannot be established.

Waivers and Consent Forms

Many coaches, players, and parents misunderstand waivers and consent forms. They believe that the two forms are the same and that the signing of either prevents legal action. These are mistaken beliefs; the forms are not synonymous and do not prevent parents and/or players from bringing legal action. The consent form, signed by the parents or guardian, gives consent (or permission) for their child to participate or do something. A waiver is used by an individual who gives up or waives the right to do something. In the case of the athlete, the coach is hoping that the right to sue is being given up by the athlete's family; however, a parent can never waive the rights of a child or minor. Therefore, even if the parents waive their right to sue, they may later bring action against the coach on behalf of their child. Athletic departments should, nevertheless, continue the use of these forms, as they do provide a degree of protection by showing the court that the parents approved their child's participation in the sport. Usually, these forms are one section of an application for participation and must be signed by both the participant and the parent or guardian. (See Figure 19-2.)

Spectator Risk

Not only must coaches be concerned with players, they must also consider spectator risk. It is clear that spectators assume the usual risk of being a spectator, but they do not assume the risk for nonroutine, nonsafe procedures or faulty facilities.

Facilities, especially bleachers or stands, have to be in good repair if they are to be used safely by fans. Coaches or athletic directors must

The Coach as an Administrator

WARNING, AGREEMENT TO OBEY INSTRUCTIONS, RELEASE ASSUMPTION OF RISK, AND AGREEMENT TO HOLD HARMLESS

(Both the applicant student and a parent or guardian must read carefully and sign.)

SPORT (Check applicable sport)

____ Football	____ Basketball	____ Track
____ Volleyball	____ Wrestling	____ Baseball
____ Cross Country	____ Golf	____ Softball
____ Soccer	____ Swimming	____ Tennis
____ Cheerleaders	____ Weightlifting	

STUDENT

I am aware playing or practicing to play/participate in any sport can be a dangerous activity involving MANY RISKS OF INJURY. I understand that the dangers and risks of playing or practicing to play/participate in the above sport include, but are not limited to, death, serious neck and spinal injuries which may result in complete or partial paralysis, brain damage, serious injury to virtually all internal organs, serious injury to virtually all bones, joints, ligaments, muscles, tendons, and other aspects of the muscular skeletal system, and serious injury or impairment to other aspects of my body, general health and well-being. I understand that the dangers and risks of playing or practicing to play/participate in the above sport may result not only in serious injury, but in a serious impairment of my future abilities to earn a living, to engage in other business, social and recreational activities, and generally to enjoy life.

Because of the dangers of participating in the above sport, I recognize the importance of following coaches' instructions regarding playing techniques, training and other team rules, etc., and agree to obey such instructions.

In consideration of the Leon County School Board permitting me to try out for the _____ School (indicate sport) _____ activity and to engage in all activities related to the sport including, but not limited to trying out, practicing or play/participating in that sport, I hereby assume all the risks associated with participating and agree to hold the Leon County School Board, its employees, agents, representatives, coaches, and volunteers harmless from any and all liability, actions, causes of action, debts, claims, or demands of any kind and nature whatsoever which may arise by or in connection with my participation in any activities related to the _____ School (indicate sport) _____ activity. The terms hereof shall serve as a release and assumption of risk for my heirs, estate, executor, administrator, assignees, and for all members of my family.

        The following to be completed only if sport is _football_, _wrestling_, _soccer_, or _baseball_. I specifically acknowledge that _____ (indicate sport) is a VIOLENT CONTACT SPORT involving even greater risk of injury than other sports. _____ (initial)

_____   _____
Date   Signature of Student

I, _____, am the parent/legal guardian of _____ (student). I have read the above warning and release and understand its terms. I understand that all sports can involve many RISKS OF INJURY, including, but not limited to, those risks outlined above.

In consideration of the Leon County School Board permitting my child/ward to participate at _____ School (indicate sport) _____ activity and to engage in all activities related to the team, including, but not limited to trying out, practicing, or playing/participating in (indicate sport) _____, I hereby agree to hold the Leon County School Board, its employees, agents, representatives, coaches, and volunteers harmless from any and all liability, actions, causes of action, debts, claims, or demands of every kind and nature whatsoever which may arise by or in connection with the participation of my child/ward in any activities related to the _____ School (indicate sport) _____ activity.

        The following to be completed only if sport is _football_, _wrestling_, _soccer_, or _baseball_. I specifically acknowledge that _____ (indicate sport) is a VIOLENT CONTACT SPORT involving even greater risk of injury than other sports. _____ (initial)

_____   _____
Date   Signature of Parent or Legal Guardian

Figure 19-2 Student permission and acknowledgment form

Courtesy of Jeff Dukes, Director of Student Activities, Leon County School District, Tallahassee, Florida.

inspect them regularly; faulty ones must be repaired or not used. The area surrounding the stadium or gymnasium must also be free of hazards, with periodic checks for proper lighting, good paving, and slippery surfaces. Dangerous areas need to be fenced or warning signs with flashers erected for temporary hazards. Daily exposure to a facility may blind a coach to potential or actual hazards; the hazard becomes a normal part of the area and is not noticed. Arrangements with another coach for an exchange of safety inspection tours may be an eye-opener for both parties.

Arrangements for appropriate crowd control must be provided. Ushers, officers, or other personnel should be available. Crowd control arrangements include the use of ropes or barriers to manage spectator movement and traffic officers to supervise traffic and parking. Alert coaches can anticipate foolish and thoughtless action and then attempt to forestall it. Also, plans for emergency medical care of spectators must be formulated. Injuries or illnesses that may occur to members of the public should be anticipated and preparations made.

Liability Insurance

How to obtain liability insurance and stay solvent in the process is a major problem for organizations. The vast majority of state high school associations have approved (and require schools to be members of) the so-called Ruedlinger Plan, which provides lifetime care for catastrophically injured athletes and protection from suits by schools. This Student Protection Trust Plan provides medical and rehabilitation expenses and other costs, including payment of lost parental wages and lost student wages. Payment begins when other insurance may end.[5]

Other agencies, such as the Reston (Virginia) Homeowners Association (RHOA), are requiring leagues to have their own insurance. Leagues using the RHOA-owned and maintained recreation facilities must have a minimum of $500,000 insurance. Also, individuals participating in league play have to sign a waiver stating that they will not sue the association.[6]

Some school districts have opted for self-insurance. An amount of money, 2.0 million dollars for example, is set aside against possible lawsuits. Coaches are required to have personal liability insurance that can be purchased for a rather nominal fee through coaching and teaching associations.

PRODUCT LIABILITY

Product liability refers to the liability of manufacturers to the user of its products for personal injury or property damage resulting from the use of those products. For many years, consumers suffered the rule of caveat emptor in the use of a manufacturer's goods. This implied that the buyer was responsible for the inspection of the items purchased and assumed the risk of injury caused by any defect in the products bought. In the 1970s, though, more of the burden of responsibility shifted to the producer, and it became a responsibility of the manufacturer to discover defects in products before they were sold or distributed. "Protection of the consumer" became an attitude of the court; and, even though a large share of the burden is now being returned to the agency and individual coach, the producer remains vulnerable.

In product liability, the producer, as an individual, is charged with the responsibility of using the reasonable degree of care that every ordinary, careful, and prudent person would use in the designing, manufacturing, testing, inspecting, packaging, and labeling of a product to make it reasonably safe when used by the average, ordinary consumer. If manufacturers can be proved to have failed in this respect, they can be charged with negligence for injuries suffered by the user.[7]

Guidelines for Defense

The industrial world, including manufacturers of sports equipment, is facing an increase in product liability cases. In answer to the many suits that have been filed, the sporting goods producers have attempted to build their defense around several points.

1. The defect in the product was one that could not have been avoided by exercise of reasonable care or that, under the circumstances, all reasonable care had been exercised.
2. The product had been altered after its sale in a manner to cause it to become defective as the result of the alteration.
3. The product was not used by the buyer or user in accordance with the manufacturer's instructions regarding proper wear and safety.
4. The product was used beyond its life expectancy or was being used in a state of disrepair.

Guidelines for Coaches

The last three points in the previous list covering product misuse have particular significance for coaches. They must be very careful to follow rules concerning the use of the product.

1. Avoid adding items to equipment or altering it.
2. Ensure the proper fit of all safety items.
3. Make frequent checks of all equipment to ensure its being in good repair.
4. Discard items that are not suitable for use.
5. Inspect equipment to ensure that players have not altered items for their convenience.

Effect on Sports

There are serious problems facing sport because of the rash of product liability suits. The very existence of many sports is threatened because suppliers of sports equipment may be forced out of business. The financial structure of the companies that makes sports possible by supplying the needed equipment is endangered.

Law Suits

Examples of legal problems are not difficult to find. In 1976 the equipment manufacturers were stunned when a high school football player was awarded $5.3 million in damages against a football helmet manufacturer. A more recent suit involving defective or poorly designed helmets sought $16 million in damages. Gymnastic equipment manufacturers have been

Legal Aspects **283**

sued for approximately $100 million; most of these suits have concerned the trampoline. Litigation has involved other pieces of equipment, but the damages sought have been somewhat smaller.[8] In many cases the suppliers do not bear the problems alone; coaches and schools are named as co-defendants in many instances.

Survival

Testimony in the United States Senate by a president of the Sporting Goods Manufacturers Association reported that, unless laws were changed, there would be no sports of any kind as there would be no equipment. The doctrine of liability is now being interpreted to mean that a manufacturer's product does not have to be at fault for the manufacturer to be guilty, but simply needs to be involved in the accident. Insurance rates are becoming prohibitive. Suppliers may reach a point where they cannot afford to pay the insurance nor the damages that may be awarded a user of their products. Coaches must expect good equipment, but they also must assist in avoiding destructive litigation if athletics are to remain a part of programs.[9]

CIVIL RIGHTS

The federal civil rights statute provides that:

> Every person, who under color of any statute, ordinance, regulation, custom, or usage, of any State or Territory, subjects, or causes to be subjected, any citizen of the United States or other person within the jurisdiction thereof to the deprivation of any rights, privileges, or immunities secured by the Constitution and laws, shall be liable to the party injured in an action at law suit in equity, or other proper proceeding for redress.[10]

The implication of this law affects all persons who act under the "color" of a state statute. Coaches, whether volunteers or employed by a school district or an agency, must act under the color of the state statute, as well as federal laws, because they are agents of the state or local government. Private organizations—those that are not local, state, or federal governmental—are frequently considered to be quasi governmental and, therefore, also cannot discriminate.

Student Rights

Students are not expected to give up their constitutional rights when they enter a school building. This is particularly true when students are attending in response to compulsory attendance laws. For many years, the burden of truth in the civil rights violation suits fell on the students to prove that their constitutional rights were unreasonably limited or taken away, and it was quite difficult for such charges to be proven. In 1969 the United States Supreme Court shifted a great degree of the burden of proof from the student to the school. Where first amendment rights—speech, press, association, and religion—are involved, the school district bears the burden of fact of showing that the limitation of the student's constitutional rights is necessary to the conduct of the school or school activity. A coach can limit the exercise of constitutional rights but must be prepared to show some reasonable relationship to school purpose, health and welfare of participants, performance of the individual or team, or moral effect upon students when this is done.

Considerations

Two areas of particular concern for coaches involve formulating rules for the athletes and providing for due process when taking disciplinary action or enforcing the rules. Care must be taken in these potential problem areas.

Rules

Rules and regulations established by coaches, discussed in Chapter 11, are quite likely to be challenged as arbitrary and unreasonable by athletes who do not want to abide by them. Training rules, rules of general conduct on and off the court or field, and standards of eligibility are most likely to be contested. It is important in the development of the rules and regulations that the coach establishes only those that follow sound guidelines. Following are some recommended procedures:

1. Develop and publicize the need and reasons for the standard or regulation before it is adopted.
2. Relate reasons to health and welfare of participants, performance, moral effects, and educational factors.
3. Involve representatives of all groups or individuals, as far as practical, who will be affected.
4. Provide copies of rules and regulations to all individuals to whom the standard will apply and make certain that they are understood. It is recommended that each athlete be required to sign a statement signifying that he or she has studied the standards, understands them, and agrees to abide by them.
5. Outline policies for enforcing standards and regulations and enforce them fairly and consistently.[11]

Due Process

Due process is that procedure which is required to bring about a fair decision after balancing all the competing interests. The coach must ensure that the athlete has had an opportunity for due process when action is taken. In other words, the courts have insisted that where action is taken against a player, the school is required to ensure that the player has been treated fairly. Athletes must be permitted to present their side of the issue and to hear the reason for any action taken. Six important elements of due process to be remembered, particularly when dealing with eligibility and discipline cases, are as follows:

1. Athletes must have ample opportunity to know the standards and/or regulations they are to meet.
2. When there is evidence that a violation has occurred, there must be adequate notice of the charges.
3. Adequate time must be allowed for the athlete to prepare an answer to the charges and evidence on his or her behalf.
4. There must be an appropriate hearing to consider evidence against and on behalf of the athlete.
5. A fair and impartial decision must be made and the decision put in writing.[12]

The necessity for engaging in a due process encounter can be avoided if the coach will expend every effort to make decisions and take actions regarding athletes fairly in every case of misbehavior or rules violation. The courts stress three points in due process concerns. They are:

1. Notice. Did the athlete have prior notice of the rules, and was the athlete told of the alleged facts that constituted the violation?
2. Discussion. Did the athlete have a reasonable opportunity to admit, rebut, explain, or deny the facts known?
3. Fair Decision. Did the decision maker reach a fair, unemotional decision based on the facts known?

Integration

The civil rights concerns for racial equity have generally been satisfied in athletic programs. When participation is based on ability and not on skin color, the integration problem fades. Most coaches look for the best players they can find, and they are always searching for the winning combination, regardless of race. There may still be some vestiges of prejudice on playgrounds, in schools, and on teams, but coaches and athletes value skill above many things. If a person can make a victory possible, he or she will usually be accepted, at least on the playing field.

This is not to say that there will not be some personality conflicts within a team. Varying life styles create misunderstandings, but these are not necessarily racial in character. Coaches will have to work to keep conflicts down, regardless of the make-up of the squad, and many will have to make a concerted effort to keep their own biases from showing. Charges can be brought against a coach for racial discrimination, but it would be difficult to prove if skill were the determining factor in squad selection or contest participation. Rational, logical procedures that cannot be misunderstood should be used.

Sex Equity

A continuing concern for coaches is the effect of Title IX on athletic programs. This concern, and subsequent confusion, is fed by a lack of firm guidelines coming from the federal government and its agencies. The law itself merely states that there will be no discrimination on the basis of sex. It is a simple statement, but the interpretations are confusing. Rulings by the federal courts and re-interpretations by the federal government have indicated that enforcement of Title IX, and other equity legislation, will continue to be a major issue well into the 1990s. A major ruling was that institutions may selectively implement Title IX according to the funds received, but the courts have consistently supported affirmative action and women's efforts to achieve equal status with their male counterparts. Therefore, coaches must be as careful not to discriminate on the basis of sex as on any ethnic or racial basis.

Players

High school activities associations are generally supportive of Title IX and provide an extensive program for girls. Participation by girls in high school sports increased 600 percent between 1970 and 1984.[13] Some of the progress has resulted from the belief in equality by people "in charge," while some has resulted from legislation and suits filed by girls and women to gain access to athletic programs. A summary of major cases in this early struggle for sex equity can be found in *Equality for Women in Sport*.[14]

The sex equity law applies to males as well as females. There have been few incidents involving the male and equity; however, males seeking equity have faced problems in some areas. Generally, it has been the question of boys playing on girls' teams (such as volleyball and field hockey) because there is no comparable activity.

Coaches

Equity between and among coaches implies and requires similar assignments, responsibilities, and salaries. Tradition suggests that males coach males and females coach females; equity suggests that gender need not be the only factor in making coaching assignments. The position should be considered and the best person selected for it. When the concept of equity is abused to increase the number of men, or the number of women, on an athletic staff for some reason other than advancing sport and opportunities for participants, then there is no equity. A current reduction in the number of women coaches and athletic administrators, reported to be supported by Title IX, clearly violates the concept of equity and leaves young women with few role models or mature women leaders and advisors.

Salaries and supplements became more equitable as the 1980s began. This was a result of federal legislation, with suits brought under a variety of affirmative action, equal opportunity, and sex equity laws confirming equal pay for equal work. Now both men and women can work equally hard for comparatively little, but equal, amounts of money.

Redress of Grievance

There are several methods of filing a complaint under sex equity legislation. The Equal Employment Opportunity Commission (EEOC), the Office for Civil Rights (OCR), and the Wage and Hour Division of the Employment Standards Administration of Labor will all receive complaints by letter, telephone, and/or written statements. Coaches and players may file grievances. They can go directly to court, as grievances do not have to be filed with equity groups before action can be taken. Grievances may also be filed under state laws; information can be secured from the office of the state attorney general.

SUMMARY

Coaches have responsibilities to their players and to themselves to provide safe environments, to inform of injury possibilities, to consider the rights of all concerned, and to avoid charges of negligence. Acting as a prudent person and a reasonable professional will prevent a great deal of difficulty. Good common sense, foresight, and a real concern for the players should keep the coach out of the courts and in the playing arena.

ENDNOTES

1. *U.S. News & World Report* (27 January 1986): 35.
2. S. H. Adams and M. A. Bayless, "How the Seattle Decision Affects Liability and You," *Athletic Purchasing and Facilities* (July 1982): 12.
3. M. A. Bayless and S. H. Adams, "A Liability Check List," *Journal of Physical Education, Recreation and Dance* (February 1985): 49.
4. B. van der Smissen, "Legal Liability," *Coaching: Women's Athletics* (January/February 1979): 50.
5. R. Berg, "Catastrophic Injury Insurance: An End to Costly Litigation?" *Athletic Business* (November 1984): 10.
6. C. O'Kane, "Insurance May Sideline Athletes," *The Fairfax Journal* (March 3, 1986): A-5.
7. D. E. Arnold, "Sports Product Liability," *Journal of Physical Education and Recreation* (April 1978): 25.
8. Ibid.
9. T. Ecker, "Will We Allow Courts to Kill Sports?" *Athletic Journal* (May 1977): 12.
10. J. Gradwold, "Legal Concepts," *Proceedings of the Eighth Annual Conference of High School Athletic Directors*, Omaha, Nebraska, 1977, p. 26.
11. I. Keller and C. Forsythe, *Administration of High School Athletics*, 7th ed. (Englewood Cliffs, N.J.: Prentice-Hall, 1984), p. 367.
12. Ibid., p. 368.
13. The Women's Sports Foundation, *Headway,* Newsletter (San Francisco, Winter 1985-86).
14. P. Geadleman, "Court Precedents," in P. Geadleman, *Equality in Sport for Women*, ed. C. Grant, Y. Slatton, and N. P. Burke (Washington, D.C.: AAHPER, 1977), pp. 72-75.

20

Transportation

VEHICLES
POLICIES AND PROCEDURES
SUMMARY

If all contests were at home, there would be no need to worry about transporting a team from one school, sports facility, or community to another. But since most schedules require home and home games or contests at a neutral site, coaches must concern themselves with the logistics of going away and returning home. It can be a very complex business, dealing with vehicles, policies, and procedures.

VEHICLES

There are several forms of transportation, with buses or vans being the most popular with local schools or agency groups. Planes are quick but expensive and are rarely used by high school teams except in such places as Alaska, where destinations can be reached only by plane. Trains that once carried many teams even short distances are no longer available in most areas.

School Vehicles The majority of schools satisfy their transportation needs by buying buses (and vans), leasing them, or contracting with public carriers. Their biggest advantage is the capacity to carry a large number of players economically, but their greatest disadvantage is that they do not always carry players in comfort.

Drivers Because the bus will not go without a driver, the first thing to consider is securing a careful, licensed bus driver. A regular school bus driver is quite familiar with the task and would be an ideal person for the sports bus. Coaches frequently learn to drive buses, get chauffeur's licenses, and then drive the teams themselves. Whoever is selected or found must be reliable, safe, and skilled and must like young players. No one who is irritated by young people's antics should be chosen.

Insurance The school should insure all their vehicles and drivers, not only for collision but also for medical costs and for liability at the maximum limits allowed. If the system or agency is self-insured, it would be helpful if drivers also carried personal liability insurance. Insurance companies, as well as school systems, require periodic review of the transportation system and vehicles. This is one way to be certain that vehicles are in good condition. Being insured does not stop accidents, but it may alleviate some of the problems they cause.

Reserving Vehicles

Most agencies and schools have great demands placed on their vehicles. This makes it absolutely necessary to reserve the bus or van early in the year. As soon as a contest is scheduled, the coach should go to the principal, athletic director, or transportation officer and reserve a bus and driver. A coach can never assume that a bus will be available just because the team wants it; it will be available only if and when it is reserved. There will be times when there are unavoidable conflicts and alternative means of transportation must be sought.

Maintenance

If it is not the coach's bus, it should not be the coach's problem; however, if the vehicle is not properly maintained, it can break down and become the coach's problem. The transportation supervisor, driver, or some designee should keep the bus clean and in good mechanical condition. It may prevent problems if the coach will take a look at the maintenance and repair records of the vehicles and try to use only those whose records indicate good care.

If coaches are responsible, a routine can be established for caring for the bus—oil and lube jobs when due, repairs when needed, washing and cleaning after each trip. If one person in the school district is named to schedule trips, make repairs, keep tanks filled, and keep the keys, the transportation system can be more efficient and reliable. At the end of each road trip, it is helpful to require all drivers to make a list of items that need to be repaired or checked.

Use of Private Cars

Many sports programs do not have access to buses and vans and cannot afford commercial transportation. These must rely on vehicles owned by parents, players, friends, and coaches. Private vehicles are used only when all other modes of transportation have been eliminated. Even though private owners may not charge for use of their vehicles, the ultimate cost in money and remorse if an accident occurs can be very great.

If such vehicles are used, certain guidelines should be adhered to. Only licensed vehicles and adult, licensed drivers should be used. The vehicle must be fully insured—extensive medical, collision, and liability coverage should be carried by the owner. Vehicles must not be overloaded with passengers and/or equipment. All should stay together, and the coach, or another responsible adult, should drive or ride in the lead vehicle to establish the safe and legal traveling speed. A form, such as the one in Figure 20-1, can be used to prevent possible problems in this area.

Coaches or any who use their vehicles to transport athletic personnel ought to check their policy to know its complete meaning. If the details of the policy are not clearly understood, the individual should check with his or her insurance agent. Those who drive passengers and are reim-

```
┌─────────────────────────────────────────────────────────────────────┐
│              JEFFERSON COUNTY PUBLIC SCHOOLS                         │
│                                                                      │
│                   SENIOR HIGH SCHOOL                                 │
│                                                                      │
│  Authorization to drive student participants to a scheduled school   │
│  activity by private vehicle.                                        │
│  (The School District does not insure private vehicles.)             │
│                                                                      │
│  Activity _____ date _____ destination _____    │
│  Activity _____ date _____ destination _____    │
│  Activity _____ date _____ destination _____    │
│                                                                      │
│  I certify that I am eighteen (18) years of age (or over) and a      │
│  legally licensed driver in the State of Colorado. I will transport  │
│  assigned students to the above named school sponsored activity      │
│  subject to the following conditions.                                │
│                                                                      │
│      The vehicle to be driven will be in good running condition and  │
│         meet Colorado State legal requirements.                      │
│      The driver must be insured and maintain the required minimum    │
│         liability insurance as required by law.                      │
│      The number of passengers carried shall not exceed the capacity  │
│         of the vehicle.                                              │
│                                                                      │
│  The insurance company providing coverage for my vehicle is:         │
│  _____  │
│                                                                      │
│  I verify that the conditions outlined above will be met by the      │
│  vehicle used on this school activity trip.                          │
│                                                                      │
│                                                                      │
│                                       _____    │
│                                       Student Driver's Signature     │
│                                                                      │
│                                       _____    │
│                                       Date                           │
│                                                                      │
│                                                                      │
│  _____                                        │
│  Parent's Signature                                                  │
│                                                                      │
│                                                                      │
│  _____                                        │
│  Date                                                                │
│                                                                      │
│  I have authorized the student driver indicated above to transport   │
│  student participants to the school activities specified.            │
│                                                                      │
│                                       _____    │
│                                       Principal's Signature          │
│                                                                      │
│                                       _____    │
│                                       Date                           │
└─────────────────────────────────────────────────────────────────────┘
```

Figure 20-1   Travel form for private vehicle

Courtesy of Alice Barron, Coordinator of Athletics, Jefferson County Schools, Lakewood, Colorado.

bursed for some or all of their expenses may consider taking out a "rider" policy on their liability insurance.

Commercial Transportation

The best alternative to using school-owned and/or -operated vehicles is to rent, lease, or charter commercial vehicles. This may even be the first choice of mode of transportation for extensive travel. Commercial vehicles are usually well maintained and insured, and chartered buses also have licensed and insured professional drivers.

Buses

Regular touring buses can be chartered for short or long trips, but they are most practical when there is considerable distance to go in unfamiliar territory, when extensive night driving is involved, and/or when the traveling squad is a large one. They are generally comfortable, have room for luggage, and frequently come equipped with restrooms. Teams can travel all day, play, and sleep on the way home. Coaches can leave the driving to others and be relieved of the strain, fatigue, and responsibility of this task. Though comparatively expensive when compared to a school bus, chartered buses are relatively economical of time, energy, and money.

As with school buses, arrangements must be made for the charter well in advance. As soon as the schedule is made, the coach should call the local or interstate bus line. The coach may make all the arrangements by phone if that is convenient, but all agreements need to be confirmed in writing, with copies of all contracts filed in the office before departure.

One way to cut down on the expenses is to "sell" seats to team fans. Many boosters will pay for two seats, theirs and an athlete's. This is an advantage to the boosters in that they do not have to worry about driving and parking and they still get to see the contest.

Planes and Trains

Most school athletic programs cannot afford plane fares and most communities do not have access to passenger train service (except in certain areas served by Amtrak or by commuter lines), but they need to be considered. They are not as flexible in arrival and departure times or location as motor vehicles are, but, generally, they are safe and sure.

POLICIES AND PROCEDURES

In addition to securing a vehicle, the coach must keep in mind policies and procedures about the passengers and the use of the vehicle. These include supervising the passengers, preparing the travel schedule, setting up emergency plans, and establishing codes of player conduct.

Supervision

When teams travel to other communities for contests, adult supervision is a must. Someone has to be responsible for the vehicle and passengers. These supervisors are usually coaches, parents, faculty, or staff.

Coaches

The typical team bus is controlled and supervised by the coaches of that team. One coach, usually the head coach or a designee, is in charge of, and responsible for, arrangements during the trip and for player conduct on the bus. Sometimes all the coaches ride the bus, sometimes only one or two. If there is a coach on the bus, that person is expected to take charge.

Staff

Occasionally trainers, managers, faculty, or administrative staff accompany the team instead of coaches. If the principal is aboard, supervision of the bus may become that person's responsibility. Generally, some other staff person is named to supervise the group on the trip. Players should be instructed to abide by the directions and instructions of this staff member as if they were given by the head coach.

Parents

When parents drive players in their private cars, they are expected to be responsible for the athletes in their care. When they are traveling with the team and are placed in charge of a group on a bus, they should be expected, again, to be responsible for the entire team or group. One difficulty in using parents as supervisors is that they may tend to pay close attention to their own children and to ignore other players. Another problem is that they may not understand the coach's routine procedures; hence, they may require or permit different conduct than the coach expects. Most teams cannot make it without parental support, however, and the transportation area is no exception.

Coaches have to inform the parent volunteers of their obligations and of the travel plans. They give the volunteer a list including such items as passengers, a schedule, and a set of player rules. In this way the volunteers can assure that the athletes act as the coach would have them act, and that everyone arrives at the game and back home safely. Male coaches with female players should make sure that at least one, and preferably more, of the parents is a mother. The reverse holds true if the coach is female and is working with male athletes; a father or two needs to travel with the group.

Schedules

If coaches want to get to where they are going on time, they must prepare a timetable or schedule. This should include departure times, en route times, on-site schedules, and returning times. These schedules are given to all players, coaches, and staff so that there can be no misunderstanding and so that no players or coaches are left behind. The players in turn are encouraged to give the schedule to their parents.

Departure

Regardless of the mode of transportation, every trip must begin with the time of departure. In order to determine when the team must leave, the required arrival time must first be set; then the coach can work backwards to the time of departure, figuring on average speed for the distance and allowing for expected stops and unexpected delays.

Having established an absolute departure time, the coach must decide whether or not to advance the announced time by 15 minutes or so in order to be certain that all are in their seats when it is time for the bus to leave. Some coaches consider it to be the best policy to tell the squad to assemble at some predetermined time to get ready for a departure at a later time. A coach who leaves late comers will establish a reputation for promptness and probably have everyone on time for future trips.

Someone, usually the manager, is given the responsibility for loading equipment, checking uniforms and luggage, and checking the team roster or passenger list. It could be as bad to leave the uniforms as the players. The driver needs to be present as early as the staff is, at least a half hour before departure. It will take that long to load a large group and get them settled for the trip.

If at all possible, the coach should avoid having to pick up players at their homes. Leaving from some central place, such as the school, usually works better than having several stops. If, however, the bus will pass by a player's house on the way out of town, it may be foolish to have that player drive to the central departure point.

En Route

If the trip is a short one, or on a train or plane, then there will probably be no scheduled stops; but a long trip in a school bus or car needs at least one "restroom" break. This break is often scheduled with a refueling and/or eating stop. The route should be reviewed to determine when and where this can be scheduled. Passengers can probably ride for about two hours without difficulty, but a longer trip may call for a respite. Players should be informed of these plans in plenty of time for them to make adjustments to the schedule.

At the Game

Coaches determine in advance when and where the bus or cars are to unload the players. If everyone goes directly to the competitive site, there will be little difficulty; but if there is an interim stop at a restaurant or motel, the coach will have to gather up the passengers again, just as for the original departure.

If the vehicles remain at the game site, there is little difficulty, but if the drivers leave to return at a later time, the coach must establish firm returning times. Vehicles remaining at the game ensures no delay in loading after the game; moreover, they are available if needed for storage, for taking a player or coach somewhere, and for a resting area.

Return

After the game is over, time should be allowed for showering and dressing before boarding the car or bus, but the team must be well out of the dressing area before the home team has to close the facility. If there is to be a post-game meal, someone should arrange for a reservation for a specific time. The coach should not assume that an eating place can be found open by driving all over town looking for one. This prearranged stop will permit the team to keep to the schedule or timetable.

The return trip ought to be as well planned as the original departure, with checklists for equipment, uniforms, and passengers, and with the driver ready to roll. Experienced drivers check the fuel, oil, water, and tires for the return trip while the team is getting dressed or eating. Being stranded with a load of tired athletes is not a happy occasion, and it is worrisome to players, coaches, and waiting families. Parents need to be notified prior to the trip when to expect players to return, and the coach should have the players at their destination when scheduled. Unnecessary delays in returning because of careless group management is inexcusable.

If parents cannot meet players after an out-of-town trip, the coach has to arrange some mode of transportation for them to get home safely. This may mean that coaches, staff, and other parents are pressed into service, delaying everyone's final return. The bus is sometimes used to take the players to their homes, but this can prove to be expensive if the driver is being paid by the hour and the bus by the mile. Many schools have established policies concerning getting players home after returning from a road trip. Coaches are responsible for knowing and following those policies and not leaving a player stranded.

Emergencies

There are always a few transportation emergencies during a season and during a coaching career. No one can avoid them, so a wise coach will look ahead to minimize their effects. If coaches have anticipated difficulty and have considered what they would do if trouble really came, they will be better prepared to meet it.

Mechanical Failures

The most ordinary of the emergencies is to run out of gas or to have a flat tire. More complex mechanical failures involve the engine, transmission, or brakes. The best way to avoid breakdowns is to check the vehicle or to have it checked by a competent mechanic. If it fails in spite of the care, coaches still have to deal with the problem, but at least their consciences can be clear.

If the bus breaks down, it should be moved off the road and the passengers unloaded. Players should not be permitted to sit in the stationary bus, especially if it is parked on the highway or very near it. The coach and driver or a mechanically talented athlete should attempt to make repairs; but if the problem is complex, a passing motorist may be flagged down and sent for help. Usually, parents or team boosters will be traveling the same route and can lend a helping hand. Many vehicles have citizen band radios or walkie-talkies that can be very useful in emergencies. As these are generally portable, it may be a good idea to place one of these in the vehicles in the group.

If game time is rapidly approaching and the vehicle is not repaired, the coach must begin to consider ways to get the team where it needs to be. A commercial bus might be flagged down, parents or team followers could be pressed into service, or passing motorists might be asked to help. None of these methods is ideal, but they can help solve the problem. The coach should be sure to make a list of who is riding with whom and be very careful about putting players into cars with strangers. The driver should stay with the bus, but if the coach is the driver, some responsible person like an assistant coach or parent can wait until the tow truck or mechanic arrives.

Breakdowns are expensive, both for the repair itself and for the alternate transportation needed. The coach will need to have sufficient funds or credit cards and know procedures to follow to take care of this additional expense. If the coach and team have to remain overnight, funds or credit will also be needed to pay for expenses, as players rarely have enough money with them to pay for meals.

Planning with the principal or supervisor before the season begins can make the coach aware of what to do and to whom to report. Staff and parents who remain at home have to be notified of the situation. One phone call to the principal or a parent can start the procedure, especially if each person calls one other person.

Accidents

The fear of all coaches and parents is that the team might be involved in a collision or accident. Good drivers usually can avoid a wreck with defensive driving, but occasionally one occurs. The coach also plans ahead for this situation.

Injured passengers must be taken care of first. If there is a trainer with the team, some of the immediate first aid can be administered before the ambulance arrives. If the coach is the best-trained person available, he or she should do the best possible under the circumstances. All coaches should have completed first-aid and cardio-pulmonary resuscitation (CPR) courses.

Uninjured players should be moved away from the immediate site. The captain or someone responsible may be placed in charge of the team to keep them together, out of the way, and safe. They should not be permitted to attempt to get their luggage or equipment from the vehicle until a traffic officer says that it is safe to do so.

Coaches may go with their injured players to the emergency room or send the trainer and/or staff member. Other staff members may be assigned to stay with the rest of the team and, if it is feasible, go to the game. Parents and principal or supervisor should be notified immediately, as well as the coach of the opponents, if the accident occurs on the way to the contest. Some details of the accident will have to be given to parents and school and medical personnel; however, it would be wise to talk only with the police and insurance representative about certain information. Coaches must be sure to give absolutely accurate information and be sure that facts are recorded as they are reported.

Arrangements would then have to be made for an alternate method of transportation and for the vehicle to be towed in. The coach must make certain that team members are accommodated together. This is no time for the players to be off by themselves or isolated. Above all, the coach must be certain where each team member is.

As for breakdowns, there will be a need for sufficient funds or credit cards to pay for whatever is needed. Coaches should always know the upper limit of their expenditures when traveling. If expenditures go above that amount, the coach may have to pay the difference.

Missing Passengers

Checking passenger lists and taking roll is a task that must be performed with care if the coach is going to bring back all the individuals who went with the team. Time has little meaning to some young people; and if they are shopping, eating, or using the restroom, the bus may drive off and leave them there. A team may use the age-old "buddy system," but a coach should never ask, "Is everybody here?" and let it go with that statement. A roll call or head count must be taken each time a bus prepares to depart.

If the bus does leave without a passenger, it will usually be necessary to turn around and go back as soon as possible. A coach should not leave a player alone any longer than absolutely necessary. If a player is not missed until the bus is "past the point of no return," the bus is stopped at the nearest phone and a call made to the restaurant, service station, or school in an attempt to locate the athlete. The police may have to be contacted and asked to check the area where the team was when the athlete failed to board the bus. If possible, a car should be sent back immediately to locate the missing athlete and return the individual to the group.

Occasionally, a player will deliberately leave the group, either to return with someone else or not to return at all. A roll check will reveal the absence, but determining the reason for the absence and the location of the missing person will be more difficult. If the athlete just decided to go home with a friend without getting permission, another player may know something. If it can be verified that the player did, in truth, catch another ride home, then the coach can worry less and settle the matter with the player later. The parents will need to be notified of the player's actions.

If the player disappears and does not leave any message with a team member, then the coach has to try to locate the athlete to be certain of the player's safety. Local school officials and city or county police are notified if the player cannot be found after a reasonable search. The bus cannot wait for an indefinite period of time. In the meantime, the player's school and family should be contacted.

It may be necessary to return home with the rest of the team and leave the search in the hands of the local officials. If there are several staff members accompanying the team, one should stay to work with the local officers; in fact, the authorities may require that a team representative remain. Hopefully, this situation will happen rarely and then only when a player decides to stay behind for personal reasons.

Player Conduct Most coaches have their regulations for conduct on a trip. They include how to act on the bus, what to do at the game, and how to act in the host community.

En Route The basic problems in team cars and buses are noise and horseplay. If there are boys and girls on the bus, there might be additional problems of close encounters. Several fundamental rules can limit the problems of inappropriate conduct (such as keep the music down, do not shout, stay in the seat, and keep feet on the floor). If it is a mixed group, the girls may be placed in the front of the bus and the boys in the back. Young children in unairconditioned vehicles may be tempted to hang out the windows or to throw things on the road. The law requires that passengers keep heads and arms inside a bus, and the driver can stop the bus if the misbehavior continues.

At the Destination Frequently, there is a strong temptation for players to sing school songs or to shout at passersby when driving through the opponent's territory. This can be carried to the point of unfavorable behavior—bad manners as well as questionable sportsmanship. Energies should be saved for the game. Rowdy behavior at the stadium, courts, or pool, and afterward at the restaurant and/or motel must be avoided. Coaches, staff, and parents must all join to ensure acceptable player behavior.

Other Concerns There are a few problems routinely appearing each season that must be resolved. They include the questions of who rides with the team, who rides with whom (if all are not riding in the same vehicle), and does a player make the round trip with the team? Answers should be found in the team or school policies.

Passenger List The eligible passenger list must be determined before the season. All players will, of course, be provided transportation, and most coaches require their teams to use team transportation both to and from all contests. One question always arises: "Must all players ride with the team?" This answer must be decided long before the first bus rolls.

Another question to be decided is: "Will boys' and girls' teams share a bus?" This seems so economical and sensible that many coaches are agreeing to do so even though it has not been their practice in the past. "Will the cheerleaders ride with the team?" Some coaches want only serious players to travel in their group and prefer not to share a bus with this group. In light of the economic situation, however, it seems unreasonable not to include them if there is room and if a boosters' bus is not making the trip.

Can parents ride the bus with their children? Many children would prefer that their parents travel some other way, but this should not be a basis for a coach's decision unless it upsets the players to the point where they cannot play well. Most schools do not permit parents to ride school buses to school and thus generally exclude them on bus trips, unless they are serving as chaperones. The problem here may be: if parents do ride, which are included and which are excluded?

Seat Assignments If there are several cars or vans, a question that always arises is: "Who will ride with whom?" Friends may want to be together, some of the group may feel left out, all want to ride with the coach, parents may prefer certain children, or there may be ethnic conflicts. Several solutions are available if there seems to be this kind of travel difficulty. Some coaches assign cars; others assign front and back seats as well as cars. Often at stops for gas or meals, passengers are rotated from car to car or from front to back seat.

If the coach has players with a tendency toward motion sickness, taking medication and riding in the front seat can help. A coach should not hesitate to permit this special privilege.

If there seem to be problems about seat sharing or positions on the bus, the coach can assign seats and swap side to side, front to back at station breaks, or follow a rotational pattern on a long trip. If two or more noisy or rowdy types sit together, the coach may need to separate only a few players instead of moving an entire group.

In either situation, car or bus, as much personal choice as feasible should be permitted and passengers moved only to provide equity in seating or to keep peace. The less a coach has to shift players, the better.

Return   The usual policy for most coaches is that players must return in the vehicle in which they came. Some coaches refuse even to let players return with their parents, citing a need to review the game on the way home as the reason. A good rule is that, except with parents or guardians, players can return only with the team. The exception, that of riding with the parent or guardian, is granted after the coach has received both a verbal and written request from the parent or guardian. If this policy is not set and followed, the problem of a missing player can frequently arise. School policy regarding this should be strictly adhered to by the coach.

SUMMARY

A major concern for coaches is how to get a team to the contest safely, on time, and back home again. As is true for the other noncoaching areas of coaches' responsibilities, the transportation of teams must be provided so that the game can occur. They must worry about securing vehicles, drivers, and insurance, and they must establish policies and procedures that will reduce transportation problems. Planning and anticipating difficulties so that they can be avoided are necessary if a coach is to be free to coach.

PART 4

The Coach as a Personnel Manager

21

Planning with and for the Staff

> DEVELOPING PHILOSOPHY AND OBJECTIVES
> ASSESSING PROGRAM AND STAFF NEEDS
> DETERMINING WAYS TO MEET OBJECTIVES
> IDENTIFYING QUALITIES NEEDED
> SELECTING ASSISTANT COACHES
> BEING AN ASSISTANT COACH
> BEING AN ADJUNCT COACH
> SUMMARY

If the coach is to fulfill the obligation to serve as an effective personnel manager, then he or she must focus on current and long-range needs for staffing and for meeting the interpersonal needs of that staff personnel. It is incumbent upon the head coach to plan extensively and to search diligently for coaching and support personnel who will contribute to the program. This means that the coach should develop a master plan to include the needs and dreams for the ultimate staff. When the opportunity to select staff arrives, that planning will produce well-earned dividends.

In designing this master plan, the coach must develop a coaching philosophy, establish objectives for the program, assess the situation and needs of the program, determine ways to reach the objectives, and identify the qualities required for personnel in each staff assignment. Unless an agreed-on direction can be established, the program and its personnel may "ride off in all directions."

DEVELOPING PHILOSOPHY AND OBJECTIVES

The first step in any systematic plan for staffing is to determine philosophy, values and beliefs, and goals and objectives. Long-range ideals and accomplishable short-range steps make it possible to evaluate progress.

Philosophy

Philosophy is a set of values and beliefs, a way of looking at one's world, one's job, and one's players. Many coaches may have the same general view of things but differ in their specific beliefs about some things. It is this difference of opinion that makes for difference in coaching styles and for a difference in how coaches can work together. If players and coaches have the same viewpoint, it can make for harmony. If the staff views the situation from different perspectives, there can be difficulty in coming to a common conclusion.

As a personnel manager or administrator, the coach seeks to secure a staff that not only performs assigned tasks but also believes in the value of those tasks. The grudging acceptance of a system by an assistant can interfere with a smoothly running operation. Having to continually monitor the work of a reluctant subordinate will consume time and energy that ought to be spent in the actual coaching process.

It may be wise to spend time with members of the staff, exploring the values and beliefs they hold. Working through to a commonly held position is very important if everyone is to travel down the same road. The staff must come to an understanding about their views of players as persons or objects, about winning as a goal or a need, about losing as an event or disaster, and about players as students first or students last. They need to explore their roles as coaches and teachers, as coaches and volunteers, as coaches and athletes, and as leaders or drivers. For example, does success result from intensive coaching of a small select group of athletes or from building large squads of interested potential athletes (a "no-cut" policy)? Does an athlete perform best in a sport by participating in other sports activities during off-season, or is total dedication to one sport the only means to achieving excellence? Whose interest should be placed centrally—the player's, the team's, the school's, or the coach's? Priority of interest will dictate direction of effort.

Objectives   A commonly held point of view will expedite the setting of program objectives (for example, to win more games, to increase cooperation between coach-player-community, to develop the character and personality of players, to provide socialization). When there is staff agreement, the season proceeds more smoothly.

Objectives should be both long-range and short-range. Long-range goals might include building a stadium, lighting the courts, or winning the district. They are measurable, but their accomplishment will not happen immediately. Short-range objectives—those that can be realized within a short span of time, probably within the year—might include getting new uniforms, improving the conditioning program, winning more than half of the scheduled matches, or installing a new defense. These are more quickly reached and more readily checked off as completed than are long-range goals.

Objectives are steps to goals, and goals are steps to dreams. No staff can afford not to plan and not to dream.

ASSESSING PROGRAM AND STAFF NEEDS

After agreement has been reached on where the program is going and the behavior needed to get there, an evaluation of the current staff situation will help ascertain what is needed in the way of personnel and resources to reach the goals and objectives. One of the first tasks is to determine the number of people needed to do the job as it should be done and the qualities of these personnel. For instance, how many areas of specialized instruction of athletes can the head coach handle effectively and efficiently? Depending on the size of the program, its popularity, and the number of athletes, an assessment of the situation will determine a reasonable and favorable number of assistants. If there are different levels of competition, junior varsity and varsity, a decision must be made for assistants to be responsible for the level of play or for a phase of the game at both levels. This will help decide the qualifications needed for assistant coaches.

A head football coach may recognize the need for an assistant football coach, but is there also an awareness of the crucial lack of a head lacrosse coach? Can the two groups be served by the same individual? The head coach must carefully assess program needs to avoid the sacrifice of a second sport through self-serving decisions. If the budget permits the hiring of only one coach, can the assistant football position be filled by a volunteer, or will it be better to hire a coach who can reasonably assume both football and lacrosse duties?

Can a volunteer coach from a neighboring college help with the tennis team to permit the hiring of a professionally trained coach for a rapidly growing soccer program? A head coach who is able to view the needs of the total athletic program and to place the needs of a specific program in perspective is likely to reap rewards in good public relations and to gain the support of colleagues, athletes, and community for his or her own goals.

Is there limited equipment to handle or are there extensive inventories? Again, depending on the size of the program and budget, there ought to be enough equipment managers to ensure handling of uniforms and playing equipment, as well as proper maintenance and storage. The weight of the equipment and its ease of handling should also be considered when trying to determine the number of support personnel needed. As an example, if minimal strength is required for the job, there is greater latitude in the selection of equipment managers.

Can one trainer serve the entire group of athletes, or is it necessary to have four assistants to expedite training procedures? Who is responsible for the education of the student athletic trainers—the head coach, an assistant coach, the head trainer? If student trainers need to be enrolled in special classes, who handles the enrollment and fees?

How much planning and coaching time is devoted to fund-raising efforts? Is there need for a coordinator of such endeavors? Parents of athletes may be the answer for this time-consuming, but often vital, project. A friend, a colleague, or a fan of the team may be willing to volunteer to supervise fund raising.

Budget

Personnel needs are usually modified by budget considerations, and fund raising may be the only answer for affording the desired staff. Several sources of these funds are discussed in other sections of this book, but the basic sources to be explored are coaching supplements from school or agency, gifts of salary or supplements from boosters, fund-raising events by team or staff, and state or federal funds for coaches or for student assistants and managers. Of course, the legality of using such sources, determined by governing bodies such as the State High School Association or the Amateur Athletic Union (AAU), has to be studied carefully.

Direction and suggestions for finding the most simple and effective way to obtain funds for staffing must be found by consulting with agency head, principal, or athletic director. The school counselor in charge of student assistance funds or a local federal agency may be able to provide support for student trainers, equipment managers, or general "go-fors."

Booster groups or other interested citizens or parents are often helpful in supplementing assistant coaches' salaries in nonpublic school situations. There can be a "hook" in these funds, however. If the supporters pay the salary, they may want also to direct the program.

DETERMINING WAYS TO MEET OBJECTIVES

Following agreement on goals and assessment of staff needs, plans should be developed to meet the defined objectives. This planning needs to be a cooperative venture when possible—many heads are better than one. A work plan ought to be developed, in accordance with local and league regulations, that will serve as a guide for the head coach and staff throughout the season. It will be helpful to outline the staff responsibilities for specific assignments that take place during pre-season and off-season.

Pre-Season Will pre-season conditioning be incorporated into a schedule? If the athlete is to work alone or in small groups, instructions have to be developed, reproduced, and distributed. If the athlete is to work under the supervision of a coach, a schedule must be arranged for the head coach or an assistant to be available at specific times and dates. These plans have to meet association guidelines. Official approval may or may not result in coaches' being on the payroll during that time. There should be a clear understanding of legal and ethical positions if pre-season work is considered voluntary.

Off-Season Will staff participation in well-defined recreational/youth club activities be supported or attendance at a youth sports camp be encouraged? Is it feasible to organize and operate a sports camp? Staff members must understand the role that off-season preparation plays in the program and staff development plans.

Numerous school coaches find summer employment in recreation departments and continue their coaching activities on a playground. This also serves as a training opportunity for upcoming players as well as for present team members. Head coaches should be alert to the methods used by their staff who may work under another supervisor's direction. They may find it to their advantage to communicate with assistants in these off-season jobs to ensure a continuation of their system.

It is not at all unusual for a coach to establish summer sports camps. They may be one- or two-week ventures, or a summer-long experience, providing both employment and training opportunities for staff and players. A good source of additional funding for the coach, staff, and/or program, the sports camp may make possible keeping a good staff together, permitting them to polish their coaching skills while helping athletes improve.

Coaches should be careful about the effect of staff training and employment during the off-season on the players. Those who actively encourage athletes to continue the sport in the off-season are in effect telling them that extra training is needed and will probably affect their chances for success in the next season. It is highly improbable that all athletes can, or will choose to, take part in off-season programs; therefore a conscientious effort to avoid negative feelings toward these individuals may have to be made by the coaching staff.

IDENTIFYING QUALITIES NEEDED

In considering staff selection, staff development, and general personnel management, the coach must identify the qualities needed for each job assignment. A job description that outlines duties and criteria needed for the position, as well as required personal qualities, can be helpful.

Professionals Coaching, like teaching, law, or medicine, is a profession. Not only does it require extensive study, but it also demands a type of internship under the leadership of a fully qualified professional, a senior coach. These professionals are obligated to assist in the development of new or assistant coaches, and this training program is part of good, professional personnel management.

The "system" utilized by a head coach often requires very knowledgeable coaches to adopt, to learn, to understand, and to implement the strategies of a particular program. Novice coaches, or interns, may work with these teams but often find themselves working with those at the bottom of the hierarchy, such as the ninth-grade team. The novice, regardless of the assignment, must be well indoctrinated in the methods that the head coach has determined to be basic to the system.

Good personnel managers secure the best trained and the most experienced staff they can for the job to be done. They use well-trained persons for positions requiring high levels of leadership and responsibility and persons of less skill and training for subprofessional assignments. Coaches also strive to secure the best professionals available for working with young athletes and developing their sports talents.

Nonprofessionals There are valuable and valid roles for nonprofessionals to play in the athletic world. Para-professionals, like experienced groundskeepers or office personnel, are essential to a smooth-running program. As much care must be taken with their selection, training, and supervision as with coaches.

Can student leadership be utilized? The need for well-trained student managers and trainers has already been mentioned, but consideration ought to be given to the crucial role they play in making the program function. With proper guidance and instruction, students will be able to perform well in the areas of timing, scorekeeping, and statistics. The superior athlete can also be used to instruct less talented teammates in developing skill and finesse.

Are there citizens in the community with special talents who can be solicited as volunteers? An avid golfer, the recreational league tennis champion, a former football player, the coach of the youth soccer team, and many other persons who retain an interest and talent in a sport may welcome an opportunity to become involved again. These nonprofessionals can augment a staff, bring new vision to a program, and relieve a head coach of many annoying chores. They may also bring many headaches if they have been out of touch with youth activities in a sport, forgotten (or never knew) the organizational and personnel difficulties in the athletic scene, poor teaching skills, and/or low moral standards.

SELECTING ASSISTANT COACHES

There is no set formula or prescribed ratio to be followed in establishing criteria for selecting and hiring coaching assistants. Smaller school districts generally have the services of fewer assistant coaches; but, because of smaller student enrollments, the need for fielding several levels of competition (such as varsity, junior varsity, freshmen) is less. It also follows that a small school will be less diversified in its offerings in athletics and that more densely populated areas will provide a greater range of sports activities, with more levels, to meet the needs of large numbers of interested athletes. Thus, larger school systems in larger communities have more potential candidates for assistant coaches' positions and can draw from both a school staff and a community personnel pool.

A variance can exist not only in the number of sports activities and available personnel but also from one sport to another and from one school to another in the same district. Large school districts may provide eight assistants in football to coach three levels (teams), but in smaller districts only three may be allocated for the same sport for one or two levels. Schools with extensive participation in track and field for boys and girls may hire two assistants, but others may have only one coach for both boys' and girls' teams.

Regardless of the number of coaching assistants that are budgeted or not budgeted, a sports program will succeed only if the head coach receives competent, dedicated assistance. The axiom that "a coach is only as good as the staff of assistants" is very relevant.

It is apparent that selection of assistant coaches may be the most important single organizational responsibility of the head coach. A versatile head coach will be skillful in assessing the talent and personality of the assistants. One who is extremely inflexible in philosophy and techniques of training will be at a disadvantage, as will be the overly flexible coach who has no recognizable coaching plan or strategy. The capability to adjust, adapt, and vary methodology and strategy will aid in recruiting new personnel and in gaining optimum assistance from holdover personnel.

Personal and Professional Qualities

Talking with active coaches to identify the characteristics and qualifications they deem most desirable in an assistant coach will reveal almost as many differences in opinion as there are coaches responding. This vari-

Figure 21-1 Head coaches need good assistants (Courtesy of Rickards High School, Tallahassee, Florida. Photographer: Mickey Adair)

ety of responses need not indicate that certain traits are not common to all assistant coaches, but rather that the variety reflects the multifaceted personalities and needs of head coaches.

Characteristics Important characteristics of good assistant coaches often mentioned by active coaches are these:

> 1. Knowledge of the sport gained through college courses, coaching clinics, or participation as a player or coach.

2. Personality that projects and engenders enthusiasm.
3. Loyalty and dedication to the game and to the team players.
4. Capability to work long, irregular hours.
5. Ability to work compatibly with others.
6. Willingness to accept constructive criticism from head coach.
7. High moral and ethical standards.

Job Description

There must be a clearly defined job description for the coaching position to be filled, as the qualifications of the applicant are important only to the extent that they relate and interrelate to the total staff needs. Greater selectivity is possible when a head coach specifies responsibilities and necessary qualities. A job description that is general in nature is likely to attract a generalist rather than the specialist required.

Many coaches have limited input in the selection of an assistant and may be happy simply to have a warm body. However, the fortunate coach who can actively recruit could develop a job description to include the following points:

1. Area of expertise that is needed (e.g., diving, defensive line, distance events).
2. Specific duties that are assigned (e.g., pitching coach).
3. Adjunct duties that may be assigned (e.g., organize and supervise off-season conditioning program for athletes).
4. Background experience that is expected (e.g., playing experience, coaching experience, athletic training).
5. General description of type of individual preferred (e.g., willing to work long hours, interested in the welfare of the athletes, can organize and work with large groups).
6. Term of employment, reporting date, ending date.

Sources of Staffing

A lack of good assistants presents an immediate barrier to the success of the team, and frequently a head coach has to develop a competent staff from inexperienced, uninformed personnel. This is a very difficult task, and only the best head coaches can overcome this handicap. Unlike collegiate counterparts, the scholastic coach is rarely in the position to recruit and select assistants, except as teaching or other occupation vacancies occur over a period of years. It is necessary, therefore, for a head coach to work and organize within a master plan that encompasses the total sports program.

Within the System

Generally, the secondary school coaching staff is built around one or two major sports, with personnel doubling as coaches or assistants in other areas of acceptable expertise. For example, it may prove difficult to hire an assistant football coach who will assume that duty only, unless he or she is certified to teach physics or a similarly difficult-to-fill teaching vacancy. There is a better possibility of securing an assistant football coach who is also qualified and interested in coaching tennis, and who is certified to teach outside the physical education department. A tendency toward an increase in athletic opportunities and a decrease in enrollment (and thereby staffing) forces administrators to look for coaching assistance beyond the previous primary source—the physical education staff.

In addition to the difficulty of matching the person qualified for coaching with the teaching vacancy, there are other considerations that restrict hiring and firing in the school system. Some examples are: (1) the teaching vacancy must be advertised, (2) all applicants must be interviewed and given due consideration regardless of sex and race, (3) tenured teachers have seniority rights, (4) destaffed teachers within the system must be placed prior to hiring someone outside the system, (5) regulatory bodies such as the High School Federation may stipulate that a coach must be a full-time teacher, and (6) the supplemental pay scale for coaching is notoriously low.

Some head coaches are free to seek assistants from the teaching ranks of other schools (middle or junior highs and elementary) in the districts that have no athletic programs. Often, a teacher in one of these underlying schools has the needed desire and knowledge and is just waiting to be asked. Another source within the school system is the substitute teacher. Many are full-time substitutes and may be eligible to serve as coaches. Coaches who are not limited to using only personnel from their own schools may be missing a wealth of talent if they do not seek help from these additional sources.

The full use of men and women in all sports may also open up new possibilities. Many women faculty and/or staff can assist men's and boys' activities, both on the field or court as a coach, or off the field as a scout, recruiter, or statistician. Men have served as coaches in girls' and women's activities for many years, so the novelty in that area is gone but the principle is the same. Use all the qualified staff that can be found.

Outside the System

Considering the immediate and future problems of obtaining assistant coaches, an interim solution may be the employment of adjunct coaches who would either be paid or volunteer. There are many talented individuals—friends, former athletes, college students, parents—outside the school or agency who can devote time to youth teams. Utilizing outside school personnel may be necessary, and if they are employed or accepted, close attention must be given to many details in order to prevent communication and policy problems or to resolve them at a very early stage. If major problems arise, nothing or no one will operate efficiently and effectively, and, too, there could be legal repercussions.

Pre-season is the time to review and finalize all plans for the upcoming season. First, the head coach must check to make sure that all rules of the sport's governing body have been followed, to know that the assistant is "legal." At the coaches' meeting all institution and team policies, procedures, and association regulations should be discussed, and printed information given to each staff member. No coach should have a reason for saying such things as, "I didn't know that" or "No one discussed that with me." This is the time to know whether or not the staff can be loyal to a program and abide by policies and regulations.

This is also the time to establish a communication system. Having a rule that the adjunct must call the office by 11 A.M. each day could assure the head coach that all staff members know the day's agenda. If the adjunct has a message for the players and/or the coaches, he or she must call in by 7:15 A.M. so that announcements can be made. Phone numbers for reaching the off-campus coaches at different times during the day should be secured.

It is during pre-season that the head coach discovers whether or not the new assistants are capable. Frequently, although they may be willing and available, they do not possess basic information concerning the physiological, psychological, and sociological aspects of work with youth. Too, they may lack knowledge of teaching/coaching methods or not be cognizant of current rules and strategies of the game. If so, there may be time for them to attend coaching clinics and enroll in a short course. In pre-season there is also time to read books and articles, review films, study play books, and talk with experts in specific areas. If the new assistants are not interested in updating their skills and knowledge base, then they should not work with the team.

Season assignments are made now. Plans of the adjunct to carry out designated responsibility should be checked by the head coach or by the person assigned to work closely with this individual. Careful supervision of plans and actions helps to ensure that team members are receiving the best possible coaching.

Projected Needs

A look at the total program will reveal some possibilities for future changes. For example, the growth of the soccer program may indicate a need for an additional coach, and the decline of the field hockey program may dictate the loss of a coach, with the implication that the two areas may be handled by the same person. The former assistant hockey coach may assume the soccer position and perhaps voluntarily assist the hockey coach.

Frequent talks with the athletic director, principal, and other local school staff may divulge teaching vacancies that exist or are likely to occur. Contacts, direct or indirect, with the personnel office can provide information concerning vacancies in nearby feeder schools. One of the better sources for locating potential candidates is the recommendation and suggestion of respected colleagues in the absence of personal knowledge of a candidate's credentials. Active participation in the local and state coaches' associations increases contacts and knowledge of prospects in other schools and in other areas.

Most colleges and universities provide a placement bureau or some form of registry that will enable a coach or school to contact eligibles interested in coaching positions. Other sources of information are deans of colleges, the head coach of the particular sport for which applicants are being sought, and physical education department chairpersons.

Following a thorough search for applicants that meet affirmative action guidelines, the coach must base the selection of assistants on the merits of the available individuals. The coach who has publicized the position extensively, described the job in detail, emphasized the role of the position as it relates to the success of the total program, and weighed the choices will secure the assistant who can help form the ideal staff.

Interpersonal Relations

In the meantime, while waiting for vacancies to occur or for present faculty to retire or transfer, what does the coach do? Finding the right assistant is a difficult endeavor, but an equally difficult and demanding task is to build a loyal team of holdover staff. A new head coach may be an effective catalyst to mold a staff into a more efficient, cohesive unit, but the probability of disappointment, resentment, and apprehension about the coaching change is more likely. It is now that leadership and organizational ability will be tested. Regardless of the composition of the staff—newly recruited, inherited, or a combination of both—the head coach will be concerned with interpersonal relationships among and between the assistants.

Needs of Staff It is essential for the coach as leader or personnel manager to keep in mind several characteristics of people and their personal and interpersonal needs. Each assistant needs to have a sense of self-worth, to feel important, and to experience the pleasure of a positive contribution to the cause. A staff member deserves the opportunity to receive attention and direction in order to gain fulfillment of potential as a coach. The need is greatest when things are not going well and performance is not up to expectations. Many assistant coaches actively seek to be associated with a coach who can and will nurture and utilize their talents.

Equally important is the recognition that should be accorded each individual for a job well done. The head coach should make the assistants well aware of the point that recognition will be given to those who perform their assignments well. Sensitivity and cooperation among staff do not occur spontaneously but are developed through mutual understanding and appreciation of the value of each staff member.

Meeting Personal Needs It is not enough to know about human needs; they must be met if the season is to progress successfully. Various coaches use different approaches, but all the good ones follow basic rules. Generally, they are very similar to those in the following list:

1. Total staff is involved in the planning; all members have input.
2. Duties and responsibilities, administrative as well as coaching, are delegated; assistants know exactly what is expected of them.
3. Authority is delegated with the assigned responsibilities and duties.
4. Assistants are allowed to carry out their duties and responsibilities; corrections may be made, but never in the presence of team members.
5. Assistants know where they stand; they receive praise, constructive criticism, advice, and direction, depending on the situation.
6. Communication lines are kept open.

The responsibility for developing a unified group rests with the head coach. He or she may be considered as head, patriarch or matriarch, of the coaching family, leading the family members to give of themselves and to direct their efforts toward a common goal. Coaches have to earn this respect through successful leadership performance and satisfying personal relations with those with whom they work. Coaches who rule with fear and anger will earn little respect, while others who give a full measure of time and effort may expect a rewarding response from the assisting staff.

Evaluation

Evaluation is an integral part of teaching and personnel management. The main purpose for evaluation of the sports staff is to improve coaching and to provide better learning opportunities for the athlete.

Effective evaluation can be performed daily as the assistant coach carries out the routine duties assigned. Informal talks and observations, or planned conferences with the assistant coach during the season, will reveal strengths that can be immediately credited and applauded and deficiencies that can be identified and corrected.

On-the-job evaluation of an informal nature can be supplemented by using a more formal and objective written evaluation that becomes part of the coach's record. The evaluation should include items that indicate personal and professional growth and capabilities similar to those that follow:

1. Personal Responsibilities
   a. Provides a moral and ethical role model for youth.
   b. Exhibits physical well-being.
   c. Controls emotions.
   d. Is trustworthy and loyal.
   e. Displays initiative.
   f. Relates well to youth.
2. Professional Responsibilities
   a. Handles routine tasks efficiently.
   b. Works cooperatively with other staff members.
   c. Demonstrates mature judgment in professional relationships.
   d. Gives evidence of professional growth.
   e. Exhibits good judgment in interpersonal relationships.
3. Coaching Responsibilities
   a. Displays a knowledge of the game.
   b. Demonstrates expertise in a specific area of the game.
   c. Demonstrates a mastery of teaching technique in the assigned area.
   d. Organizes learning activities to achieve specific objectives.
   e. Assumes duties that relate to maintenance and care of equipment and supplies.
   f. Handles scouting assignments efficiently.
   g. Participates in public relations promotions.

BEING AN ASSISTANT COACH

Most individuals entering the coaching profession have aspirations of being a head coach of a successful team, but may begin their careers at a lower rank, as an assistant. Dedication and hard work are basic to success as an assistant and will lead to being a successful head coach. Ingredients that make an assistant coach successful are:

1. Loyalty to the head coach.
2. Respect for fellow assistants and the coaching staffs of other teams.
3. Diplomacy in discussing points of contention with the head coach.
4. Self-confidence in accepting the maximal duties and program responsibility that the head coach may assign.

To be an assistant coach is to learn by doing. This learning is presumably from a master teacher—the head coach. The knowledge and experience gained from the apprenticeship need to be sorted, evaluated, and filed in anticipation of a head coaching position in the future.

BEING AN ADJUNCT COACH

Career goals and job opportunities commonly are divergent from a long-held ambition to be involved with developing young athletes—to coach a team. A person's hopes for association with a school team may become a reality, as the relaxation of rules stipulating teacher status for high school coaches permits the use of adjuncts or nonfaculty staff as assistants or, in some instances, head coach.

In order to benefit from the experience, adjuncts must be knowledgeable about institutional guidelines and be encouraged to follow them. Too, they must be dedicated to performing routine procedures, coordinating efforts, and sharing ideas.

The forced separation of an adjunct coach from the day-to-day activities of the athletes creates a myopic view of the athlete as a person and as a student. An adjunct coach should especially try to gain insight into the personalities and daily lives of young people outside the playing fields, along with their athletic development at practices and games. Skills of listening, communicating, and understanding are essential if the adjunct is to fulfill an obligation to the total well-being of a student/athlete. These skills must also be employed with other coaches and administrators; the adjunct should strive to become as full a member of the entire staff as possible.

Most significantly, an adjunct coach can determine the very existence of a sport (if there is no coach, there is no team) or the success of a team (having expertise in areas that help team members do well). Although the disadvantages peculiar to adjunct coaching present challenges, the pleasure derived from nurturing an important aspect of a youth's life can more than compensate for these problems.

SUMMARY

The coach as a personnel manager wears many hats. He or she has to determine program direction, select and train staff, work with professionals and nonprofessionals, and get the most out of all members of the support group. Sound planning, considerate training and scheduling, and effective supervision should pay off in smooth programs, good practices, superior contests, and winning seasons.

Extensive recruiting and care in the screening and selection of assistant coaches and adjunct coaches are only the beginning for a quality staff. The ultimate test of the coach as a personnel manager will be the molding of the staff into a loyal, cohesive unit. This can be accomplished only through strong leadership that permits close supervision and continuous evaluation of assistants. A coach is only as good as the staff of assistants; the staff is only as good as the coach is willing to let them become.

22

Support Personnel

> **MANAGERS**
> **TRAINERS**
> **MEDICAL PERSONNEL**
> **MAINTENANCE PERSONNEL**
> **CLERICAL PERSONNEL**
> **SUMMARY**

To make the program function smoothly, a coach needs—in addition to good assistant coaches—support personnel. On the immediate staff the necessity for managers and trainers is very apparent if all duties and chores are to be attended to and if players are to be protected. Still necessary, but not always under the coach's immediate control, are medical personnel, maintenance staff, and clerical assistants. Everyone affiliated in any way with the athletic program influences the players, coaches, staff, and total program; therefore, much care must be taken in selecting, training, and/or interacting with the entire staff. They also should be shown appreciation for their contributions: a "thank you" note, special recognition at a banquet, a personal word, public credit for a job well done, and so on, are very important.

Although some school systems, recreational leagues, or other groups sponsoring athletics may employ an adult who serves as equipment manager and perhaps another who is a certified trainer, the emphasis here is on the great majority who do not have this assistance. More often, the coach assumes these duties and must find students or young adults who can be trained to perform managerial and training tasks.

There is general consensus that the successful head coach acquires or develops a capable staff of coaching assistants and that the coaching staff is complemented by a crew of competent managers and trainers. These personnel are considered to be basic for implementing sports programs and for ensuring the success of a coach's plan for a team. A similar parallel can be drawn with program support personnel—that is, physicians, custodial crews, secretaries. With the addition of more technically trained people, coaches' jobs become more complex, but easier. In truth, coaches cannot function well without their services; the coaching staff and players may be on stage, but it is the support staff that prepares the stage for action.

MANAGERS

Managers are the individuals who take care of all details so that the coach can coach. They sweep floors, launder the uniforms, pack equipment bags, check lockers, and keep everything running smoothly—if they are good. A coach would never be able to attend to the primary task with athletes if the manager did not perform all the routine, grubby jobs that make a program go. Managers might survive without coaches, but coaches could never survive without managers.

Desirable Characteristics

The process of selection can be expedited by having in mind certain characteristics that are desirable in a manager. Some of the qualities needed for good management are discussed in the following paragraphs, although the relative importance of any one characteristic will vary with the individual head coach and the overall organizational plan.

Dependability

A good manager can be relied on to perform the duties assigned. Of all the qualities that the manager must possess, this is the most important. Coaches cannot tolerate a manager, or anyone else, who cannot be counted on absolutely, all the time. There must be assurance that uniforms, equipment, and everything else will be ready and waiting when needed. An undependable, unreliable person should never be included on a staff. If one is inadvertently hired or accepted, it would be an error in judgment to retain him or her.

Organization

A good manager has the ability to sort out the various aspects of the job to be done and systematically to determine the order of timely completion. Managers who cannot arrange a thousand details into a logical plan for accomplishing them will be frustrated and unproductive. Pleasant as some unorganized persons are, a coach cannot afford to have them around.

Adaptability

A good manager can adjust easily to accommodate circumstances outside routine assignments. Because the only sure thing in any athletic endeavor is that it will not go smoothly, managers must be able to accept changed circumstances and situations without being upset. A cool head in a difficult situation makes a coach's problem simpler.

Creativity

A good manager improvises ways to improve efficiency or to provide an interim solution to immediate problems. Creativity involves finding innovative ways to deal with routine problems and unexpected situations. A new way to issue uniforms, a better way to load equipment on the bus, or a modification of existing storage procedures can make a manager's job easier and the coach's problems fewer.

Concentration

A good manager can perform duties during the distractions and excitement of competition. It is not easy to worry about chin straps for helmets when your team is about to go for the winning score, but devotion to duty comes before personal satisfaction. The manager must be alert to play on the field or court in the event some service is needed, but the ability to focus on the task at hand is paramount.

Knowledge

The more knowledgeable the manager, the better service that can be rendered. Managers for each sport must make it their business to know everything about equipment, facilities, and uniforms—both routine maintenance and basic repair. No coach can tolerate an ignorant or stupid manager—though ignorance can be cured.

Recruitment and Selection

The typical high school manager is a student who is interested in athletics but is not a participating athlete. Coaches may use a variety of selection techniques to choose the best students available. These procedures apply generally to all situations.

Recruitment

Perhaps the most effective way to recruit student managers is to offer a two- to three-week trial or training period. Announcements can be made through the public-address system, to classes, or by posters or fliers. Interested candidates should be given a brief orientation and assigned specific duties. Any ideas of "glamour" being associated with a team will dissipate quickly amid the routine hard work of field or court preparation, equipment repair or adjustments, and custodial duties. Many of the desired characteristics, or lack of them, can be easily observed.

Another valid system is recruitment of new managers by experienced managers. The continuing managers contact prospective recruits among their friends whom they know will be interested and willing to work with them to learn the job. The managerial staff, in effect, locates and trains its successors. Frequently this system of recruitment promotes a continuance of service-oriented responsibilities beyond secondary school as coaches of college and university teams are interested in obtaining good team managers, and the institution may offer a type of scholarship.

Members of the coaching staff may be able to identify potential managers through their classes or other contacts with the students. A student's need to be involved, lack of athletic talent to make the team roster, demonstration of qualities that reflect good management, or interest in a particular sports activity can indicate to the coach that an invitation or solicitation to join the group as a manager will be productive.

The coach should not limit the recruitment of managers by contacting only boys for male teams or only girls for female teams. It may prove expedient to involve members of the same sex because of duties in the locker rooms, but to exclude potential managers solely on the basis of sex is not only unpopular (if not illegal) but also eliminates approximately one-half of the potential recruits.

Not all managers are students. Some schools have faculty members with a specific assignment for equipment who receive supplements for their work. This person can be a coach but need not be. Managers of nonschool teams can be parents or friends of players or the coach. They may have to be urged to help and may need to be diligently sought, since not all parents, teachers, and friends volunteer as readily as students do.

Selection

When recruiting has produced the names of potential manager candidates, the selection process can begin. Each candidate should be measured against the yardstick of expected characteristics previously outlined; any who are not dependable, organized, or adaptable should be eliminated. Recommendations from faculty, coaches, students, and other managers are worthwhile; it is a good policy to consider no one who does not have someone's enthusiastic support. Some candidates are asked to serve a trial period so that their work can be evaluated. Their enthusiasm for the job and their personal compatibility with the coaches must also be assessed.

After all the information has been gathered, the potential managers should be interviewed and their duties and responsibilities outlined. When this procedure is complete, a new manager can be selected with confidence, and, with luck, several new managers may emerge from the process. There are coaches who keep a big squad of assistant managers and, to ensure a ready supply of helpers, eliminate only the obviously unqualified.

Duties

Some managers can perform many of their duties instinctively, but good management and efficient functioning of a program require direction and explicit organization. Ideally, if help is available, a squad of 50 athletes needs five managers. These persons, student or adult, have serious responsibilities, work hard, and make a practice or game run smoothly. The duties of a manager can be categorized into four general areas: facility preparation, equipment care and repair; inventory of supplies and uniforms, and locker room maintenance.

Facility Preparation

Ideally, a groundskeeper or custodian should have primary responsibilities for preparing facilities for games, but, practically, those chores usually fall to a coach and thus to a manager. Whatever needs to be done to prepare the site for competition is done by managers unless they enjoy the luxury of the service of professional or para-professional maintenance personnel. Local policies and procedures need to be examined before certain maintenance duties are assigned to the team managers; otherwise, stipulations of a union contract or a liability insurance policy could be violated.

Equipment and Uniform Care

Again, the ideal situation would have para-professionals repair uniforms and equipment, launder or dry-clean them, patch holes, clean balls, and wrap hockey grips, but usually the task falls to a manager. He or she must rescue damp uniforms from heaps on the locker room floor, clean and rack the bats, replace the spikes or cleats on shoes, collect the floating lane lines, and generally guard all the properties. The manager should be given instructions for operating the washer and dryer, authority to deal with the dry cleaners and shoe shop, and enough room and facilities to conserve and preserve all the expensive items that are necessary to operate a team.

Inventory

Closely related to equipment care and repair is the responsibility for keeping up with every item that belongs to the team and keeping an inventory record of everything. The manager's records should be so complete and accurate that the coach can tell instantly how many of each item is available and what the condition of that item is. This is necessary for pre-season preparation to ascertain that what was stored is still available and in good condition. It is necessary during the season to keep up with wear and tear and necessary replacements. It is absolutely essential at the end of the season so that there can be a final accounting and so that purchase orders can be prepared for next year's equipment and uniforms.

The inventory manager is responsible for the numbering, marking, and filing system that is indispensable for keeping an accurate inventory. He or she will receive new items, match them against the purchase order, mark them properly, and keep all records of receipts and issue up to date. No one should be permitted to use anything not officially issued. As the major cost of operation generally comes from expenditures for equipment and uniforms, a manager plays a crucial role in keeping costs down.

Locker Room Maintenance

The cleanliness, security, and general maintenance of the locker and shower area goes with the job as manager. Perhaps the regular building crew will scrub showers and sweep the locker room; but additional use by the team at odd hours, long after the regular working day, will require the manager to scrub and sweep again.

Security of the team locker room is a serious concern for the coach and thus for the manager. Individual lockers and equipment areas should be locked, equipment not in use stored, and the locker room itself locked when the players are not using it. The security of the visiting team's possessions and those of the officials are also among a manager's concerns.

Direction and Organization

The process of organizing and providing proper direction to managers is a difficult one. A head football coach at a large northern Virginia high school has assigned duties in nine categories. He uses five student managers—two seniors, one junior, and two sophomores—to carry out these assignments. Duties are detailed in Figure 22-1.

Other sports will require somewhat different specific duties, but they would be similar in the scope of organizational detail. Teams with a small number of participating athletes, less equipment, or fewer items of uniforms and supplies will require fewer managers to perform managerial tasks efficiently.

Rotation

To promote the idea of training managers for progressively higher levels of responsibilities, the assistant managers should be rotated periodically to gain knowledge of the duties performed in different assignments. For example, the basketball manager whose basic responsibility is to ready the basketball court for practice (mop the floor, periodically clean the glass blackboard, check the nets for degree of wear) could be assigned to security responsibility (check players' lockers to be sure that each is secured with a lock; close and lock equipment rooms; close and lock all exterior doors to the locker rooms; accompany players or other managers to the locker room if they need to enter during practice). This rotation system helps each manager to be thoroughly familiar with all the facets of operation and ensures that management will be efficient in the event of a manager's absence on any particular day. The rotation could be scheduled during practice sessions to avoid possible confusion of delegated respon-

1. Pre-Season Duties
   a. Keep in touch with head coach for helping set up equipment to be issued and locker room layout.
   b. Check first-aid kit to be taken to field the very first day. (Be sure Emergency Care Cards are in kit.)
   c. Prepare master locker list with lock and locker number.
   d. Prepare number of footballs, kicking tees, etc., for field. (One large bag will do.)
   e. Make sure sufficient scrimmage vests are available (22).
   f. Be familiar with VHSL eligibility form to make first check on returned forms.
   g. Sweep and swab dressing room each day after practice.
2. Daily Duties
   a. Be on time for all practice sessions. Check your duties for the day.
   b. Make certain that one manager is on the field with ball bag and first-aid kit before any player arrives.
   c. Assist coaches with extra equipment to be taken to the field by players.
   d. Be sure there is one manager (usually the one designated as trainer) in the training room with coach assigned duty.
   e. Check air pressure in balls.
   f. Be sure to report broken, lost, or needed equipment to equipment manager.
   g. Be aware of boys who quit or are cut from the squad—help check out their lockers and equipment with coaches.
   h. Be aware of injuries in the locker room and on the fields; report and assist.
   i. Consult with head coach about any problems you may be having with players and other staff.
   j. Bring towels and equipment to be cleaned to designated place.
   k. Assigned manager, last one out of locker room, lock the room before and after practice.
   l. Keep training room clean and orderly at all times. Do not allow loitering.
   m. Assist coaches and remind players to lock lockers and keep a clean dressing room. Ask players not to leave tape and trash on floors.
3. Thursday Practice (Day Before Game)
   a. Same as daily routine and/or
      1) Check cleats and equipment
      2) Have laces for shoulder pads handy
      3) Make screw drivers available
      4) Clean and buff footballs and check air pressure in each.
4. Game Night at Home
   a. All managers report at 5:00 P.M.
   b. Prepare all equipment—check for use on field, water, ice, etc. (one manager with bench.)
   c. Ready training room for taping and treatment.
   d. Lock locker rooms after teams leave rooms.
   e. Help with field marking during day.
   f. Open lecture room (201). Have chalk and eraser available.
   g. Make sure ice is available.
   h. Open locker room adjacent to gym.
   i. Designate one manager to be responsible for officials.
   j. Check with coaches about placement of balls for pregame warm up.
5. Game Nights Away.
   a. Pack all equipment and extra on Thursday or sometime on Friday before 3:00 P.M.
   b. When bus arrives to depart for trip, get all equipment on bus quickly. On arrival at site, remove all equipment quickly and check bus.
   c. When you are settled at your destination, lay out needs in dressing room for coaches.
   d. Managers going to field and bench, lay out equipment and supplies directed by coach.
   e. One manager should stay with equipment before game, during, and at half-time.
   f. See to it that all players' valuables are locked up if dressing at site.
   g. As game is ending, see to all your equipment; prepare to vacate field. Stay with equipment.
   h. Check locker room if necessary for anything left behind, and board bus with all equipment.
   i. Check bus upon vacating back home and secure all equipment in dressing room.
   j. Unpack everything upon return to school.
   k. See that rooms are locked before leaving.

(continued)

Figure 22–1   Managerial duties

Courtesy of Robert G. Hardage, Head Football Coach, Annandale High School, Fairfax County, Virginia.

> 6. Sideline Procedure During Game
>   a. Have water ready at all times, keep equipment orderly. Be able to find first-aid kit at all times.
>   b. Assist players with jackets upon entering or leaving game.
>   c. Have kicking tees ready at all times.
>   d. Be alert for needs of players and coaches.
>   e. One manager goes to open locker room three to five minutes prior to half-time. Assist at doors and see that doors are locked upon leaving.
>   f. All managers must stay within bench boundaries at all times during game.
>   g. Be alert to recognize possible injuries of players.
>   h. Have ice available at bench for injury.
>   i. One manager takes care of game balls with officials.
> 7. Half-time Procedures
>   a. One manager stays on field to guard equipment and straighten up.
>   b. Bring first-aid kit to dressing room.
>   c. Have cokes or drink for players.
>   d. Be aware of player and coach needs. Stay with the team.
>   e. Check locker room and lock up room when leaving.
>   f. One manager in charge of officials' needs.
> 8. After Game Procedure
>   a. One manager leaves field early to open up locker rooms for team and officials.
>   b. Get game balls, square away and pick up all equipment on field.
>   c. Unpack ball bag and equipment bag so nothing will mildew.
> 9. Post-Season Duties
>   a. Report Monday after last game to collect equipment.
>   b. Aid coaches in collecting, counting, and separating equipment.
>   c. Remove pads from all sleds and check for damage.
>   d. Meet with Head Coach to discuss suggestions for improvement of management for next season.

Figure 22-1 Continued

sibilities and should ensure that at least one proficient assistant is retained in each area of responsibility.

Good managers are developed over a period of years. A manager who learns the duties of an assistant in the freshman year and continues to serve in increasingly responsible positions should be an excellent head manager as a senior. Myriad responsibilities create a unique training program for an aspiring manager, as the successful completion of one level of assignments leads logically to being assigned additional duties or to a more prestigious level.

Pride

A feeling of pride in performing an important function for the team is inherent in every good manager. This quality rarely occurs spontaneously; it must be developed. The logical person to begin and to maintain this development is the head coach, who is aware of how indispensable the manager is and conveys this awareness to the manager and the team. Thoroughness of planning, implicit instruction, careful supervision, and constructive evaluation by the coach will indicate to the manager that managing is vital to a successful program.

The attitude of the coach toward the manager will likely be reflected in the attitude of the athletes toward the manager. They should join the coach in providing an atmosphere of appreciation and confidence to make certain that the manager feels a part of the total effort.

TRAINERS

The safety of players is the primary concern of every coach, not just because a player in good condition plays better but also because coaches care about their athletes. The person to whom the training and well-being of a team is entrusted is the trainer. Most teams do not have the luxury of a certified trainer to be responsible for conditioning and for the prevention and care of injuries, but this is a goal to strive for. In the absence of a certified trainer, the coach or assistant coach who has had some preparation assumes these duties or instructs a student in basic diagnosis and first-aid treatment of athletic injuries. Whoever serves as trainer should be under the instruction and supervision of a team physician.

Certified Athletic Trainers

Certified trainers are highly trained professionals who have varied skills ranging from conditioning and rehabilitative programs to counseling about nutrition programs for athletes. Most are employed by college, university, or professional sports teams. Many secondary schools, though, are becoming increasingly conscious of the need for these para-medical personnel and are making provisions for hiring them within the school district's personnel policies. This hiring policy developed from the increased awareness of a need by coaches, availability of certified trainers, and requirements by many states that each school or cluster of schools hire them. As the level of competition increases, the need for specialized, intensive coaching increases; concurrently, the amount of time that the coach can devote to athletic training duties decreases. Well-trained personnel must be available.

NATA

Ideally, the head athletic trainer should be certified by the National Athletic Trainers' Association (NATA) or be participating in a NATA-approved training program. This association permits a two-year probationary status for a trainer in an approved program, who is not yet qualified, but suspends NATA privileges if the trainer does not qualify within the probationary period.

The professional and personal qualifications of a certified trainer can be determined in ways similar to those proposed for selection of assistant coaches. Coaches may be aided in the selection process by an awareness of certain obligations and responsibilities that an athletic trainer assumes as a member of the profession, as set forth in the National Athletic Trainers' Association "Code of Ethics." Some pertinent excerpts from those basic principles state that a trainer:

1. Shows no discrimination in interest or effort to improve all sports activities.
2. Treats each athlete impartially and responsibly.

3. Cooperates fully with the medical advisor.
4. Conveys to parents of athletes, by conduct and communication, that proper care is being given to the athletes.
5. Develops a close relationship with the coach to ensure mutual respect and cooperation.[1]

Medical and Legal Concerns

School administrators are well aware of the medical and legal, as well as the ethical, ramifications of employing personnel to perform services for which they are not qualified. As a result, a number of states (13 in the mid-1980s) enacted licensure requirements for the position of athletic trainer. An individual must meet the requirements, which vary from state to state, necessary to be a licensed or registered athletic trainer within the particular state.

The influence and support of the state medical society and the state board of education are crucial to ensuring that certified athletic trainers are made available to school athletic teams. Physicians who are not involved with sports medicine need to be educated by their colleagues in this area to promote acceptance of the athletic trainer's role and the licensure for trainers. The recommendation of the state medical society will exert tremendous influence on the state board of education to initiate requirements for local school districts. If leadership is absent at the top echelons, pressure can be put on local school boards by parent and coaching groups who are convinced of a need for trainers.

The problem of liability cannot be overlooked as an important impetus in securing athletic trainers. Although proof of negligence is currently the interpretation of liability, the "sue syndrome" may lead to change in precedents and a wider base of proof. It has been speculated that injury liability suits will be easily won in the absence of trainers and other provisions that ensure optimal safety for athletes. This area is discussed more fully in Chapter 19.

Duties

The basic duties or responsibilities of an athletic trainer, as discussed by certified athletic trainers at a symposium in sports medicine, are suggested in the following outline:

1. Preparation for Practice
   a. Be present in training room area or dressing area before practice.
   b. Have supplies for taping, etc.
   c. Make sure that water/fluids and equipment are ready for the field.
   d. Be on the field or court before or at times of practice.
2. On-Field Duties
   a. Observe practices.
   b. Be ready for any injuries that take place on the playing field.
   c. Treat any injuries immediately.
   d. Make sure that there are an adequate number of fluid breaks.

3. After-Practice Duties
    a. Ask about any problems like blisters, bruises, or abrasions.
    b. Look at any injuries that took place during practice.
    c. Clean up training room area.
4. Other Duties That Are of Importance to a Trainer
    a. Let coaches know of any injuries as soon as they happen and after practices, so that they have an understanding of the player's status.
    b. Have phone numbers available of key personnel:
    Doctor _____
    Rescue Squad _____
    Area Hospitals _____
    c. Keep records of all injuries, and have some general information on each player. Usually players' physical form will be a good source.
    d. Keep some school insurance forms for accidents on the playing field for use when a player needs medical attention from a doctor or from a hospital. Become familiar with this form so that it will be easy to use.
    e. Make sure you have telephone numbers of players' parents to be used when an injury occurs and you need to get in contact with them.

Sources of Aid If it is not feasible for a coach to have a certified trainer for the team, there are options available. A few schools have hired certified athletic trainers to serve in the capacity of school nurse, classroom teacher, permanent substitute, or administrative assistant. At the end of the school day these individuals are free to work with the athletes and may also be available for consultation at a time earlier in the day. There are schools that have pooled their resources to hire a certified trainer who is available to athletic personnel from a cluster of schools. A few coaches are fortunate to be near a university or college whose athletic trainer shares time and expertise with the young athletes in the area; or there may be graduate students specializing in athletic training who would love to work for a little money and a lot of experience. Occasionally, Sports Medicine Centers have a visiting trainer program and would be pleased to add a school to its list.

These are viable options for a coach. If requesting trainers, a coach must have a well-designed plan to present. Just saying "we need" or "I want" is not enough to justify an approval of the request.

Noncertified Athletic Trainers Duties of these personnel are very much like those of the certified trainer. Since they do not have the same level of expertise as the certified trainer, they should be closely supervised by licensed medical practitioners. The extent of this supervision should depend on the background of the noncertified trainer.

Staff Using coaches or other staff for training duties is a common practice. They usually are experienced in dealing with athletic injuries and may have taken courses in first aid, workshops in athletic training conducted by equipment manufacturers, or instruction in cardio-pulmonary resuscitation (CPR). Although not NATA-certified, they may serve their teams well.

Students

The head trainer is assigned the responsibility of selecting, training, and supervising a staff of student or assistant trainers. These persons should also be prepared in first aid and CPR. The use of unsupervised student trainers, a practice in some schools, is not encouraged, as they are inexperienced and limited in their training.

During practice times the head trainer should assign a student trainer to the locker room or training room and a separate trainer to each team. They should be expected to be on duty every time a team reports for practice.

Figure 22-2 Trainers are indispensable members of an athletic staff (Courtesy of Kentucky State University, Frankfort, Kentucky)

Other Personnel

Athletic programs may avail themselves of the services of emergency medical technologists (EMTs), who are more numerous than certified trainers are. Some solicit the services of a physical therapist; others routinely use the school nurse for injuries and illnesses.

MEDICAL PERSONNEL

The need for a trainer has already been discussed—and there can be no doubt that the trainer is important—but the person who has the authority and responsibility for medical direction of the program is the team physician. The team doctor can supervise pre-season physical examinations, establish acceptable routine treatment procedures, and work with the coach and trainer to maintain the health and safety of the players.

The welfare of the athlete must always be a primary concern of the coach. Appropriate professional medical care indicates to the athlete, to the parent, and to all observers that the coach's priorities are in proper order. Establishing a positive relationship with a team physician will improve a coach's odds for accomplishing all the priorities involved in building a successful team; it will also provide another disciple for the program.

Although it is desirable to have a team physician in attendance at all athletic contests, practicality dictates that this situation rarely occurs. The need for a physician to monitor contact sports, where more serious injury is likely to occur, is clearly indicated and should be met if at all possible. In the absence of a certified athletic trainer and/or emergency rescue assistance on the spot, or even with this help, the coach is assuming an enormous responsibility for player welfare unless a physician is present.

Regardless of the organizational set-up, be it school or agency, a concerted effort needs to be made to engage a physician in an advisory capacity, if not on a game-by-game basis, for all sports-related injuries. It is a matter of good coaching practice as well as good public relations to inform and involve as many professionals as possible in the athletic programs.

A new medical specialty, sports medicine, emerged in the 1970s and is pursued by physicians and surgeons with a particular interest in the medical and surgical aspects of sports participation and injuries. Because these doctors are better prepared to service youth sports than is a doctor in general practice, their services should be sought.

Securing a Team Physician

Locating a physician who is willing to volunteer many hours of precious free time is not an easy task. Some of the sources that may yield results are:

1. A physician who is the parent of an athlete and would probably attend some of the games in a parental role anyway.
2. A physician who is the parent of a student who is a loyal fan of sports.

3. A local physician who is the family doctor for many students in the school.
4. A physician who has an interest in athletics as a fan or because sports medicine is of interest.
5. A clinic specializing in orthopedics that is used in referral for athletic injuries.
6. A Health Maintenance Organization (HMO) interested in performing community service.

In seeking the services of a medical director for the athletic program, the principal, athletic director, or supervisor might first try to secure these services at a reduced cost or on a voluntary basis. If all else fails, a standard retainer might be offered if funds are available. It can be pointed out that the doctor may use the contribution of time and effort as a part of his or her community service activity or, in the case of nonprofit agencies, that there is a tax-deductible advantage in rendering services. Most schools and agencies do not have funds sufficient enough to support adequate medical services on a day-to-day basis, but the student or participant insurance can pay for actual services needed in case of injury. Many doctors are willing to serve first and seek funding later.

Policies

The assumption is that the local school is seeking a physician who will volunteer time and professional services at games and/or be on call for emergencies at other times. The school, therefore, is obligated to provide the necessary support to make the physician's job easier.

Policies about the entire medical program must be established mutually by the team physician, the coach, the trainer, and the school or agency administrator. For example, the objectives of the physical examination must be detailed in order to differentiate it from the traditional health screening examination. Five such objectives are to:

1. Determine the general health of the athlete.
2. Disclose defects that may limit participation.
3. Uncover conditions predisposing the athlete to injury.
4. Bring the athlete to an optimal level of performance.
5. Classify the athlete according to individual qualifications.[2]

Coaches and trainers know the particulars involved in each sport and should have a form, such as the one illustrated in Figure 22-3, to share with medical personnel. Physicians may choose to use their own forms; if so, they will need to sign a statement similar to the one shown in Figure 22-4. Regardless of the form they use, they may need to be reminded of areas to be checked closely for a specific activity. Runners are particularly vulnerable to back, hip, knee, ankle, and foot injuries; volleyball players place extreme stress on their wrists and knees; softball/baseball players have frequent problems with elbows and shoulders; football players are subject to head, neck, and knee injuries, and so on.

Decisions should be made about these general concerns: areas of responsibility, emergency procedures, need for personnel at games, training room operation, and stocking supplies and medication. The medication of

```
┌─────────────────────────────────────────────────────────────────────────────┐
│              SUGGESTED HEALTH EXAMINATION FORM                              │
│                                                                             │
│ (Cooperatively prepared by the National Federation of State High School     │
│ Athletic Associations and the Committee on Medical Aspects of Sports of the │
│ American Medical Association.) Health examination for athletes should be    │
│ rendered after August 1 preceding school year concerned.                    │
│                                                                             │
│           (Please Print)         Name of Student        City and School     │
│ Grade _____ Age _____ Height _____ Weight _____ Blood Pressure ____ │
│ Significant Past Illness or Injury _____│
│                                                                             │
│ Eyes _____ R 20/    ; L 20/   ; Ears _____ Hearing R /15; L /15│
│ Respiratory _____│
│ Cardiovascular _____│
│ Liver _____ Spleen _____ Hernia _____│
│ Musculoskeletal _____ Skin _____│
│ Neurological _____ Genitalia _____│
│ Laboratory: Urinalysis _____ Other: _____│
│ Comments _____│
│ Completed Immunizations: Polio _____  Tetanus _____         │
│                                    Date                      Date           │
│ Instructions for use of card  Other _____ │
│                                                                             │
│ "I certify that I have on this date examined this student and that, on the  │
│ basis of the examination requested by the school authorities and the        │
│ student's medical history as furnished to me, I have found no reason which  │
│ would make it medically inadvisable for this student to compete in          │
│ supervised athletic activities, EXCEPT THOSE CROSSED OUT BELOW."            │
│ BASEBALL          FOOTBALL         ROWING         SOFTBALL       TRACK      │
│ BASKETBALL        HOCKEY           SKATING        SPEEDBALL      VOLLEYBALL │
│ CROSS COUNTRY     GOLF             SKIING         SWIMMING       *WRESTLING │
│ FIELD HOCKEY      GYMNASTICS       SOCCER         TENNIS         OTHERS ___ │
│ * Estimated desirable weight level: _____ pounds.                      │
│ Date of Examination: _____ Signed: _____│
│                                               Examining Physician           │
│ Physician's Address _____ Telephone _____│
└─────────────────────────────────────────────────────────────────────────────┘
```

Figure 22–3   Health examination form

Courtesy of the American Alliance for Health, Physical Education, Recreation and Dance, Reston, Virginia.

players requires close medical supervision, and all drugs must be administered only with the approval of the team doctor. Coaches should not administer any medicine or drugs without authorization. All medical and training activities are conducted with the welfare of the athlete at heart; nothing is to be done to cause harm or increase risk.

MAINTENANCE PERSONNEL

Building and grounds maintenance crews, custodians, electricians, plumbers, and other personnel lend the special touch needed for a first-class, quality program. Conversely, less than dedicated attention by support services often seriously impedes the development of a program.

Any team can achieve a winning tradition and a pride in accomplishment in spite of facilities that are inferior, or at best barely satisfactory. But developing pride is easier when there is tangible evidence that others

☐ Initial physical examination

☐ Medical Re-evaluation

*STATEMENT BY PHYSICIAN FOR ATHLETIC PARTICIPATION

I hereby certify that I have examined _____ and that the student was found physically fit to engage in baseball, basketball, cross country, football, golf, gymnastics, soccer, softball, swimming, tennis, track, volleyball, wrestling, other. (Please cross out any sport in which the student should not participate).

DATE: _____ SIGNED: _____
(Valid for 365 days unless   Physician (must be signed by a
 rescinded)   physician)

Summary Information for Physicians

Rule 1, Section 9, Page 32

No pupil shall represent his school in inter-school athletics until there is on file with the superintendent or principal a statement signed by his parents or legal guardian and a practicing physician certifying that he/she has passed an adequate physical examination within the past year; that in the opinion of the examining physician he/she is physically fit to participate in athletics; and that he/she has the consent of his parents or legal guardian to participate. A student who has received an adequate physical examination at least once upon entering 9th grade may elect to have a Medical Re-evaluation instead of a physical examination in subsequent years, unless significant injuries or illnesses have occurred the past year.

Note: It is strongly recommended by the Colorado Department of Health that individuals participating in athletic events have current tetanus boosters. Tetanus boosters are recommended every 10 years throughout life. Boosters are recommended at the time of major injury if more than five years have elapsed since the last booster.

If significant intervening illnesses and/or injuries have occurred, a more complete physical examination should be conducted. The physical examination form must be signed by a practicing physician.

If a student athlete has been injured in practice and/or competition, the nature of which required medical attention, the student athlete should not be permitted to return to practice and/or competition until he/she has received a release from a practicing physician.

Note: The CHSAA urges an adequate physical examination be given when a student athlete changes levels of competition, i.e. Little League to Junior High, Junior High to High School, etc.

Figure 22-4   Physical examination form

Courtesy of Alice Barron, Coordinator of Athletics, Jefferson County Schools, Lakewood, Colorado.

believe that what the coach is doing is important and deserving of support. Good relationships, arrangements, and mutual understanding with maintenance personnel are necessary if a program is to function at its best.

Building Personnel

No athletic program can operate without the hard work done by the building custodian and staff. They are responsible for opening and closing the building; keeping the gymnasium and locker rooms clean, lighted, and warmed or cooled; and seeing that the facilities are painted, repaired, and mowed. No coach can get along without the full support and cooperation of this group.

Custodians can make a coach's life easy when they are interested in the program and go the extra mile to help and cooperate. They can make coaching very difficult if they choose not to be helpful, doing only the minimum cleaning and repairing that may be stipulated in their contracts. Although students and other coaches may be enlisted to help with such tasks as groundskeeping, floor scrubbing, and light-bulb changing, this diverts time and energy from coaching tasks to maintenance tasks. The friendship and talents of the custodial staff should be cultivated, and they should be given recognition for a job well done. Custodians, like athletes, thrive on positive reinforcement. Sending a note to the individuals involved and their supervisors will reap dividends.

System Personnel

Most school systems and recreation departments have central maintenance staffs for specialized repairs and for maintenance jobs too big for the building personnel. Plumbers, painters, carpenters, mechanics, and electricians fall into this category, as do bus drivers and big equipment operators. The services of these staff are generally secured by request from the custodian or building administrator to the central office. It may be necessary for the system supervisor to present a list of construction and repair needs to the school board or city commissioners for approval before anything can be done. A list of athletic department needs, in order of priority and due dates for delivery of each service, should be prepared for incorporation into the system-wide list.

The good will of the maintenance supervisor is very important because that office frequently determines priorities. If fields need to be regraded in time for the opening season, it may be possible for him or her to rearrange the heavy equipment operator's schedule to take care of that problem. All assistance rendered by the supervisor and central staff should be suitably acknowledged. They, too, savor appreciation.

Cooperative System Personnel

In many communities the school system and recreation department cooperate in providing and maintaining good athletic facilities. Knowing the procedures for securing these services is most important for coaches working in this situation.

If the youth sports program is offered by the recreation department on school grounds and in the school gymnasium, the responsibility for maintenance and repairs can be shared. The school board and recreation board have to work out cooperative agreements; but, generally, the school provides the facilities and utilities in exchange for maintenance of floors, fields, courts, and pools. Thus, during the school year, schools use facilities during school hours and during sports seasons, while the recreation departments use them in the summers and at times not in conflict with sports seasons.

Cooperative use saves money for agencies and taxpayers; it can also pay off in better facilities and maintenance. Prompt attention to the coach's needs by the joint supervisors is necessary; procedures for making requests and making repairs must be mutually established for expedited action.

Special Needs On the rare occasion when there are special needs, like a new lighting system for a football field, a contract must be made with a company that deals with those special needs. Sometimes these can be arranged for through booster members who own such companies, or sometimes they must be contracted for through the bid process. In many communities, county officials share heavy equipment and manpower with schools to build a new facility or to renovate a present one.

However the special needs are to be met, the coach must make particular efforts to know the personnel and to explain the use of, and need for, the items. Personal contact can help improve the service.

When All Else Fails In many situations, there is no outside assistance at all; the head coach is directly responsible for the maintenance of the facility used for a particular sport. Whether the sports facility preparation consists of marking fields or floors, mowing grass to the appropriate height, or bailing water and adding absorbent material to rain-soaked fields, the coach must plan ahead to meet routine and emergency obligations so as to provide optimum conditions for practices and games. Maintenance may be delegated to students or other youths under the coach's direction, to volunteer adults in the community, or to assistant coaches. In any case, the head coach has to know what the maintenance requirements are for the sport.

A corollary for having the knowledge of maintenance requirements is to possess the foresight to make the necessary preparation to handle emergencies as quickly as possible. The knowledge that a certain type of absorbent material will take care of the muddy pitcher's mound will be of little use unless a bag of it is handy when needed. Knowing how to replace burned-out bulbs in the scoreboard is only part of the responsibility; having replacement bulbs on hand makes that knowledge useful.

CLERICAL PERSONNEL

All the world floats on a sea of paper, and the coach's world is no exception. Although the majority of coaches are field types, not office types, necessary clerical office work has to be done to ensure proper correspondence, record keeping, purchasing procedures, inventory, and accounting. Good, reliable, cooperative assistance in the athletic office, the building office, and the system office is essential so that the necessary paper work can be handled efficiently, freeing the coach to work with the team.

Secretarial Staff A good secretary is a prize who can relieve the coach from routine distractions and who should be diligently sought and carefully nurtured. It would be nice if each coach had a private secretary to greet parents, faculty, and students, making them feel welcome; to handle routine correspondence; to type; to keep eligibility records; and to assist with game schedules and contracts. The fact of life is that assistance will probably have to be obtained from secretaries in the offices of the athletic director, principal, and/or supervisor. It is advantageous for the coaches to know the other office staffs and work; this ensures a mutual understanding of, and respect for, each other's problems. The work load of the clerical staff probably will not permit prompt attention to all the needs of the coaching staff. Both limitations and potential should be clear to all personnel, and courtesy demands that as much time as possible be allowed for secretarial requests. Courtesy and good sense also require that appreciation be shown for assistance given by all clerks, typists, bookkeepers, and secretaries.

Purchasing Staff Some buildings or centers have their own purchasing officers through which orders for equipment must be submitted, but it is doubtful if the athletic department will have its own purchasing clerk or agent. Regardless of the location of the purchasing officer or clerk, it is imperative that he or she is interested in the athletic program, informed about special needs, understands written specifications, and processes purchase orders promptly. As with secretaries, it is important that the coach and whoever prepares purchase orders for athletics share an understanding with the purchasing personnel about problems involved in buying goods and services.

Accounting and Pay Office Staff Coaches deal with large sums of money coming from many sources, including the school and gate receipts. All these funds have to be properly received and expended to avoid any charge of misappropriation.

There may be a bookkeeper for the athletic program, a secretary may be appointed to serve in that capacity, or the coach may be responsible for handling the money. Regardless of the personnel involved, the basic rule is: "Receipts are given for funds received and are received for funds expended."

The building office may have a student or activities account bookkeeper who will handle these funds for the coach. The central or system office may have an internal auditor to verify all accounts through the system and to ensure that established procedures are followed. Members of the accounting staff can be very helpful in all fiscal transactions and should be consulted and used to the fullest extent.

Student Assistants For most coaches, a need for student clerks may be as pronounced as the need for student trainers and managers. The business education department is aware of well-trained students who can be helpful or who can be trained to do the work required.

Students can type rosters, answer the phone, cut stencils, and run errands as well as handle the usual office chores. They cannot replace a well-trained, full-time secretary, but they can be fair substitutes or augment the full-time staff.

SUMMARY

Recruiting and training managers and trainers are the responsibilities of a head coach. Successful coaches give attention to details and explicit instruction to develop a "winning" athlete. No less energy should be expended to develop a good manager or trainer, as failure to do this may lead to the creation of more problems for the head coach than does trying to handle the details without help. Support staffs play a major role in determining the success or failure of an athletic program. A good program has the backing and cooperation of medical, maintenance, and clerical personnel.

Principles of good personnel management should be followed to promote the concept of teamwork. The coach who organizes and pre-plans for personnel responsibilities and expectations can reasonably anticipate a team effort with a limited number of conflicts. The ingredient for success is mutual respect. It takes time and patience to select, organize, coordinate, and supervise support staff, but the good coach takes the necessary time.

The good coach also takes time to acknowledge the many contributions that a fine staff can make. Mutual respect and cooperation among and between all personnel should be a primary administrative goal.

ENDNOTES

1. National Athletic Trainer's Association, "Code of Ethics."
2. F. L. Allman, D. B. McKeag, and L. M. Bodner, "Prevention and Emergency Care for Sports Injuries," *Family Practice Recertification* 4 (1983): 4.

23

Support Groups

SCHOOL GROUPS
BOOSTER CLUBS
OTHER SUPPORT GROUPS
COMMUNITY ORGANIZATIONS
SUMMARY

All athletic programs—school, community, and agency—need encouragement and assistance from a variety of support groups. Parents, boosters, students, community organizations, interested citizens, and fellow staff members all can provide the extra assistance that makes the difference between a poor program and a superior one. Extracurricular programs, particularly athletics, cannot function fully without enthusiastic support that includes funds, equipment, awards, labor, and cheers.

Coaches need to work with all such groups, including governmental units, to improve the total athletic program as well as a specific sport. School, parental, and community support are imperative for growth, success, and survival.

SCHOOL GROUPS

The area of influence most likely to provide the greatest impact on an athletic program will be found in the institution with which the coach and team are associated. The scope of an athletic program (the sports included as well as the emphasis placed on a particular sport) is affected by the institution's rules, regulations, financial situation, and basic philosophy. Even though a particular sport may be currently included or may have top priority in regard to financial support, there is no assurance of perpetual popularity as there is a continuous assessment by the institution and by groups promoting changes.

Positive influence from school or institutional groups will most likely be exercised when there is awareness that the coach has a plan of action that will provide sound experiences for the total school population as well as for the team. Active interaction between coach and team and all other student or school-related groups is imperative if the athletic program is to be understood and supported.

Faculty and Staff

The entire school may exist for the students, but it cannot operate without teachers, administrators, and staff. Athletic programs are in need of their support, their interest, their hard work, and their cooperation. As an "in" member of this group, the coach shares with them in accomplishing the mission of the school as well as the mission of the athletic program.

Faculty

According to the rules of many state high school associations, the interscholastic coach is required to be a member of the teaching staff, or to be certified to teach if employed in a nonteaching capacity. The head coach is usually a faculty member and, in this position, is aware of concerns and attitudes that could affect the athletic program.

A coach's example in meeting teaching responsibilities sends an indirect but important message to the faculty. The positive image of the educator carries over to promote a positive image of the coach to both faculty and athletes. It can be conveyed that coaching duties will not be used as an excuse for not meeting classes on time, not using instructional time properly, not participating on committees, not attending faculty meetings, and not assuming noninstructional duties as assigned.

Most faculty are supportive of all student endeavors, including athletics, and can be relied on to do all they can to be cooperative and helpful. Coaches will encounter only a few faculty who are anti-athletics, believing that the program interferes with the true purpose of the school—education. The behavior of the coach and the good performance of athletes as students should minimize and alter negative attitudes.

The faculty need to be informed about what the coaching staff will be doing to achieve maximum effort from the student/athlete. They may like to know that he or she is expected to succeed in classwork and to follow rules of good school citizenship. Most skeptical teachers will welcome the knowledge that the coach considers extracurricular activities to be a privilege that is granted deserving students rather than a right that takes precedence over all else.

Student/athlete accomplishment is most important. A consistent insistence by the coach on responsible student/athlete behavior may indicate to fellow faculty members that the practice of using sports participation as an excuse for lazy classroom effort will not be condoned. Requiring players to attend classes, except in unusual circumstances and under administrative directive, will demonstrate that the coach is concerned with their academic status. The degree of difficulty of requirements, timely completion of assignments, time periods for make-up work, and standards for performance evaluation should be the same for the athlete and nonathlete. A request for favoritism is an unethical coaching practice and an injustice to all students. It is wrong for coaches to seek special consideration for an athlete in classwork or grade inflation to protect player eligibility. Rather, they should join with other faculty in helping students reach their academic potential. A national trend toward increasing academic requirements for participation in extracurricular activities has received varying degrees of support from parents, athletes, and coaches. In the absence of specific legislation or regulations, a grade policy for athletes may be established such as the one shown in Figure 23-1.

Faculty support for the coach may be more available if they understand the coaching role. Some faculty will need little encouragement to be supportive of the athletic program. They already hold an appreciation

Our purpose in having a grade policy is to help the student/athletes keep their eyes on the main reason they are in school—to gain an education, to strive for good grades, and, in the end, to receive a diploma which will aid them toward their life goals they have set for themselves. Our policies are as follows:

1. The student/athlete should receive a grade sheet from the Athletic Department during the first day of the week.
2. This grade sheet is to be taken to each teacher that the student/athlete has classes with during the day.
3. Each teacher should fill out the grade sheets completely to help us better evaluate the student/athlete's progress in class.
4. Each teacher should initial the comments and/or grades.
5. Each teacher should evaluate the student/athlete's conduct in class; these grades are extremely important so they need to be evaluated carefully.
6. Grade stipulations include:*
   a. If a student/athlete receives three consecutive "D's" (3 weeks in a row) in the same class and receives an "O.K." or a negative comment, he or she will be suspended for one game.
   b. If a student/athlete receives an "F" and then a "D" in the same class, then he or she will be suspended for one game.
   c. Three consecutive suspensions will result in dismissal from the team for the rest of the season.
   d. If no academic grade is given for that week, the conduct grade will be the lone criterion.

*Special note:

1. No student/athlete will be suspended until the head coach or sponsor has discussed the situation with the individual's teacher.
2. If a student is honestly working hard in class and can not do any better than "D" work, the coach, after consultation with the individual's teacher and with either the athletic director or principal can reserve the decision to suspend the player as long as it does not conflict with FHSAA grade policy.
3. Any forgeries will result in immediate dismissal from the team for the school year.

Teachers, if you have any comments on how to improve upon this grade policy, please let us know. Your ideas will be greatly appreciated.

Orlando Falvo
Athletic Director

Figure 23-1   Athletic grade policy

Courtesy of Orlando Falvo, Athletic Director and Head Football Coach, Rickards High School, Tallahasse, Florida.

for the intrinsic values of extracurricular activities and strive to eliminate weaknesses in the programs rather than to eliminate programs with weaknesses. These people are actively involved and need only cooperation and communication from the coach to be a positive influence for athletics.

A large portion of the faculty will probably be passive in their support of athletics. This is not aversion to the activity, but may represent a stronger interest in other programs. A lack of past experience or involvement in the excitement of athletic competition is a common reason for their disinterest and inactivity. Coaches may stimulate interest by providing opportunities for this segment of the faculty to become part of the action.

Spectator involvement may be an accomplishment for an otherwise passive colleague, but it may not be the stimulus necessary to evoke active influence. An area to explore is voluntary assistance; the need for numerous auxiliary support personnel to stage athletic contests can provide an avenue for enlisting faculty aid. Plans should be made well in advance to request assistance for timing track events, selling tickets for a gymnastics meet, scoring a wrestling match, supervising crowd control at a cross-country meet, and similar responsibilities. These duties may be viewed as time-consuming chores, and the possibility that a one-time acceptance might become a regular job will turn off some faculty. A coach must exercise caution in the approach used and in the number of requests made of each teacher. The objective is to expose the uninitiated to athletics rather than to acquire reluctant assistance at athletic events.

Often, there are paid positions available such as ticket sellers and takers, crowd controllers, and officials. Having an opportunity to earn additional funds by being placed on a priority list may serve as an incentive for some. Faculty members can develop a strong interest in, and an appreciation for, sports while earning a little extra money.

Coaches' support for faculty endeavors is demonstrated by showing an interest in the work being done in areas other than their own. Concerned coaches seize every opportunity to comment to an individual teacher about a particularly successful class session, project, or event that was shared by an athlete or that was personally experienced. They attend as many nonathletic events, such as drama productions and dances, as possible. Answers are provided to reasonable questions concerning the upcoming contest, the playing status of specific athletes, interesting match-ups of opposing teams or players, and special arrangements that may have been made to accommodate faculty spectators.

Make it easy for the faculty member to attend a contest. If reserved seating is available, colleagues are accommodated. If parking is a problem, times and areas are specified to minimize frustration. A personal touch is important to most people, so an invitation by the coach to specific teachers may be effective. Whatever the means, the purpose is to convince the faculty of the importance of their presence to the program.

The coach is obligated to reciprocate in responsibility and willingness to assist colleagues in nonathletic events. Supervising or chaperoning extracurricular events are usually considered routine duties for faculty members and are established by various schemes such as voluntary subscription, administrative assignments, or sponsor recruitment. The coach's name on the duty roster and his or her presence at these events should be routine. Such action indicates an appreciation for the kind of efforts of others that is being sought for athletics.

Administration An athletic program needs the enthusiastic support not only of the faculty but of the administrative staff as well. Principals, assistant principals, counselors, and deans are all important personnel who can help the program succeed or merely survive.

The principal is the person with total authority in the school. He or she is responsible for program, discipline, budget and maintenance, and, as top personnel officer, for determining which faculty go or stay. Support of the principal and encouragement in the form of moral support, funds, and services are essential for a successful program. Coaches will work with, and for, no other person who is as influential and should, therefore, treat him or her with due respect and extend every courtesy.

Principals' professional staffs of assistant principals, deans, and counselors represent them in their official capacities and thus are very influential. These staff members frequently have faculty assignments and will respond to efforts of the coach to improve the academic program as well as the athletic program.

The principal or someone from the professional administrative staff is expected to attend every school event, including athletic events. All game procedures (such as ticket sales, parking, security) need to be communicated to this person so that he or she can review them with the coach to be sure that all eventualities are planned for. Close understanding and cooperation are imperative.

Athletic Administration An athletic director, assistant athletic director, or director of student activities has the resources to supervise, delegate, and organize a multitude of minor and major assignments that are crucial, in particular, to game and tournament management. Student assistants, off-season coaches, maintenance crews, and custodial personnel can be contacted and engaged to perform tasks that will free the coaching staff and players to concentrate on the game. When coaches and players must bear the brunt of preparation for an event, their fatigue and frustration may result in lowered performance.

Most coaches want to have some, if not total, control over aspects concerned with hosting a contest or tournament. Assuming total control may result in a coach spending too much time on nonessentials such as sponging water off the tennis courts or attaching nets to a goal. At this point, the need for control overrides the benefits of assistance. Someone else should be doing these tasks.

Support from the athletic administration in handling arrangements is especially vital for adjunct or part-time coaches who are not on campus during the school day. It is virtually impossible for these personnel to establish a proper environment themselves, as they may not arrive at the site until it is time for the teams to take the field. Athletic directors should assume the responsibility for securing assistance for these and other coaches. Coaches may find it necessary to make specific requests

Support Groups 343

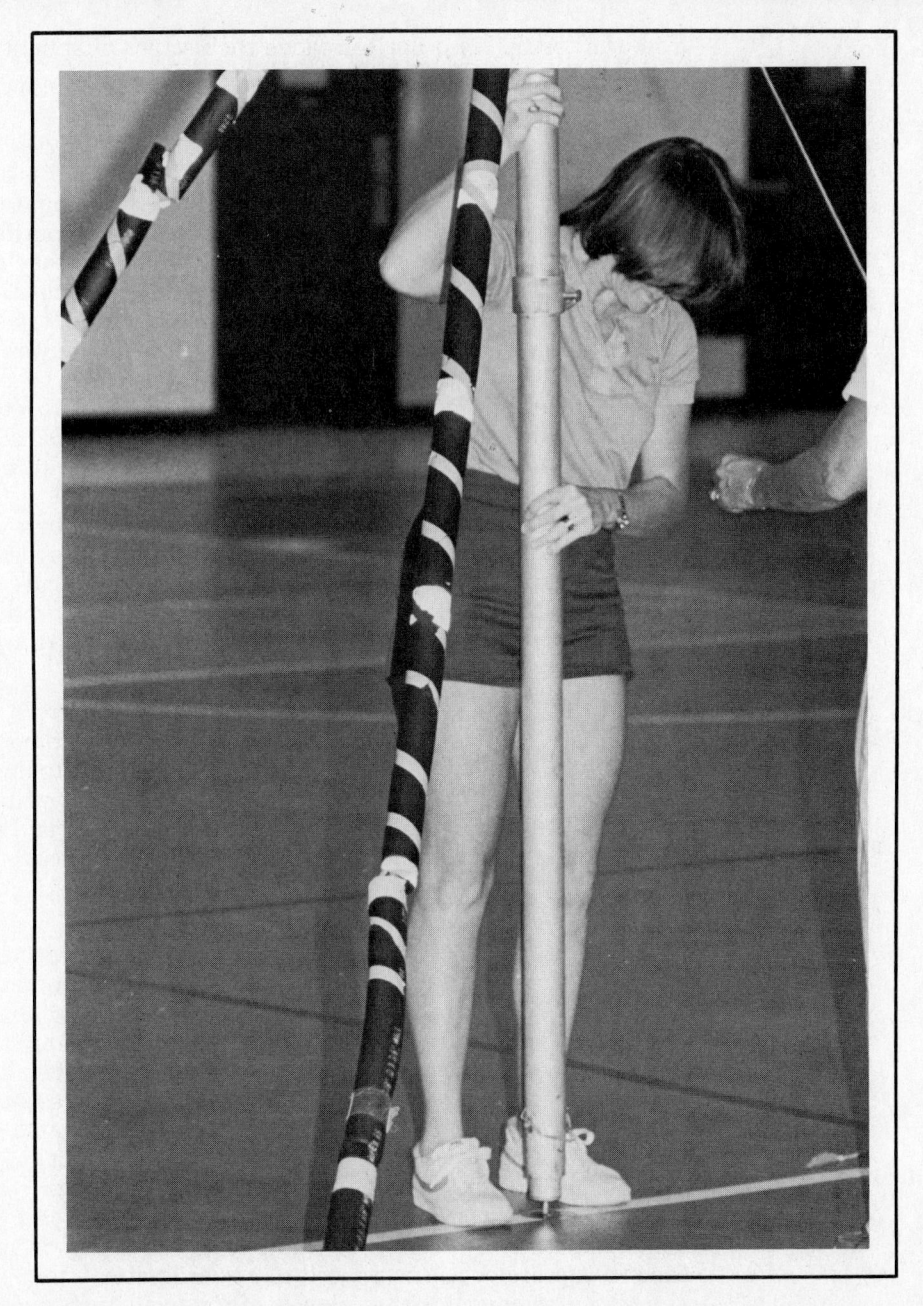

Figure 23-2 Many coaches have to do everything (Courtesy of Maclay School, Inc., Tallahassee, Florida. Photographer: Mickey Adair)

from the "A.D." in order to relieve themselves of some time-consuming noncoaching tasks.

Staff

Members of the school staff—including office personnel, custodial crew, lunchroom staff, and bus drivers are important and influential groups that the coach must work with cooperatively. The important role of the purchasing and bookkeeping staff has already been outlined, but it cannot be emphasized too strongly. They can make life easy or hard when it comes to getting and helping with money and equipment. The need for a good custodial crew and a superior maintenance staff has also been discussed, but it should be recalled, again, that they are necessary for success.

Secretarial staffs are also influential and important. They process correspondence and phone calls, greet the guests to the school, know the people in the system, and know how the system works when something needs to be done.

All of these staff personnel are full-fledged members of a school family. They deserve to be treated with the same courtesy and the same appreciation as faculty and administrators do. They get parking privileges, special rates, and all the benefits that faculty receive. The coach might make it without total faculty support, but the program will be in trouble without full staff support.

The Band

A marching band and athletic team share many common traits and requirements. Both are performing groups, work hard to develop skill, and respond to cheers of spectator appreciation by performing better in the best tradition of showmanship. The two groups can and should complement each other when appropriate attention is given to the needs and objectives of each.

Band Director

Administrative direction may establish basic expectations for the band director and marching band to perform at athletic events; that is, to stage a half-time show at football games, to provide a "pep" band for pep rallies, and to participate in homecoming parades. Without cooperation and mutual respect, the band director and coach may have unnecessary confrontations to the detriment of both programs. It is essential to establish the logistics of practice times, facilities, finances, game schedules, and procedures for the resolution of student/athlete/musician conficts.

Regardless of the delegation of responsibility for coordination, the coach needs to establish rapport with the band director. Personal contact helps alleviate any feeling of competition, creating an opportunity for each to express concerns related to a coordinated effort.

Practice areas for the sole use of the band, or for any one organization, are not usual. It is unlikely for a football team to have exclusive use of a practice field that meets all the needs of pre-game preparation. Thus, the game field may become the essential area for final rehearsal for both groups on the same day, usually the day before the game, and this conflict has to be resolved. The preferred practice time and use of a designated facility should be mutually agreed upon prior to the start of the season. Weather conditions and field conditions that would preclude one or both from using the game field should also be predetermined and alternative indoor facilities for practice fairly assigned.

Funding for the band may conflict with funding for athletics. It is common practice for all extracurricular activities, including band, to be self-supporting, primarily through gate receipts and fund-raising projects. Coaches should not feel resentment if the band expects or requests a small fee for performing at athletic events. In lieu of a fee for each performance, the band director often requests a fixed amount needed to purchase uniforms or equipment items, or a percentage of the gate receipts for the date of performance. If the revenue from concessions at sports events goes to athletics, the band parents or boosters could be given the option for operating part or all of the concessions to provide a lucrative income. The primary consideration must be that both groups are served in their quest for financial independence and ability to fulfill their goals.

Dual participation by a student in both band and athletics is another area of possible disagreement. Generally, the practice and performance times of the marching band and fall sports are concurrent, which makes it rather difficult for the student to hope for success in either. Assuming that there are times when the musician can practice and the athlete can practice and not be in conflict, the coach and the band director should try to accommodate the student's dual roles. To promote consistency, a policy needs to be established to remove the student from conflict, insofar as possible. A primary consideration ought to be the relative importance of the student to the performance of the band or to the team. For example, if the student is the leading scorer for the basketball team and fourth chair violinist for the concert band, the student should play in the game and miss the concert. If the student is first chair flutist and reserve rightfielder for the softball team, he or she should play in the concert and miss the game.

For many students and their parents, the concept of dedication and sacrifice of time needed to produce excellence may not be easily understood. It becomes the duty of the professional to provide sufficient experience for the youth to decide where to direct his or her greatest talent and interest. Forcing a youth to specialize in a particular sport, or in music, or in any phase of concentrated study seems inappropriate to furthering the total development of a young player.

Student Groups

Students, who provide important support with their contributions—both tangibly with funds and work and intangibly with "spirit"—can determine the success of a program. Typically, they are members of school organizations such as student government, cheerleaders, pep club, and special interest groups. These groups provide moral and fiscal support for a team and can contribute greatly to the festivity of an event.

Student Government

Basic to the formation of most student groups are the elected officers and representatives who provide the impetus, approval, and implementation of many functions promoting "school spirit." Without the support of the student population and the influence of their organizations, that spirit would be difficult to foster.

Class skits for pep rallies; parades and floats for "homecoming" games; class and student body gifts to the school; donations of money for special projects; and innumerable hours of labor are routine contributions from this group. Student government activities promote the spirited involvement that makes a competition a special event.

The head coach's enthusiastic acceptance of requests to speak at student body meetings and functions is indicative of the value he or she places on the students' contributions. Any coach will enjoy the cheers from the bleachers filled with students who radiate excitement and pride.

Cheerleaders This group, whose primary responsibility is to lead cheers, generally also assumes the responsibility of promoting good sportsmanship. The coach would be wise to arrange for frequent meetings with the cheerleaders, or captains, and their sponsor if there are activities in conflict with the coaching plan or if there are helpful recommendations to be made. To make sure that the cheerleaders understand what the specific sport requires of the group, it may be necessary to provide briefing sessions to discuss such items as the rules of the sport, when to cheer and when to be silent, whether or not to decorate the team locker room, the preferred format for a pep rally, and guidelines for expected behavior if traveling with the team to game sites. It is necessary for coaches to take the opportunity to express appreciation of the role the cheerleaders play. At the same time they can interject the expectations of the coaching staff for the positive influences that can result from cheering.

Pep Clubs These clubs tend to form in the same manner that cheerleading groups have developed. Groups who are dedicated to sports—to one sport in particular—and attend events regularly to cheer on the team decide to form a club to promote the efforts of those athletic teams. This spirit group comprises a strong cheering section at contests and is responsible for publicizing the sport and for stimulating interest and support. A successful, winning team may generate its own following, needing little additional encouragement; however, this situation does not usually occur spontaneously but as a result of concerted effort initiated and nurtured by the coach.

Once an interested group of fans becomes involved in promoting a sport, the coach must be continually responsive to the growth and enthusiasm of the spirit group. Frequent acknowledgment of the importance of their support and of the need for expanding their influence is vital to maintaining momentum. The molding of a loyal support group requires close direction and cooperation by the coach. Without that leadership, a spirit group may become spiritless and look for other outlets.

Special Groups Some teams have "special" supporters, a group that is unique to that team. Baseball teams have bat and ball girls, softball teams have bat and ball boys, wrestling teams have mat maids, swimming teams have deck siders, and track teams have field hands. Membership in such groups is usually small, with support given in the form of work as well as of cheers. The coach may decide that help is needed with certain aspects of practices or contests, such as keeping score or time, getting equipment in place, chasing balls, flashing scores of judges, and hosting visiting squads. These are necessary tasks that a coach does not want to worry about for each practice or contest. A coach may begin by talking with two or three people who overtly support team events about starting a small, select support group. If these people respond favorably, the needs of the team and what members of such a group could do to help can be outlined and their input requested. If coaches are really interested in forming a support group, they will be enthusiastic in making the organization's importance known.

BOOSTER CLUBS

Most coaches find it extremely difficult to assume all the tasks of coaching without the assistance of adult volunteers—team boosters in effect. These volunteers are most likely to be relatives of athletes, but friends of the coach or former patrons of the school whose children have graduated are also part of the group. Professional athletes who live in the area, former students in the school, college students, and business or professional persons frequently lend their support.

Booster clubs are composed of individuals from the entire community who want to have strong athletic programs and who put their time, energy, and money to work to that end. They are frequently highly organized, composed of persons of means and/or great energy, and are only loosely connected with the school or agency. Whatever the association with the coach or team, all are united by a common bond—an interest in athletics.

Functions

In local school or recreation youth leagues in small communities, boosters sometimes function on an informal basis. A telephone call can arrange for a parent to transport the tennis team, a visit to the hardware store can solicit materials for a softball backstop, and a letter can arrange for a football professional to speak at the awards dinner. Even on a limited basis, however, these contacts are time-consuming and fragmented, and there is a tendency to repeat requests of previously successful sources rather than to approach new prospects for their assistance. This calls for the formation of a booster group.

A logical progression might be to organize parents and other interested adults into a booster group for a specific sport. Again, it becomes the coach's duty to give purpose and direction to the promotion of the sport. Some of the goals that the organization may wish to accomplish are in these areas:

1. Financial—to provide supplementary funds for maintenance or an operating budget that would provide for basic equipment, uniforms, officials, and transportation
2. Personnel—to provide assistance for crowd control, ticket selling, scoring, timing, and other game management duties

3. Special projects—to conduct a fund-raising program for acquiring major, permanent equipment items such as bleachers, pitching machine, blocking sled, basketball rebounder, or electronic timers.

The local school's Athletic Booster Club has the opportunity to support all athletic teams. Service is rendered in varied ways and as needed for any sports activity. Fund-raising projects are conducted for the benefit of athletics rather than for a particular team. If political action is needed to improve coaching supplements, improve facilities, or provide additional personnel for coaching, the Boosters Club often has the necessary clout to get the issues before the public and the appropriate offices.

Club members learn of the needs and concerns of all teams from their coaches and the athletic director, so quality of input plays a major role in determining the club's support, both financial and political. The school's administrative liaison officer assigned to work with the boosters must also understand the needs and concerns of the entire athletic program.

Organization

There are probably as many ways to organize a booster club as there are teams to boost. A sagacious coach will let the boosters actively work for the program but with the staff's goals and plans for the team in front of the group. Some groups are for one activity only, whereas others support an entire athletic program. Whatever the focus, there should be clearly stated procedures such as those found in organizational bylaws.

A booster club that organizes in support of athletic pursuits will need bylaws and statements to delineate objectives and to provide guidelines for responsibilities of the leadership. Bylaws of one school's booster club are given in Figure 23-3.

Boosters usually work directly with the athletic director. A variation of the same format might have an assistant principal, or principal, as the administrative advisor or liaison. Regardless of who advises, the primary thrusts are to promote, assist, and support in ways that are indicated by the school's liaison officer. The direction of the student activities programs remains with the school.

The Boosters Clubs of America, an organization formed to bring local boosters clubs together to share ideas, held its first national meeting in 1979. It continues to provide a nationwide forum for the improvement of high school athletics as well as for support groups.

Advantages

Advantages secured from a booster organization are, or can be, enormous. They can change the mood of the community toward athletics; build tennis courts or stadiums; buy uniforms; assist in transportation, officiating, and chaperoning; and generally make the coach's job much easier. Properly conducted, with the best interests of athletes at heart, they are of immeasurable benefit; no coach would want to be without one.

The coach can further the cause of athletics generally (and enhance the support for a specific sport) by being available to speak at booster meetings, by meeting informally with parents of team members, by providing game commentary for boosters, and by preparing a positive manu-

>
> The Ram Booster Club
> of
> The James W. Robinson (Jr.) Secondary School
> Fairfax County, Virginia
> By-Laws
>
> I. *Name*
>
> The name of this organization is THE RAMS BOOSTER CLUB, hereinafter referred to as the Boosters, of the James W. Robinson (Jr) Secondary School of Fairfax County, Virginia, hereinafter referred to as the School.
>
> II. *Purpose*
>
> a. It shall be the purpose of the Boosters to foster the highest standards of citizenship in the community by encouraging the growth and development of all programmed student activities of the School.
>
> b. It shall further promote, assist, and support the Director of Student Activities and his staff with financial assistance, manpower, and consultive advice to improve the student activities of the School.
>
> c. It shall stimulate and guide community interest in, and support of, the School and its programmed student activities.
>
> d. The Boosters shall cooperate with the Student Parent Teachers Organization (SPTAO) and other duly constituted organizations of the School.
>
> III. *Policies*
>
> The Boosters shall have two types of membership. (1) Regular (2) Honorary. All persons who have a constructive interest in the student activities of the School are eligible for membership. Membership dues shall be $3.00 and is effective for the school year in which issued.
>
> a. *Regular Membership.* Any person interested in the objectives of the Boosters and is willing to uphold its policies and subscribe to its By-Laws may become a member upon payment of the dues.
>
> b. *Honorary Membership.* The Executive Committee may bestow honorary membership upon individuals or organizations in appreciation of support or services rendered to the Boosters.
>
> IV. *Officers, Term of Office and Duties*
>
> The officers of the Boosters shall be President, First and Second Vice Presidents, Recording Secretary, Corresponding Secretary and Treasurer. All shall serve without pay or remuneration for services.
>
> *(continued)*

Figure 23-3   Booster club bylaws

Courtesy of the Ram Booster Club of The James W. Robinson (Jr.) Secondary School, Fairfax County, Virginia.

a. *Term of Office.* The term of office shall run from *May* of one calendar year to *May* of the next year. All officers shall be elected to serve for one year. No one may serve more than 2 consecutive years in the same office. The term of office shall begin immediately following their election and installation at the regularly scheduled May meeting.

b. *Vacancy.* The President shall appoint another officer to assume the duties of a vacant office pro term. Except that if the office of President becomes vacant, the First Vice President shall succeed on a temporary basis.

A special election shall be held for any vacancy at the next meeting of the Boosters after the vacancy occurs or the President may call a special meeting for this purpose.

c. Officers and Duties
   1. President
      (a) Preside at all meetings
      (b) Appoint chairman and members of all committees
      (c) Appoint a member to assume the duties of a vacant office until a special election can be held.
      (d) Represent the Boosters at meeting of outside groups or individuals.
      (e) Approve proposed operating expenditures not to exceed $25.00.
   2. Vice Presidents
      (a) Act as President in the absence of the President
      (b) Serve as an executive assistant to the President and carry out those duties assigned to him by the President
      (c) Coordinate the work of all committees.
   3. Recording Secretary
      (a) Record, prepare, and read the minutes of all meetings
      (b) Maintain a complete file of all minutes of all meetings
   4. Corresponding Secretary
      (a) Prepare and sign correspondence as designated by the President
      (b) Maintain a complete file of all correspondence
   5. Treasurer
      (a) Act as the custodian for all funds
      (b) Set up and maintain proper bookkeeping records
      (c) Issue authorized checks
      (d) Deposit all cash receipts to an account in a convenient bank
      (e) Read the financial report at all meetings

(continued)

Figure 23-3 Continued

V. *Election and Recall of Officers*
a. *Election.* The President shall appoint a nominating committee at the April meeting who shall submit a slate of Officers at the May meeting. Additional nominations may be made from the floor at the election meeting. Written ballots shall be used. Only those members present at the election meeting shall be eligible to vote. A plurality of votes shall be required for an election.
b. *Recall.* Any officer who without good reason fails to attend two successive meetings shall be recalled from office, and the office shall be declared vacant.

VI. *Committees*
The standing committees of the Boosters shall consist of the following with a chairman and a minimum of two members. Other special committees may be appointed by the President.
Standing and Special Committees shall meet as directed by their Chairman. It shall be the responsibility of the chairman to assure prompt action and to follow through on all tasks within the committee's spheres of responsibility. Executive Committee shall meet as directed by the President.
a. *Executive Committee.* Shall consist of the officers of the Boosters, all chairmen of current standing committees and the Director of Student Activities of the School. The purpose of this group is to transact necessary business in the intervals between club meetings and such other business as may be referred to it by the membership.
b. *Ways and Means Committee.* Shall devise and implement ways and means of raising funds to carry out the purpose of the Boosters.
c. *Membership Committee.* Shall devise and implement methods for increasing membership in the Boosters.
d. *Athletic Events Committee.* Shall provide manpower for all athletic events as requested by the Director of Student Activities.
e. *Activity Committee.* Shall plan and organize special events, arrange for space, decoration, music, etc. and provide adult supervision.
f. *Concessions Committee.* Shall plan, organize, and provide soft drinks, candy, popcorn and other miscellaneous food and refreshments for sale at student activity events.

VII. *Meetings and Quorum*
a. The regular Booster meetings shall be held in the School on the 4th Tuesday of every month.
b. Special meetings may be called at any time by the President. The calling of a special meeting shall be mandatory as a result of a petition signed by one-fourth of the membership.

(continued)

Figure 23–3 Continued

> c. One-eighth of the Regular members of the Boosters present at a meeting shall constitute a quorum to transact business.
> d. Each Regular member in good standing at a meeting is entitled to one vote on each notion considered at the meeting. Honorary members are not voting members. A favorable vote of the majority shall carry a motion.
>
> VIII. *AMENDMENTS*
> a. These by-laws may be amended at any regular meeting of the club by a two-thirds vote of the members present and voting, provided notice of the proposed amendment shall have been given at the previous meeting.
> b. A committee may be appointed to submit a revised set of by-laws as a substitute for these by-laws only by a majority vote at a meeting of the club, or by a two-thirds vote to the executive committee.

Figure 23-3   Continued

script for honoring athletes at awards ceremonies. Athletic boosters want to know about the program, the philosophy and objectives of the coach, and the good things that the teams are accomplishing.

For numerous coaches there is no choice. They must cooperate with booster groups to get sufficient funding for equipment and facilities and travel. For many booster club members there is no choice. If they are to have good programs for their children, this is the way to get them.

Disadvantages Whether booster efforts on behalf of a sports team are continuous or a one-time project, this concentrated effort to promote a specific sport may spawn adverse effects for the coach and for other sports as well. Although the focus of attention should be on the objectives promoted by the coach, the boosters may turn their attention to the coach, particularly if team progress is not meeting expectations. The same zealousness that was so effective in gaining needed and requested support can be applied to securing a new coach.

A person who gives time, talent, or money to a program that needs all three is, in a sense, buying a piece of that program. At least that may be the view of the donor. The person making the gift may want to make the decisions; thus, a coach receiving booster money may be selling a piece of his or her life. The organization should safeguard against this, as there are persons of wealth and position who also like power. Coaches are well advised to avoid large gifts with strings attached if at all possible.

There are also other problems to be faced. For example, basketball might flourish under the enthusiastic leadership of its boosters to the extent that available gymnasium space could be allocated almost exclusively to this sport to the detriment of a volleyball league that enjoys less rigorous backing. Each club and each coach must work very hard to achieve mutual respect and equal consideration in sharing resources.

OTHER SUPPORT GROUPS

It is unfortunate that the cost of athletics or other extracurricular endeavors cannot be completely borne by the sponsoring agency or school, but that is generally the situation. Thus parents' clubs, special sports clubs, or adopt-a-team groups must be organized to provide support.

Parents' Clubs If a team cannot fully fund its activities, parents join together to raise money for uniforms, trip expenses, and awards. This is especially true for activities with low or no gate receipts.

Parent clubs seem to be more frequently found with the band or other nonrevenue producing enterprises, but the need for them varies from situation to situation. If there is a strong booster club, then the parents' club seems to be absorbed in it; but regardless of the organizational structure, the athletic program needs the support of the team members' parents.

Parents not only take good care of their athletic young people but also chaperone, drive, arrange transportation, manage pre- and postgame meals, fry fish, bake cookies, keep time, and raise money. Because disinterested, unsupportive parents can bring a program to its knees, smart coaches cultivate the parents of the athletes and encourage them to support their players and the team.

Sports Club A club that organizes and operates with the objective of serving the needs of an individual sport will probably function best with youth club activities, recreational leagues, or a sports activity at a high school. Youth club basketball, for example, may require the services of parents or other adults to schedule games, to provide transportation, to keep score and time, and to officiate. A recreational soccer league may depend on parents of the participants to solicit funding from the business community for team uniforms. Parents of members of a newly formed lacrosse team at the high school may undertake a major fund-raising event to help defray equipment costs.

Efforts of sports clubs are directed to promoting and enhancing athletic opportunity for youth in a particular sport, but involvement with one sports activity often stimulates an enthusiasm for sports in general. Thereby, all sports benefit from their efforts.

Adopt-a-Team Concept With the inauguration of the Partnerships in Education in 1983, Adopt-a-School emerged as a way to enlist the community's aid in meeting school needs. Sponsors provide a broad spectrum of talents and interests among their volunteers. Examples of their services are tutoring, counseling, providing school supplies, lecturing, and judging science fairs.

Similar benefits can accrue from an Adopt-a-Team concept. Contractors may provide equipment and services to prepare or repair facilities, and area police or military personnel may assist in fitness testing and off-season conditioning. Not all contributions need be business-related, however; professional and civic groups can meet many needs capably and responsibly.

Before the adoption, the coach and sponsor must agree on the anticipated outcomes. The role of the adopting group, or individual, must be definitive, with frequent evaluation conferences set to ensure success.

COMMUNITY ORGANIZATIONS

There are many other community organizations that can be influential. In fact, many small communities would not have youth sports programs without the assistance of civic clubs, veterans groups, churches, or community action associations. Members of these organizations have the best interest of their community at heart and will work long and hard to provide good programs for their young people. The governing bodies of communities also are influential in program development; in fact, without their support and approval less would be accomplished. Coaches need to seek support from the total community as both school and nonschool programs depend on their friends for survival.

Civic Clubs

Every community has its share of civic clubs, groups of men and/or women who meet regularly and who have community betterment as their goal. Clubs such as the Kiwanis, Rotary, Pilot, Business and Professional Women, and Lions have an interest in anything that improves the quality of life for the citizens in the city or area. These groups have built playgrounds, installed lighting for fields, sponsored teams, and sent champions to tournaments. They are eager to be of help, and the needs of the team should be made known to them.

A community group is easily stimulated to become associated with success. Special effort is required to bolster a program that is struggling or to initiate programs that may not be as popular or well known in the community; therefore, the coach has to be a good salesperson, representing and publicizing these athletic programs as often as the opportunity arises. The coach who is available and able to speak at luncheons and dinners can provide the push to enlist community support that might otherwise be diverted. A reciprocal invitation to a club member to speak at an awards program or to attend a contest as a guest may further acquaint civic groups with a program. The important consideration is that a community club needs information and direction to become a supportive faction for athletic programs. Without these clubs, a program may suffer loss of moral, financial, and political support that most successful programs must have to survive.

Patriotic Clubs

The American Legion and the Veterans of Foreign Wars (VFW) have been noted for their support of athletics in sponsoring teams and programs and in providing facilities. The American Legion baseball programs provides national level competition for boys of high school age and works closely with school and agency coaches to assure high level supervision and play.

Many communities use indoor and outdoor facilities provided by the VFW or Legion, and these veterans' groups can be counted on to be supportive of all kinds of sport programs. It is important to seek assistance from these groups for a worthwhile program.

There are other patriotic groups who have been more supportive of good citizenship than of athletics. These local organizations for civic service, such as mounted posses or volunteer patrols, can also be of assistance.

Community Development Groups

Those organizations whose primary function is civic betterment are additional sources of support for athletic activities. Chambers of Commerce, for example, are totally immersed in community development. They are eager to have successful athletic teams at every level, both for the favorable publicity and improvement of business for the community and for the value to the participants themselves. Besides being a source of some funds, they can provide names of individual businesses that might be helpful and can suggest good public relations techniques.

Business associations can serve a similar function. The local retailers' association or the businesses in a mall can help an athletic program while they are helping themselves.

Neighborhood associations, whose prime purpose is neighborhood development, can assist with funding and in building facilities. Civic pride and interest in youth sport programs is not always just citywide. It may be more intense in smaller community divisions, and much assistance may be gained on a local basis.

Churches

No longer are sport and vigorous activity considered immoral, un-Christian, or nonreligious by most denominations. In fact, youth sport is a major concern of many church groups. They provide indoor and outdoor facilities for the youth and adults in their congregations and participate in all community programs and church leagues. Denominations who value athletic programs support coaches and youth leaders to the extent that they can.

Catholic Youth Organization, Jewish Community Centers, and Christian Life Centers involve members of the religious community in sport and other activities. If the coach is a part of these congregations or programs, athletic endeavors may be encouraged and funded.

Governments

The governing bodies of schools, cities, counties, states, and the nation are the most influential groups that coaches must deal with; however, their closest relationship may be with school and recreation boards or city councils. These groups form front-line power groups with full authority to fund or not to fund, to permit or not to permit program and facility development. Some county governments are also in this front-line position. Coaches ought to know their board members and commission or council members and help these members become cognizant of, and understand, the proposed athletic program.

Local delegations to the state legislature can also be influential. They are in a position to support state bills that improve athletic programs, or they can serve locally as backers of what the coach is attempting to do. Although state representatives and senators do not usually have the immediate authority that local boards and commissioners do, they know how to influence decisions.

Members of Congress are even farther away from local decision making, but their support can be very useful on the local level. Their power is exerted, of course, on the federal scene and they are involved with funding national sports programs like the Olympic Development Committee. They also are involved with all forms of equal rights legislation dealing with nondiscrimination for race, sex, or mental/physical condition. Coaches and their associations need to make their problems known to state and national governing bodies.

SUMMARY

When a coach considers all the influential groups that can help or hinder a program, the first group of supporters can be found close at hand—in the school. Cooperation with faculty, staff, and students is essential to success. Since the entire athletic endeavor is to promote the best interests of the school—faculty and students alike—it needs to be a mutual effort. Professional staffs—administration, clerical, and maintenance—are partners in the program. When the entire group cooperates and accommodates, the job of the coach will be much easier.

Student support is also necessary. Athletes, of course, are expected to work hard, but the additional cooperation and participation by the band, cheerleaders, pep club, and special groups are the icing on the cake. A coach must work with influential community groups, booster clubs, and other associations both within the institutional confines of a school and in the broader field of the city, county, state, and nation. The impact of their influence can be beneficial in the area of funding, securing facilities, gaining personnel, and increasing acceptance for programs.

24

News Media

VARIETIES
RELATIONSHIPS
PROCEDURES
SUMMARY

Athletics are news. Each team, coach, athlete, and contest provide stories in themselves. They are a source for a continuous variety of news to arouse and satisfy public interest and to inform and convert both the knowledgeable fan and the uninitiated.

There can be no greater allies than the members of the press or their radio and television counterparts. There are also no groups that can be more harmful to a program than the news media, whether inadvertently or intentionally. Because they need publicity and good public relations, coaches must learn to work with reporters and photographers on a cooperative, friendly basis. Newspapers, as well as radio and television stations, need sports news because much of their audience is interested in sport and sporting events. Thus, a coach and the local sports writers and reporters need each other and should form a mutually supportive group with free interchange of information.

VARIETIES

Most coaches traditionally think of newspaper reporters and sports columnists when they think of news media. There are broader horizons to be expanded, however, and coaches must consider not only the power of the press but the power of radio and of television.

Print Media

There are several kinds of press or print media available to work with; and, as the circulation of these publications varies, so does the influence they wield. The usual forms of print media are newspapers, school or agency papers, and magazines.

Newspapers

Papers have a marked advantage over the nonprint media in that time limits for reporting are not such a great factor as they are for a sportscast. They have another advantage in that complete episodes can be perused at the reader's leisure. Coaches can get scores placed in a newspaper when a broadcast is too brief to include them; however, since space is limited, newspapers tend to report only the contests of interest in their readership area.

Although school papers are usually not printed daily and their readership is limited primarily to the school, they have one prime advantage. They can enter every home served by that school and thus equal the readership of a county weekly. Coaches should extend the same courtesy to young school reporters as to their professional counterparts, as programs need complete coverage and young reporters become older professionals. Also, most sports programs are school programs, by and for students, and they deserve full consideration.

Magazines Only a few unusually successful coaches are approached for stories or articles, but it happens often enough for all to be aware of the possibilities. Many kinds of sports magazines exist, and one may be seeking a story. There are those that focus on a single sport, others are general in nature, some report on general coaching concerns, and several are involved with sport and physical education. All are seeking information, articles, and features about good procedures and programs. Many are also interested in action pictures for their cover pages. A coach with a story to tell, a system to describe, or an idea to develop can look to these magazines as a place to publish. Too, those who are looking for new ideas can find many in these publications.

Nonprint Media Nonprint media have the opportunity for instant, on-the-spot reporting that papers cannot have. Radio and television broadcasts can describe or show the action as it happens and thus command a wide audience of listeners and viewers.

Radio Radio has the great advantage of being portable; listeners tune-in in their cars, homes, or offices. Many schools use radio broadcasts of contests, and stations want to do so because it is relatively inexpensive and can be very exciting and profitable. A good play-by-play announcer and assistants are imperative if the public is to continue to listen. It could be helpful to a program if the coach assisted in their selection or at least made recommendations for selections. During broadcasts team members on the injured list or managers often assist in providing color or in identifying players.

Television Sport has become the darling of television broadcasters because of its exciting and dramatic quality and its unusual appeal. Unfortunately, local videocasts of community sports activity are generally limited to educational television stations as networks seek collegiate, professional, and Olympic activities for viewing.

Most coaches below the collegiate level will work with TV only occasionally, but the opportunity for the game to be viewed "live" should be pursued when possible. The regular sportscast, however, can contain game results, interviews, and short action news, so it is essential to maintain good relationships with TV sports reporters and broadcasters.

Film

Rarely do coaches participate in the making of a news film or video, but they routinely take movies of their team and others for study purposes. These game films can provide an opportunity for the public to see the action long after it happened, and the showing of these movies might provide a real public relations, as well as money-making, opportunity.

RELATIONSHIPS

In giving and receiving information what is important, besides accuracy, is a cooperative, friendly, and responsible relationship between the media and the athletic staff and program. In fact, the words *public relations* designate an area of endeavor that attempts to inform, to explain, and to persuade. Coaches and reporters have to be honest, fair, and reasonable with each other if an unbiased story is to result.

Central Information Source

It is generally advisable to channel news releases and requests from the media for news information through one individual or office. This designation of a public relations officer or a sports information director (SID) may better ensure that the press is informed of newsworthy items and that all sports activities and sports-related stories are given appropriate coverage. That individual might be the athletic director, a principal, a coach, a student reporter, an agency supervisor, or a public relations director. The SID plays an important role for a school or agency in gathering all sports information and providing one source and one version of a program and its results. This can relieve the athletic director and the coaches of part of their public relations tasks and can provide accurate data in consistent style to all media.

Coach's Responsibilities

Regardless of the scope of the athletic program and the availability of an SID and interested news media, the most important source of news and potential promotion of a sport is the head coach. Positive reporting results from positive information supplied. If reporters have a good relationship with the coach, they will emphasize the good things that a team is accomplishing and will ignore, or at least minimize, happenings that could be counterproductive for the sport.

Because the coach is the ultimate source of all information, special relationships have to be established so that the coach's position is made clear. A sportswriter has suggested that attention given to the following recommendations can improve rapport between the coach and the media.

1. Establish a first-class program—get yourself and your program "together."
2. Ask for inservice training with media specialists.
3. Prepare, have available, and distribute information, including photos, about the program, players, and coaches.
4. Think of information that might be of interest to the public.
5. Compile, and have available, statistics throughout the season.

6. Build trust and confidence by being honest and providing accurate information.
7. Be available and ready to comment on bad situations as well as good ones.
8. Organize materials before sending them in.
9. Call reporters at appropriate times—when they say they will be available.
10. Address any problem to the person responsible—do not "go over heads" or complain to their peers.
11. Arrange for reporters to be well taken care of at contests.
12. Get information in quickly, before deadlines.
13. Develop a list of the right things to say in a variety of situations—crucial losses, controversies, player difficulty.
14. Return reporter's calls. Deal with them courteously.[1]

Being the immediate contact person for the media is often very time-consuming, however, and can divert a coach from the primary job of coaching. Many schools and agencies work with a coach in deciding how much time can be spared for this public relations function and the limitations on actual contact with reporters.

Ethical/ Responsible Behavior

All parties involved in creating and reporting sports news should conform to reasonable ethical standards. Responsible journalism requires accuracy and unbiased reporting, and ethical coaching practices put the welfare of the participant foremost. Within these guidelines of accuracy and concern, standards of ethical and responsible behavior can be established.

Reporters

Reputable reporters are dedicated to public service and are not inclined to exploit youth in athletics or otherwise to inflict damage to athletes, their coaches, or the community for the sake of a news story. Numerous examples of reporting can be found that seem to contradict the image of sensitive reporters, but a close scrutiny will probably show a valid reason for those news items.

Reporters, both in print and nonprint media, seek the facts, but sometimes publication of information has permanently harmed a young player, coach, or program. Coaches inadvertently abet this practice by being careless in giving facts both "on" and "off" the record when attempting to provide full information; facts can be misinterpreted.

Coaches

Coaches have a primary responsibility for their players and their welfare and for the school or agency and its welfare. Protecting students and players from inaccurate or harmful reporting and protecting successful players from an admiring press are serious tasks. In all situations coaches should strive to be fair, honest, and protective.

A coach, hoping to share in the news and information process and benefits, must participate as a full partner, but the goal should always be the promotion of team interest and player interest—not self-interest. Ethical standards require that honor be given where honor is due, with assistants and players duly credited for their good work. Ethical standards also require that the coach not try to share any blame but assume it personally.

Coaches should be available to all reporters on a regular basis and offer information on an equal basis. They should be open and honest, without having to "tell all" to the media, and neither expect nor give preferential treatment. When firm professional and friendly relationships are established with all the media, the coach might then anticipate some advantage or breaks in reporting; but neither party is entitled to violate the standards of responsibility and truth.

Players

If a team is very successful or has exceptional athletes, team members will be approached directly by the media unless mutually satisfactory arrangements for interviews and pictures can be made. Players sometimes need to be protected from exploitation by reporters, but, in many instances, players would like to exploit the media. Fair and even-handed management is required.

Should a team member be a highly publicized or popular athlete, the coach may need to provide protection against inroads on his or her time or school work and may also need to protect the family from an invasion of privacy. Some coaches and families have to be reminded that the welfare of the athlete is the primary concern.

News, Publicity, Public Relations

Coaches must learn to differentiate between news, publicity, and public relations and try to follow responsible and ethical standards of behavior for each. News consists of the facts. Papers may prefer to publish startling rather than routine facts; while they may decide which facts to print, the coach is expected to give all that can be printed.

Publicity is the art of getting a team mentioned for any good reason and for a sufficient number of times so that they are not forgotten. Most coaches provide information, but many also use rumor, wild guesses, and make-believe. Responsible ones attempt to get good publicity for valid successes and avoid the "name in the paper at all costs" syndrome. Good contests and enthusiastic players generate good publicity.

Public relations is the art of gaining support or a favorable impression. At its best, it is based on sound programs and accurate reporting; at its worst, it is a fraud. Coaches are public relations targets, regardless of their personal preference, as their actions bring favor or disfavor to the school or agency. Coaching staffs, as well as the team members, have to be concerned about behaving in a manner that creates a good public image.

PROCEDURES

Every coach and athletic department ought to develop a set of procedures to use with the media. These procedures, ranging from pre-season plans through actual game arrangements to the end of the season and its wrap-up, can be jointly prepared by all coaches, an administrator, and consultants from the media. All possible eventualities should be considered and included in the set of procedures.

Guidelines — If everyone knows what is expected, the work of both the coach and media is expedited. General guidelines for a coach include being courteous to all, knowing the newspeople, making contact with these people, and being available to assist them.

Courtesy — Treat all representatives of the media courteously and with equal access to information. The coach who lacks the patience to provide routine details to an inexperienced reporter for a newspaper of limited circulation, or who lacks the courage or temerity to contact the area's major television sports commentator, may forfeit the opportunity for future publicity and good public relations.

Knowledge — Know the sports reporters for all the papers and all the stations. It is important for the coach to have at least a speaking acquaintance with every reporter and sportscaster in the vicinity so that they can be contacted when necessary.

Contact — Make a personal contact with each reporter. Paying a visit, writing a letter, or phoning to communicate necessary information such as telephone numbers, best times to call, deadlines for publication or broadcast, preferred format for routine coverage, and potential feature stories are priority actions. It is often necessary to make the contact more than one time in more than one way.

Availability — Be available during the season to assist reporters. Reply promptly to questionnaires, and respond quickly to all correspondence received. Most publicity reflects the quality of information provided by the coach during practice, before the game, after the game, at work, and even at home.

Pre-Season — Preparing a team before the season begins is not only a process to develop skill and condition or to select a team but also to develop a relationship with the media. News releases, picture days, interviews, posters with schedules, programs, special features, and all the details that go along with trying to increase public awareness and interest in the program need to be arranged.

News Releases — Some coaches request a pre-season interview or submit copy that previews the team's capabilities for the coming season. Appropriate comments include the names of the returning letter winners; a statement about a rebuilding year with young, inexperienced athletes; and a statement about a strong nucleus of veterans of championship caliber that promises a successful season. Also frequently mentioned are outstanding accomplishments of individual athletes or the team as a unit, as well as strategy that will be employed to utilize talents of the current group (especially if the strategy is notably different from the past year).

To facilitate working with reporters of all kinds, coaches should prepare rosters with player information. A vignette on each player, including name, class, height, weight, parent's name, hobbies, academic record, number of years lettered or played, special abilities, special athletic accomplishments, and future goals, will assist reporters in their write-ups.

Team records should be made available, and a brief summary or handout of several years' results will also make it easier for reporters to do their job. Win-loss records, series results with traditional rivals, and highlights of last year's season are important bits of information. It is also a good idea to have pictures (black and white) of each player readily available.

Interviews

Not all coaches are interviewed, but it is not unusual and the opportunity can be anticipated. Information for the interview can be taken from material prepared for pre-season handouts. Seasoned coaches take care that their remarks are accurate, reasonably moderate in tone, supportive of team and school or agency, supportive of staff members, and never derogatory of opponents. They attempt to make only accurate, courteous statements and avoid those that might be misconstrued when quoted out of context.

Features

A classic pre-season feature is picture day, which is a ritual for football teams but is also widely used in other sports. On this occasion all players are in uniform and are photographed as a team, in groups, and individually. The coach arranges for the setting, players, uniforms, and any posing or staging that will take place. Players should be given direction concerning their appearance, their language and gestures, and the topics to be discussed if they are interviewed.

Other features might include a piece on traditional rivals, in which most coaches walk the line trying to keep the rivalry intense yet not antagonizing the opponent. A plea or pitch for better facilities often results in a feature story and generally includes pictures, facts, and comparisons with other local or rival's facilities. Additional picture stories or newscasts could be prepared jointly by the coach and reporter on almost any topic that needs some depth in preparation and presentation; the list is endless.

Season

Procedures for media coverage during the playing season should be carefully thought out and mutually planned by athletic staff and media. Not only coaches but administration and maintenance staff must participate if game coverage is to proceed smoothly. These procedures can be considered in three phases: pre-game, game, and post-game.

Pre-Game

Regardless of how simple or elaborate, the press box ought to be furnished with necessities including good visibility, protection from weather, desks or provisions for writing, power sources for lights and electrically operated equipment, and a telephone if possible. The coach's responsibility is to see that the maintenance personnel clean, repair, and set up the structure correctly and that additional touches be provided where possible.

In addition to checking on the physical facilities for media use, the coach should be certain to provide accurate player information. This includes possible starting line-ups, injury reports, and any special items of

Figure 24-1 Keep the remarks accurate and supportive (Courtesy of Eastern Kentucky University, Richmond, Kentucky).

interest that might appeal to the public. Information about opponents and their strengths and weaknesses is appropriate, as is any information concerning how the team intends to meet these strengths and weaknesses.

Game

Procedures at game time include providing a starting line-up and list of substitutes with correct numbers and with proper spelling of names. The coach can also provide hints for the pronunciation of difficult names. If transmission of messages is required, spotters and runners are assigned. Refreshments in the pressbox show appreciation.

The primary concern of the coach during the game is the game itself; communication with the media is rare unless, as in some collegiate and professional games, interviews are conducted on the sidelines. Generally, after information and facilities are provided, the coach's responsibility is over until after the game.

Post-Game

When reporters come around after the game, it is the coach's responsibility to talk with them and attempt to answer logically questions that may seem illogical. The best plan is to respond plainly and simply, trying to avoid making any comments in the heat of anger or frustration. Players may need to be encouraged to respond in the same manner if they are interviewed post-game or in the locker room.

If it is an away contest, and the squad is not accompanied by a reporter or someone else who is responsible for news, the coach usually calls in to report the scores. It should already be known which papers and/or stations expect or will accept the report; therefore, the report is prepared in response to their needs as well as to the team's needs. Basics—score, players, summaries—are submitted first, then additional information is given because space or time may be suddenly available. The vital thing is to be sure that the scores are called in immediately.

Post-Season

In concluding a season, successful or not, there is information that must be prepared for the coach's own use and for media use. These include season summaries and special feature stories.

Summaries

Every good coach maintains records on team play and individual player accomplishments. These become a part of the permanent record for the team, but they can also be used in post-season stories for the media. Although winning teams seem to be more interesting to reporters than losing teams are, materials are prepared regardless. Final batting averages, golf scores and handicaps, free throw percentages, goals scored, and similar records must be kept. These can be compared to those of previous years and matched with win-loss records. They also provide the basis for preparing news stories at the beginning of the next season.

Features

Any special event or interesting happening can become a feature story. Features can be written on a superior player, a winning season, a new record, a mother-son accomplishment, or a collegiate scholarship awarded. Any human interest event is a good topic for a feature story; funny, memorable, or important subjects appeal to media subscribers. People seem to remember the feature stories long after the season record is forgotten.

SUMMARY

All coaches, regardless of level of play, work with the media and should be prepared to do it accurately, courteously, and cooperatively. Because public support may depend on factual reporting and good public relations, the coach must devote time and energy to this responsibility, which is off-task from the actual coaching job.

Responsible and ethical behavior on the part of the coaches and media representatives will ensure interesting stories, and will also serve the best interest of players. No program, no paper, no station, no coach is more important than the participants are. The media can be useful to all athletic programs and should be given every consideration so that they can do their job. A mutually cooperative relationship can be a profitable investment.

ENDNOTE

1. J. Roberts, "Game Plan for Media Coverage" (mimeographed material, 1987).

PART 5

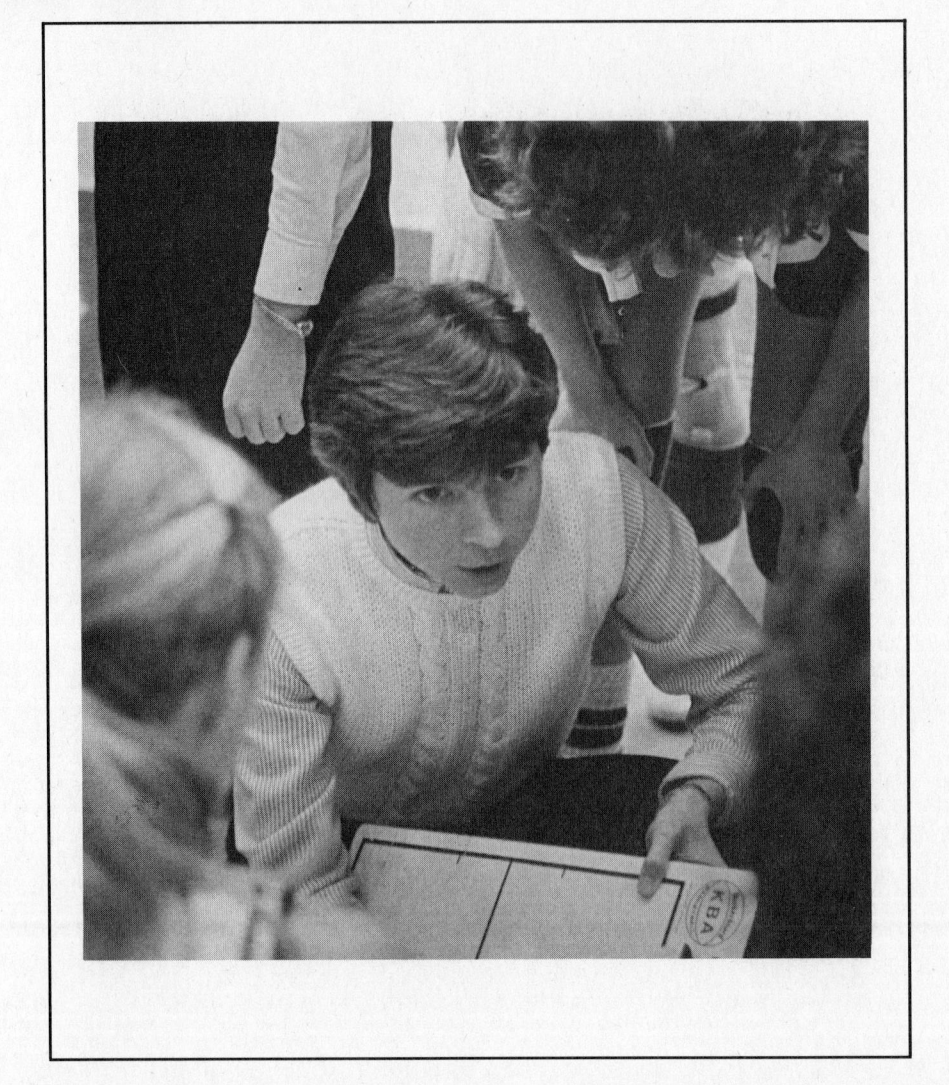

The Inner Nature of Coaching

25

Why Coach?

> ADVANTAGES
> DISADVANTAGES
> WHY COACHES REMAIN IN COACHING
> WHY COACHES LEAVE COACHING
> WHY YOU SHOULD COACH

This book has presented a broad picture of the duties, responsibilities, pleasures, and conflicts in coaching. There is a need to sum up the advantages and disadvantages involved in the profession and to consider why some coaches stay in the field while others leave. A look at the inner nature of this special occupation by the new or pre-service coach can help determine one's potential for a satisfactory coaching career.

ADVANTAGES

A coaching position brings with it many built-in advantages. Not all coaches benefit from all of them, but each gains some. Included among the advantages are satisfaction from both player and personal growth and accomplishment; challenges that are met; the intangible rewards of pleasure and fun; and tangible rewards of community appreciation, reasonable salary, and business and professional opportunities.

Satisfaction   Coaches can be proud of their efforts and be satisfied that they have succeeded when their players improve and mature and when they, themselves, accomplish their goals. Being satisfied and pleased with a job well done is one of the great rewards.

Player Accomplishment   To be able to work with talented, interested, and hard-working players—at any level—and to see them develop their skills is truly satisfying. These team members can achieve almost unbelievable heights with good teaching and coaching; some move on to college and professional teams, and a few become international competitors. Their accomplishments are a credit to them and to their coaches and constitute one of the better "payoffs."

Player Growth   Not only do players grow in skill, they also grow socially, academically, and as human beings. It is deeply satisfying to watch and help a young, unformed athlete develop into a fine man or woman with character and maturity. To see a player become a leader in the school or a former player become a leader in the community or state helps make coaching worthwhile. Physical development is gratifying to observe, but the molding of an athlete as a person is, for many coaches, a greater obligation and pleasure.

Coaches' Accomplishments

One of the more pleasing advantages in coaching is to succeed in developing superior players and helping them put together a winning season. Coaches' visible accomplishments are recorded in a win-loss chart, titles won, and champions produced. Another accomplishment that can give equal satisfaction (which cannot be placed on a chart) is the impact on players' lives. The public may not know, but coaches know how important their influence is on the player's total development.

Coaches' Growth

The opportunity to develop professionally and personally is a distinct advantage. Gaining full membership in the coaching fellowship is a happy outcome. Novice coaches become experienced, accomplished veterans. All coaches mature, become wiser, and learn more every day that they work. The personal and professional interaction coaches must experience with other staff, townspeople, and players can provide a laboratory for personal development.

Challenges

The coaching field is a land of opportunity for those individuals who enjoy being challenged. Many young people enter the profession for this reason: for the opportunity to be tested and to overcome difficulties. Those who do not mind facing obstacles relish the idea of doing something that few others have achieved; those who believe that they can make positive things happen will enjoy this line of work.

Player

It is a challenge to take a boy, girl, man, or woman and develop the potential that is found in each. True satisfaction comes when a coach discovers a "diamond in the rough" and polishes that player until he or she performs brilliantly. It also is a challenge to take those players who are unpolished as persons and develop them into cooperative team members and contributing citizens.

Team

Trying to make a team out of a collection of athletes is a challenge that most coaches face. Trying to make a cooperative, effective, highly skilled, and winning team is a bigger one. To prepare players so that they have the winning edge is a challenge faced every day, and, when the task is performed properly, victory is sweet.

Coach

Coaches meet challenges beyond those presented by players and the team. They have the opportunity and necessity to come up with the perfect system, to outwit their opponents, and to find new ways to improve the skill and competency of their players. The coach is always on stage in public view and has the perfect opportunity to show the public what good coaching is.

Why Coach? 373

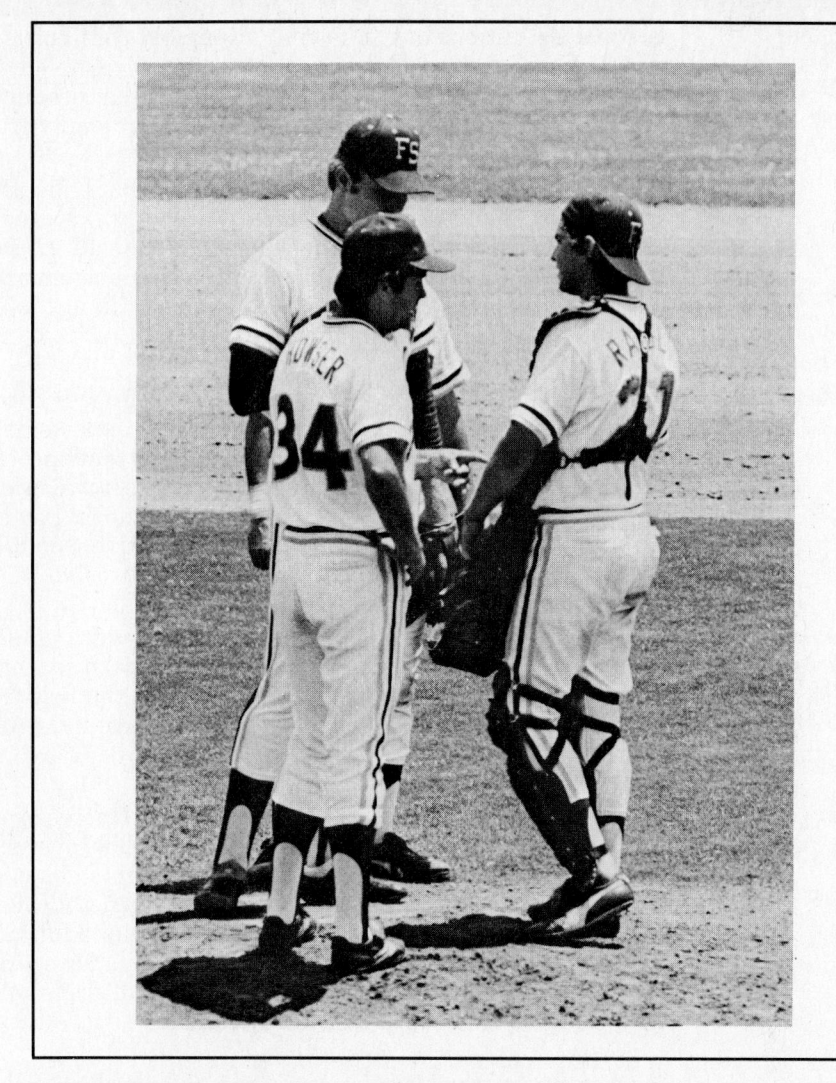

Figure 25-1 Some college coaches become big-league managers (Courtesy of The Florida State University, Tallahassee, Florida)

Intangible Rewards

Among the major advantages of coaching are those called intangible—the things that cannot be seen or touched. They include appreciation, joy at success, and fun in work. If it were not for those happy intangibles, many would not coach.

Fun

Most coaches coach because they like it. They like the work, the people contacts, the sense of achievement, and professional and community interaction. "Fun" can be defined in many ways. Each coach may have a personal definition, but it is this intangible that turns hard work into play, fields and courts into playgrounds, and teams into happy associations of players. As long as the job is satisfying, productive, happy, and fun, coaches will work long hours and undergo many frustrations.

Joy

Joy is also defined by each person, but it is a kind of suffusing glory that can be experienced when everything is properly executed and there is the exhilaration of beauty in motion. It can also result from winning, but it is not limited to that. Joy can be addicting as players and coaches strive for that one clear moment again and again. Ordinary jobs have few occasions for joy; coaching may have many.

Appreciation

Sometimes knowing that a good job has been done is not enough; coaches thrive on expressions of appreciation. These expressions come in many forms—phone calls, letters, conversations, attendance at contests, dinners, awards, and so on. Players, other coaches, townspeople, and parents all join in telling a coach how valuable he or she is. Fan support is one of the special intangible rewards a coach can receive, and it is often a strong reason for many to continue their efforts.

Tangible Rewards

Not only are there tremendously satisfactory intangible rewards, there are those more tangible considerations that make coaching a worthwhile profession. Some individuals are attracted to the field because of salary and supplements, social benefits, and business and professional opportunities.

Fiscal

The fiscal or monetary rewards that coaches receive are usually greater than those of most other teachers or staff in school systems. Supplements may add several thousand dollars each year to a coach's income. Those at the collegiate and professional levels are generally very well paid for their services. There are limited opportunities for additional revenue with camps, concessions, radio and television shows, newspaper columns, and advertisements. Many coaches have the use of driver education cars or those donated by boosters or business firms.

Social

Coaches are sought after for social and civic events; opportunities for interaction are unlimited. Tangible social rewards may take the form of membership in country clubs, civic clubs, or social groups. There is much written about the upward mobility of athletes, but little is said about the obvious upward mobility of coaches. There is also considerable mention of the banquets and other gatherings that coaches attend; they get to eat many chicken and roast beef dinners.

Business and Professional

Coaches frequently find themselves in positions of professional leadership, which can lead to publication of articles or books and, in limited cases, to commercial advertising. Business opportunities may come the coach's way from interested boosters. Summer employment is often forthcoming. What may begin as a side-line business may become quite lucrative and provide a generous livelihood when coaching days are over. Contacts made during the coaching years are also contacts for business years.

DISADVANTAGES

Not everything in a coach's life is pleasurable. Of the many disadvantages in coaching, some are just the opposite side of the advantage coin. What is an advantage to one coach in a particular situation may be a disadvantage to another. Often, the conditions in a specific community or school are not suitable, and a change of jobs can result in mutual satisfaction and growth for all concerned.

Dissatisfaction Those areas of player and coach growth and accomplishment that bring satisfaction can also bring dissatisfaction. If the course of events does not run smoothly and the outcomes are disappointing, it is difficult to be pleased with results.

Player Accomplishment In a situation where there is lack of player interest and limited skill, a coach must work harder to get results. There are innumerable players who are not interested in learning. Not all coaches can be successful as teachers of skills and strategies to players of minimal skill and experience. Some can be content only with players who already possess skill and knowledge. When players develop slowly, success is long in coming, wins are few and far between, and many coaches become very dissatisfied.

Player Growth Player development is not only in skilled performance. Some are superior in skill, strength, and endurance but never develop socially or morally or show behavior that is accepted by the school, team, and community citizens. Coaches whose jobs take them into areas where nonsporting and illegal behavior is the norm for young people can be gravely disappointed, disillusioned, and dissatisfied. All players cannot be reached; for many coaches the lack of satisfaction caused by these failures lasts longer than the hurt of a lost title.

Coaches' Accomplishments When coaches do not accomplish their goals—whether to improve skills, to help athletes grow, or to win contests—they are displeased, disgusted, and miserable. The level of accomplishment required for satisfaction varies with each coach. Those accustomed to winning seasons are depressed with a couple of losses; others accustomed to losing seasons are pleased with two consecutive wins. Being displeased with one's own efforts is a great dissatisfaction.

Coaches' Growth Good coaches must continue to develop as professionals and as persons. When job conditions do not permit opportunities for upgrading skills and knowledge, stagnation sets in. No coach can stand still; he or she will be passed quickly in the race. Many find that the communities or situations in which they are employed are too limited in social, professional, or personal opportunities for growth. A coach not matched to the life style of a community can be very unhappy and usually chooses to leave at the first opportunity.

Lack of Challenge

If coaches thrive on challenge, then they will wither on the vine that does not put enough spice and zip in their lives. As in other areas, the view of what is challenging and what is not rests with the individual; however, if there is no challenge, there is no thrill of victory.

Players

Some coaches find no challenge in dealing with players with limited ability and motivation, and they cannot afford the time to wait for long-range development growth. Others are not challenged by the age group with which they work; this limits potential for development. If there are obstacles to achievement that are not of the coach's making, it may be so difficult to meet the challenge that continued efforts are useless.

Team

If the team as a whole is limited in ability and motivation, some coaches are not challenged, but others are. There are a few who have teams of such high ability, or who compete against such weak opponents, that their schedule offers no challenge. After a period of years with no improvement in quality or quantity of material or competition, many coaches feel a lack of challenge.

Coaches

Some coaches become tired. They have seen it all, have done it all, and are no longer enthusiastic about meeting any challenge. This lack of challenging situations can be actual or in the coach's mind. Either way, this condition is a real disadvantage. When a challenge is no longer present, it may be time to leave the field.

Lack of Intangibles

When the fun is gone, coaching becomes a disagreeable chore for the overworked coach. It is the intangible emotional satisfaction that keeps a coach working longer hours than does almost anyone else in the community. Joy and satisfaction in a job well done have kept coaches "hooked" on coaching for years, but when it is no longer fun, it is no longer worth the effort.

Disappointment

Idealistic concepts may be rudely shattered when a coach learns that everyone in the profession is not honest, rule-abiding, cooperative, or fair-minded. Cheaters do win. When merit and accomplishments are not recognized by peers and public, disappointment of being overlooked can be great. It is difficult to be pleased when the person named coach of the year is well known for unethical and illegal practice. It is equally difficult to be pleased when all-star teams are composed of players who possess better press agents than skill. When the community, school, or agency fails to support the athletic endeavors of the program, a coach can be disenchanted and disappointed.

Frustration

When it appears impossible to set reachable goals or to move toward them, frustration appears. Roadblocks consist of player apathy, community apathy, or general disinterest in athletics by the school or agency. The coach's sport may be going out of fashion (as wrestling and field hockey have in some locations), organized sport may be giving way to sports clubs, or agency programs may be conflicting with school programs. Players are often not dedicated to the coach's style and rebel against the coaching methods. Whatever the cause, frustration continued over a period of time can turn individuals away from coaching.

Loss of Support

A definite disadvantage and extreme disappointment comes when there is loss of financial and moral support from the school, agency, or community. Fiscal support must be adequate for a program to continue. As the number of programs increase and the value of the dollar decreases, there is reduced support for all athletic endeavors for boys and girls, men and women. Coaches working together cooperatively can overcome some reduction in financing, but it may be more difficult to overcome a loss of moral support or confidence. When communities doubt the value of an athletic program or doubt the competence or effectiveness of a coach, the program and/or coach are in deep trouble. Coaches are especially vulnerable to loss of fan and community support, which can grow or die quickly, and are at a distinct disadvantage if their jobs rest on the performance of immature adolescents at any given time.

Lack of Tangible Rewards

It is difficult enough to coach when the fun is gone, but if the money is limited, too, that becomes an even greater disadvantage. Coaches may be expected to work for less because they are dedicated to their jobs, but they have to pay for food, housing, energy, and education for their children like everyone else. If social, business, and professional benefits prove to be less than generous, coaches cannot be faulted for being frustrated and seeking appropriate recognition elsewhere.

Fiscal

If salaries, supplements, and fringe benefits do not provide sufficient income for a reasonable standard of living, then the advantages found in coaching dwindle. Families often tell young couples that they "can't live on love." This is also true for coaches. Many continue to coach for low salaries and minimal supplements because they love what they do, but eventually the time comes when the disadvantages of low or moderate incomes have to be weighed against the advantages of a more lucrative livelihood.

Social

It is nice to be recognized and included in local social activities, but this requires both time and money. Coaches rarely have enough of either. Some find having to meet social obligations and to meet and work with civic clubs a tremendous disadvantage. These obligations can interfere with work, as well as personal choices and activities, and diminish precious family time. They also can be expensive unless a fan or booster member provides memberships, fees, or expenses.

Business and Professional

Although there are coaches who receive tips on the market, shares of a business, or sport camp directorship, most do not. Additional business revenue is difficult to secure and takes time from coaching responsibilities. Professional advantages come to the talented few, with most coaches following the leaders. Time to write, produce films, and give clinics is limited to the minority. Chances for professional advancement from school, to college, and to the professionals are minimal. Many aim high, but most stay at a level where they began.

The ultimate disadvantage of all is that coaches lose their jobs; they get fired. Tenure as a teacher may be retained, but when the title, role, and supplement are gone, the joy may also be gone. This lack of stability turns coaches away from the profession.

WHY COACHES REMAIN IN COACHING

When all the advantages and disadvantages are weighed, there are still countless men and women who choose to remain in the profession. There must be many satisfying and rewarding aspects to be found in the profession to have such a large number of members. Some of these have been outlined as advantages. They include pride, satisfaction, challenge, pleasure, enough money, and a habit or addiction to coaching.

Pride

Coaches are proud people who strive to instill a sense of personal dignity and worth in their athletes. They are proud to be a coach, proud to work with young people, and proud of their achievements. Pride keeps a coach or team hustling when there is little to hustle about. Pride also helps a coach smile at a winning opponent when it hurts to lose and stiffens the backbone in the face of adversity. The majority take great pride in the statement "I am a coach."

Satisfaction

Coaches keep on coaching because it pleases them to do so. They gain immense satisfaction from their work, their players, and their successes. It is a thrill to win, a pleasure to watch athletes develop, and gratifying to receive accolades from the fans. It is fun to coach, and for most it is more than work; it is what they would do even if it were not their job. The emotional reward of being admired, respected, and loved is important. This position in the community is very satisfying.

Challenge

Most coaches remain in coaching because there is one more game to win, one more player to develop, one more program to straighten out. Veteran coaches know that they can meet any challenge—that is why they are veteran coaches. It takes a stout heart, a strong back, a keen mind, and a tough skin to deal with problems and opportunities that a coaching career brings. Those who continue to coach are assured, competitive, experienced, and comfortable in their ability to meet any situation; they relish the challenge.

The Money Is Adequate

No coach ever entered the field to get rich, but those who continue in the profession have found the salaries and fringe benefits sufficient for their needs and those of their families. (Frequently the spouse works, so there are two incomes in the family.) Many coaches are reasonably content with

Why Coach? 379

Figure 25-2　　Champions (Courtesy of The Florida State University, Tallahassee, Florida)

a moderate, average life style. They find that satisfaction gained from coaching far outweighs the need for above-average recompense. Like everyone else, they would rather have more than they make, whatever it is, but they find the money adequate.

They Would Miss It

If all coaches were released from their positions tomorrow, the world would be filled with frustrated men and women whose lives would have large, empty holes. Coaching can be so all-consuming and fulfilling that many individuals cannot envision their lives without it. Their work, their play, and their profession are all tied up in one package—coaching.

When coaches do retire or step down, they often continue to frequent the athletic scene. They may retire their clipboard with its X's and O's, but they do not give up their interest. Most continue to work within the area in a paid or voluntary position.

They Are Winning

Generally, as long as a coach is winning, he or she is not very likely to hang up the cap and whistle. Fans, students, players, and administrators value, applaud, and reward this type of success. It is gratifying to the ego, rewarding to the pocketbook, and fills the heart with personal pride. Winning is fun, too.

Sometimes those with a long history of winning do decide to retire; but, when it happens, there are banquets, speeches, gifts, and accolades to last a lifetime. Continuing to coach is easy when one has a winning tradition, and it is nice to go out in a blaze of glory when the coaching days are over.

WHY COACHES LEAVE COACHING

Individuals do stop coaching and return to the classroom, move up to an administrative position, or go out into the business world. Their reasons for leaving the field are similar to the disadvantages discussed previously in this chapter. The primary reasons seem to be that coaching has lost its charm, family needs are greater than coaching positions can satisfy, and there has been a series of unsuccessful or losing seasons.

The Fun Is Gone

A common statement by ex-coaches or by those who contemplate leaving the field is, "The fun is gone." They imply that the satisfactions they once had are either no longer present or are not strong enough to overcome the job difficulties they are experiencing. Some say that athletes are different and no longer work as hard or show respect as they once did. Others say that they are tired of working long hours. There are those who say that coaching is a young person's game, that the fatigue level increases with years on the job, that they are burned out.

Whatever the "fun" was, it appears that when it is gone the strong attraction that coaching had is also gone. Unless the great intrinsic value of satisfaction and enjoyment is present, coaches leave the field.

The Challenge Is Over

Somewhat akin to fun is the pleasure of meeting and overcoming a challenge. Some coaches have met all the challenges they want to meet and now want a less stressful occupation. Continued stress may have resulted in health problems or in chronic fatigue. It may be that an individual has reached a plateau in his or her position; there is no hope of moving to a larger school or from a school to a college. There are a few coaches who have already "done it all" and find there are no challenges remaining.

Family Obligations

The need to meet family obligations appears to be a dominant reason for leaving coaching. A statement frequently made by departing coaches is, "Now I will have time for my family." The great demands on coaches' time makes it impossible for them to be with their families as the ordinary 8:00 to 5:00 o'clock workers do. Spouses and children may not receive enough attention from coach/parent, and this can create stresses that pull on the fabric of a marriage or child relationship.

The financial needs of a family also have to be considered. When the per hour rate for work is calculated, it is far below minimum wage. The same amount of time in a less stressful situation could produce considerably more income. It is little wonder that families urge the coach/parent to do something other than coach, both to gain more time and increased financial resources.

They Lose

Unfortunately, many coaches do not leave the field voluntarily. They are encouraged to do so by fans, boosters, athletes, and administrators when losing seasons appear. These groups do not consider the lack of available material, limited fiscal support, or better opponents. All they see is the scoreboard and record.

If a coach is also a tenured teacher, then he or she continues teaching without a supplement or is moved "upstairs" to an administrative position. Some choose to continue in this manner, while others prefer to leave the educational profession and enter private business.

Good coaches can get caught up in this win-at-all-costs syndrome and decide to leave the profession before they are fired. These, too, remain educators or find a business venture.

WHY YOU SHOULD COACH

After considering the advantages and disadvantages and personal abilities and interests, individuals will have to decide if they should coach. The reasons for being a coach have been given, as well as the reasons for not entering the field. It is not a profession for everyone; not everyone has the drive, stamina, personality, skill, and interest to be a coach. Some reasons why a person might choose to enter the profession include possession of the necessary personal qualifications, need to meet a challenge, use of coaching as an entry-level position leading to a different vocation, and a strong desire to coach and work with athletes.

Assist in Securing a Position

Being willing and able to coach is, in some systems, a necessary requisite for a teaching position. As the need for coaches increases and the pool of qualified applicants decreases or remains stable, an interest in coaching may ensure a teaching position. Frequently, coaches are hired as permanent substitutes to meet the standard of being employed by the school board. This permanent substitute position can lead to a permanent teaching position.

Some young coaches intend to use coaching as a springboard to business opportunities. They know that they have to develop management and fiscal skills to coach and that they can make good contacts with the business community as they coach. This can lead to other job offers or to their own business.

Figure 25-3   A way of life (Courtesy of Eastern Kentucky University, Richmond, Kentucky)

Satisfaction

Each person must decide where personal satisfaction can be secured. Many young people and novice coaches get their greatest satisfaction from participating in athletics. One who enjoyed being a player will likely enjoy remaining on the athletic scene as a coach. Others have observed their coaches' obvious enjoyment and high-status position and want a share in the values inherent in the role.

Athletics can be all-consuming and provide pleasure in participation and pride in success. This satisfaction in a job well done may be the most attractive aspect of coaching.

Drive to Succeed

Many entering coaches are convinced that they can succeed where others have failed. They believe that they can improve behavior, increase skill, win games, and rise in the profession. This confidence in their abilities is characteristic of most coaches and is the mark of all successful ones. The necessity or the ability to meet challenges by athletes, teams, community, and other coaches may be a basic aspect of coaching that attracts young people to it. Certainly no one can be successful who lacks drive, energy, and assurance.

Because competition is fundamental in athletics, coaches must be fierce competitors. Those who thrive on competition and all its stresses and joys will probably thrive if they enter the field.

Association

Many individuals enter and stay in the coaching profession because they enjoy working with people. This interest in coaching provides a lifelong opportunity not only to work with young people but also to watch them grow and develop into strong, mature, competent men and women. It is very rewarding to know that one's efforts have been successful. Some say that working with the youth keeps them young. Whatever it is, youth work is rewarding.

Way of Life

Most coaches are former athletes or would-be athletes who have followed a competitive path since they were youngsters. They have built their lives around the sports world and find it rewarding and satisfying. When the time comes to make a choice for a life's work, it is only natural that they would return to the exciting scene they know so well.

Athletics and coaching are a way of life. They are set apart from all other activities and they have a meaning and significance all their own. Coaches and players know this, and, although they may try, they can never communicate their own devotion to sport to nonparticipants.

Yes, coaching is a way of life and rewarding to those who choose that way. It is a high calling; to become "coach" is to earn a respected place in an honored profession. What is in a name; a rose by any other name would smell as sweet? Not so. The name, the title "coach," does smell sweeter to those who have earned it. To hear a former player say "Hi coach. Remember me?" is something special. John Wooden, the renowned coach of the UCLA men's basketball team, entitled his book *Call Me Coach* for that reason. Calling someone "coach" says it all—respect, affection, fear, nostalgia, joy—for the person who changed a life.

Index

Abuse, 123
Academics. *See* Education; Professional preparation
Accidents, 296
Accounting staff, 335
Acromegaly, 164
Adjunct coach, 311, 315–316
Administrative duties, 31–32, 181–300, 342. *See also* Management
Administrative support, 342
Adolescence
 biological considerations, 73–81
 conflicts in, 19
 injuries in, 74
Adopt-a-School, 353
Adopt-a-Team concept, 353–354
Advertising campaigns, 192–193
Agency training, 50

Age of athlete
 and equipment, 209–210
 and scheduling considerations, 246
Alcohol, 23, 164, 165
Amateur Athletic Union (AAU), 3–5
Amenorrhea, 80, 81
American Alliance for Health, Physical Education and Recreation (AAHPER), 45, 46
American Alliance for Health, Physical Education, Recreation and Dance (AAHPERD), 51, 72
American Coaching Effectiveness Program (ACEP), 47
American Legion, 354–355

American Society for Testing and
  Materials (ASTM), 212
Amphetamines, 165
Anabolic steroids, 164
Announcements, 89, 90
Anorexia nervosa, 76
Applebee, Constance, 41
Aspiration levels, and
  performance, 114, 128
Assistant coach, 17
  job description, 33, 92, 176, 305,
    310
  personal and professional
    qualities, 14, 47, 153,
    308–312
  selecting, 308–314
  success as, 315
Athletic director, 342–344
Athletic programs
  costs of, 184–186, 248
  equipment needs, 208–209
  goals and objectives, 304
  staff needs, 304–306
  status of, 34
  support groups and, 338
Athletic trainer. See Trainers
Attendance, 123, 153
Auditing, 226–227, 335
Authoritarianism, 15–16, 18
Awards
  end-of-season, 134
  forms of, 140
  as a motivating factor, 134, 140

Band, 344–345
Barbiturates, 165
Basketball, 235, 322
Behavior. See also Discipline
  acceptable, 155, 156
  American model of, 149
  coach's, 16–17, 149
  codes of, 151
  control procedures, 154–160
  control variables, 155, 158–160
  game, 16–17
  neutral, 155, 157
  in practice sessions, 106–107
  on trips, 297–298

unacceptable, 16–17, 155, 156–
  157, 167–168
Bias, personal. See Favoritism
Bidding, 225–226, 229
"Bill of Rights for Young
  Athletes," 9
Biological considerations
  adolescents, 73–81
  children, 65–73
  race, 81–84
Blacks
  biological considerations, 82
  cultural differences, 82–84
Body build
  and choice of sport, 67
  gender differences in, 74–76
  and maturation rate, 67
  and performance, 112–113
  and selection of players, 104
Body building, in adolescence, 77
Body fat, percentage of, 80
Body language, 172
Books, 52
Booster clubs
  advantages of, 190, 292, 306,
    348–352
  by-laws, 348, 349–352
  disadvantages of, 41, 306,
    352–353
  functions, 347–348
  organizing, 348
Boosters Clubs of America, 348
Bryant, Paul "Bear," 18
"B" teams, 101
Buckley Amendment, 93
Budget
  balanced, 200
  cost analysis, 200–201
  expenditures, 196
  finalizing, 201–202
  long- and short-range, 195–196,
    228–229
  for new programs, 208
  for new staff, 305–306
  preparation of, 196–202
  sample worksheet, 197–199
Bulimia, 76
Business arrangements. See Game
  management; Legal aspects

Business community, 189, 192, 262, 355

Caffeine, 165
Call Me Coach (Wooden), 384
Camps, sports, 51, 306
Canada, certification in, 47
Captains, team, 97
Cardiopulmonary resuscitation (CPR), 328
Cardiovascular system
  in adolescents, 76-77
  in children, 68-70
Careers, 54-61, 381-383. *See also* Coaching
Ceremonies, pre-game and half-time, 263-264, 268 344-345
Certification
  in Canada, 47
  obtaining, 47
  programs, 50
  requirements, 46-47
  for trainers, 325
Cheerleaders, 264, 346
Chemical Health Resource Center, 164
Children
  biological considerations, 65-73
  of coaches, 26-27
  injuries of, 71
  at practices, problem of, 25
Chilling, 206
Church support, 355
Civic clubs, 354
Civil rights, 283-286
Clearance forms, 96-97
Clerical personnel, 334-336, 344
Climate
  equipment and uniforms and, 206
  practice and, 78-79
  scheduling games and, 247, 248
  travel and, 247
Clinics, 48
  coach's, 51
  commercial firms, 52
  high school, 50

Clothing, 72, 215-217. *See also* Uniforms
Coach, title of, 4, 10, 384
Coaches' Manual, 7
Coaching
  advantages in, 55-56, 371-375, 378-380
  aptitude for, 56, 60, 381-383
  careers, 54-61, 381-383
  challenges, 372-373
  disadvantages in, 55-56, 375-378
  intangible rewards of, 373-374, 376-378
  leaving, 380-381
  personal qualifications, 4-5, 7-8
  personal roles and conflicts, 12-29
  professional roles and conflicts, 30-43
  remaining in, 378-380
  responsibilities in, 9-10, 34, 175
  styles, 7, 14-15, 122-123
  tangible rewards of, 374-375, 377-380
Cocaine, 165, 166
Cold temperatures, 79, 206, 248
College
  athlete's choice of, 37, 176-177
  coach's preparation at, 45-48, 51-52
College coaching, 40, 45
Comaneci, Nadia, 113
Commercial firms, training assistance, 52
Communication skills, 171-172
Community
  coach's role in, 17, 143
  players' images in, 151
  standards of conduct, 28
  support, 143, 186, 354-356
Community organizations, 354-356
Competition
  children and, 68
  equitable, 245-246, 250, 253
  traditional rivalries, 18, 247, 249
Computer use, 196, 232, 243

Concessions, 194, 260–261, 268
Conditioning
  in child athletes, 71
  need for, 150, 325
  pre-season, 306
Conditioning equipment, 210–211
Conduct. *See* Behavior; Discipline
Conferences (leagues)
  games, 249–250, 252
  meetings, 252
  policies on scheduling, 246–247, 250
Confidentiality, player/coach, 22–23
Consent forms, 279, 280
Contest. *See* Games
Contracts
  clarity in, 255
  competent parties, 254
  game, 253–256, 260, 268
  legality of, 255
  mutual assent, 254
  officials', 260, 261
  sample, 255, 256
  valid considerations, 255
  violating or breaking, 254, 277
Cost analysis, 200
Counselor, coach as, 20–23
Court testimony, 22–23. *See also* Legal aspects
"Crack," 166
Criticism, coach's, 123
Crowds
  control of, 281
  drawing, 249, 251
Cultural factors
  in behavior control, 157
  black athletes, 82–84
  female athletes, 74
Cutting policy, 101–102

Depression, 23, 171
Development, human. *See* Maturation rate; Motor development
Discipline
  basic areas of, 150
  coach's role in, 18–19
  consistency in, 154
  defined, 18, 149
  developing codes of behavior, 151–152
  penalties, 154
  rule making, 152–154
  self-, 14, 18, 150
Doctorate degree, 52
Drills, 121, 122
Drug Enforcement Administration (DEA), 166, 167
Drugs. *See also* Drug use
  alcohol and tobacco, 23, 164
  mood enhancing, 165–166
  performance enhancing, 24, 39, 165
Drug testing, 167
Drug use, 23, 24
  by coaches, 166
  coaches' actions, 23, 166–169
  coaches' concerns, 164–166
  peer pressure and, 158
  prevention programs, 164
  recognizing, 23, 24, 167
  school policies, 167, 168
  statistics on, 163–164
  symptoms and effects of, 164–167
Dysmenorrhea, 80, 81

Economy, effect on programs, 185
Ectomorphs, 67
Education
  coaches' actions, 22–24, 35, 38, 96
  coaches' concerns, 24, 38, 173–175
  eligibility standards, 24, 96, 173, 340
  social issues of, 173, 244–245, 339
  state standards, 174
  and stress, 170
  versus scheduling of games, 244–245, 246
Education Amendments of 1972, 185

Eligibility, academic, 24, 340
  coach's responsibility, 96, 173, 263
Emergencies
  money for, 269
  transportation, 247, 295–297
Emotional level, and performance, 113–114, 150
Endomorphs, 67
Endurance
  adolescents and, 76–77
  children and, 71
  gender differences in, 72, 77
Energy costs, 185, 248
Ephedrine, 165
Equal Employment Opportunity Commission (EEOC), 286
Equipment
  categories of, 210–211
  conditioning, 210–211
  luxury items, 219
  as a motivating factor, 132–133
  practice, 238–239
  protective, 36, 206, 207, 212–214
  quality in, 227
  reconditioned, 230
  for team meetings, 91
Equipment management, 220–227, 231–241. *See also* Purchasing
  care and maintenance, 36, 132–133, 236–241, 321
  for games, 211, 263, 265–266, 269, 272
  gathering information, 221–223
  inventory, 209, 221, 321–322
  inventory forms, 221, 222
  issuing, 235–236, 237
  loss, 194, 232
  marking and coding, 234–235
  player needs, 209–210
  program needs, 208–209, 219
  receiving procedures, 233–234
  requisition forms, 223–225
  rules requirements, 206–208, 211
  safety and performance criteria, 205–206, 227
  selection, 210–217
  standardization, 227–228
  storage, 235, 238, 239–240
Equipment managers, 305, 321
Equipment manufacturers, 52, 229, 281, 282
Ethics
  academic integrity, 176, 339
  bending the rules, 153
  in coaching, 9–10, 16–17
  code of, 9–10, 325–326
  player/coach confidentiality, 22–23
  of recruiting, 37–38
  in reporting sports news, 361–362
  of stimulants, 39
  in training, 325–326
Exercise
  in childhood, 70–71
  physiological effects of, 70, 78–79
Experience factor, 48, 112

Facilities, game
  cost of, 188
  hazard-free, 36, 116, 279–280
  management responsibilities, 263, 272–273
  as a motivating factor, 132–133
  multiple-use, 255
  preparation of, 266, 321, 334
  reserving, 247, 263
  special, 268
Faculty support, 338–342
Family
  as cause of stress, 169–170, 173
  changing role of, 24–25
  of coaches, 26–28, 381
  influence on players' behavior, 157–158
  single-parent, 25
Favoritism, 22, 153, 339
Feedback
  in motivation, 128, 136
  in skill learning, 119–120
  timing in, 159
Field hockey, 41

Films, game and practice, 119–120, 136, 139, 360
Financial situation, players', 97, 193
Financing, 184–195. *See also* Fiscal management; Funding
Fiscal integrity, 32
Fiscal management, 31–32, 183–203
  auditing, 226–227
  the budget, 31, 195–202
  estimating revenue, 186, 187
  factors affecting costs, 184–186
  financing, 32, 184–195
  purchasing criteria, 205–217
  purchasing procedures, 219–230
  sources of revenue, 186–195
Florida, 171
Florida State University, 47
Fluids, replacing, 72, 79
Football, 101, 206, 330
Football Coaches Association, 51
Fosbury, Dick, 41
Funding. *See also* Fiscal management
  problems, 101, 184
  school, 187
  sources, 185, 186–195
Fund raising, 32, 40–41
  advertising campaigns, 192–193
  commercial companies, 190–192
  fees, 193–195
  permission card, 191
  personnel, 305
  season ticket sales, 189–190
  for staff needs, 3–5

Game management, 259–273
  business arrangements, 260–261, 268, 272
  equipment, 263, 269, 272
  facilities, 247, 263, 266
  guests, 266, 272
  home team, 265–268, 270
  medical services, 264–265
  officials, 260, 261, 266, 272
  player eligibility, 263
  post-game, 270–273
  pre-game, 263, 264, 265–269
  pre-game and half-time activities, 263–264, 268, 271
  pre-season, 259–265
  publicity, 261–262, 267
  public relations, 259, 261–262, 267, 364–365
  schedules, sample, 270, 271, 343
  security, 262–263, 266, 273
  visiting team, 266–267, 268–269, 270
Games
  half-time pep talks, 145–146
  motivation in, 145
  preparation for, 138–139, 150
  scheduling (*see* Scheduling games)
  simulated, 122
Gate receipts, 188–190
  splitting, 249
Gender differences
  in adolescence, 74–76, 78
  in childhood, 72
  in performance, 113
  in personal equipment and uniforms, 210
  in sports participation, 186, 285–286
Genetic factors, 70, 82, 112
Glasses guards, 214
Gloves, 212–213
Goals and objectives
  of coaches, 303–304
  of players, 128, 131
  of the program, 304
  of the team, 92
  ways to meet, 306–307
Golf, 48, 101
Governments, support of, 355–356
Graduate degree, 52
Gramm-Rudman Bill, 186
Grove City College v. *Bell*, 185
Gymnastics, 205–206, 216, 227, 282
Gymnastics Association, 50

Gynecological considerations, 79-80

Hair length, 151
Half-time activities, 263-264, 268, 344-345
Handicapped, 185-186
Hazards
　at facilities, 36, 116, 279-280
　player awareness of, 36
Hazeldon-Cork Sports Education Program, 164
Headgear, 212
Health forms, 331, 332
Heat exhaustion, 71-72, 78
Heat stroke, 72, 78
Heroin, 165
High school association clinics, 50
High school coaching, 8, 22
Home games, 133, 239, 249
Home team, 256, 265-268, 270
Hormones, 75, 77, 79, 164
Hot temperatures, 72, 78, 206
Human growth hormones (HGH), 164
Humid conditions, 78
Hypothermia, 71

Iba, Henry "Hank," 41-42
Identification, player and team, 208
Illinois State High School Athletic Association, 186
Image
　public, 151
　team, 150
Immaturity, of players, 18
Impressions, first, 89
Individualization
　in discipline, 151
　in motivation, 131
Inflation, 185
Injured players
　playing of, 39
　treatment of, 296
Injuries
　in adolescence, 74
　checking for, post-game, 270
　in childhood, 71
　legal aspects, 35, 275
　medical services for, 264-265
　preventing, 35-36
Insurance
　liability, 36, 275, 277, 281
　players' medical, 96
　rates, 283
　transportation, 289-290
Integration, 285
Intelligence, as a factor, 113, 150
Interpersonal relations, 312-314
Inventory, 209, 221, 321-322
　forms for, 221, 222
Iowa High School, 170

Jerseys, 211, 215-216
Junior varsity teams, 101, 251

Kurland, Bob, 42

Landry, Tom, 111
Laundry, 194, 238, 239, 241, 272, 321
Law suits, 47, 282-283. *See also* Legal aspects
Leadership
　qualities for, 13-14, 16
　styles in, 7, 14-15, 122-123
　workshops, 133
Leagues. *See* Conferences
Learning
　ability levels, 113
　critical periods of, 141
　and environment, 116
　overlearning, 120
　principles of, 20, 112, 150
　rate of, 114
　visual and verbal cues, 118
Legal aspects
　assumption of risk, 276, 281
　breach of contract, 277
　civil rights, 283-286
　coach's defense, 22-23, 279, 282
　contracts, 253-256, 260, 268

392 Index

Legal aspects (*continued*)
  due process, 284–285
  legal liability, 276–281
  litigation trends, 275, 282, 326
  negligence, 275, 276, 279, 326
  product liability, 281–283
  redress of grievance, 286
  risk management guidelines, 277–279
  tort liability, 277
  waivers and consent forms, 279, 280
Liability. *See also* Legal aspects
  for injuries, 35, 326
  insurance, 36, 275, 277, 281
  product, 281–283
  tort, 277
Life management, 22, 23–24, 163–179
Lifestyle, coach's, 17, 28
Listening skills, 172
Little League, 45, 48, 169
Litwhiler, Danny, 41
Lock and locker fees, 195
Locker room
  guests in, 272
  maintenance of, 132–133, 156, 322
  security, 322
Lombardi, Vince, 18, 142
Lordosis, 76
LSD (Lysergic acid diethylamide), 165, 166

Magazines, 52, 359
Maintenance
  building, 266, 333
  cooperative system of, 333–334
  costs of, 188
  equipment and uniforms (*see* Equipment; Uniforms)
  locker room, 132–133, 156, 322
  personnel, 331–334
  systems, 333
  vehicle, 290, 294
Management
  administration, 31–32
  equipment, 220–227, 231–241
  fiscal, 31–32, 183–203

game, 258–273
  legal aspects of, 253–256
  personnel, 33–34, 302–368
Managers, 270, 318–325
  desirable characteristics in, 319–320
  duties, 305, 321–322, 323–324
  recruitment and selection of, 320–321
  rotation of, 322–324
  student, 307, 320
  volunteer, 320
Maravich, Press, 8
Marfan's Syndrome, 75–76
Marijuana, 23, 165–166
Married coaches, 26–28
Married players, 25
Massengale, J. D., 35
Master's degree, 52
Maturation rate
  of adolescents, 6
  of children, 67–68
Media
  coach's relationship with, 40, 262, 267, 358, 360–362, 363
  interviews, 364
  news releases, 272, 363
  players and, 362
  seasonal procedures, 262, 272, 362–366
  varieties of, 358–360
Medical aspects, 81, 326
Medical insurance, 96
Medical personnel, 329–331
Medical services, 36
  for injured players, 264–265, 267
  for spectators, 265, 281
Medication, 331
Medicine, sports, 38, 326, 329
Meetings
  agendas, 91–92, 97–98
  conference, 252
  equipment for, 91
  first of the season, 88–98
Menopause, 79, 80
Menstrual cycle, 79–81
Mental health agencies, 166, 167
Mental readiness, 150

Mesomorphs, 67
Minnesota, 50
Motivation
  extrinsic, 127
  fear as, 172
  generalizations, 127, 131
  incentive, 128
  intrinsic, 127, 141
  and performance, 112, 114, 126
  optimal arousal level, 128
Motivational approaches
  analysis of athletes and the sport, 128-131
  awards and rewards, 134, 140
  change in routine, 143
  feedback, 128, 136
  in game situations, 138-139
  gimmicks, 142
  good facilities and equipment, 132-133
  personal philosophy and, 127
  personal touch, 135-136
  planning, 126-131
  in practice, 134
  pride, 141
  recognition, 130, 133-134
  reinforcement, 128, 134, 138
  researching methods in, 127-128
  slogans, 142-143
  sports rituals, 140
  team supporters, 143-145
  team togetherness, 141-142
  timing, 132
Motor skills
  development of, 68
  learning of, 20
Mouth protectors, 214
Multi-sport athletes, 124
Muscle cramps, 71
Muscular systems
  in adolescents, 77-78
  in children, 70, 72

National Athletic Trainers' Association (NATA), 325-327
National Children and Youth Fitness Study, 72
National Code of Ethics, 9-10, 325-326
National Collegiate Athletic Association, 170-171, 174, 245
National Federation of State High School Associations (NFSHSA), 5-7, 165, 185, 186, 212, 246, 305
National Operating Commission for Safety in Athletic Equipment (NOCSAE), 212
National Recreation and Park Association (NRPA), 47, 51
National Youth Sport Coaches Association (NYSCA), 47
Negligence, 35-36, 275, 276, 279, 326
News media. See Media
Newspapers, 358-359
No-cut policy, in selection, 101
Notices
  for first team meeting, 88-89
  for tryouts, 90

Office for Civil Rights (OCR), 286
Officials
  contracts with, 260, 261, 266, 272
  judgments of, 16
  volunteer, 260
Off-season activities, 306-307
Olympics, 113
Optimal arousal level, 128

Padding, 212
Pain, point of, 165
Pants, 216
Parent(s)
  coach as substitute, 24-26
  expectations of, 169-170, 173
  involving, 145
  and selection of players, 108
  traveling with teams, 293, 298
Parents' clubs, 353
Participation fees, 97, 193
Partnerships in Education, 353

Patriotic clubs, 354–355
PCB (polychlorinated biphenyl), 165, 166
Peer evaluation, 107–108
Peer pressure, 157–158, 159, 170
Pep clubs, 346
Performance
  arousal levels, 128
  aspiration and, 114, 128
  emotional level and, 113–114, 150
  form in, 115
  motivation and, 112, 114, 126
Permission forms, 96, 279, 280
Personal data, of players, 93, 94
  forms, 94, 96, 130
Personality development, sports and, 19
Personality tests, 105, 130
Personality traits
  of coaches, 4–5, 7–8, 60
  of players, 105, 106–107, 130
Personal touches, 135–136
Personal values, coach's, 151, 152
Personnel
  assistant coaches, 308–315
  auxiliary staff, 33
  clerical, 334–336, 344
  maintenance, 331–334
  managers, 305, 307, 318–325
  media, 40, 360
  medical, 329–331
  non-professionals, 307–308
  professionals, 307
  support, 267, 305, 317–336, 341
  trainers, 305, 307, 318
Personnel management, 303–368
  budget considerations, 305–306
  coach's roles and conflicts, 33–34
  evaluation, 314
  interpersonal relations, 312–314
  job descriptions, 306, 310
  pre-season activities, 311–312
  staff needs, 293, 304–306, 312
  support groups, 337–356
Philosophy, personal, 127, 303–304, 376
Physical abuse, 123

Physical education
  certification requirements, 46–47
  major programs, 46, 47, 52
  minor programs, 47
Physical examination
  forms, 96, 331, 332
  objectives, 330–331
Physical readiness, 150
Physiological factors, 68–72
Picture-taking, 134
Pitching, 41
Player selection. *See* Selection of players
Playing experience, 48, 112
Posters, 262
Post-game activities, 262, 270–273, 366
Post-season activities, 239–240, 366
Postural conditions, 76
Practice areas, 344–345
Practice films, 119–120
Practices
  attendance at, 123, 153, 156
  behaviors in, 106–107
  care of uniforms and equipment, 211, 238–239
  creating a learning environment, 134
  demands of, 102
  emphasis in, 117–118
  evaluation in, 118
  length and frequency, 120–121
  mental, 122
  as a motivating factor, 134
  and reinforcement, 122–123, 134
  simulated games, 122
Pre-game activities
  ceremonies and rituals, 263–264, 268, 344–345
  home team responsibility, 256, 265–268
  media contact, 364–365
Pre-menstrual syndrome (PMS), 80, 81
Pre-season activities
  conditioning, 306
  equipment check, 238, 263, 322

game management, 259-265
personnel management, 134, 311-312
news releases, 363-364
Pride, instilling, 141
Principals, 342
Problems, players', 20, 21-22. *See also* Drugs; Education
Product liability, 219, 281-283
  effect on sports, 282-283
  guidelines for defense, 282
Professional Golf Association, 50
Professional organizations, 48
  training opportunities, 50-51
Professional preparation
  additional study, 51-52
  areas of study, 46, 47
  certification requirements, 46-47
  competencies required, 46
  field experience, 46, 48
  in-service, 48-53
  pre-service, 45-48
Professional sports, 14, 51
Progesterone, 79
Programs, 194, 267
Proposition, 48, 174
Protective equipment. *See* Equipment
Psychiatric problems, drug-related, 166
Psychological factors
  in coaching of players, 19-20, 113-114
  in learning theory, 20, 113, 114
Puberty, 71, 72, 73, 79
Publicity, 40, 41, 133, 261-262, 362
Public image, 151
Public Law 94-142, 185
Public relations
  with business community, 192, 262
  in management procedures, 259, 261-262
  with media, 40, 41, 360, 362
  methods, 40-41, 261-262
  speaking engagements, 262, 346, 354
Punishment, 154, 158, 159

Purchasing
  bidding, 225-226, 229
  bulk, 225-227
  criteria, for, 204-217
  guidelines, 227-230
  justifications for, 205-210
  long-range planning, 228-229
  order forms, 226
  procedures, 218-230
  staff, 335

Race
  biological factors in, 81-82
  cultural factors in, 84
Racial discrimination, 285
Radio, 359
Recognition. *See* Awards; Motivation; Rewards
Records, 89
  access to, 106
  of equipment and uniforms, 236, 237, 321-322
  personal data, 93, 94
  physical examinations, 96-97
  player and game, 272
Recreation departments, 50
Recruiting
  for additional team members, 102-103
  staff, 307-308, 320
  by universities, 37-38
Reinforcement
  of behaviors, 157, 158, 159
  consistency in, 138
  as a motivation factor, 128, 134, 138
  purpose of, 122-123
Relationships
  coach/athlete, 21-22, 24-25, 163
  coach/faculty, 34-35
  coach/staff, 312-314
  with sexual connotations, 22, 28
Requisition forms, 223-225
Reston Homeowners Association (RHOA), 281
Retton, Mary Lou, 113
Rewards. *See* Awards

Risk
  assumption of, 276, 281
  spectator, 279-280
Risk management, 277-279
Rituals, sports, 140
Rivalries, traditional, 18, 247
Road games
  care of equipment, 239
  scheduling, 245, 249
  on school nights, 245
Role model, coach as, 16-18, 166-167, 175
Role(s)
  defined, 12
  conflicts, 12-29, 35
  expectations, 13
  overload, 13, 35
Routine, change in, 143
Ruedlinger Plan, 281
Rules. *See also* Behavior
  enforcement of, 153
  exceptions to, 153
  fairness in, 153
  legal aspects of, 284
  setting up, with players, 152, 519
  team standards, 93-95
  violation of, 16, 284, 285
Running, 77, 330

Safety
  competition and, 250
  in equipment and uniforms, 206, 208, 212
  priorities, 36, 116
Salary, 188, 374, 378-380
SATs (Scholastic Aptitude Tests), 174, 176
Schedules, transportation, 293-295
Scheduling games. *See also* Game management
  academic considerations, 244-245, 246
  at coaches' meetings, 252
  computer use in, 243
  contract guidelines, 253-256
  equitable competition and, 245-246, 250, 253
  factors affecting, 246-248
  game balance, 249-250
  joint, 250-251
  long-term planning, 243-248
  partial, 252-253
  policies and regulations, 246-247, 249-250
  for a winning season, 253
Scholarships, athletic, 37, 38
Schools. *See also* Education
  budget allocations, 187-188
  policy on drugs, 167-168
  training programs, 48-50
Scoliosis, 76
Scrimmages, 134, 135
Season, preparation for, 88-89
Seattle Decision, 275, 276
Secretarial staff, 335, 344
Security, 262-263, 266, 273, 322
Seed money, 188
Selection of players, 97, 100-109
  cutting policies, 101-102
  informing methods, 108
  objectives, 103-105
  peer evaluations, 107-108
  personal traits, 106-107
  recruitment, 102-103
  size of squad and, 100-101, 102
  skill evaluation, 103-104
  structured, 103-108
  subjective evaluation, 105
  unstructured, 101-103
Self-assessment, 8
Self-control, 150, 152, 157
Self-cut policy, in selection, 102
Self-discipline, 14, 18, 150
Sex differences. *See* Gender differences
Sex discrimination, 185, 285-286
Sexual relationships, 22, 28
Shoes, 212, 234
Shorts, 216
Sickness, 240
Single coaches, 28
Single-parent families, 25
Size of athlete. *See also* Body build
  and choice of sport, 67
  and equipment, 209-210
  and scheduling considerations, 246

Skeletal system
  in adolescents, 74-75
  in children, 70, 72
Skills. *See also* Motor development
  age and, 114
  developmental levels, 20, 114-115
  evaluation, 103-104, 114-115
  learning, 120
  performance of, form in, 115
  teaching, 112, 115-120
  transfer of, to other sports, 123-124
Slogans, as motivation aids, 142-143
Slumps, 143
Soccer, 101, 129, 266
Socks, 214
Softball, 206
Somatotype, 67
Speaking engagements, 41, 262, 346, 354
Spectators
  medical care for, 265, 281
  risk to, 279-280
  as team motivators, 130
Sports
  cycles in popularity, 129
  participation statistics, 186, 285
  role of, in personality development, 19, 130
  team, 152
Sports associations, 48, 50-51
Sports camps, 51, 306
Sports clubs, 353
Sports information director (SID), 40, 360
Sportsmanship, 16, 17
Sports medicine, 38, 326, 329
Sportswriters, 40, 41
Squad, size of, 100-101, 102. *See also* Selection of players
Staff. *See* Personnel; Personnel management
Stagg, Amos Alonzo, 41
Statistics
  on sports participation, 186
  utilizing, for motivation, 136

Steroids, 164
Stimulants, 39, 165
Storage, of equipment, 235, 238, 239-240
Strategy
  coach's role, 41-42
  defined, 41
Stress
  academic, 170
  benefits of, 169
  causes of, 169-173
  coaches' actions, 25, 171-173
  coaches' concerns, 169-171
  of competition, 25
  peers and, 170, 173
  physiological, 70, 169
  psychological, 169, 170-171
  reducing, 173-174
Student activity fees, 193
Student clerks, 335-336
Student groups, 345-346
Student managers, 307, 320
Student Protection Trust Plan, 281
Student rights, 283-284
Student trainers, 305, 307, 308
Suicide, 23, 171, 173
Summer employment, 306
Support groups
  band, 344-345
  booster clubs, 347-353
  coaches and, 338
  community organizations, 354-356
  effective on motivation, 143-145
  school groups, 338-347
  student groups, 345-346
Swimming
  coach's duties, 57-59
  meets, 265-266
  time demands, 130
  uniforms, 205, 216

Tactics
  coach's role, 41-42
  defined, 41
  in motivation (*see* Motivational approaches)

Teacher, coach as, 34–35, 111–112, 115–120, 175, 339
Teague, Berath Frank, 111
Team physician, 329–330
Team(s)
  benefits of membership, 19–20
  diverse versus homogeneous, 107
  image, 150
  togetherness of, 141–142
Team standards, 93–95
Team supporters. *See* Support groups
Teamwork, 152, 156
Television, 359
Temperature regulation
  in adolescents, 78–80
  in children, 70
  gender differences in, 78–79
Tennis, 90
Testosterone, 77
Texas, 174
Thompson, John, 111
Tickets, 189, 261, 262
  season, campaigns for, 189–190
  sellers and takers, 267
Tights, 216
Title IX, 285, 286
Tobacco, 164, 165, 166
Towel fees, 194
Track teams, 101
Traffic management, 268
Trainers
  certified, 325–327
  duties, 269, 326–327
  medical and legal concerns, 326
  noncertified, 318, 327–328
  professional and personal qualifications, 325
  student, 305, 307, 328
Training
  cardiovascular endurance, 76–77
  for coaches (*see* Professional preparation)
  coach's role in, 38–40
  conflicts, 39–40
  regimens, biological considerations, 38
  rules, 39

Training equipment, 210–211, 227
Transportation, 133
  commercial, 292
  costs of, 188, 248, 250–251
  drivers, 289
  emergencies, 247, 269, 295–297
  equipment management, 239
  insurance, 289–290
  maintenance of vehicles, 290, 294, 295
  missing passengers, 296–297, 299
  overnight, 245
  passenger lists, 264, 298
  by plane and train, 292
  player conduct, 297–298
  by private car, 290–292, 293
  readiness, 269
  reserving vehicles, 290
  schedules, 293–295
  by school vehicles, 289–290
  supervision, 292–293
  travel forms, 291
Travel. *See also* Transportation
  environmental conditions and, 247
  restrictions, 246
  value of, 245
Tryouts, 103–104. *See also* Selection of players
Tunics, 216
Tyler, Suzanne, 41

Uniforms, 132. *See also* Equipment
  care of, 238, 240–241, 272, 321
  coding, 235
  freedom of movement in, 205–206
  rules requirements, 206–208, 211, 215
  selection of, 214–217
  sex differences in, 210
  standardization of, 227–228
U.S. Field Hockey Association, 50
Ushers, 267–268

Vehicles. *See* Transportation
Vending machines, 195

Veterans of Foreign Wars (VFW), 354–355
Video taping, 120, 136
Violence
  spectator, 247
  in sports, 16
Visiting fans, 267
Visiting teams, 266–267, 268–269, 270
Volleyball, 206, 330
Volunteers. *See also* Booster clubs
  as coaches, 48, 50, 305
  as managers, 320
  as officials, 260
  recruiting, 307–308, 341

Waivers, 279, 280
Warmup clothes, 216
Waterproof gear, 206, 217
Weather. *See* Climate

Webb, "Spud," 113
Win
  pressure to, 170–171, 381
  scheduling to, 253
Winning
  psychology of, 19
  sportsmanship in, 17
Women athletes. *See* Gender differences
Women coaches, 25, 26, 286
Wooden, John, 384
Workouts. *See* Exercise
Workshops. *See* Clinics
Wrestling, 216

Yost, Fielding, 41
Young Men's Christian Association (YMCA), 9
Youth Sports Guide for Coaches and Teachers, 9